Eighteenth-century landscape description was a discourse in which the nature of liberty and authority was debated – a vital discourse in a Britain defining its nationhood in the contexts of growing imperial power and rapid economic change. Tim Fulford examines this discourse in the writings of Thomson, Cowper, Johnson, Gilpin, Repton, Wordsworth, Coleridge and others, arguing that it is the site of culturally revealing tensions which arose as writers both struggled for authority over the public sphere and sought to redefine the nature of that authority.

Dr Fulford investigates political and aesthetic writing as well as poetry and throws new light upon the legacy of Commonwealthsman and Country-party ideas of liberty. He discusses the significance of the Miltonic sublime, the politics of the picturesque and the post-colonial encounter of the Scottish tour. He intervenes in the critical debate over the politics of Romanticism by showing Wordsworth's and Coleridge's early radicalism and later conservatism to have been shaped as much by their ambivalent emulation of/definition against the political and literary authorities of eighteenth-century England as by their response to the French Revolution and the rise of Napoleon. Containing both historicist and rhetorical criticism of canonical and non-canonical writers, Dr Fulford's quietly innovative study will be of interest to all those looking for an understanding of literary and political influence that cuts across conventional periodization and finds new links between the early eighteenth and nineteenth centuries.

CAMBRIDGE STUDIES IN EIGHTEENTH-CENTURY
ENGLISH LITERATURE AND THOUGHT 30

Landscape, Liberty and Authority

CAMBRIDGE STUDIES IN EIGHTEENTH-CENTURY
ENGLISH LITERATURE AND THOUGHT

General editors
Professor HOWARD ERSKINE-HILL LITT.D., FBA,
Pembroke College, Cambridge
Professor JOHN RICHETTI, *University of Pennsylvania*

Editorial board
Morris Brownell, *University of Nevada*
Leopold Damrosch, *Harvard University*
J. Paul Hunter, *University of Chicago*
Isobel Grundy, *University of Alberta*
Lawrence Lipking, *Northwestern University*
Harold Love, *Monash University*
Claude Rawson, *Yale University*
Pat Rogers, *University of South Florida*
James Sambrook, *University of Southampton*

Some recent titles

Poetry and Jacobite Politics in Eighteenth-Century Britain and Ireland
by Murray G. H. Pittock

The Story of the Voyage in Eighteenth-Century England
by Philip Edwards

Edmond Malone: A Literary Biography
by Peter Martin

Swift's Parody
by Robert Phiddian

Rural Life in Eighteenth-Century English Poetry
by John Goodridge

The English Fable: Aesop and Literary Culture, 1651–1740
by Jayne Elizabeth Lewis

Mania and Literary Style
The Rhetoric of Enthusiasm from the Ranters to Christopher Smart
by Clement Hawes

A complete list of books in this series is given at the end of the volume

Landscape, Liberty and Authority

Poetry, Criticism and Politics from Thomson to Wordsworth

TIM FULFORD

The Nottingham Trent University

CAMBRIDGE
UNIVERSITY PRESS

Published by the Press Syndicate of the University of Cambridge
The Pitt Building, Trumpington Street, Cambridge CB2 1RP
40 West 20th Street, New York, NY 10011–4211, USA
10 Stamford Road, Oakleigh, Melbourne 3166, Australia

© Cambridge University Press 1996

First published 1996

Printed in Great Britain at the University Press, Cambridge

A catalogue record for this book is available from the British Library

Library of Congress cataloguing in publication data
Fulford, Tim, 1962–
Landscape, liberty, and authority: poetry, criticism, and
politics from Thomson to Wordsworth / Tim Fulford.
p.   cm. – (Cambridge studies in eighteenth-century English
literature and thought; 30)
Includes index.
ISBN 0 521 55455 1 (hardback)
1. English poetry – 18th century – History and criticism.
2. Landscape in literature.   3. Politics and literature – Great
Britain – History – 18th century.   4. Wordsworth, William, 1770–1850 –
Political and social views.   5. Thomson, James, 1834–82 –
Political and social views.   6. Political poetry, English – History
and criticism.   7. Picturesque, The, in literature.   8. Authority in
literature.   9. Description (Rhetoric)   10. Liberty in literature.
I. Title.   II. Series.
PR555.L27F85   1996
821′50936 – dc20   95–40538   CIP

ISBN 0 521 55455 1 hardback

For my mother and father

Contents

Acknowledgements

Without the unflagging support of Professor H. H. Erskine-Hill this book would never have appeared. I am most grateful to him and, for their scholarly help and advice, to: Professor Fredric Bogel, Professor Raimonda Modiano, Dr Lucy Newlyn, Professor Morton D. Paley, Professor Reeve Parker, Dr Nicholas Roe, Mr Frank Salmon, Professor James Sambrook. For help of other kinds I thank my parents, my wife, Paul Butler and Annie Ng, Paul Lawrence. Jesus College, Cambridge, and the Nottingham Trent University provided sabbaticals and financial support to enable me to complete the essential research work. The editors of *Romanticism* kindly allowed me to reprint the discussion of 'Yew-Trees' from volume one of their journal (1995).

Abbreviations

B Corr	*The Correspondence of Edmund Burke*, ed. Thomas W. Copeland et al., 10 vols. (Cambridge, 1958–78)
BL	*Biographia Literaria*, ed. J. Engell and W. Jackson Bate, 2 vols. (London and Princeton, NJ, 1983). *CC* VII
Boswell	*Boswell's Life of Johnson*, ed. G. B. Hill, rev. L. F. Powell, 6 vols. (Oxford, 1934, rpt. 1971)
BWS	*The Writings and Speeches of Edmund Burke*, gen. ed. Paul Langford, 17 vols. (Oxford, 1981)
CC	*The Collected Works of Samuel Taylor Coleridge*, Bollingen Series LXXV (Collected Coleridge)
CL	*The Collected Letters of Samuel Taylor Coleridge*, ed. E. L. Griggs, 6 vols. (Oxford, 1956–71)
CM	S. T. Coleridge, *Marginalia*, ed. George Whalley, 5 vols. (London and Princeton, NJ, 1980–). *CC* XII
CN	*The Notebooks of S. T. Coleridge*, ed. Kathleen Coburn, 5 vols. (London and Princeton, NJ, 1957–)
CoL	*The Letters and Prose Writings of William Cowper*, ed. James King and Charles Ryskamp, 5 vols. (Oxford, 1979–86)
Cowper	*The Poems of William Cowper*, ed. John D. Baird and Charles Ryskamp (Oxford, 1980)
CPW	*The Complete Poetical Works of Samuel Taylor Coleridge*, ed. E. H. Coleridge, 2 vols. (London, 1912)
Darlington	William Wordsworth, *Home at Grasmere*, ed. Beth Darlington (Ithaca, 1977)
Dennis	*The Critical Works of John Dennis*, ed. E. N. Hooker, 2 vols. (Baltimore, 1939–43)
ELH	*English Literary History*
EOT	S. T. Coleridge, *Essays on His Times*, ed. David V. Erdman, 3 vols. (London and Princeton, NJ, 1978). *CC* III
Friend	S. T. Coleridge, *The Friend*, ed. B. Rooke, 2 vols. (London and Princeton, NJ, 1969). *CC* IV
Goldsmith	*Collected Works of Oliver Goldsmith*, ed. Arthur Friedman, 5 vols. (Oxford, 1966)

J Letters	*The Letters of Samuel Johnson*, ed. Bruce Redford, 3 vols. (Oxford, 1992)
JPP	*Johnson Prose and Poetry*, ed. Mona Wilson (London, 1950)
JW	*The Works of Samuel Johnson*, gen. ed. John H. Middendorf, (New Haven, 1958–)
LB	W. Wordsworth and S. T. Coleridge, *Lyrical Ballads 1798*, ed. W. J. B. Owen, 2nd edn (Oxford, 1969)
Lects 1808–19	S. T. Coleridge, *Lectures 1808–19 on Literature*, ed. R. A. Foakes, 2 vols. (London and Princeton, NJ, 1987). *CC* v
Lives	Samuel Johnson, *Lives of the English Poets*, ed. G. B. Hill, 3 vols. (Oxford, 1905)
LPR	S. T. Coleridge, *Lectures 1795 on Politics and Religion*, ed. L. Patton and P. Mann (London and Princeton, NJ, 1971). *CC* I
LS	S. T. Coleridge, *Lay Sermons*, ed. R. J. White (London and Princeton, NJ, 1972). *CC* vi
MLQ	*Modern Language Quarterly*
MLR	*Modern Language Review*
Observations	William Gilpin, *Observations relative chiefly to Picturesque Beauty made in 1772, in several parts of England; particularly the Mountains and Lakes of Cumberland and Westmoreland*, 2 vols. (London, 1786 (facsimile rpt. Richmond, 1973))
PE	Edmund Burke, *A Philosophical Enquiry into the Origin of our Ideas of the Sublime and Beautiful*, ed. J. T. Boulton (London, 1958)
Pope	*The Twickenham Edition of the Poems of Alexander Pope*, gen. ed. John Butt, 11 vols. (London, 1961–9)
Prelude	*William Wordsworth, The Prelude, 1799, 1805, 1850*, ed. Jonathan Wordsworth, M. H. Abrams, Stephen Gill (New York and London, 1979)
Price	Uvedale Price, *An Essay on the Picturesque as compared with the Sublime and the Beautiful: and on the use of Studying pictures for the purpose of improving real landscape*, 3 vols. (London, 1810 (facsimile rpt. Farnborough, Hants, 1971))
Prior	*The Literary Works of Matthew Prior*, ed. H. Bunker Wright and Monroe K. Spears, 2nd edn, 2 vols. (Oxford, 1971)
SiR	*Studies in Romanticism*
Task	William Cowper, *The Task 1785* (Ilkley and London: facsimile edn, 1973)
Thomson	James Thomson, *The Seasons*, ed. James Sambrook (Oxford, 1981)
TLS	*Times Literary Supplement*
TWC	*The Wordsworth Circle*

Watchman	*The Watchman*, ed. Lewis Patton (London and Princeton, NJ, 1970). *CC*, II
WL(EY)	*The Letters of William and Dorothy Wordsworth*, ed. E. de Selincourt, *The Early Years, 1787–1805*, 2nd edn, rev. C. L. Shaver (Oxford, 1967)
WL(MY)	*The Letters of William and Dorothy Wordsworth*, ed. E. de Selincourt, *The Middle Years, 1806–17*, 2nd edn, 2 vols., rev. Mary Moorman (Oxford, 1969)
WL(LY)	*The Letters of William and Dorothy Wordsworth*, ed. E. de Selincourt, *The Later Years*, rev. Alan G. Hill, 3 vols. (Oxford, 1979–81)
W Prose	*The Prose Works of William Wordsworth*, ed. W. J. B. Owen and J. W. Smyser, 3 vols. (Oxford, 1974)
WPW	*The Poetical Works of William Wordsworth*, ed. E. de Selincourt and Helen Darbishire, 5 vols. (Oxford, 1940–49)

Introduction

Arguments

The chief concerns of this book are eighteenth-century discourses on landscape and the nature of the authority which those discourses conferred upon their writers and readers. It will be my argument that these discourses have complex and at times conflicting ideological and political functions which criticism needs to explore if it is to understand the changing constructions of and relationships between poetic, critical, natural, and political power in the period, constructions which were instrumental in shaping a sense of national identity. First, a definition: by the term 'discourses on landscape' I shall refer not only to representation which claims simply to describe nature, but also to writing which uses the motifs and scenes of landscape-description in the course of critical and political arguments. I begin with Thomson as the first major poet to make an extended treatment of the British landscape in the post-Miltonic period, and I end with Wordsworth and Coleridge as the last to do so. But I shall not be treating their verse simply as a collection of prospect-views or picturesque scenes. Instead I shall try to put it in the contexts of contemporary debates in politics, aesthetics and criticism, to show that it was one of many efforts (with some of which it was in competition) to define the proper nature of moral and political authority for a nation whose physical and social organization was changing rapidly. And I shall suggest that we need to understand that the competition between these efforts occurred at the level of style as well as genre, so that the way in which landscape was organized by different forms of writing was less stable and harmonious than many eighteenth-century authors and some contemporary critics would have us believe. Within the polite and tasteful description of a scene in which natural (and national) order could be viewed was a struggle for authorial power that left its mark upon the description itself and on the shared taste to which the description appealed. This book will examine the different forms of that struggle for power within and between different writers on landscape in order to reveal how anxieties and tensions came to destabilize their discourse until it became a challenge to, as much as a reinforcement of, the hegemony of

1

gentlemanly taste. This destabilization made the work of the earlier writers studied here – Thomson, Cowper, Gilpin – available to the later – Wordsworth, Coleridge – for their explicit attack on the aesthetic and political values of gentlemen. This attack was made through landscape poetry that was itself unstable since its authors needed to gain popularity and reputation with a readership which still largely espoused the values they were criticizing. I shall not, it follows, be presenting the discourse on landscape as a progressive development in which the primitive forms of the earlier eighteenth-century writers reach sophisticated and self-conscious maturity in the works of the Romantics. On the contrary, I intend this book to provoke a reconsideration of Wordsworth and Coleridge as writers who, if they were able to make explicit what largely remains implicit in earlier landscape poetry, were nevertheless similar to their predecessors both in their vexed relationship with a public sphere over which gentlemanly values held sway and in their effort to depict in nature patterns of order on which a harmonious Britain could be founded. British nature, whether the landscaped estates of the Whig gentry, the woods of rural Buckinghamshire, the hills and valleys of the Lake District, or the wilds of Scotland toured by several of the writers studied here, had a complex and changing political significance in debates within and about the nation.

Contexts

Nature's political significance emerged clearly at the start of the eighteenth century in relation to the consolidation of the landed interest. The constitutional settlement of 1688 and the development of a system of patronage in the hands of the King's ministers, most notably Sir Robert Walpole, created what J.H. Plumb has called 'a paradise for gentlemen, for the aristocracy of birth'.[1] Power remained predominantly in the hands of the landed nobility and gentry, many of whom increased their wealth and influence by investment in commercial activities in the City and on their estates (iron, stone, coal, timber). But it was the possession of an independent income from heritable property, giving both freedom from labour and a continued stake in the country, that was seen as conferring upon the landed interest their legitimacy as legislators. Walpole himself, at the height of his power, wrote 'it can never be conceived but that a gentleman of liberal fortune and tolerable education is fitter to serve his country in parliament than a man bred to a trade, and brought up in a shop'.[2]

For such gentlemen the proper source of power and stability in the nation

[1]   J.H. Plumb, *The Growth of Political Stability in England 1675–1725* (London, 1967), p.187.

[2]   Sir Robert Walpole, draft of a pamphlet, quoted in J.P. Kenyon, *Revolution Principles: The Politics of Party 1689–1720* (Cambridge, 1977), p. 206.

was the possession of land, and the organization of the prospect-view was an expression of their authority over the national landscape which they owned. It was also a patriotic celebration of the resultant stability given to Britain, a stability itself seen as the foundation of trading and imperial success. Through landscape-gardening, through painting, and through the descriptions of prose writers and poets, views of the landscape owned by gentlemen became representations of the legitimacy of their power and the benefits it brought the nation. Such representations were not wholly new; as James Turner has shown, since Sir Philip Sidney poets had been adapting classical forms of topographical poetry to present prospects of the British landscape.[3] But with the civil war over and with the blank verse of *Paradise Lost* as an example, eighteenth-century writers were able to rework Virgilian epic and georgic into a panegyric on the national benefits deriving from a landscape 'naturally' productive of wealth, viewed from the commanding position of the noblemen and gentlemen who owned it. Nature, in such representations, predominant in eighteenth-century culture, was a ground on which the legitimacy of gentlemanly power and taste could be tested and confirmed, above that of 'a man bred to trade' and despite particular political disputes that might occur within the landed interest. The country estates were enlarged and remodelled in the century to an unprecedented extent. As Stephen Daniels has noted, the paintings and poems that represented them did not eclipse their owners' economic and political interests; 'rather they codified these interests in terms of landscape'.[4]

Crucial to that codification was the semblance of disinterest given to the owner/viewer of the prospect by means of the appeal to taste. Through the prospect-view, the propertied classes were able to present their political dominance as confirmed by the natural scene. The ability to distinguish and possess shared standards independent of self-interest (standards of aesthetic value or taste) in agreement about the beauty and sublimity of landscape seemed not only a mark of the viewer's gentlemanliness but a criterion for the exercise of legitimate social and political power. And that ability was itself seen to depend upon the capacity of the observer to take a distant, extensive and detached view of the scene, to be above self-interest. Bishop Berkeley discussed the matter in 1712:

It is true, he who stands close to a palace can hardly make a right judgment of the architecture and symmetry of its several parts, the nearer ever appearing disproportionably great. And if we have a mind to take a fair prospect of the order and general well-being which the inflexible laws of nature and morality derive on the world, we must, if I may say so, go out of it, and imagine ourselves to be distant spectators of all

---

[3]   James Turner, *The Politics of Landscape: Rural Scenery and Society in English Poetry 1630–1660* (Cambridge, MA, 1979).

[4]   Stephen Daniels, *Fields of Vision: Landscape Imagery and National Identity in England and the United States* (Cambridge, 1993), p. 80.

that is transacted and contained in it; otherwise we are to be deceived by the too near view of the little present interests of ourselves, our friends, or our country.[5]

The ability to take a distant prospect of nature, which depended in practice upon the freedom from labour that came with land ownership (the master looking down on his domains rather than working within them), was offered as a criterion of the disinterest regarded necessary for proper government of 'ourselves, our friends, or our country'. Adam Smith made the most careful formulation of the argument in *The Wealth of Nations* (1776). Distinguishing between those with sufficient revenue to be men of leisure and those compelled to labour, he used metaphors of viewing to suggest the importance to the nation of the former:

These varied occupations present an almost infinite variety of objects to the contemplation to those few, who, being attached to no particular occupation themselves, have leisure and inclination to examine the occupations of other people. The contemplation of so great a variety of objects necessarily exercises their minds in endless comparisons and combinations, and renders their understandings, in an extraordinary degree, both acute and comprehensive. Unless those few, however, happen to be placed in some very particular situations, their great abilities, though honourable to themselves, may contribute very little to the good government or happiness of their society.[6]

Representations of landscape, which offered such varied contemplation and commanding prospects at secondhand, also reproduced the detached view in that they asked to be read and seen as 'just representations of general nature' (*JW*, vol. VII, p. 61), to be judged disinterestedly as reflections of the scene rather than approved as rhetorically persuasive social or political argument. They appealed to taste and defined it as they did so as a capacity for disinterested judgement, possession of which in the aesthetic realm legitimized the exercise of authority in the nation at large.

By the end of the century the argument had become more explicitly ideological. Defending gentlemanly taste (and the landscape gardens it enjoyed) against corruption from within and attacks from the increasingly political self-representations of the 'lower orders', Humphry Repton wrote that the man of good taste

Knows that the same principles which direct taste in the polite arts, direct the judgement in morality; in short, that a knowledge of what is good, what is bad, and what is indifferent, whether in actions, in manners, in language, in arts, or science, constitutes the basis of good taste, and marks the distinction between the higher ranks of polished society, and the inferior orders of mankind, whose daily labours allow no

5 *Passive Obedience*, in *The Works of George Berkeley, Bishop of Cloyne*, ed. T.E. Jessop, 9 vols. (London, 1948–57), vol. VI, pp. 32–3.
6 *The Wealth of Nations* (Oxford, 1976), bk. V, ch. i, fol. 51.

leisure for other enjoyments than those of mere sensual, individual, and personal gratification.

And he continued by quoting Kett's *Elements of General Knowledge* to show that the possession of extensive views depended upon the possession of taste, which in turn depended upon freedom from labour: 'the department of taste is consequently confined to persons enlightened by education and conversant with the world, whose views of nature, of art, and of mankind, are enlarged and elevated by an extensive range of observation'.[7] Aesthetic criticism itself, as well as landscape gardening, helped to set out the ideological and social importance of such observation. Such criticism not only defined the rôle of taste but often discussed the representation of landscape directly (as when Johnson discussed Thomson's poetry). William Enfield, writing of artistic representations of landscape, declared

whatever is grand or beautiful in nature; whatever is noble, lovely, or singular, in character; whatever is surprising or affecting in situation; is by the magic power of genius brought at pleasure into view, in the manner best adapted to excite correspondent emotions. A rich field of elegant pleasure is hereby laid open before the reader who is possessed of a true taste for polite literature, which distinguishes him from the vulgar.[8]

Enfield's vocabulary reveals the exclusive circularity of the languages of criticism and art at this historical juncture: he uses metaphors drawn from the observation of landscape to describe the aesthetic, moral and social distinction conferred upon the reader by art which is itself an observation of nature. For Enfield, then, a polite education in aesthetics is a matter of acquiring a critical vocabulary which reproduces, rather than challenges, that of the art it examines. Criticism comes to share the ideological function of an art that serves the interests, as it views the estates, of the leisured landed classes – as Sir Joshua Reynolds put it: 'a hundred thousand near-sighted men ... that see only what is just before them, make no equivalent to one man whose view extends to the whole horizon around him'.[9]

The authority conferred by the prospect-view was to greater and lesser degrees always precarious. The representation of landscape was never simply a disguised ideology presenting gentlemanly aesthetic judgement as naturally, and by implication socially and politically, valid. It was also a discourse in which that judgement could be redefined, challenged and even undermined – as it was in much of the work of Johnson and Wordsworth that deliberately confronts the contemporary aesthetic conventions. For Thomson, Cowper and Coleridge landscape-description was, I shall suggest, also a means of making interventions in current political debates. Each of these writers

---

[7]   Humphry Repton, *Observations on the Theory and Practice of Landscape Gardening* (London, 1803), p.11.

[8]   William Enfield, 'On Reading Works of Taste', in *The Speaker* (London, 1799), p. xxxiii.

[9]   In F.W. Hilles (ed.), *Portraits by Sir Joshua Reynolds* (London, 1952), p.129.

explicitly politicizes natural scenes in order to gain authority for his arguments about the government of the nation. Often, I shall suggest, such scenes stand in conflict with the apparently unpolitical representation of natural power that occurs elsewhere in the text, leaving it divided as the readership detects the writer imposing a partisan political argument on the landscape as well as deriving a moral pattern from it. Explicitly political scenes threaten to undermine the hidden politics of apparently purely natural scenes by suggesting that landscape-description is not an observation of a natural order but an imposition of a party line. Such texts are, as a result, indeterminate, having both an apparent reinforcement of gentlemanly authority and a destabilization of it encoded within them. As such they should serve to remind us that forms as varied and complex as these discourses on landscape were never simply means to perpetuate an ideology, but constituted a place in which ideologies were proposed and contested. They formed part of the debates by which a nation defined itself, challenged its definitions and changed.

In examining the part which these discourses played in these debates I shall place poetry, aesthetic theory, literary criticism and the prose tour narrative in the context of contemporary politics. In particular, I shall be concerned with the arguments made repeatedly through the century and developed by Wordsworth and Coleridge as young radicals, that the independence and disinterest on which depended the gentry's and nobility's legitimacy as the people's representatives in parliament was being undermined. As early as 1709 Sir John Pakington had articulated the fears of Tory squires when he spoke of the danger of 'the moneyed and military men becoming lords of us who have the lands'.[10] During the ascendancy of Walpole (1721–42) such fears were greatly increased as a system of placemen, pensioners and patronage was perfected, producing in parliament large numbers of men who were indebted to the Crown and ministry for their own, their family's and their friends' income and status. Independent country gentlemen, of both Tory and Whig leanings, felt that parliament, a necessary counterweight in the constitutional balance against arbitrary rule by Court and/or army, was being compromised. Whilst Walpole was still able to retain the support of many of these backbench MPs by playing on their fears of aiding, or appearing to aid, disloyal Jacobitism, he was increasingly opposed by members of the landed interest who felt that it was being corrupted from within by the blandishments of pay and patronage offered by him. By the mid-1730s the necessary disinterest of the landed gentry in parliament was seen to have been threatened by corruption, and an opposition emerged which sought to replace Walpole with a ministry defined neither by its use of

---

[10] Quoted in Geoffrey Holmes, 'The Achievement of Stability: the Social Context of Politics from the 1680s to the Age of Walpole', in John Cannon (ed.), *The Whig Ascendancy: Colloquies on Hanoverian England* (London, 1981), pp. 1–22 (p.18).

corrupt means nor by its party nature. The 'Patriot' group, assembled around Bolingbroke, Chesterfield and Lyttelton, attempted to appeal beyond the Tory/Whig denominations to the gentry's loyalty to the nation as a whole. The nation was to be safeguarded by a parliament of disinterested and patriotic gentlemen free from corrupt links to the ministry and Court.

The 'Country' ideology of the Patriot opposition has been the subject of much scrutiny by historians of the period. I shall be examining two of the aspects revealed by that scrutiny in the course of this book. First, following the arguments made by J.G.A. Pocock and the modifications made of them by John Brewer and by Isaac Kramnick, I shall suggest that Country ideology, and the seventeenth-century Commonwealthsman arguments that it adapted, continued to shape opposition to the power of ministry and Court until the end of the century – that it, as much as rationalist and natural rights arguments, shaped radical thought in the 1790s.[11] Coleridge and Wordsworth were, as the Patriots had done before them, modifying a tradition of anti-monarchical radicalism found in Harrington and Algernon Sidney – a modification which was itself a recognized motif of eighteenth-century radicalism. This tradition emphasized the inherent danger to liberty stemming from the natural tendency towards corruption. Such danger could only be averted by a balanced constitution, in which the tendency of each power group to despotism was checked by the others. In Britain this meant opposition to a standing army, to arbitrary monarchy, to the manipulation of parliament by Court and ministry through bribery, placemen and pensions. An independent parliament, a popular militia and regular elections were necessary checks, as was a restraint on the financial interests of the City. The Roman republic and Hebrew commonwealth were idealized by contrast with Walpole's Britain.

The second aspect to be examined concerns the strain which Country ideology revealed at the heart of the hegemony of the landed interest. Chesterfield claimed that the Patriots stood for loyal gentlemen as a whole, men who, valuing independence against the encroachments of ministry and monarch, were preservers of British liberty. Yet this claim, and the very existence of the Patriot opposition, emerged from a division in the landed interest. In face of Walpole's continued majorities in the Commons, obtained with the votes (votes bought and freely given) of backbench Country gentlemen, Chesterfield could not simply speak for all the landed indepen-

---

[11] See J.G.A. Pocock, *Politics, Language and Time: Essays on Political Thought and History* (London, 1972), pp. 125–33 and *Virtue, Commerce, and History* (Cambridge, 1985), pp. 257–61. See also Caroline Robbins, *The Eighteenth-Century Commonwealthman* (Cambridge, MA, 1959). Pocock's reading of all opposition in the eighteenth-century as essentially 'Country' in its Commonwealthsman neo-classical republicanism has been modified by John Brewer, *Party Ideology and Popular Politics at the Accession of George III* (Cambridge, 1976), pp. 250–63 and Isaac Kramnick, *Republicanism and Bourgeois Radicalism: Political Ideology in Late Eighteenth-Century England and America* (Ithaca and London, 1990), pp. 164–97.

dents against the corruption of the Court. His claims seemed to reveal a
gentry and nobility deeply split – the argument that on the basis of the
disinterested views given them by land ownership they could discern the best
interests of the whole nation was threatened by its appearance in partisan
campaigns against Walpole and his supporters. These disinterested and
extensive views appeared too shaped by party politics for the nation's best
interests to be agreed upon or mutually discerned. And furthermore, the
Patriots seemed to many to be appealing to the virtues of disinterest for
reasons of self-interest – from their own desire to supplant Walpole and enjoy
power.

The results of these splits and tensions on the representation of landscape
were far-reaching. They were evident in the magnates' organization of their
estates. Walpole's own improvements to his house and lands at Houghton
were funded by the diversion of public money: to Harley in 1732 they
epitomized the tainting of gentlemanly values by financial corruption,
showing 'very great expense without either judgement or taste'.[12] Cobham,
one of Walpole's opponents, included a headless statue of him in the ruinous
'Temple of Modern Virtue' built in his gardens at Stowe. The representation
of landscape had become a means of symbolizing a ruling class divided in its
view of the proper scope and nature of its power – in Cobham's hands a
means of criticizing a resultant decline in moral and imperial authority. For
Thomson, as a poet patronized by the Patriots in the 1730s and 1740s,
landscape poetry ceased to represent an uncontroversial ground of liberty in
which a providentially arranged natural order could be observed at leisure,
thus perpetuating the taste and disinterest by which the gentry might
reproduce that liberty and independence in wise government. It became
instead a means of making particular political arguments: the freely owned
land upon which taste might be exercised was shown as falling prey to
invasion and tyranny. Cowper was influenced by Thomson's verse and was
himself an independent Whig. Suffering a mental breakdown at the prospect
of public office he retired from London to a country retreat, whence he
perpetuated this Country treatment of England's fields. He used Virgil's
Roman exile as a model for a poetry that criticized Court from the country.
But in arguing that the country was itself subject to the self-serving corruption
of a newly commercial gentry, he developed Thomson's critique of the
extension of Court patronage over the land as a whole. Johnson's Tory
idealization of the vanishing independence of the Scottish clans and, later,
Uvedale Price's, Humphry Repton's and William Gilpin's rural paternalism
can all be seen too as critiques from supporters of the landed gentry of its
corruption from within by financial self-interest.

Critiques of this kind could only be made at a cost – the critic had to bear

---

[12] Quoted in Nigel Everett, *The Tory View of Landscape* (New Haven and London, 1994), p. 47.

the tension of having been seen to abandon the sustaining convention that
tasteful observation of landscape could speak uncontroversially for a united
British nature properly represented by the gentry for the nation. Later
politicians accepted that cost as the price of retaining integrity in face of a
corrupt parliament, in a way Bolingbroke and Chesterfield did not. As
Charles James Fox began to think of secession from a House of Commons
dominated by the alliance of Pitt and George III, he quoted Cowper's
conscious choice of a position of marginality, longing 'for a lodge in some vast
Wilderness'.[13] Fox had learnt from Cowper that gentlemanly independence
could only be preserved by withdrawal from arenas in which all opposition,
however principled, was construed as self-interested. He was able from his
rural retreat (as Cowper also was) to generate a powerful critique of the
corruption of gentlemanly independence. He had, however, no arena other
than parliament in which the power of a disinterested landed interest could
be revived. A meeting of 4 June 1793 suggests the value still placed by his
supporters on this disinterestedness: they raised money to pay Fox's debts,
arguing that 'it deeply concerns and may effectually promote the service as
well as the Honour of the Nation that the example of disinterestedness held
out to the future by Mr F–'s publick conduct, should not descend to posterity
unaccompanied by some evidence of the general impression it has made &
the sense which His Country entertains of it'.[14] That disinterestedness, made
possible by the subscriptions which ensured Fox did not need place or
pension, was itself seen more cynically by the increasingly articulate radicals
who sought the reform of a parliament of landed gentry. Francis Place later
saw Fox's meetings with such radicals as an insincere attempt to win support
enough from a new constituency to get himself a place in power again.
Cowper had been able to persuade a readership of his continued disinterest
by an uncompromising rejection of corrupting influences which left him,
however, anxiously and vulnerably presenting views of a shrinking rural
refuge in which liberty and independence might still be observed. Fox, a
politician rather than a poet, was neither content with the cold comforts of so
isolated an integrity nor able to make common cause with radicals who
campaigned outside parliament for representation to be open to other classes
than the traditional ruling elite. He returned to the Commons in 1801.

By 1801 the pressure upon the values and authority of the landed interest
was seen to have intensified, as a result both of the increasing commercialization of the gentry and of the radicals' campaigns for reform. I shall be
reading the debate about the picturesque that raged at this time in the
context of this pressure, suggesting that the Country ideology of independent
Whigs was redefined by it, as were Cowper's vision of landscape and the
prose tour narrative. The picturesque responded also to the changing

---

[13] *The Task*, bk II, line 1 quoted in L.G. Mitchell, *Charles James Fox* (Oxford, 1992), p.132.
[14] Philip Francis, quoted in Mitchell, *Charles James Fox*, p.105.

relations between the landowner, his tenants and the labourers on the land. As enclosure, improvement and more commercial estate management replaced a more traditional paternalist authority, those wishing to preserve that authority idealized the old-fashioned squire. And they tried to compensate for his disappearance by institutionalizing the watchful and disinterested view he had taken of his lands and those who lived on them. What had been presented as an attribute of the gentleman essential for a government protective of national liberty, was now seen, in the work of Thomas Gilbert, as a requirement of committees convened to oversee the potentially rebellious poor:

> The district committee, standing thus upon a vantage-ground, from whence they may ascertain, at one view, the necessities of the whole district, are the proper persons to pronounce what sum of money is requisite for carrying on the maintenance and employment of the poor.[15]

This argument shows the disinterested and commanding view available to gentlemen as no longer either purely aesthetic or an emblem of their personal paternal authority over their estate. The prospect-view is instead made a justification of an official and institutionalized supervision, by which the poor are as much controlled as relieved, a justification which shaped the presentation, visible in Repton, Malthus and Bentham, of workhouse and prison as models of paternal superintendence.

For writers less uncompromising in their country independence than Cowper the representation of landscape involved anxieties that their own authority would be undermined by their use of poetry for less worthy motives than disinterested appeals to taste. This anxiety took the form of vexed relationships with patrons and with the market. These relationships, difficult for the majority of the writers studied here, will be a recurrent theme of my discussion. Smith had argued that it was the leisured man's freedom from labour that gave him the opportunity for varied contemplation. But the disinterested and extensive views of a gentleman were, in the cases of the writers who represented them, endangered both if they were labourers for the market, and if they were responsible to a patron. In the former case, as Wordsworth and Coleridge found, manly independence of view could be compromised by the self-interested need to conform, for money and fame, to fashionable taste. In the latter, independence was threatened by the need, for the sake of continued support, to conform to the patron's view. What might be accepted as a disinterested view if held by Chesterfield might, as Thomson found, seem self-interested and insincere if espoused in the hope of patronage. This difficulty was exacerbated in Thomson's case since Chesterfield's appeal beyond party divisions to patriotism was seen by some as self-serving. The

---

[15] Thomas Gilbert, *Considerations on the Bills for the Better Relief and Employment of the Poor* (London, 1787), p. 30.

apparently disinterested landscapes of patriotic liberty that Thomson depicted for his Patriot patrons thus seemed doubly contentious, enmeshed as they were in the divisiveness of a political campaign which might appear less than sincere and in Thomson's own need to please his paymasters.

Texts

The texts examined here are linked by the sense common to all that the writer's authority as an observer of nature is in some respects threatened (even whilst in others it is enhanced) by his participation in the politics of the day and by the unstable relationship with patrons and market. For Thomson, Cowper, Johnson, the theorists of the picturesque, Wordsworth and Coleridge the representation of a commanding view was a means of establishing their own authority over the objects of their contemplation and the whole cultural field. But it was also a process in which their own authority, and that of disinterested and extensive views in the nation more generally, came to be challenged and redefined. The writers' involvement in particular political disputes and their precarious existence between patrons and reading public put their gentlemanliness – and the ideology of the landed gentry – in doubt. By 1798 Wordsworth and Coleridge were deliberately exposing the ideological nature and limited exclusivity of gentlemanly taste even as Repton was bemoaning its perversion by the contemporary gentry. Neither he nor they, however, could afford to ignore it: they might hope to question and reform it but they needed the support of patrons and public who still, as Enfield's essay reveals, espoused it.

The writers studied here are not only linked by their common difficulties with the politicization of landscape and the demands of patrons and market. They are linked by their development of, and resistance to, each other's representations. For Cowper the poetry of Thomson was itself an organization of landscape which he both imitated and resisted as he sought to appear before the public with a style both recognizable and original. For Wordsworth and Coleridge too the verse of Thomson and Cowper was a model to be imitated, revised and challenged in a process by which they defined their own poetic styles, ambivalently, as indebted to but also independent of their predecessors'. Johnson – the strongest critic of the century – and the picturesque theorists – the aestheticians who sought to revise taste by a discussion of landscape – were also writers to be both imitated and challenged. In their writings on landscape and on the representation of landscape in art they set out the limits of taste and marked out the patterns, natural and literary, to be accepted as the foundation of good order. They also disturbed those patterns as their own allegiances were subjected to tension. For Johnson the duty to perpetuate established patterns of order came into conflict with his need to derive his authority from his own rhetorical efforts, a conflict I shall compare with the similar battle staged in Wordsworth's landscape poetry. In these (self-) conflicts, existing authorities – whether they were aesthetic conventions or the works of other writers – were often subordinated to the author's need to derive from himself alone his power to speak morally to the nation. For these writers their promotion of this power through landscape-description came to depend on the suppression of the discourses that already marked the scene – both those that challenged their conceptions of order and those that made their descriptions possible. In the process other writers (in Johnson's case Shakespeare, Milton and Thomson – in Wordsworth's, Thomson, Cowper, Milton and Coleridge) were acknowledged only to be subordinated respectively to Johnson's and Wordsworth's own discourses. Subordinating discourses of this kind were, for Cowper observing Johnson's critical power over the poetry he wished to imitate, for Coleridge viewing Wordsworth's poetic domination of the landscape he wished to describe, too authoritative to be confronted directly. Instead each designed landscapes in which authority is shown to arise in the acceptance of weakness, in an acknowledgement of vulnerability that undermines the commanding position from which the writer presents his view. Confessions of vulnerability as these landscapes are, they are also implicit critiques of Johnsonian and Wordsworthian authority and its subordination of others. They remain, therefore, struggles for personal authority as well as debates over the proper nature of authority in the fields of Britain at large.

Such, then, is an outline of some of the complex relationships between the texts examined in this book. By deliberately including aesthetic and critical writings in the discourses on landscape under investigation I intend to show that poetic authority should not be understood as being produced simply by the struggle of a poet with his strong poetic predecessors. Harold Bloom's theory of poetic influence tends to understand it in such terms and in so doing removes from the account the often vexed relationship between poetry and criticism, as well as that between poetry and the public realm with its competing political and social discourses. Moreover, in construing poetic influence via a Freudian model in which the desire to master the father is repressed, Bloom fails to account for the productive influence of weak predecessors. The eighteenth-century landscape poem is not only to be seen as shaped (as I shall show of Cowper's *The Task*) by emulation of and deference towards Milton, but also by absorption of discourses (poetic, critical, political) whose very instabilities made them attractive. It was, I shall suggest of Thomson, of Gilpin, of Cowper himself, precisely because their representations of landscape seemed indeterminate, ambivalent, even self-contradictory, that later writers were able to develop their own discourses from them, borrowing from them whilst criticizing them. As well as the desire to master the father, eighteenth-century landscape-description was driven by sibling rivalry (Wordsworth and Coleridge) and by past writing (poetry and aesthetic theory) whose indeterminacy allowed it to be easily used, often for ends opposed to those the original author had intended.

Chapters

This book begins with a consideration of Thomson, since it is in *The Seasons* that the prospect-view and the sublime are first combined to transform the georgic and the Miltonic epic into a celebration of an order observable in the fields of Britain. Considering the naturalization of power-relations made in *Winter*, I shall suggest that what was at stake was nothing less than the definition, for the enfranchised classes who formed the larger part of the reading public, of Britishness. This definition was more powerful and more inclusive the more that conflicts and tensions were shown to be containable within a national landscape in which disorder was present within a natural (and providential) order. The later poetry of Thomson, which used landscape to speak of political division, was an attack upon a ministry which had, he believed, made the foundation of national unity on natural order impossible. It was less popular than his earlier work in which such a foundation had been made, but it dramatized the increasing difficulty, as political divisions came more sharply into focus, of endorsing by apparent observation an order embracing the whole national scene. For the later writers on whom I shall concentrate, the difficulty increased still further and was a major source of tensions in their work and in their conceptions of themselves as authors. In Cowper's landscape poetry the divisions that beset his attempt to speak for a moral order observable in the whole British scene themselves became the main-spring of the poem. I shall show him striving to imitate but unable to sustain the religious and natural sublime that Milton and Thomson practised, an inability which he turned into a critique of the absence of morality from politics in the land of which he wished to speak patriotically. In Cowper, the poet's inability to generate from landscape poetry an authoritative vision of order was offered as evidence of the displacement of that order to marginal retreats and lives. Cowper, under-mining with humour his own pretensions to a language of religious or political power, nevertheless made a political comment. He bore for his readership the burden of their inability, in the face of political division and corruption in the gentlemanly classes themselves, to read in the landscape of Britain a national order in which their power and judgement were endorsed. Internalizing political and religious division, Cowper made impotence a token of moral sensitivity, a moral sensitivity which was also dependent upon his retreat from the market – evidenced by his departure from London and his attacks upon commercialism. Authority, in the face of a disordered realm, came to reside in the acceptance of its loss – the gentleman read in nature his inability to read himself into a position of power in and for the nation. Disinterested views were seen to survive only in the genteel poverty of the rural margins.

Central to my arguments is the account of Samuel Johnson given in the second chapter. For Johnson writerly authority, linguistic order and national identity were bound up together. His mastery of the English language, exhibited in the Dictionary, was portrayed as an extension of order and conquest over the whole island of Britain. Yet Johnson questioned his own authority, testing it against the landscape poetry of Thomson and the unfamiliar language and landscape of Highland Scotland. Johnson addressed the politics of landscape explicitly – discussing issues of land ownership, social subordination and the clan system. And his interest in Gaelic whilst on his Scottish tour was part of his desire to test the limits of a British identity based on the hegemony of the language, law and culture of England. I shall examine this tour in detail, comparing it with those made following its path by Gilpin, the Wordsworths and Coleridge.

Johnson made from his discourse on landscape a rhetoric which appeared to grant power to others only to retain it in his own hands. His critical authority was built upon rhetorical strategies of this kind, and they were strategies which later writers adapted to their own ends – including that of subjecting Johnson's own discourse to their own critical and poetic power. Cowper and Wordsworth both sought to make room for their own landscape poetry by criticizing Johnson, and they used the motifs of landscape-description to subordinate him to a critical and poetic discourse which could then speak for a national/natural order in a style unthreatened by his authority over English language and poetry. And so the politics of landscape-description were critical politics too: subordination of Johnson was necessary if nature was to be made to represent social and political views of which he disapproved. And since for Cowper and Wordsworth representing the power of landscape necessitated a modification of the poetry of Milton, it became vital that Johnson's criticism of *Paradise Lost* be answered. To adapt Milton it was necessary not only to disagree with Johnson's views on his blank verse but to dislodge the authority with which Johnson aligned poetic order with a Tory politics of traditional paternalism. Cowper, seeking a familiarization of Miltonic style in political poetry, and Wordsworth, representing revolutionary patterns in landscape, sought to overcome the power of Johnson's view that Milton's republicanism was a disordered discontent in politics and prosody. They did so by reducing Johnson to an object in scenes which they controlled, a rhetorical battle intended to diminish Johnson in the eyes of the reading public.

After my discussion of Johnson, I shall make an analysis of the picturesque, arguing that this aesthetic theory was an attempt to appeal to and perpetuate the power of gentlemanly taste: by agreeing to enjoy a landscape that

presented disorder in palatable and safe form, readers could retain faith in
the ability of their judgement to discover, disinterestedly, an order within the
world, despite its wildness. The picturesque was also a discourse of struggle
between writers who advocated paternalism and those who, vindicating the
taste of gentry and nobility, nevertheless were haunted by visions of natural
and social forces beyond the limits of that taste. William Gilpin's picturesque
was in tension with that of Uvedale Price as it articulated, through reports of
natural destructiveness, his sympathy with the rebellious power of the lower
orders who resisted the authority – and aesthetics – of gentlemen. Similarly
Humphry Repton was in dispute both with Price and with Richard Payne
Knight over the proper place of the poor in the landscape and over his own
position. As a man of commerce, he seemed to them precluded by his self-
interested relationships with patrons from possessing the disinterested
landscape-aesthetics of the gentleman squire. Like Johnson writing resentfully
to his prospective patron Chesterfield, Repton replied by asserting his
independence in a form of writing from which he did not expect to gain
money or patrons.

It is one of my contentions here that, viewed as they rarely are in the
context of the eighteenth-century writers with whom they compared
themselves, Wordsworth and Coleridge can be seen to be developing many
of the power-seeking verbal strategies of their predecessors. As well as
wrestling with Milton, Wordsworth was adapting Thomson and Cowper, as
was Coleridge as he attempted to create a landscape of political unity for a
nation whose divisions undermined his own position. Recent critics have
suggested that responses to the French Revolution caused divisions in the
political field of Britain to which Wordsworth's and Coleridge's landscape
poetry was an often evasive (or even denying) reaction.[16] I will suggest
however that their reaction was overwritten by their involvement in conflicts
and strategies that had driven landscape-description in Britain since the start
of the eighteenth century. Learning from Thomson, Johnson and the
picturesque writers ways of seeking authority over the British reading public
by locating social and political order in the landscape, they learnt also to
borrow from past writers and to subordinate their rivals. For Wordsworth
these rivals included the gentlemen who owned landscape and those writers,
including Johnson, Price and Knight, who had endorsed such ownership in
their representations of nature and art. In the *Lyrical Ballads* and *Home at
Grasmere* the conflicts and strategies present in these earlier writers are not
only as significant as those presented by the French Revolution but help to
shape Wordsworth's discussion of the violence of political insurrection. In
'Yew-Trees' in particular it is by a consideration of the historical violence
symbolized by an English landscape that Wordsworth seeks, in speaking for a

---

[16] See Alan Liu, *Wordsworth: The Sense of History* (Stanford, 1989), Marjorie Levinson, *Wordsworth's
Great Period Poems* (Cambridge, 1986).

natural scene, to give himself a voice whose authority to speak for the nation is increased by his exploration of its inscription in political conflicts and divided loyalties. The authority that this poetry claims is founded not on evasion of the French Revolution but on an examination of poetry's relationship to English rebellions made by a radical reworking of the opposition's traditional use of the arguments of the seventeenth-century Commonwealthsmen.

The battles for power waged by the writers examined here were, it should by now be clear, conducted as part of a struggle to present an authoritative view of the proper social, cultural and political order for the nation. Wordsworth's radical revision of the long landscape poem and Coleridge's poetry of radical community placed that order beyond the limitations of the disinterested gentlemanly view, beyond its representation in the bounded prospect. That they were able to do so is a testament to the poetry of Cowper, which was pivotal in its use of gentlemanly aesthetics of landscape against the social and political course taken by (and in the name of) the majority of the landed interest. The politicization of the landscape view as a mode of criticism, uneasily begun by Thomson, sacrificed the illusion that the landed gentry and nobility was united and that its view was identical to the interests of the nation. But it allowed, in Cowper's hands as in Johnson's suspicion of Chesterfield's disinterestedness, a demonstration of the complacency and self-serving exclusivity of gentlemanly taste. When Country opposition to the corruption and commercialization of the gentry was also taken up by radicals, speaking for the urban middle classes and for the small farmers and labourers disadvantaged by the gentry's commercial improvements of their land, then the authority of taste and of its representation in disinterested views was challenged from below. As part of this challenge Wordsworth's and Coleridge's landscape poetry seems like a critical reworking of a tradition that effectively brings it to an end. Their Romanticism brought about the destruction of the poetry of the prospect-view in so far as that poetry was aligned with the taste and power of the landed interest. In this respect, if their work heralded the end of a tradition of gentlemanly authority, it was also seminal in a way they recognized but disliked. From Wordsworth's landscapes of the self grew Shelley's and Byron's iconoclastic scenes of individualism. But Wordsworth and Coleridge turned after 1815 to an idealization of the landed interest whose claims they had helped to undermine. They did so out of concern that the further undermining of the ruling classes by their own commercialism and by radical individualism would cause revolutionary anarchy. Both urged the gentry, for the sake of a national stability in which British liberty would be protected by traditional order, to return to a disinterested and benevolent paternalism. By then, partly through their own earlier efforts, to represent that kind of landscape of liberty was to espouse a politics of nostalgia (a politics further compromised in Wordsworth's case by the fact that he was writing to serve the political interests of his patron, the landowner Lord Lowther).[17]

It is, however, not with Wordsworth but with Thomson that I begin, examining the means by which he sought authority by staging implicitly (and often explicitly) political landscapes in a language which adapted what John Dennis called the masterful style of the religious sublime (Dennis, vol. I, pp. 359–64). Landscape in Thomson becomes in a new way a naturalization of moral force yet also a ground of political dispute – a divided scene cloaked in apparent order, a realm whose hidden conflicts remained to be expressed and redefined by the writers who succeeded him, adapting and criticizing, renewing but also undermining his ideological vision of the fields of Britain.

[17] A phrase used by Isaac Kramnick to designate an earlier Country idealization of the landed gentry: *Bolingbroke and his Circle: The Politics of Nostalgia in the Age of Walpole* (Cambridge, MA, 1968).

1

Thomson and Cowper: the 'stubborn Country tam'd'?

Born in 1700 in Scotland, Thomson came to London in 1725. His poem *Winter* was published in 1726, followed by poems named after the other seasons. They appeared in one volume, *The Seasons*, in 1730, incorporating revisions to the original texts. Widely popular for the next one hundred years *The Seasons* was praised both for its accurate depiction of the details of the rural scene, and for its capacity to lead the reader to moral reflection.

The means by which *The Seasons* leads the reader will be my subject here, and I shall be examining these means by detailed criticism of particular rural views and incidents narrated by Thomson. I shall be examining them too in the context of the critical arguments about poetry's persuasive power made by Thomson himself and the circle of which he was part, a circle for whom the ideas of John Dennis about the sublime in general and Milton in particular were important. I shall be arguing that, through Dennis's discussion of 'enthusiastic passion' in poetry, Thomson developed a discourse on landscape intended, as Dennis argued such poetry should be, to appeal to and renew the taste of gentlemen. Thomson's loco-descriptive verse, I shall contend, formed an ideology the more powerful for its apparent naturalness and the more effective for the contradictions it included. Amongst these contradictions was that in which power is refigured as powerlessness, a reversal staged by Thomson in the theatre of nature, but with relevance to the theatre of society since it presents submission to authority as an inevitable and universal lot. Thomson reminds gentlemen-readers of human power-lessness by presenting them with generic rural figures, rustics who stand for vulnerable man-in-general crushed by the forces of nature. He simultaneously enforces a moral with an implicitly political message – that subordination is necessary – and leaves the reader with his power enhanced by the reminder of vulnerability. For the gentleman-reader is invited both to pity the poor rustic (who may represent man-in-general but is socially inferior to the reader) and to associate himself with the narratorial energy with which nature's crushing force is represented. And so, by a contradiction that paradoxically increases his authority, the reader vicariously imagines himself crushed only to regain a position of safety and power as he is asked to pity the rustic who stands in for him. The invitation to be compassionate removes the vulnerability which identification with the rustic brings. It reassures the reader of his virtue whilst he enjoys the dramatization of destructive power.

The contradiction I have outlined is implicit in the sublime as Dennis describes it, and in sensibility as delineated in the philosophy of Shaftesbury and Hutcheson, who were also influences on Thomson. It is itself in tension with Thomson's tendency, increasingly marked as he grew older, to read landscape politically. In the revised *Seasons* and a number of other late works Thomson explicitly represents cultivated landscape as an index of the virtues of a particular patron whose politics he shared. He also, in a related movement, makes wild landscape a source of a native British freedom, a naturally occurring national characteristic endangered, he claims, by the extension by Walpole's government of corruption, bribery and court-influence across the land. Whilst these politicized landscapes allowed Thomson to make rhetorical interventions in current debates, they endangered his ideological naturalization of power-relations by revealing the landscape to be a political (and even party political) fiction. It can thus be argued not only as Johnson argued that Thomson's nature-descriptions were better than his political poems, but that his recognizably political landscapes endangered his ostensibly unpolitical ones, which were them-selves more politically (if 'politically' is understood in a broad sense) powerful the more they represented subordination as a pitiable 'fact' of nature.

I shall investigate Thomson's explicitly politicized landscapes later in the chapter, after a detailed reading of his account of a shepherd lost in and killed by a winter storm. I begin, however, by looking at the criticism of John Dennis and the use Thomson and his circle made of it. By 1726 Dennis was a long established critic, no stranger to controversy. For the young Thomson, recently arrived in London from Scotland, Dennis was an older figure whose ideas, discussed by his friends Aaron Hill and David Mallet, were impressive. Thomson wrote to Dennis and sought an introduction to him in August 1726, shortly after the publication of *Winter*. Before this, however, he had become enthusiastic about ideas derived from Dennis in the work of Hill, a poet whose encouragement the young Scot sought. In the Preface to his poem *The Creation* (1720) Hill had advocated the sublimity of Hebrew poetry as a model for English verse. Like Dennis he found such sublimity in the Psalms and declared that it *'frightens, astonishes,* and *ravishes* the Mind of a Reader'.[1] He suggested, in the manner of Dennis, that it was by 'enthusiasm' in the poetry that the reader was astonished, ravished and transported. Hill praised *Winter* on its first appearance in April 1726 and, after meeting Thomson for the first time at the end of that month, began an acquaintance

---

[1]   *The Creation* (London, 1720), p.viii, quoted in Robert Inglesfield, 'James Thomson, Aaron Hill and the Poetic "Sublime"', *British Journal of Eighteenth Century Studies*, 13 (1990), 215–21 (p. 215). My discussion of Hill and Thomson is indebted to this article.

that led to his writing a prefatory poem for the second edition. Thomson on his part quoted Hill's poem 'Judgment Day' as an example of poetic seriousness in the Preface that he added for the second edition.

Thomson's Preface reflects the ideas of Hill and Dennis; it views Hebrew poetry as a model for English verse, cites Milton as an example of poetry's charm and exalting force over the reader and advocates the treatment of serious subjects so as to 'please, instruct, surprize, and astonish' (Thomson, p. 304). Thomson used, as had Hill, Dennis's definition of the response obtained by poetry from readers: 'I know no subject more elevating, more amusing; more ready to awake the poetical Enthusiasm, the philosophical Reflection, and the moral Sentiment, than the *Works of Nature*' (Thomson, p. 305). It is nature that 'enlarges, and transports, the soul' – there is no thinking of it 'without breaking out into POETRY'. Here Thomson borrows Dennis's critical language, but applies it directly to nature rather than to classical or Miltonic poetry as had Dennis himself. Poetry becomes, on this account, an outburst or transport of excited thought in direct response to landscape, which itself takes on the power to exalt the viewer into a state of high moral feeling, a power possessed by religion in the critical account Dennis had given of classical cultures.

What was there in Dennis's work that made Thomson keen to adapt it to define his own purpose in writing landscape poetry? In *The Advancement and Reformation of Modern Poetry* (1701) Dennis had adopted many of the ideas of Longinus, whose treatise *On the Sublime* was itself concerned with the capacity of figurative language (especially that found in religious and poetic texts) to persuade audiences by swaying them emotionally.[2] Whilst Longinus was interested too in how figuration might be used rhetorically in political and legal arenas, Dennis intensified his treatment of poetry's emotional power. Dennis suggested that it both stemmed from and in turn strengthened the passionate power of religion: 'for Passion in a Poem, is Genius and the Power of exciting Passion, is Genius in a Poet; to the raising of which, Religion, as we have shown above, gives a very great Advantage' (Dennis, vol. I, p. 246). Poetry, by transporting and exalting its readers' minds through its figurative language, could renew the religious culture from which it emerged – becoming a moral and even spiritual rhetoric. Dennis, in a detailed analysis of Augustan Rome, showed that poetry, in its style, subject-matter and moral authority was shaped by the conjunction of particular sets of historical circumstances. The 'Language of the Country in which he writes, and which he finds made to his Hands', 'Art ... those Rules, and that Method' and Religion all needed to be at their height for great poetry to be written. For

---

[2] See *Longinus On the Sublime*, tr. and ed. James A. Arieti and John M. Crossett (New York and Toronto, 1985) and, on the importance of Longinus in the eighteenth century, see Samuel H. Monk, *The Sublime: A Study of Critical Theories in Eighteenth-Century England* (Ann Arbor, Mich., 1960).

Dennis all were so, or were nearly so, in the reign of Augustus when, in
particular, religion had 'more Force, more Authority, and more Majesty,
than it had had for some time before' (Dennis, vol. i, p. 246).

Dennis's criticism offered Thomson a way of endorsing a poetry of strong
emotional effect. After the *Advancement ... of Modern Poetry* and *The Grounds of
Criticism in Poetry* (1704) Hill, Mallet and Thomson himself were able to claim
a moral and semi-religious purpose for their sublime landscapes, whilst also
maintaining that their style emerged from the language of the country in
which they wrote, rather than from a diction imported from books.[3] Dennis
had asserted that a more forceful translation of Hebrew religious poetry
would 'attract the Gentry, and particularly those of the most extraordinary
Parts among them, whose Examples would influence the rest, as the rest
would influence the People' (Dennis, vol. i, p. 372). Thomson was able to find
in this view a combination of religion, moral teaching and ideological
function that he could apply to his own poetry. In his case the translation (or
'outburst') of nature into passionate poetry in a style derived from current
language and the latest art (Milton's religious poetry in particular) replaced
the direct translation of Hebrew texts.[4]

Much of Thomson's *Winter* can be usefully seen as an exemplification of
the sublime, as derived from Longinus but modified by Dennis.[5] In *The
Grounds of Criticism* Dennis makes 'the Wrath of Infinite Power' and the
'Vengeance' of 'the great universal Monarch' sources of terror and passion,
and advocates a poetry that by imagining such power in action will 'surprise
and astonish the soul' (Dennis, vol. i, p. 362). The subordination of the
reader to images of God's retributive hand is a moral education by emotional
effect – an education with implications for the maintenance of the social
hierarchy, as Dennis's hope that the gentry will influence the people suggests.
Dennis, moreover, explicitly views natural objects as divine works worthy of
poetic treatment, sources of the passionate responses of admiration, astonishment, and terror: 'the glorious Works of the Creator, which next to Himself,
are worthy to move with Admiration all who are worthy to be called wise,
because these, when they are reflected upon by the Great and the Wise,
never fail to declare His Eternal Power and Godhead' (Dennis, vol. i, p. 345).
Such works, treated with the 'great Passion' that 'must be the Characteristical
Mark of the greater Poetry' produce 'Enthusiasm', and chief amongst the
enthusiastic passions are 'Admiration and Terror' (Dennis, vol. i, p. 363).

[3] For a discussion of the religious purpose of Thomson's landscapes see David R. Anderson,
     'Emotive Theodicy in *The Seasons*', *Studies in Eighteenth Century Culture*, 12 (1983), 59–76.
[4] On Milton and Thomson see David R. Anderson, 'Milton's Influence on Thomson: The Uses of
     Landscape', *Milton Studies*, 15 (1981), 107–20 and Dustin Griffin, *Regaining Paradise: Milton and the
     Eighteenth Century* (Cambridge, 1986), pp. 182–202.
[5] In *James Thomson 1700–1748: A Life* (Oxford, 1991), James Sambrook compares Thomson's
     sublime with that of John Dennis, and notes that in 1726 the poet tried to cultivate Dennis's
     acquaintance (p. 49). On the importance of Dennis's ideas see Monk, *The Sublime*, pp. 45–50.

Dennis plays at length upon the paradox that viewers and readers should feel enthusiasm for that which terrifies them, declaring that 'no Passion is attended with greater Joy than Enthusiastic Terror, which proceeds from our reflecting that we are out of danger at the very time that we see it before us' (Dennis, vol. I, p. 361). It is a contradiction which Thomson exploits to give the gentlemanly reader the illusion of vulnerability before a nature which represents divine wrath whilst maintaining a safe literary and social distance. And Thomson exploits it by representing a landscape in which not only is danger suffered by rustics rather than the gentry, but power and violence are contained within a larger structure of order. Order is present in Thomson's presentation of landscapes owned and organized by economically improved agriculture (a commercial order associated with the gentry who govern it and benefit from it). But it is also present in the episodic structure of his poem, which ensures that terrifying scenes remain set-pieces that do not endanger the overall authority of the surveying narrator and reader.

It is on such a set-piece that I wish to focus first in order to examine how Thomson stages the power-relations of his contemporary rural society, and more particularly the power-relations operative between the writer, his readers and the largely illiterate rural labourers he wrote about. Scenes of disorder allowed Thomson to dramatize the tensions that occurred within those relations as scenes on the terror- and joy-inducing stage of God's creation. Challenges to the authority that the author, on behalf of his readers, exerts over rural society are dramatized as forces of nature emanating from an omnipotent Deity before which all must submit. Injustice and vulnerability to power become through such scenes an apparently common fate shared by the reader with the rural poor, obviating the need for analysis or large-scale reform of the social and political structure which helped to cause them. The writer and his gentlemanly readership are left with their social position confirmed. Thomson included more expanded versions of such scenes in later editions of his poetry. One, made in 1730, was taken into the 1744 and 1746 texts of *Winter* almost unaltered. It describes a shepherd overwhelmed by a snowstorm:

> Then throng the busy Shapes into his Mind
> Of cover'd Pits, unfathomably deep,
> A dire Descent! beyond the Power of Frost;
> Of faithless Bogs; of Precipices huge,
> Smooth'd up with Snow; and, what is Land unknown,
> What Water, of the still unfrozen Spring,
> In the loose Marsh or solitary Lake,
> Where the fresh Fountain from the Bottom boils.
> These check his fearful Steps; and down he sinks
> Beneath the Shelter of the shapeless Drift,
> Thinking o'er all the Bitterness of Death,

Mix'd with the tender Anguish Nature shoots
Thro' the wrung Bosom of the dying Man,
His Wife, his Children, and his Friends unseen.
In vain for him th'officious Wife prepares
The Fire fair-blazing and the Vestment warm;
In vain his little Children, peeping out
Into the mingling Storm, demand their Sire
With Tears of artless Innocence. Alas!
Nor Wife, nor Children, more shall he behold,
Nor Friends, nor sacred Home. On every Nerve
The deadly Winter seizes, shuts up Sense,
And, o'er his inmost Vitals creeping cold,
Lays him along the Snows, a stiffened Corse,
Stretched out, and bleaching in the northern Blast.

(lines 297–321; Thomson, p. 218)

Thomson works diligently to achieve his effects. There are deliberate distortions of syntax and word-order intended to reproduce for the reader the dizzying disorientation to which the shepherd is subject: 'Then throng the busy Shapes into his Mind / Of cover'd Pits, unfathomably deep, / A dire Descent! beyond the Power of Frost; / Of faithless Bogs ... ' (lines 297–300). The displacement of the genitives until after the indirect object 'into his mind' reserves them as unexpected surprises at the start of the next lines, just as they also describe a hidden pitfall. The deliberate unfamiliarity of the Latinate word order adds to the strangeness of the discourse and invites comparisons with the English poet agreed by Addison and Dennis to be most sublime – Milton. Similarly, the looseness of the grammatical connection between the plural 'pits' and 'A dire Descent!' (which, the reader infers, must describe the fall) mimics the ability of nature to contain abysses which surpass the ordinary and recognizable. It is as if the pit is almost beyond the connective power of grammar as it is beyond that of frost. The violent shift from this statement to 'Of faithless Bogs', a phrase we are forced to relate back to 'throng the busy Shapes into his Mind' further disrupts the flow of sense and betrays the expected procedure of English syntax, just as the bogs betray conventional expectations that nature is morally organized (faithful). For a moment it seems as if syntax and sense are conjoining to force an experience of reading in which landscape becomes profoundly disturbing, since for reader as for shepherd both nature and the discourse in which it is framed lack conventional order. On the face of it lines 300–4 ('of Precipices huge') are supplemented by more radical innovations, as when 'of the still unfrozen Spring' causes the reader again to return to 'throng ... into his Mind', disrupting the temporal and spatial sequentiality of reading down and across the page. At the same time semantic ambiguities create a landscape of strange opposition. Does 'still' indicate temporal continuity or spatial stasis,

an apparent contradiction of the motion implied by 'unfrozen Spring'?
Likewise the phrase 'where the fresh Fountain from the Bottom boils'
introduces the unexpected notion of violent heat, at odds with both the
stillness and the coldness of the scene hitherto. Thomson's language is
straining all its resources to register an apprehension of chaos, which if it
were taken further, would question the very existence of recognizable (and
readable) order.

Thomson does not take his language further. The apprehension of chaos
remains a small set-piece, within the context of a larger poetic order, an
order which is presumed to correspond to a natural order (the passage of the
seasons) and ultimately to a divine order (providence). Within the providential scheme present disorder is shown on Judgement Day to have been part of
the divine plan. As a result of this implicit correspondence the hidden and
apparently objective narrator of the storm-scene can strain his description to
articulate nature's and God's destructive power without endangering the
belief in a wider order. He can safely move the reader to that joyful
participation in terror which Dennis had suggested should be the response to
poetry of great passion.[6] By a paradox which Dennis had identified as a
hallmark of the sublime, nature is staged by the poet so as to produce terror
at man's vulnerability and participation in destructive wrath at once. In this
winter scene, as in Dennis's theory, it is the reminder that the reader is at a
safe distance that allows powerlessness to be refigured as power. Thomson
shows the storm as a tableau, a scenical representation in a theatre of
landscape, a theatre in which moral purpose reinforces social hierarchies.
The narrative supposedly reproduces the shepherd's mind at a moment of
panic, and it is therefore not offered as the author's own questioning, but as
an affecting and pathetic scene, which we can read within the conventional
terms of sympathy and of sensibility.[7] The shepherd becomes a spectacle
giving an awe-inspiring sense of man's insignificance in comparison with the
great objects of nature. He is, in fact, an object-lesson in the kind of general
moralizing about man's place in nature that the rendering of his panic and
confusion seemed to challenge. He is, it turns out, a poetic example, a 'swain'
in whom Thomson has little interest other than in his emblematic rôle as the
representative of insignificant man and innocent rustic. We do not learn his
name, history or circumstances; his family appear as a pathetic example of
innocence: 'th'officious Wife prepares / The Fire fair-blazing and the

6   For a discussion of the conflicting schemes of order in *The Seasons* see John Barrell, *English Literature
    in History 1730–80: An Equal, Wide Survey* (London, 1983), pp. 51–109.
7   For a discussion of the conventions of sensibility see Janet Todd, *Sensibility. An Introduction* (London
    and New York, 1986) and Louis I. Bredvold, *The Natural History of Sensibility* (Detroit, 1962) .
    Douglas Grant, in *James Thomson: Poet of The Seasons* (London, 1951) has shown that Thomson's
    stress on sensibility led to his poem's favourable reception by women readers. The influence of
    Shaftesbury on Thomson's account of the shepherd is noted by Robert Inglesfield, 'Shaftesbury's
    Influence on Thomson's "Seasons"', *British Journal of Eighteenth Century Studies*, 9 (1986), 141–56.

Vestment warm' (lines 311–12). Here the noun 'vestment' transforms the shepherd's smock into the robes of a priest, idealizing the household as one of holy perfection in order to increase the pathos of its destruction and move readers to sympathize. But this sort of destruction is assimilable, as the shepherd's panic was not, to conventional notions of sympathy and pity: the innocent family allow Thomson a moralizing exclamation but then disappear from the poem.

> A H little think the gay licentious Proud,
> Whom Pleasure, Power, and Affluence surround;
> They, who their thoughtless Hours in giddy Mirth,
> And wanton, often cruel, Riot waste;
> Ah little think they . . .
>   . . . Sore pierc'd by wintry Winds,
> How many shrink into the sordid Hut
> Of chearless Poverty. How many shake
> With all the fiercer Tortures of the Mind,
> Unbounded Passion, Madness, Guilt, Remorse;
> Whence, tumbled headlong from the Height of Life,
> They furnish Matter for the Tragic Muse.
>
> (lines 322–42; Thomson, pp. 218–19)

The shepherd and his family, deserted and poor, function as a poetic device, able to produce the catharsis that the tragic muse demands by arousing terror and admiration at nature's power, and pity for its victims.[8]

Thomson moves from the family and its circumstances into a lament at human pain in general, drawing the general lesson that charity and sympathy are necessary to alleviate it, but implying that the family's fate is simply one part of the universal lot of pain and insignificance before the forces of nature. The shepherd and the other manifold examples of human pain 'furnish Matter for the Tragic Muse'. No specific remedies for the rural poverty that made shepherds more vulnerable to natural disasters than gentlemen are offered, although Thomson's next scene is a prison, the jailer of which has been charged with cruelty by a parliamentary committee. The sympathy raised by the account of the shepherd is harnessed to encourage readers to approve of legislation to end the man-made oppression of extortion and torture in prison. In this respect Thomson shows himself a reforming Whig, keen to oppose injustices which, unlike that of the shepherd's death in the

---

[8] The influence on this poetry of sensibility of Shaftesbury's philosophy is discussed by Chester Chapin, 'Shaftesbury and the Man of Feeling', *Modern Philology*, 81 (1983), 47–50. Mary Jane W. Scott, in *James Thomson Anglo-Scot* (Athens, GA and London, 1988), makes a convincing case that it was less Shaftesbury than his Scottish follower Francis Hutcheson, with his Calvinist view of benevolence, who stood behind Thomson's recommendation of sympathy as a social duty (pp. 158–62). Ralph Cohen, in *The Unfolding of The Seasons* (London, 1970), p. 265, distinguishes Thomson's benevolence from Shaftesbury's by suggesting that it is a response to his recognition of man's 'dependence upon fortune, the inevitable uncertainty of man's temporal condition'.

snowstorm, he believes to be remediable. His social imagination is limited, however, by his assumption that the shepherd died from unavoidable natural causes. In fact, as Stephen Duck and other 'peasant-poets' showed, the farmworker's need to labour in all weathers was determined by a social and economic order in which farmers and landowners demanded it of him.[9] Thomson's conclusion is limited by the absence of such facts from its moralizing application of the shepherd's case to man in general:

> How many, rack'd with honest Passions, droop
> In deep retir'd Distress. How many stand
> Around the Death-bed of their dearest Friends,
> And point the parting Anguish. Thought fond Man
> Of These, and all the thousand nameless Ills
> That one incessant Struggle render Life,
> One Scene of Toil, of Suffering, and of Fate,
> Vice in his high Career would stand appall'd
> And heedless rambling Impulse learn to think;
> The conscious Heart of Charity would warm,
> And her wide Wish Benevolence dilate;
> The social Tear would rise, the social Sigh;
> And, into clear Perfection, gradual Bliss,
> Refining still, the social Passions work.
>
> (lines 345–58; Thomson, pp. 219–20)

Here it is enough for the readers to feel these emotions; there is no question of being urged to take any preventative action. The readers can instead congratulate themselves on their improved sympathy without acting other than by occasional charity. The poem flatters the vanity of sensibility; it neither disturbs the social hierarchy within which rural hardship was present, nor does it question gentlemanly values by articulating the thoughts of the shepherd in a language derived from his colloquial speech. He remains a generalized rustic, treated in a Latinate language which makes him merely an affecting example. Both he and the nature that crushes him are read according to a pre-existent and undeclared set of moral assumptions: he as a symbol of innocent honesty designed to stimulate compassion, it as a retributive power reminding man of God's authority in a fallen world (although Thomson characterizes 'faithless' Nature as female).

In Thomson's poems the reader is comfortably insulated from nature's cruelty. Others are crushed by it, just as others work in the fields. They provide vicarious experiences of human misery without seriously threatening the comfort of the reader's position. Their lesson in general human vulnerability is given to an audience whose physical and social remoteness from the scene leaves them cossetted. The pity and sympathy aroused then

---

[9] On Duck, labour and the social and economic order see Raymond Williams, *The Country and the City* (London, 1973), pp. 68–71.

turns easily to condescension, patronage and even enjoyment of others' pain, the sort of delight that, because it does not issue in action, worried theorists of sensibility when they found it to be a response to the fictional scenes of tragedy. A representation aiming at sentimental sympathy in its readers risks prompting, as here, affected self-pity over human ills that are not shared in any detailed way. And further questions about the apparent cruelty and indifference of nature to human needs are checked by the fact that Thomson moves on to the next scene rather than develop the implications of this one. By the episodic nature of his work and by a final reference of all questions to providence, Thomson prevents his poetic landscape from causing any lasting disorder, and avoids detailed consideration of the tensions within it.[10] Viewing nature as God's providential agency, Thomson relocates patriarchal authority there. Nature's disasters and cruelties are an expression of God's will which can only be understood when nature is remade after the second coming:

> Ye vainly wise! ye blind Presumptuous! now,
> Confounded in the dust, adore that POWER,
> And WISDOM – oft arraign'd: see now the Cause,
> Why unassuming Worth in secret liv'd
> And dy'd neglected . . . why licens'd Pain,
> That cruel Spoiler, that embosom'd Foe,
> Imbitter'd all our Bliss . . . yet bear up a While . . .
> The Storms of WINTRY TIME will quickly pass,
> And one unbounded SPRING encircle All.
>
> (lines 1050–69; Thomson, p. 252)

By providing a literary practice by which experience of natural disorder could be safely controlled, Thomson allowed submission to be confined to an area kept separate from the social realities of his readers. The noble and gentlemanly classes could, through his poetry, experience the self-righteous pleasures of submission to power without abandoning their social and political authority and without having to enter a binding relation with a scriptural God. Confirming the power of the landowners of and for whom he wrote, Thomson also, however, appealed to their patriotic love of British liberty in the cause of reforming the oppressive enforcement of the law against the victims of poverty. Capitalist rather than feudal, Whig rather than Tory, Thomson turned class relations into a transaction, economic as well as aesthetic, in which the poor man gave his labour, pain and suffering for the rich man's edification, entertainment and wealth. In return he received

---

[10] John Barrell and Harriet Guest have suggested that the deliberately episodic and digressive nature of Thomson's *The Seasons* makes it one of many popular eighteenth-century poems intended to be of 'mixed genre', allowing it to be read (and reviewed) as a collection of noble passages. 'On the Use of Contradiction: Economics and Morality in the Eighteenth-Century Long Poem', in Felicity Nussbaum and Laura Brown (eds.) *The New Eighteenth Century* (New York and London, 1987), pp. 121–43 (p. 139).

charity and a stable society within which oppressive laws were tempered by compassion. Thomson endeavoured, however, to root that transaction into the landscape so that it appeared as part of the natural order rather than as a social construct.

The apparent naturalness of the order which Thomson read in the landscape and the ideological function which depended on that appearance of naturalness were both endangered by his development of more explicitly politicized scenes. These included the ostensibly uncontroversial and conventional dedication to Sir Spencer Compton, a loyal Whig who had been Speaker of the House of Commons since 1715, and was created Earl of Wilmington in 1730. He became Prime Minister briefly in 1742 after Walpole's long period of government. Seen by some as an ineffectual and acquiescent absorber of sinecures and titles, he was not publicly viewed, as Thomson flatteringly suggests, as a 'firm, unshaken' statesman (line 33) behind whom the nation could unite, but as a figurehead for the Patriot opposition centred in the Prince of Wales's court – men such as Bolingbroke, Chesterfield, Pitt, Lyttelton. Thomson had first sought his patronage when an unknown poet in 1726. He added the verse compliment in 1730, dedicating not only his poem but nature itself to the Whig peer. The Muse, Thomson declares, dedicates the forces of nature – winds and floods – to an articulation of Wilmington's sublimely patriotic political activities (his 'awful schemes' (line 30)).

Thomson's willingness to use the vocabulary of his natural sublime to flatter Whig politicians can be understood as the result of a tradition of formal compliment of patrons, expected of the poet and not necessarily judged by readers for its sincerity and veracity. Despite the existence of this tradition, Thomson, in protesting too much for his patron, threatens the apparent sincerity with which, in the poem as a whole, he dramatizes the forces of nature as morally exemplary instances of the power of God. As he revised *The Seasons* in the 1730s and 1740s he increasingly dedicated its landscapes as tributes to those Whig politicians who opposed the ministry of Walpole, thereby preventing his nature-descriptions from seeming to speak disinterestedly for the nation in general (or, in practice, for the gentry as a whole).[11] A passage added to *Winter* in 1744 extravagantly praises the Earl of Chesterfield, the Whig politician opposed to Walpole and critical of George II.

> O Thou, whose Wisdom, solid yet refin'd,
> Whose Patriot-Virtues, and consummate Skill
> To touch the finer Springs that move the World,
> Join'd to whate'er the *Graces* can bestow,
> And all *Apollo's* animating Fire,
> Give Thee, with pleasing Dignity, to shine

[11] On Thomson and Walpole, see Christine Gerrard, '*The Castle of Indolence* and the Opposition to Walpole', *Review of English Studies*, 41–161 (1990), 45–64.

At once the Guardian, Ornament, and Joy,
Of polish'd Life; permit the *Rural Muse*,
O CHESTERFIELD, to grace with Thee her Song!
Ere to the Shades again she humbly flies,
Indulge her fond Ambition, in thy Train,
(For every Muse has in thy Train a Place)
To mark thy various full-accomplish'd Mind:
To mark that Spirit, which, with *British Scorn*,
Rejects th'Allurements of corrupted Power . . .
O let me hail thee on some glorious Day,
When to the listening Senate, ardent, croud
BRITANNIA'S Sons to hear her pleaded Cause.
Then drest by Thee, more amiably fair,
Truth the soft Robe of mild Persuasion wears:
Thou to assenting Reason giv'st again
Her own enlighten'd Thoughts; call'd from the Heart,
Th'obedient Passions on thy Voice attend;
And even reluctant Party feels a while
Thy gracious Power: as thro' the vary'd Maze
Of Eloquence, now smooth, now quick, now strong,
Profound and clear, you roll the copious Flood.

(lines 656–90, Thomson, pp. 234–5)

By the end of the tribute Chesterfield is not only an embodiment of paternalistic power, a 'guardian' under whose authority the rural muse finds shelter. He is also a national father-figure who tempers his sternness, thus subduing party strife by 'gracious power'. But this is wishful thinking: it locates in the landscape party-divisions and political complaints, but produces in Chesterfield a figure only nominally able to unite the field of Britain beyond such divisions. Chesterfield's speech becomes, in Thomson's final metaphor, a force of British nature, a powerful 'flood' or stream of language. The metaphor gives Chesterfield, by analogy with the irresistible forces of nature described throughout the poem, the power to subordinate political opponents ('reluctant Party'). But this, after those natural forces had been treated as instances of a providential order that is the expression of God's will, seems a reduction of an omnipotent divine authority to flattery of a political figure, a diminution of Thomson's sublime staging of nature to the tendentious victories scored in a limited political theatre. The reader will not be humbled in 'enthusiastic terror' before Chesterfield's 'copious flood' since, after reading Thomson's representations of floods in nature, the discrepancy in scale and effect suggests that the politician is clothed in a language of borrowed authority, its power having been established in larger – and more apparently disinterested – contexts.

Thomson's tribute to Chesterfield reflects the patronage he had received from the mid-1730s from the Country and Patriot opposition to Walpole.

The persistence of the ideology espoused by the Patriot group in subsequent opposition to Court and ministerial power will be a recurrent theme in this book, so I shall offer here a summary of it. I shall also assess the importance of Chesterfield in that group and examine Thomson's relations with it. From the late 1720s Bolingbroke and Pulteney had been writing in the journal *The Craftsman* of the need for the opposition to Walpole to overcome Tory/Whig divisions. The opposition, they argued, should recognize that a defence of the constitution against encroachment on parliament's independence by Court and ministry required a united Country party. Its readers were urged to

act like wise Men; and remember that *Liberty* is the same divine Blessing, whether it be dispensed to us under a *Whig* or a *Tory* Administration; and that *arbitrary Power*, or any Degree of it, cannot alter its Nature; but is equally destructive of the *British* Constitution, by whatsoever Hands or under whatsoever Shapes, it shall be imposed on us.[12]

By 1737 Frederick, Prince of Wales, had fallen into a dispute with the King and Queen and set up his own rival court as a Patriot prince, declaring his interest in the liberty of all his people. Bolingbroke, Pulteney and the young William Pitt and George Lyttelton, joined by Chesterfield (who had held office under Walpole but had been removed after opposing his excise scheme in 1733), gathered around the Prince. They adapted their Country cross-party platform to a vision of a Britain united under him as a Patriot king. Patronage was extended, through Lyttelton and Chesterfield, to Whig and Tory writers including Mallet, Glover, Thomson and Pope.

The works written by these authors reflected the political ideas of the Country, now Patriot, opposition. Walpole was seen to be ruling by corrupting with place, pension and sinecure inside and outside parliament, by buying elections, by smearing opposition with the taint of disloyal Jacobitism. His ministerial alliance with the Court was endangering the liberty which Whigs and Tories had protected in guaranteeing a balanced constitution at the 1688 settlement. That constitution, native and ancient but threatened by the Stuarts' arbitrary rule, was a balance of Court and Country, with both represented in parliament, the Court by the ministry, the Country by independent men of property. On parliament's preservation of the disinterest and liberty that stemmed from property ownership depended independence in the nation. In 1729 Chesterfield had written of his reluctance 'to be a gainer' by any employment for his country: 'whatever my actions may be, interest shall never be thought to influence them'.[13] For Country opponents of Walpole such disinterest could only be ensured by regular, uncorrupt parliamentary elections, and by resistance to corruption within the parliament. This demanded men of independent wealth and property as a

---

[12] *The Craftsman*, xvii (30 January 1726/27).
[13] Quoted in W.H. Craig, *Life of Lord Chesterfield* (London, 1907), p.108.

necessary check against the blandishments of the ministry. Means by which Court and ministry could exercise power and raise money without parliament – standing armies, excise duties – had also to be resisted.

The Country and Patriot opposition developed their arguments about property and the balanced constitution in part from the work of James Harrington. In *Oceana* (1656) and *The Art of Lawgiving* (1659) Harrington had argued that the tendency of all constitutions was to degenerate into a despotism of the Court, the nobility, or the people.[14] Only a constitution balanced between groups by a distribution of power commensurate with the distribution of land could prevent this tendency. Although Harrington favoured a republican commonwealth and an agrarian law which ensured that large landholdings were periodically redistributed, eighteenth-century readings of him did not. They linked his ideal commonwealth with the ancient English constitution, consolidated in 1688, threatened by Walpole, dependent upon the existence of a propertied and therefore independent gentry and nobility. This neo-Harringtonian argument, as it has been termed,[15] expressed in the writings of Moyle and Neville after 1688, remained at the forefront of Patriot language.[16] In September 1737 Thomson wrote to Andrew Millar of his wish that his Ode on the birth of the Prince of Wales's daughter might appear in the Patriot journals *The Craftsman* and *Common Sense*. And he asked for 'another Harrington'.[17] Millar had recently published an edition of *Oceana*, and the Commonwealthsman's importance to the opposition was well enough known for it to be singled out in a pro-Walpole satire on Pope and other Patriot poets. Millar also published in January 1738 Milton's *Areopagitica* with a preface by Thomson fearing 'an Administration' that might erect 'arbitrary Jurisdiction over the Press'.[18] Both publications, and others later that year, showed the Patriot campaign as a revival of a native tradition of resistance to the encroachment on liberty by arbitrary power.

The danger to the liberty of the Press had been precipitated by the publication, in *Common Sense* (the journal Chesterfield and Lyttelton had begun), of the 'Vision of the Golden Rump', a scurrilous attack on Walpole and the Court. A version intended for the stage, shown to Walpole, led to the passing of the Licensing Act on 24 June 1737. After this the Patriot writers, as Harrington and Milton had done, turned to ancient subjects. Writing of the

[14]　Harrington's *The Commonwealth of Oceana* and *The Art of Lawgiving* had been published in 1700 in an edition by the radical Whig John Toland: *The Oceana of James Harrington* (London, 1700). See also J.G.A. Pocock (ed.), *The Political Works of James Harrington* (Cambridge, 1977).

[15]　By J.G.A. Pocock in *Politics, Language and Time: Essays on Political Thought and History* (London, 1972), pp. 130–1.

[16]　For Moyle's and Neville's works see Caroline Robbins (ed.), *Two English Republican Tracts* (Cambridge, 1969).

[17]　A.D. McKillop, *James Thomson (1700–1748) Letters and Documents* (Lawrence, KS, 1958), p.114.

[18]　Quoted in Sambrook, *James Thomson: A Life*, p.186.

Roman republic and England under King Alfred they were able to idealize a constitutional liberty under threat without risking having their plays banned. Chesterfield had opposed the Licensing Bill in a powerful speech in the Lords, and in pamphlets and opposition journals he attacked Walpole's influence. In the Lords he spoke of the 'slavery and arbitrary power' certain (and intended by the Crown) to be produced by the increase of the standing army. After the fall of Walpole Chesterfield continued to attack the succeeding ministry, composed mostly of Walpole's followers. In the Lords he opposed, as he had ten years earlier, the maintenance of Hanoverian troops at British expense. After an indecorous remark on the Elector of Hanover's 'obscurity' before he was 'exalted' to the throne by the British nation, a remark which lost him the support of the House, he appealed to the people in the pamphlet *The Case of the Hanover Forces* (1743). He declared that Walpole's ministry had shown 'notorious Corruption and Waste of the public treasure at home, for the support of the said Minister's own Power and Projects; and the open and manifest Sacrifice of the *British* Interest and Glory abroad'. The 'People of England had stooped like a Camel to be loaded, and Pensioners to hang upon them like so many Horse-Leeches'.[19] It was to this patriotic Chesterfield, powerful speaker in the Lords, pamphleteer and negotiator with foreign powers, that Thomson paid his tribute in the 1744 *Seasons*.

Yet Thomson had a difficulty when making such tributes: the perception that the Patriot politicians were, for all their vision of a united Britain renouncing Whig and Tory divisions for a nation secure in gentlemen of independent property, less than disinterested in their arguments for disinterest. Chesterfield had accepted place and a gartership under Walpole. To many his arguments looked, as did those of Bolingbroke, Lyttelton and Pitt, like cynical attempts to play the Prince of Wales against King and Queen to win power for themselves. On 26 April 1745 the *Daily Post* offered a 'true Picture of modern Patriotism' in the spectacle of Lyttelton, Pitt and others 'all very lately most flaming Patriots' but now newly members of the ministry, attending the first night of Thomson's play *Tancred and Sigismunda*. By this time Chesterfield had also accepted a place in the new 'Broad-Bottom' ministry, which included Whigs and Tories as the Patriots had wished. But the inclusion of men of both parties did not satisfy the *Daily Post* that the Country principles of the Patriots had been upheld:

Well Sir, this unwearied Opposition was, at last, attended with Success; and most of these Patriots are in the Administration of Affairs. And now, Sir, follows the material Question, – *What has been done for the People? Has any one Grievance been redress'd?* I am afraid, Sir, it would be no difficult Task to prove that our Grievances have been made the Subject of Ridicule even by some of these very Heroes! – But they are in

[19]   *The Case of the Hanover Forces* (London, 1743), pp. 1, 11.

good Places, and therefore *all Opposition* is to cease, or be construed into Party, and, now, treated as criminal.

The article concludes with a warning that '*strict Adherence* to their *former Principles*' will be required, and with a critique of the play, which had been supervised in rehearsal by Pitt and Lyttelton themselves: 'But tho' thy tedious Scenes are void of Fire, They'll do, if P__tt and Ly__n admire.' Thomson was seen as a talentless playwright and, worse, as the creature of patrons, putting his words blatantly to their own partisan and insincere use. The article notes that Pitt and Lyttelton applauded the following speech, and recommends the substitution of the word 'PLACE' for 'time':

> I here renounce those *Errors* and *Divisions*;
> That have so long disturb'd our Peace, and seem'd
> Fermenting still to threaten new Commotions;
> By Time instructed, let Us not disdain
> To QUIT MISTAKES.[20]

Attached so closely to the interests of a party, Thomson's verse seemed doubly dubious: not only did it make easy points for politicians whose own conduct was in doubt, but it seemed to do so for the sake of patronage. In 1739 Thomas Edwards wrote of Thomson's earlier tragedy *Edward and Eleonora,* banned from performance by the Chamberlain for parallels with current politics, and published by subscription: 'many of the Subscribers ... are ashamed of their patronage. I cannot tell how far party prejudice may carry an audience, but I think nothing else could have saved these pieces ...'[21] Thomson himself realized the danger of being a poetical placeman in the fickle world of politics. He lost his pension from the Prince of Wales after Lyttelton and the Patriots joined the King's ministry and declared, 'not entirely trusting to the Broad Bottom, I will try to subsist upon the narrow but sure one of Self-Independency'.[22]

The nearest Thomson came to a language of 'self-independency' in these years was in his letters to Elizabeth Young. Writing from Lyttelton's country estate at Hagley in 1743 he portrayed the scene, for the benefit of the woman he wished to persuade to marry him, as more charming for 'it's sweet embowered Retirements' than its 'grand extensive Prospects'. He rewrote the landscape, itself designed as a demonstration of the disinterested protection of liberty by propertied gentlemen, as a retreat. Whilst this portrayal is in line with Country party ideals of a virtuous and free landed commonwealth, it is also a visualization of the life he wished to live with his wife: 'this is the truly happy Life, this Union of Retirement and Choice Society: it gives an Idea of that which the Patriarchal or Golden Age is supposed to have been; when

---

[20] *Daily Post* quoted in McKillop, *Letters and Documents*, pp. 178–9.
[21] In *ibid.*, p. 129
[22] In *ibid.*, p. 181.

every Family was a little State by itself, governed by the mild Laws of Reason, Benevolence, and Love'. This familiar classical topos is given poignancy and sincerity by its almost immediate qualification. Anxious that so retired a life will worry rather than woo Elizabeth, he tells her 'I would rather live in the most London Corner of London with you, than in the finest Country Retirement ... without you'. In the face of his anxiety that his vision of retirement will not be shared, the 'sweet embowered' dale, 'overhung with deep woods' seems a fragile refuge, all too violable by the 'dear exquisite Mixture of Pleasure and Pain' of the hopeful/hopeless thoughts of love.[23] To an extent Thomson does not explicitly acknowledge it is a retreat of fear and loneliness rather than a landscape conventionally emblematic of pastoral love or political idylls. Thomson used some of the images of the letter in a revision of *Spring* but there they are incorporated in a tribute to the garden's owner Lyttelton, using landscape to celebrate his variety of view and height of vantage. The garden becomes a landscape of Patriot politics, providing its master with 'Benevolence of Mind' 'unwarp'd by Party-Rage' but losing the more acute personal meaning it had possessed in the letter (lines 928–9; Thomson, p. 46).

Thomson's tributes to Patriot politicians known to be his patrons and thought by many to be trimmers in search of places in power are unconvincing in their context in *The Seasons*. They claim too much for their subjects; they cast doubt on the disinterestedness of the rest of the poem; the language in which they are written lacks the context that, in the letters, had allowed it to indicate complex emotional states. Sitting uncomfortably in what he had announced in 1726 (in the Preface to *Winter*) as a poem meant to make readers muse on the greatness of nature, they threaten to reduce his sublime to bathos: Pope, of course, turned this threat into a mode of political attack in his mock-heroic poetry written against the Walpole ministry. Thomson, attempting to make landscape heroic rather than to satirize, threatened to undermine his own authority by a misappropriation of his 1726 discourse just as Pope undermined that of the political and poetical placemen of Walpole. Thomson's uneasily politicized landscapes found little favour with the public which had continued to buy *The Seasons* in large quantities: parts four and five of his more explicitly Country poem *Liberty* (1735–6) were printed in editions of 1,000 each when 2,000 of parts two and three and 3,000 of part one had been issued. Despite this failure Thomson remained convinced that *Liberty* was his best work.

Yet the increasing politicization of landscape in Thomson's later work should not simply be attributed to his critical blindness – nor wholly to his desire to flatter the Whig magnates whose patronage he enjoyed. That the

---

[23] In *ibid.*, pp. 165–6.

fields of Britain are in his later work presented to a gentlemanly readership as places, real and symbolic, of political division reflects his sense that the moral and religious patterns that gentlemen disseminated to their social inferiors were being disrupted by a culture of corruption originating in minister and King. At his best he makes landscape speak of a British liberty retreating to rural margins, the wildness of which left them uncultivated – as if the subordination of cultivated farmland to a culture of profit was increasingly symbolic of a landed gentry who were willing to prostitute their independence and traditional paternalism in order to reap the financial rewards Walpole offered supporters. Whilst such landscapes are, in Thomson, compromised by the question of his and the Patriots' sincerity and disinterest, they opened a way which Cowper and Wordsworth, unattached to any party or patron, could follow.

In *Alfred* (1740), a masque composed by Thomson and David Mallet, Alfred is viewed as the protector of a native British liberty, a Patriot king threatened by arbitrary and foreign rule.[24] Yet nature's uncontrollable wildness is protective of the King, hostile only to the invading Danes who have defeated him in battle:

> Nature's own hand
> Hath planted round a deep defence of woods,
> The sounding ash, the mighty oak; each tree
> A sheltering grove: and choak'd up all between
> With wild encumbrance of perplexing thorns,
> And horrid brakes. Beyond this woody verge,
> Two rivers broad and rapid hem us in.
> Along their channel spreads the gulphy pool,
> And trembling quagmire, whose deceitful green
> Betrays the foot it tempts. One path alone
> Winds to this plain, so roughly difficult,
> This single arm, poor shepherd as I am,
> Could well dispute it with twice twenty *Danes*.
>
> (Act I, Scene I, lines 24–36)[25]

In the revised *Winter* a landscape of hostile wildness is shown to encourage a society of independence and liberty that rejects the blandishments of pleasure and ambition (lines 834–50). It is significant that this landscape is foreign: independent power is nourished by the stern forces of nature in Lapland and Russia rather than in Britain. Whereas the British landscape

24 Michael Cohen, in 'The Whig Sublime and James Thomson', *English Language Notes*, 24:1 (Sept 1986), 27–35, identifies the Northern wilds of Thomson's plays as anti-Walpole landscapes, grounds whose rugged independence is emblematic of the ancient and native origin of liberty.

25 *Alfred: A Masque* (London, 1740), p. 3. On this work and others which derived British liberty from northern barbarian tribes rather than Roman culture see Howard D. Weinbrot, *Britannia's Issue: The Rise of British Literature from Dryden to Ossian* (Cambridge, 1993), p. 499.

is divided, its fields of national liberty portrayed as marginal refuges from conquering forces, foreign landscapes still offer Thomson a rhetorical location in which national liberty, limited monarchy and cultural harmony can jointly be based on a ground of stubborn resistance. Thomson's tribute to Peter the Great's Russia, added to *Winter* in 1744, implicitly a critique of Walpole's Britain, allows him to present a united natural and political field. Russia provides a cultural ideal which the poet can represent as a model for his erring nation and for his potentially corruptible readership:

> WHAT cannot active Government perform,
> New-moulding Man? Wide-stretching from these Shores,
> A People savage from remotest Time,
> A huge neglected Empire ONE VAST MIND,
> By HEAVEN inspir'd, from Gothic Darkness call'd.
> Immortal PETER! First of Monarchs! He
> His stubborn Country tam'd, her Rocks, her Fens,
> Her Floods, her Seas, her ill-submitting Sons;
> And while the fierce *Barbarian* he subdu'd,
> To more exalted Soul he raised the *Man*.
> Ye Shades of antient Heroes, ye who toil'd
> Thro' long successive Ages to build up
> A lab'ring Plan of State, behold at once
> The Wonder done! behold the matchless Prince!
> Who left his native Throne, where reign'd till then
> A mighty Shadow of unreal Power;
> Who greatly spurn'd the slothful Pomp of Courts;
> And roaming every Land, in every Port,
> His Scepter laid aside, with glorious Hand
> Unweary'd plying the mechanic Tool,
> Gather'd the Seeds of Trade, of useful Arts,
> Of Civil Wisdom, and of Martial Skill.
> Charg'd with the Stores of *Europe* home he goes!
> Then Cities rise amid th'illumin'd Waste;
> O'er joyless Deserts smiles the rural Reign;
> Far-distant Flood to Flood is social join'd;
> Th'astonish'd *Euxine* hears the *Baltic* roar;
> Proud Navies ride on Seas that never foam'd
> With daring Keel before; and Armies stretch
> Each Way their dazzling Files, repressing here
> The frantic *Alexander* of the North,
> And awing there stern *Othman's* shrinking Sons.
> *Sloth* flies the Land, and *Ignorance*, and *Vice*,
> Of old Dishonour proud: it glows around,
> Taught by the ROYAL HAND that rous'd the Whole,
> One Scene of Arts, of Arms, of rising Trade:

For what his Wisdom plann'd, and Power enforc'd,
More potent still, his great *Example* shew'd.

(lines 950–87; Thomson, pp. 247–8)

Here the land yields prosperity to the 'active government' of those who, patriotically inspired by their active King, harness its natural sublimity for the end of national unity and power. Peter the Great, and Thomson representing his monarchical power over terrain contested by the Swedes and by the Turks, put into action the characteristics that are seen elsewhere to make God the creator sublime: 'Of what his wisdom planned and power enforced, / More potent still his great example showed'. In Russia, but apparently not in Britain, the independent power found in the land is not prostituted by the gentry who own it for reward from a corrupt minister. Instead it is a source of national power patriotically used in war – a criticism of Walpole's reluctance to involve Britain in foreign campaigns.

Thomson's foreign landscapes, interventions in home politics, did not overcome the difficulty that politicizing the British landscape undermined his ability to speak for it with apparent disinterest. His location of political divisions in the familiar fields which he had previously represented as places of natural power questioned his own authority as a moralizing poet. His poetry had, in the manner of Dennis's theory, enshrined a contradictory relationship between power and powerlessness, enthusiasm and terror, as a fact of nature rather than a production of society. But it was disturbed by explicitly politicized scenes which implied that landscape, and the discourse by which Thomson staged it for the public, was shaped by structures and languages that sought political power. And so Thomson's natural scenes became ambivalent, his poem indeterminate, posing the question for readers of his revised work (and for landscape poetry in the eighteenth century) of how poetry can be a discourse of moral instruction by means of the natural sublime when it reveals its own partiality, its own manipulation for political effect of a landscape in which disorder and contradiction are apparently signs of nature's and God's law?

Thomson did not answer the question posed by his later work. In posing it so strongly, however, that work offers the critic a means of interrogating the discourse of landscape as it appears elsewhere in the eighteenth century. For poets, critics and moralists Thomson's difficulties were problems to be overcome, and/or tensions that recurred, in a discourse that the indeterminacy of his poetry encouraged them to use as they sought authority over nature and society. Wordsworth and Coleridge adapted Thomson, whilst differing from him politically, as they tried to negotiate conflicts in society by representations of landscape that raised questions concerning cultivation, ownership, patronage and power. And Coleridge and Johnson, in different ways, questioned the very discourse that used landscape to seek authority in critical and political debates – Coleridge through a nature poetry he viewed as a revision of Thomson and Cowper, Johnson by, amongst other means, criticizing Thomson's diction.

Closest to Thomson in method, subject-matter and the conflicts of power he narrates is William Cowper (1731–1800). Of the many landscape poems that were published after the success of *The Seasons*, Cowper's *The Task* (1785) best sustained the variety of subjects, attitudes, and tones that had characterized Thomson's work. Yet it also reflected Cowper's own anxieties. He had suffered a breakdown in 1763 and (apparently) attempted suicide. He withdrew from public life to rural retirement in Huntingdon and then in Olney and Weston Underwood, where he was sheltered by friends including Mrs Unwin and Lady Austen. Though he found some solace in the beauty of rural Buckinghamshire he continued to suffer from depression, believing himself damned. This depression deepened into crisis in the early 1790s when friends, afraid that he would take his life, persuaded him that a move to Norfolk would improve his health. He died there after years of misery.

The Task was written in Cowper's Olney years in a verse derived from Milton via Thomson that gave him rhetorical power over the landscape and those who dwelt and worked in it. If it gave that power it also questioned it, for Cowper, often unable to find evidence of a moral order in the nation of and for which he was writing, frequently made the landscapes represented in his poetry places of division and loss. His own position as a writer on landscape was often undermined in the process: unable to base a vision of shared moral or social order in the fields he surveyed, he refigured the landscape poet's authority as an anxious marginality and vulnerability. By this means he avoided, however, the taint of identifying with or writing for political patrons. My discussion of Cowper will focus on this refiguring of authority, suggesting that it dramatized, in a way that Wordsworth and Coleridge learnt from, the collapse of the consensus in which gentlemanly values were seen as legitimate criteria for government. For Cowper the corruption of those values endangered the political and social realm, and made it impossible for the poet to perpetuate them by depicting the presence in the rural scene of a natural order to be appreciated by taste. In his verse he retreats from the task of making such depictions almost as soon as he begins it, establishes commanding views only to undermine them, criticizes his gentlemanly readers as soon as he appeals to them. The realm of taste and the disinterested view survive, in a critical condition, at the self-isolated margin.

Cowper's refiguring of authority takes several related forms, and I shall examine each in a separate section, looking at his reworking of Thomson, his emulation of and deference towards Milton, his undermining of the picturesque view and his politicization of the rural scene, his writing on public affairs, and his struggle with the critical power of Johnson. I begin with a discussion of his relations with previous poets, arguing that because he identifies his relationship with his contemporary society and readership as one of critical marginality and anxious retreat, Cowper does not seek to master his authoritative predecessors but to propitiate them, accepting his own voice as a lesser version of theirs. In so doing he should lead us to rethink the theory of poetic authority provided by Harold Bloom.[26] Cowper finds a style recognizably his own in which authority depends not on the subordination of other poets but on an imitation of them which accepts its secondary and comparatively minor status. That status is presented as all that is possible in a sinful and divided society likely to ignore poetry's claim to preach to and have authority over it. Such, at least, was the case when Cowper compared himself with Milton; he was more confident of his ability to stand alongside (rather than above) Thomson. He adapted Thomson's verse in his own, borrowing but often undercutting its assumption of authority through the prospect-view.

In December 1784 he discussed *The Task* with his friend and mentor, the evangelical divine John Newton:

Milton's manner was peculiar; so is Thomson's. He that should write like either of them, would in my judgement, deserve the name of a Copyist, but not of a Poet. A judicious and sensible Reader therefore like yourself, will not say that my manner is not good because it does not resemble theirs, but will rather consider what it is in itself. Blank verse is susceptible of a much greater diversification of manner, than verse in rhime. And why the modern writers of it have all thought proper to cast their numbers alike, I know not. Certainly it was not necessity that compelled them to do it. I flatter myself however that I have avoided that sameness with others which would entitle me to nothing but a share in one common oblivion with them all.

(*CoL*, vol. ii, p. 308)

In 1788, more confident after the success of his poem, Cowper declared 'Thomson was admirable in description, but it always seemed to me that there was somewhat of affectation in his stile, and that his numbers are sometimes not well harmonized' (*CoL*, vol. iii, p. 180). He remained, however, an admirer of *The Seasons* and John Johnson noted a conversation about Thomson on the journey from Weston to Norfolk in 1795: 'alas, alas – during all the years that he lived after this, I never heard him talk so much at ease, again'.[27]

Within *The Task* Cowper takes advantage of the verbal strategies by which Thomson renders observation of landscape a source of rhetorical authority for the narrator. The fourth book, *The Winter Evening*, courts comparison with *The Seasons* as Cowper apostrophizes a Winter which is personified as, at first sight, an awesome paternal power:

---

[26] In, for example, *The Anxiety of Influence* (London, 1973).

[27] John Johnson's Diary, 28 July 1795, quoted in James King, *William Cowper: A Biography* (Durham, NC, 1986), p. 268.

> Oh Winter, ruler of th'inverted year,
> Thy scatter'd hair with sleet like ashes fill'd,
> Thy breath congeal'd upon thy lips, thy cheeks
> Fring'd with a beard made white with other snows
> Than those of age; thy forehead wrapt in clouds,
> A leafless branch thy sceptre, and thy throne
> A sliding car indebted to no wheels,
> But urged by storms along its slipp'ry way
> I love thee, all unlovely as thou seem'st,
> And dreaded as thou art. Thou hold'st the sun
> A pris'ner in the yet undawning East,
> Short'ning his journey between morn and noon,
> And hurrying him impatient of his stay,
> Down to the rosy West.
>
> (*Task*, pp. 143–4; Bk IV, lines 120–33)

As it did in *The Seasons*, Winter here appears to stand for the authoritarian God, before whose 'dreaded' might the narrator is humbled. Submission is apparently presented as an observed fact of nature rather than as a moral duty – if Winter can hold the sun 'a pris'ner' then his power cannot be resisted. And Cowper, like Thomson, goes on to palliate social ills by presenting them as instances of man's inevitable submission to natural power.

Before he does so, however, he implicitly raises questions about the location of authority and the morality of power with a greater intensity than occurs in Thomson's more impersonal narrative. In the apostrophe to Winter quoted above the nakedness of the declaration 'I love thee' threatens to make submission to natural authority into a masochistic adoration of an acutely and unusually personal kind. The degree of enthusiasm shown by Cowper unsettles the appearance that submission to nature is inevitable – a common fate of writer and readers – and makes obedience into an act strangely compounded of sympathy and desire. Cowper's imagery and syntax invest the dreaded patriarch of Winter with a disturbing ambiguity, which the narrator does not attempt to resolve. The imagery of decrepitude that describes Winter suggests, despite 'made white with other snows / Than those of age', that he is infirm – 'scatter'd hair' – 'A leafless branch thy sceptre' – a tottering king. The declaration 'I love thee, all unlovely as thou seem'st' indicates a sympathy for an ugly ravaged figure, pathetic in that it is felt for a father-figure more infirm than powerful. It is as if Cowper quietly rewrites personified nature, even as he acknowledges its dreaded power, in his favourite image of himself, that of a broken man. By so doing he can sympathize with it as a companion in decrepitude, as a fellow 'unlovely' outcast, even as he seems to worship its authority. At the same time his syntax insistently repeats vocative phrases addressed to Winter ('Thy scatter'd hair' / 'Thy breath congeal'd') suspending forward progress towards a main verb so that when the verb finally appears it does so with a sense of decisive and climactic resolution of stasis: 'I love thee'. The intensity thus given to the emotional declaration makes it both passionate and powerful: it is the centre of active energy in the sentence. And so it is on Cowper's love, both a masochistic desire to know the master by obeying his authority and an act of perverse sympathy for decrepitude, rather than on a general and passive submission to natural force, that emphasis comes to lie.

The passage is characteristic of Cowper in that it presents through landscape-description a relationship with power that is more complicated and contradictory than the narrator explicitly acknowledges.[28] Winter is an absolute monarch, a decrepit father, a generalized nature and a recipient of passion. Here Cowper's observation of the scene presents shifting and unstable relationships with paternal authority, with God and with the past poet (Thomson) whose scene Cowper is adapting. By implicitly personalizing the narrator's relationship with the personified season Cowper introduces notes of love, desire, passion and complicity with destructive (and even self-destructive) power that are discordant with his own Thomsonian tendency to portray man as a generalized and passive victim of natural (and divine) force. Instead his discourse about nature is composed of a complex mixture of needs, desires and fears that are seen to be in tension with each other. His attempts to gain rhetorical power by speaking on behalf of a generalized nature retain signs of this mixture – and this both undercuts and redefines nature too – making it unreliable and elusive since it is simultaneously represented as a scene invested with the Master's crushing power and as a place attractive in its wounded vulnerability.

The extent of Cowper's dependence upon the voice shaped by Thomson is apparent in a description of a carter in which Cowper echoes Thomson's portrait of the shepherd lost in winter snows:

> He, form'd to bear
> The pelting brunt of the tempestuous night,
> With half-shut eyes, and pucker'd cheeks, and teeth
> Presented bare against the storm, plods on.
> One hand secures his hat, save when with both
> He brandishes his pliant length of whip,
> Resounding oft, and never heard in vain.
> Oh happy! and, in my account, denied
> That sensibility of pain with which
> Refinement is endued, thrice happy thou.
> Thy frame, robust and hardy, feels indeed
> The piercing cold, but feels it unimpair'd.
> The learned finger never need explore

---

[28] On the ambivalence and insecurity of Cowper's poetry see P.M.S. Dawson, 'Cowper's Equivocations', *Essays in Criticism*, 33 (1983), 19–35.

Thy vig'rous pulse; and the unhealthful East,
That breathes the spleen, and searches ev'ry bone
Of the infirm, is wholesome air to thee.
Thy days roll on exempt from household care;
The waggon is thy wife; and the poor beasts,
That drag the companion to and fro,
Thine helpless charge, dependent on thy care.
Ah, treat them kindly! rude as thou appear'st,
Yet show them thou hast mercy! which the great,
With needless hurry whirl'd from place to place,
Humane as they would seem, not always show.

(pp. 155–6; bk IV, lines 350–73)

Through the georgic convention Cowper portrays the carter as an emblem of the healthy virtues of hard rural work, a man more fortunate than the indolent refined with their greater sensibility of pain – although they would be loth, as Cowper admits of himself earlier in the poem, to change places with him. It is, however, to that refined sensibility that Cowper appeals as, like Thomson before him, he presents the picture of the generalized rustic battling against hostile nature in order to remind his readers of a world 'where none / Finds happiness unblighted' (bk IV, lines 333–4) but where we may learn to 'bear our mod'rate ills, / And sympathize with others, suff'ring more' (bk IV, lines 339–40).

As he continues the portrait Cowper outdoes Thomson at his own sentimental game, idealizing domestic bliss and female innocence but ensuring that compassion towards the poor is directed towards the encouragement of charitable relief rather than advocacy of large scale reform or analysis of its social and political causes.

Poor, yet industrious, modest, quiet, neat,
Such claim compassion in a night like this,
And have a friend in ev'ry feeling heart.
Warm'd, while it lasts, by labor, all day long
They brave the season, and yet find at eve,
Ill clad and fed but sparely time to cool.
The frugal housewife trembles when she lights
Her scanty stock of brush-wood, blazing clear
But dying soon, like all terrestrial joys.
The few small embers left she nurses well,
And while her infant race with outspread hands
And crowded knees, sit cow'ring o'er the sparks,
Retires, content to quake, so they be warm'd.
The man feels least, as more inur'd than she
To winter, and the current in his veins
More briskly moved by his severer toil;
Yet he too finds his own distress in theirs.

The taper soon extinguished, which I saw
Dangled along at the cold fingers end
Just when the day declined, and the brown loaf
Lodged on the shelf half-eaten without sauce
Of sav'ry cheese, or butter costlier still;
Sleep seems their only refuge. For alas!
Where penury is felt the thought is chain'd,
And sweet colloquial pleasures are but few.

(pp. 156–7; bk IV, lines 374–98)

Cowper imitates Thomson here as he views the rustics from the position and in the language of their social superiors. Yet he differs from him in several respects. He relaxes Thomson's self-consciously Miltonic and Latinate diction, whilst retaining much of the syntactical variety that characterized *Paradise Lost*. He removes much of what he called the 'affectation' in Thomson's style, thus making the scene quietly corrective of the scene in *The Seasons* which it resembles. Cowper makes his diction approximate to gentlemanly conversation, so that the narrator seeks the sympathy of the educated classes in their own terms, rather than declaiming to them or exhorting them in the lofty rhetoric of epic. He is then able to increase the pathos of the scene by revealing in the household a lack of that which he and his readers share through his poetry: 'sweet colloquial pleasures'. At the same time the introduction of the first person in 'I saw', with the detailed observations of poverty that follow it, makes the narrator's distress less a generalized response to an emblematic scene and more a cry which recognizes in the impoverished cottagers fellow-beings forced like the poet himself into the imprisoning isolation of their separate thoughts. Poverty is for Cowper, in a way it is not for Thomson, an acutely and particularly represented condition of mental as well as material diminution and confinement. Here, however, he does not pursue at length this understanding of poverty, either in his own or the cottagers' case. Instead he has recourse to an increasingly popular socio-political discourse in a way that reveals the cultural shift that had occurred between Thomson, writing in the 1740s, and the 1780s.

Thomson had appealed to gentlemanly charity and had advocated reform of legal abuses as means of alleviating the plight of the poor. Cowper makes similar appeals, but also introduces distinctions which carefully limit the sympathy and the duty owed by gentlemen to the poor. First he offers a grandiloquent but empty promise, speaking on behalf of nature through a pompous rhetoric:

But be ye of good courage. Time itself
Shall much befriend you. Time shall give increase,
And all your num'rous progeny well-train'd
But helpless, in few years shall find their hands,

And labor too. Meanwhile ye shall not want
What conscious of your virtues we can spare,
Nor what a wealthier than ourselves may send.
I mean the man, who when the distant poor
Need help, denies them nothing but his name.

(pp. 158–9; bk ɪv, lines 420–8)

Assuming the power to speak for future time is easy: it allows Cowper to make a pledge which by its nature cannot be soon called in. He is enabled by it to reassure his gentlemanly readership that their charity is only a temporary stopgap. In fact Cowper strives to reassure potential givers – they are flattered by an implicit comparison with the Good Samaritan whilst remaining at a safe distance from the poor they help. And charitable relief, as the next verse paragraph makes explicit, will be dependent upon the perceived virtue of the recipients: 'But poverty, with most who whimper forth / Their long complaints, is self inflicted woe' (bk ɪv, lines 429–30). Cowper distinguishes between the deserving poor (industrious, dutiful and temperate), and the undeserving (lazy, thieving, drunken), in a manner which resembles that of his fellow evangelical author, Hannah More. More's *Cheap Repository Tracts* encouraged the poor to adopt a lifestyle the Christian virtues of which were those which made them suffer their condition without rebelliousness. Cowper admired More's work, and here he echoes its priorities: relief could be properly limited to those paupers who met the cultural criteria which, in the name of Christianity, gentlemen and gentlewomen set for them. Reviling as immoral those who did not endure poverty with uncomplaining fortitude and frugality, Cowper abandoned his earlier implicit identification with the poor man's mental and social confinement. He adopted instead a view that was increasingly prevalent in late eighteenth-century Britain as agricultural change and population increase made poor relief a growing burden upon landowners.

Redrawing the limits of gentlemanly paternalism and shifting between implicit identification with and distance from the poor, Cowper successfully redefined Thomson's winter scene by his own. He removed much of the Miltonic diction without, finally, closing the social and linguistic distance which ensured that his readership remained safely superior to the distressed poor, who were presented generically, viewed as objects of enquiry in the varied rural landscape that the poet surveyed. At its most limited, the Miltonic style which Thomson had applied to nature became in Cowper a means of banishing, by pompous moralizing, the disturbing identification with poverty that he was elsewhere inclined to make. This is so in the following passage, which presents the kind of detached and general view against which Wordsworth was later to define his own poetic voice in ballads which presented the same situation from the poor man's perspective and in an approximation of his words:

> But poverty, with most who whimper forth
> Their long complaints, is self inflicted woe,
> Th'effect of laziness or sottish waste.
> Now goes the nightly thief prowling abroad
> For plunder; much solicitous how best
> He may compensate for a day of sloth,
> By works of darkness and nocturnal wrong.
> Woe to the gard'ner's pale, the farmer's hedge,
> Plash'd neatly, and secured with driven stakes
> Deep in the loamy bank. Uptorn by strength,
> Resistless in so bad a cause, but lame
> To better deeds, he bundles up the spoil
> An asses burthen, and, when laden most
> And heaviest, light of foot steals fast away.
> Nor does the boarded hovel better guard
> The well stack'd pile of riven logs and roots
> From his pernicious force.
>
> (pp. 159–60; bk ɪv, lines 429–45)

Here the word 'resistless' for the more common 'irresistible' is part of a deliberately lofty style, the Latinate diction and inverted syntax of which invokes that of *Paradise Lost*. 'Resistless', however, is a word rarely used by Milton; it is, however, applied by Thomson to the night which closes around the poor shepherd in the winter snowstorm, bringing about his death.[29] Cowper, his discussion of winter's effect on the rural classes shaped by Thomson, makes the thief who steals the firewood seem as menacing as the nightstorm is in *The Seasons*. This reflects his fear of social rebellion at home, a fear springing from his personal need for an inviolable rural refuge but one which came increasingly to be shared by the landowning classes. It also, paradoxically, provides reassurance as part of a discourse which presumes that the activities and experiences of the poor can be comprehended and criticized by a traditional poetic style, originally framed for very different purposes. Cowper seeks the authority of Miltonic epic without resolving the contradictions that occur as he adapts it to new fields with regard to which he has sympathies more divided and conflicting than he acknowledges.

Cowper, Milton and God the father

Those contradictions arose at least partly because seeking Miltonic authority produced in Cowper a mixture of embarrassed deference and asserted power. And the process was complicated by Cowper's need to surpass Thomson by using Miltonic style to convey the epic seriousness of the moral and religious truths 'discovered' in the rural scene. Cowper was unable,

---

[29]   *Winter*, line 294.

despite his claim in a letter of October 1784 that 'my descriptions are all from Nature ... Not one of them borrowed from books' (*CoL*, vol. ii, p. 285), simply to reflect the landscape in a polite language of his own. His pastoral retreat into a rural refuge was threatened by the very poetry which describes it, since even at its least assertive his style is marked by his uneasy attempt to develop from Milton a representation of nature as morally perceptive as that of *Paradise Lost* but without the 'affected' diction of Thomson's version of that discourse. Fundamental to Cowper's sense of identity as a poet and as a man was the struggle to find a discourse which he could feel he was authorized to use by father figures – Milton in poetry, God the father everywhere.[30]

Fearing rejection by these figures, he alternated between anticipating the worst by regarding himself as the subject of their indifference (or contempt), and carefully propitiating them by ensuring that his imitation of their words was offered with self-deprecation as a humble echo rather than a usurpation of their voices. He adopted in his religion the language of evangelicals, finding in John Newton, the former slave-trader turned clergyman, a mentor willing to exercise paternal authority over him – even to the extent of adjudicating upon his poetry. Newton also offered Cowper a discourse of apparent certainty, an evangelical interpretation of life in which events were understood as indicators of the pleasure or displeasure of God with the individual. This discourse was reassuring for Cowper in that it provided, supposedly on religious and even divine authority, rhetoric which confidently spoke for God's hand in the world. Rather than presenting a scene of bewildering complexity, producing a self of conflicting sympathies and divided loyalties, evangelical theodicy referred all to an authoritarian God, through a dualism of good/evil and punishment/redemption. Newton put it thus in his spiritual autobiography, the *Authentic Narrative* (1764): 'I was prevented from every harm, and having seen many fall on my right hand and on my left ... the Lord was pleased to lead me in a secret way.'[31] For Cowper, Newton's certainty, constricting although he came to find it, was preferable to the distress of uncertainty. Moreover Newton, as a preacher of evangelical Christianity, became a father-figure through whose language the ultimate father, God himself, could be propitiated.[32] In *The Task* Cowper made clear his need for such a figure:

> Some friend is gone, perhaps his son's best friend,
> A father, whose authority, in show
> When most severe, and must'ring all its force,
> Was but the graver countenance of love.

---

[30] On Cowper's poetic struggles with his Calvinist God see Morris Golden, *In Search of Stability. The Poetry of William Cowper* (New Haven, Conn., 1960), pp. 78–118.

[31] Quoted in King, *William Cowper, A Biography*, p. 66.

[32] On his idealization of the preacher and his need for father and mother figures see Andrew Elfenbein, 'Cowper's *Task* and the Anxieties of Femininity', *Eighteenth Century Life*, 13 (1989), 1–17.

Whose favour like the clouds of spring, might low'r,
And utter now and then an awful voice,
But had a blessing in its darkest frown,
Threat'ning at once and nourishing the plant.
We loved, but not enough the gentle hand
That reared us. At a thoughtless age allured
By ev'ry gilded folly, we renounced
His shelt'ring side, and wilfully forewent
That converse which we now in vain regret.
How gladly would the man recall to life
The boy's neglected sire! a mother too,
That softer friend, perhaps more gladly still,
Might he demand them at the gates of death.
Sorrow has, since they went, subdued and tamed
The playful humour; he could now endure,
(Himself grown sober in the vale of tears)
And feel a parent's presence no restraint.
But not to understand a treasure's worth
Till time has stol'n away the slighted good,
Is cause of half the poverty we feel,
And makes the world the wilderness it is.

(pp. 233–4; bk vi, lines 29–53)

On Cowper's need for a benevolent substitute father, this passage suggests, depended his sense of productive order and meaning in the world. But the discourse of evangelical Christianity as mediated through Newton proved a dangerous paternal law. For although it represented God in reassuringly ordered terms, it also made him so severe and threatening that Cowper, as Newton's influence upon him began to wane, felt unable to deserve God's love. Without a substitute parent to propitiate and mediate God's sublime authority Cowper found that he was unable to discover in the world evidence of divine favour towards him, only signs of God's wrath and his own damnation.[33] The comfort of a series of substitute parents became essential to his sanity.

It was a language capable of mediating paternal authority without being crushed by it that Cowper needed. Recognizing authority as 'an awful voice' of a father, needed to govern but also to nourish the writer, he understood it to be produced by a male discourse over and in nature. Unwilling to challenge the authoritarian God whom he believed was the ultimate source of such discourse, he found others whose representations of divine law he could more easily absorb and make his own.[34] He formed an unusual relationship

---

[33] As Felicity Nussbaum has remarked, 'Cowper finds himself unable to present a coherent and convincing rational identity' – the 'traditional pattern cannot accommodate the vacuum of authority'. In 'Private Subjects in William Cowper's "Memoir"', *The Age of Johnson*, 1 (1987), 307–26 (p. 323).

[34] On Cowper's absorption of divine law into a vulnerably subjective language, see Vincent Newey, *Cowper's Poetry: A Critical Study and Reassessment* (Liverpool, 1982), p. 161.

with Samuel Teedon, a tradesman who, at Newton's instigation, had settled at Olney, becoming a schoolmaster there. Teedon was paid £30 a year by Cowper, in return for which he interpreted Cowper's dreams and attempted, on the basis of his belief that God revealed his will to him in special notices, to assure Cowper that forgiveness and salvation remained possible. Cowper, himself suffering from voices which assured him of his damnation, was in effect buying a language which claimed the authority to reveal God's will and which had the confidence to believe in its worthiness to reflect a pattern of saving grace present in the world. Teedon was ultimately unsuccessful in reassuring Cowper, who plunged further into religious despair. Their relationship, moreover, revealed the very instability of Cowper's position – social and religious. Cowper saw himself as a gentleman giving charity to a poverty-stricken social inferior, whose conduct merited patronage: 'The poor man' (he wrote of Teedon) 'has gratitude if he has not wit, and in the possession of that one good quality has a sufficient recommendation' (*CoL*, vol. III, p. 40). This is a distant and lofty view similar to that in the passage, already examined, in *The Task* in which charitable relief of the deserving poor is seen as a virtuous duty. But the developing relationship changed the position – Teedon, though he was still liable to be patronized (and threatened by Cowper's protector, Mrs Unwin, with a cut in his allowance) became a confessor upon whose greater religious certainty and authority Cowper depended. Cowper's spiritual impoverishment made him the supplicator whilst he retained the financial power to determine the extent of Teedon's services and shape his discourse. Not surprisingly, the relationship was full of social and religious tension and ultimately ended with Cowper's belief that Teedon was sent by God to deceive him with false hope.

Cowper's use of Teedon can be seen as an attempt to create in his daily life a figure and language of authority ultimately controllable by him. Seen in such as way it appears as a microcosm of his larger attempt to strengthen his poetic voice through that of Milton. The most direct expressions of this attempt were Cowper's translation of Milton's Latin poems and his commentary on *Paradise Lost*, embarked upon but left incomplete in the 1790s. A remark from the latter makes clear Cowper's sense of Milton's strength. Speaking of Milton's description of Satan and the Council in Hell he comments:

It was doubtless a happiness to have fallen on a subject that furnished such scenery and such characters to act in it, but a happiness it would not have been to a genius inferior to Milton's; such a one on the contrary would have been depressed by it, and in what Milton reaches with a graceful ease, would have fallen short after much and fruitless labour.   (*CoL*, vol. v, p. 155)

Milton's 'Divine subject', he notes, 'afforded him opportunities of surpassing in sublime description all the poets his predecessors' (*CoL*, vol. v, p. 153). But it was Milton's grandeur of mind that allowed him to succeed: his language was powerful enough properly to represent the sublimity of its subject matter, to justify the ways of God to man – 'he not only does not degrade his subject, but fills the mind of his reader with astonishing conceptions of its grandeur' (*CoL*, vol. v, p. 154). Cowper sees in Milton a writer capable of being sustained rather than crushed by the task of representing the authority of God the Father and the terrors of Hell.

He viewed Milton as a father capable of mediating for him, and for mankind in general, with the divine father, one whom he could, in the words of *The Task* quoted above, demand 'at the gates of death', so powerfully had Milton represented those gates and the scenes of Hell without being overwhelmed by them. In a letter of 1793 to William Hayley he described a dream in which Milton returned from death:

Oh you rogue! what would you give to have such a dream about Milton as I had about a week since? I dream'd that being in a house in the city and with much company, looking toward the lower end of the room from the upper end of it, I descried a figure which I immediately knew to be Milton's. He was very gravely but very neatly attired in the fashion of his day, and had a countenance which fill'd me with those feelings that an affectionate child has for a beloved father. Such for instance as Tom has for you. My first thought was wonder where he could have been conceal'd so many years, my second a transport of joy to find him still alive, my third, another transport to find myself in his company, and my fourth a resolution to accost him. I did so, and he received me with a complacence in which I saw equal sweetness and dignity. I spoke of his Paradise Lost as every man must who is worthy to speak of it at all, and told him a long story of the manner in which it affected me when I first discover'd it, being at that time a school-boy. He answer'd me by a smile and a gentle inclination of his head. I told him we had poets in *our* days, and no mean ones, and that I was myself intimate with the best of them. He replied – I know Mr Hayley very well by his writings. He then grasp'd my hand affectionately and with a smile that charm'd me said – Well – you, for your part, will do well also.   (*CoL*, vol. iv, p. 297)

Milton's paternal blessing sanctions Cowper's own poetry and allows him to feel that he is a legitimate son of a great poetic father. The letter was written two days after a much grimmer letter sent to Teedon in which Cowper's memory of Charles II's indifference towards Milton is seen as a divinely-sent 'notice' of God's indifference towards Cowper.

I waked the other morning with these words distinctly spoken to me.

Charles the second, though he was or wished to be accounted a man of fine Taste and an Admirer of the arts, never saw, or express'd a wish to see the Man whom he would have found Alone superior to all the race of man.

But in such a notice as this I find nothing to comfort, nothing spiritual. A thousand such would do me no real service. A single word of Christ is worth all that can be said either by men or Angels concerning all the men of genius that ever lived. But such a word I seldom hear.   (*CoL*, vol. iv, p. 295)

Here Cowper appeals to Teedon to provide what his dream of Milton blessing him had of itself been inadequate to provide, a discourse capable of overcoming for more than a brief moment his sense that his own poetry had failed to propitiate a cruelly indifferent kingly/godly father.

Milton's blessing was, despite this letter, of greater value than Teedon's. His justification of God was incomparably greater, if less immediately controllable, than was that offered by the Olney schoolmaster. In Cowper's more confident periods Milton was a father with whom he could come to terms, one who could propitiate in powerful words the stern authority of God the father, one, crucially, whose words Cowper could imitate, so becoming in his own eyes a true descendant but also achieving a certain independence. He placed limits upon his imitation, so as to prevent deferential adaptation of Milton's style becoming a challenge to the power of the epic poet. Self-deprecating irony ensured in *The Task* that Cowper undercut his pretensions to an epic grandeur that would court comparison with past epic poets. His self-deflating opening, absurd by comparison with Virgil, begins the process: 'I sing the sofa. I who lately sang / Truth, Hope and Charity, and touch'd with awe / The solemn chords, and with a trembling hand / Escap'd with pain from that advent'rous flight, / Now seek repose upon an humbler theme ... ' (bk I, lines 1–5). He continues with a mock-Miltonic description of the historical progress towards the sofa:

> At length a generation more refined
> Improv'd the simple plan, made three legs four,
> Gave them a twisted form vermicular,
> And o'er the seat with plenteous wadding stuff'd
> Induced a splendid cover ...
>
> (pp. 2–3; bk I, lines 29–32)

Later he includes a mock epic description of cucumber growing, in which Latinate style is devoted to a subject so domestic and trivial that Cowper the cultivator of prize vegetables becomes a comic rather than epic hero.

Yet the jokes are not wholly destructive of Cowper's authority. Instead, by highlighting his limitations they enhance it, showing that he is aware that authority cannot be sustained by borrowing an epic style if the perspective of the poet and his resultant subject-matter are self-consciously marginal. By mocking his own claims to the discourse of epic he admits his own inadequacy, enlisting his reader's sympathy. This sympathy allows Cowper's self-deprecating mock epic to be read as the minor heroism of a damaged personality. In a landscape in which desolation and confusion threaten the writer the growing of cucumbers is a triumph over adversity made more successful and poignant because Cowper, through the mock epic, exposes his awareness of the gap between the small scale of the achievement and its difficulty and seriousness for him. At the same time it shows that he can imitate Milton but will not pretend to match, still less outdo, him. And by demonstrating this it allows him to use Miltonic rhetoric to enhance his ability to speak for God-in-nature in localized areas of his digressive poem. Meditating on an earthquake and subsequent tidal wave which had killed many in Sicily and Calabria, he adapts Milton's descriptions of Eden, of Hell and of the bridge built between them into an evangelical's reading of a world in which disorder in nature is a 'notice' of God's wrath at man's sinfulness:

> While God performs upon the trembling stage
> Of his own works, his dreadful part alone.
> How does the earth receive him? – With what signs
> Of gratulation and delight, her king?
> Pours she not all her choicest fruits abroad,
> Her sweetest flow'rs, her aromatic gums,
> Disclosing paradise where'er he treads?
> She quakes at his approach. Her hollow womb,
> Conceiving thunders, through a thousand deeps
> And fiery caverns roars beneath his foot.
> The hills move lightly and the mountains smoke,
> For he has touch'd them. From th'extremest point
> Of elevation down into th'abyss,
> His wrath is busy and his frown is felt.
> The rocks fall headlong and the vallies rise,
> The rivers die into offensive pools,
> And charged with putrid verdure, breathe a gross
> And mortal nuisance into all the air.
> What solid was, by transformation strange,
> Grows fluid, and the fixt and rooted earth
> Tormented into billows heaves and swells,
> Or with vortiginous and hideous whirl
> Sucks down its prey insatiable. Immense
> The tumult and the overthrow, the pangs
> And agonies of human and of brute
> Multitudes, fugitive on ev'ry side,
> And fugitive in vain. The sylvan scene
> Migrates uplifted, and, with all its soil
> Alighting in far distant fields, finds out
> A new possessor, and survives the change.
> Ocean had caught the frenzy, and, upwrought
> To an enormous and o'erbearing height,
> Not by a mighty wind, but by that voice
> Which winds and waves obey, invades the shore
> Resistless.

(pp. 49–51; bk ii, lines 81–115)

In this description Cowper adapts Milton in a Thomsonian manner to represent natural violence as divine anger, reproducing it in a syntax of convoluted development and abrupt transition, so that it seems structured by an inherited epic style. In the process he acquires authority, for although he goes on to suggest that all sinful men should be warned by such events, his discourse is so energized by the attempt to represent such violent energy that he seems to direct the retributive force rather than to be a sinful victim of it. Milton and Thomson, as elsewhere Newton, allow Cowper to glory in being the prophet in whose verse doom becomes an articulate power. Through his carefully limited imitation of them he was able briefly to speak authoritatively for the dreadful power of God.

It was a dangerous as well as limited achievement since, without the complacent conviction that he was one of the elect predestined to be saved, Cowper's prosodic identification with retributive wrath rebounded upon him. Imagining God's power gave him a vicarious poetic authority in the short term but ultimately depressed him with a sense of his own likely subjection to that wrath, even when he could fend off feelings of inadequacy by portraying himself as the dutiful son of his father-figure Milton. By his last years Cowper was again in the depths of the spiritual crisis which had begun in his twenties, leading him then to attempt suicide. Convinced of his damnation by 1773, he had nevertheless been able to achieve a degree of stability, setting his despair in order by writing poetry. Yet, as Dustin Griffin has shown, Milton, like Teedon, became in the 1790s a source of images of damnation. Hearing voices which assured him that he was condemned, Cowper was again close to suicide. In 'Lines Written on a Window Shutter at Weston' he portrayed his coming move to Norfolk as a hellish exile, quoting Milton's Satan: 'Me miserable! How could I escape / Infinite wrath, and infinite despair!' (cf. *Paradise Lost*, bk ɪv, lines 73–4).[35] And in his commentary on *Paradise Lost*, written at the same late period in his life, Cowper linked the awesomeness of the portrait of Death with its obscurity. By choosing not to delineate the menacing figure exactly Milton had made it more threatening, leaving the reader to see for himself and to suppose the worst (*CoL*, vol. v, pp. 166–7). Cowper, despite his ability to exert a certain control over Milton's rhetoric of heaven and hell by editing, translating and imitating his poetry, had come to find him not a benevolent substitute for the Calvinist God, able to propitiate him in a language from the strength of which Cowper could draw, but another power confirming his inadequacy and despair.

The fields of contradiction: the politics of retreat

Convinced of his damnation, in retreat from public life, Cowper nevertheless made public interventions in the contemporary politics of language. His

---

[35] Dustin Griffin, 'Cowper, Milton, and the Recovery of Paradise', *Essays in Criticism*, 31 (1981), 15–26 (p. 17). For the full text of Cowper's poem see *The Poetical Works of William Cowper*, ed. H. S. Milford, 4th edn (London, 1934), p. 428.

poetry suggested that the polite language of the gentlemanly classes and the terms of evangelical Christians were adequate to represent and judge the poor. At the same time the act of composition was important for Cowper's readers, for whom his ability to find a quiet order of his own in the face of almost overwhelming anxiety at the abandonment by the gentlemanly classes of their duty to govern rural society, was a token of poetry's continued moral and social efficacy. *The Task* served to displace the tensions and insecurities of English culture – over the place of God in the world, over the American Revolution, over political corruption in London and India, over rural discontent – into the poet's (mock-) heroic battle for a style which would give him his own discourse of virtuous security, a discourse which accepts that gentlemanly virtue has largely turned to vice in the fields of Britain.

Cowper's poetry became pivotal in its use of the prospect-view and a disinterested stance to challenge, rather than legitimize, the values of the landed interest as they appeared in practice. Attacking their corruption by commercialism, by places at Court, by the wealth of the City, by the luxury of the spa towns, Cowper appeared as a traditional Country independent who regarded critical scrutiny of power, even when exercised by Whig ministers, as the duty of a truly patriotic Whig. He regretted the gentry's abandonment of the independent views that stemmed from land ownership. And he reconstituted this Country ideal more vulnerably in the prospect-views that he, a gentleman suffered to walk through estates owned by others, was able to take. However, in a reversal of the traditional Country equation of disinterest with land ownership, it was now only Cowper's landlessness, his poverty, that kept him independent and immune from temptation. The results of succumbing to that temptation were, for Cowper, all too visible in the surrounding scenes: improved land organized to create profit and to symbolize the wealth of its owner rather than his duty to his tenants as their squire and representative in parliament.

Cowper's critical stance changed the poetry of retirement. The urbanity with which Pope and the wistfulness with which Thomson manipulated the classical topos was replaced by a radical, but also anxiously self-doubting, separation of Country from City. This separation was implicitly political in that it suggested that integrity could not be preserved in the political realm, where the compromises and petty victories of party battles and the temptations of fame and wealth corrupted all. A last-ditch Country politics, in that it regarded independence and liberty (as Neville, Moyle and Pakington all had done) as threatened by Court and City corruption now colonizing the country too, it was reactionary in that it demanded a return to a patriotic disinterest portrayed as a virtue of the past. *The Task* showed William Pitt as an embodiment of that past virtue. Pitt, of course, had been one of the 'boy Patriots' seeking to unite Whigs and Tories in a Country party to defend the liberty of the nation against Walpole's ministry. With Lyttelton he had patronized Thomson's Patriot plays. Later, ennobled as the Earl of Chatham, he had, for Cowper, served his country's rather than his own or his party's interests:

> Praise enough
> To fill th'ambition of a private man,
> That Chatham's language was his mother tongue,
> And Wolfe's great name compatriot with his own.

(p. 57; bk II, lines 235–8)

Pitt, 'consulting England's happiness at home', naturally defended the national interest abroad, as did General Wolfe, the hero who had died taking Quebec (bk II, line 236). For Cowper Country, rather than party, City, or Court values were a source of national manliness and a cause for patriotic pride. Chatham was contrasted with the 'effeminates' unable to conduct successful war against the alliance of France and the American colonies.

Charles James Fox, abandoning parliament for his country estate in the 1790s, recognized Cowper's retirement as a retreat from Westminster party divisions and machinations. Gilpin, Wordsworth and Coleridge, as I shall show, all recognized Cowper's voice as an important model because it made retirement a critique both of London politics and of the contemporary country gentry. By finding a voice to narrate the anxiety that a divided realm produced in a poet seeking moral authority, Cowper moved beyond his own outbursts of nostalgia for the idealized paternal gentleman as local and national leader. For the young Romantic poets who followed him he had transformed Country party politics by relocating the moral authority to speak for the nation. Authority appeared neither in London politicians nor the traditional landed gentry, but in the retired, landless, isolated poet pondering his own vulnerability and limitations. It was not by poetry tied to a party (as Thomson's had come to be), nor by direct intervention in current political events that Cowper's poetry became authoritative for his own and subsequent generations. It did so by an implicitly critical view the disinterested patriotism of which was evinced by its marginality in a predominantly corrupt nation. In 1781, for example, he had renounced the writing of poems explicitly concerned with specific political events (*CoL*, vol. I, p. 551). They were, he thought, always too likely to be disproved by the changing course of public affairs. He did not, however, need to discuss current issues in detail since his moralizing commentary on his own retreat from contemporary society effectively held up for scrutiny the public realm and the difficulty of finding undivided and untainted authority within it.[36] Cowper, admitting his own and, self-referentially, his own poetry's unfitness for public authority, became

---

[36] Here I differ from Richard Feingold who, in analysing the public aspects of *The Task* sees retirement as evidence 'of the poet's need to escape, to isolate himself from the battleground of nature and art in life in order to comprehend nature morally as a creature of grace'. See *Nature and Society: Later Eighteenth-Century Uses of the Pastoral and Georgic* (Hassocks, Sussex, 1978), p. 133.

a model of worthy anxiety as he showed himself as an ordinary man struggling to resolve common dilemmas. His personal struggle and his provisional solution – a place of peace represented in the vocabulary of polite conversation – vindicates gentlemanly discourse but also shows that, in the face of the actual corruption of the gentlemanly classes by commercialism and self-interest, such discourse covers a reduced area. It is a guarantor of security and shared domestic values, a bastion (or, more appropriately, a garden hedge) against larger social and political anxieties:

> Since pulpits fail, and sounding-boards reflect
> Most part an empty ineffectual sound,
> What chance that I, to fame so little known,
> Nor conversant with men, or manners much,
> Should speak to purpose, or with better hope
> Crack the satyric thong? 'twere wiser far
> For me, enamour'd of sequester'd scenes,
> And charm'd with rural beauty, to repose
> Where chance may throw me, beneath elm or vine,
> My languid limbs when summer sears the plains,
> Or when rough winter rages, on the soft
> And shelter'd Sofa, while the nitrous air
> Feeds a blue flame and makes a chearful hearth;
> There undisturb'd by folly, and appriz'd
> How great the danger of disturbing her,
> To muse in silence, or at least confine
> Remarks that gall so many, to the few
> My partners in retreat. Disgust conceal'd
> Is oft-times proof of wisdom, when the fault
> Is obstinate, and the cure beyond our reach.
>
> (pp. 92–3; bk iii, lines 21–40)

Continuing in Miltonic vein Cowper declares 'Domestic happiness, thou only bliss / Of Paradise that has surviv'd the fall!' (bk iii, lines 41–2). This happiness, however, itself proves vulnerable to pressures from without and from the temptation to make verbal war on 'the fault ... obstinate', despite his confessed inability to cure it. In July 1785 a local landowner felled trees, removed scrub and reorganized as an orderly plantation a wood near Olney through which had run one of Cowper's favourite walks. He mourned for its loss in terms that make of the picturesque glade a sanctuary of spiritual community shared between Cowper and his domestic circle:

this pleasant retreat is destined never to be a pleasant retreat again ... I have promised myself that I will never enter it again. We have both pray'd in it. You for me, and I for you, but it is desecrated from this time forth, and the voice of pray'r will be heard in it no more. The fate of it in this respect, however deplorable is not peculiar; the spot where Jacob anointed his pillar, and which is more apposite, the spot once honoured with the presence of Him who dwelt in the bush, have long since suffer'd similar disgrace, and are become common ground.   (*CoL*, vol. ɪɪ, pp. 362–3)

Here the comparison with the holy sites in which God became manifest suggests that Cowper had made a deep spiritual investment in the local spinney.[37] When he reflects on similar despoliations in *The Task* he is tempted to move from the peaceful discourse of domestic retirement to discuss current affairs. This contradicts his renunciation of intervention in public debates, tempting him to wield a power-seeking rhetoric that allusions to *Paradise Lost* suggest he found Satanic:

> Oh blest seclusion from a jarring world,
> Which he thus occupied, enjoys! Retreat
> Cannot indeed to guilty man restore
> Lost innocence, or cancel follies past,
> But it has peace, and much secures the mind
> From all assaults of evil, proving still
> A faithful barrier, not o'erleap'd with ease
> By vicious custom, raging uncontoul'd
> Abroad, and desolating public life.
> When fierce temptation seconded within
> By traitor appetite, and arm'd with darts
> Temper'd in hell, invades the throbbing breast,
> To combat may be glorious, and success
> Perhaps may crown us; but to fly is safe.
>
> (pp. 125–6; bk ɪɪɪ, lines 675–88)

Milton's Satan fathers Death, 'terrible as Hell' who 'shook a dreadful Dart', whilst his Adam, after falling into sin, advises escape from God's anger (*Paradise Lost*, bk ɪɪ, lines 671–2). Nevertheless Cowper is tempted to the combat, and he takes up arms against the despoliation of rural refuges, transforming his anger at the loss of his own sylvan retreat into an indictment of the political values and cultural fashions of his contemporary Britain. The Earl of Northampton had spent heavily trying to secure the election of his favoured candidates to parliament. He had gone bankrupt in 1774. His landscape gardener Lancelot 'Capability' Brown, one of his creditors, took a charge on the timber on his estate at Yardley Chase, near Cowper's residence. Cowper viewed the fate of the woodland as a symptom of the national triumph of greed over traditional paternalism:

> Mansions once
> Knew their own masters, and laborious hinds
> That had surviv'd the father, serv'd the son.
> Now the legitimate and rightful Lord

---

[37] For an analysis of *The Task* which views the poem as an attempt to invest human words with the divine spirit or Logos, see W. Gerald Marshall, 'The Presence of "the Word" in Cowper's *The Task*', *Studies in English Literature*, 27 (1987), 475–87.

Is but a transient guest, newly arrived,
And soon to be supplanted. He that saw
His patrimonial timber cast its leaf,
Sells the last scantling, and transfers the price
To some shrew'd sharper, 'ere it buds again.
Estates are landscapes, gazed upon a while,
Then advertised, and auctioneer'd away.

                              (p. 129; bk iii, lines 746–56)

For Cowper such a gaze is exploitative and it uproots not only the trees but the landowning classes, to their own detriment and that of the rural society of which they had been masters. They are lost to gambling and luxury; it is without government or care. Richard Feingold comments 'in the new polity of power and wealth ... the moral basis of politics is destroyed along with the old order of society because the former guardians also now join in the new riot of luxury'.[38]

Cowper singles out for attack Capability Brown and the fashion for landscape-gardening, echoing Pope's 'Epistle to Burlington' as he makes the practice an emblem of the degradation of the nobility by commerce. Milton is again invoked: Brown's control over the landscape is reminiscent of Satan's sinuous penetration of Eden and fascination of Eve:

Improvement too, the idol of the age,
Is fed with many a victim. Lo! he comes -
Th'omnipotent magician, Brown appears.
Down falls the venerable pile, th'abode
Of our forefathers – a grave whisker'd race,
But tasteless. Springs a palace in its stead,
But in a distant spot; where more exposed,
It may enjoy th'advantage of the north,
And aguish East, till time shall have transform'd
Those naked acres to a shelt'ring grove.
He speaks. The lake in front becomes a lawn,
Woods vanish, hills subside, and vallies rise,
And streams as if created for his use,
Pursue the track of his directing wand,
Sinuous or straight, now rapid and now slow,
Now murm'ring soft, now roaring in cascades –
Ev'n as he bids! Th'enraptur'd owner smiles.
'Tis finish'd, and yet finish'd as it seems,
Still wants a grace, th'loveliest it could show,
A mine to satisfy the enormous cost.
Drain'd to the last poor item of his wealth,
He sighs, departs, and leaves the accomplished plan
That he has touch'd, retouch'd, many a long day

---

[38] Feingold, *Nature and Society*, p. 145.

Labor'd, and many a night pursued in dreams,
Just when it meets his hopes, and proves the heav'n
He wanted, for a wealthier to enjoy.
And now perhaps the glorious hour is come,
When having no stake left, no pledge t'indear
Her int'rests, or that gives her sacred cause
A moment's operation on his love,
He burns with most intense and flagrant zeal
To serve his country. Ministerial grace
Deals him out money from the public chest,
Or if that mine be shut, some private purse
Supplies his need with an usurious loan,
To be refunded duely, when his vote,
Well-managed, shall have earn'd its worthy price.

                                   (pp. 130–2; bk iii, lines 764–800)

Brown is here a personification of the danger that Cowper recognized attended the representation of landscape for popular taste – the danger that, like Satan, the artist becomes sinfully proud of the subordination of nature to his own discourse. Brown's subordinative power is more direct than that of poets or painters and Cowper both envies him this ('Ev'n as he bids!') and attacks him for imposing commercial values inimical to the local particularity of the place. Cowper, by contrast, speaks from a landscape paced and measured in a verse that tries to reflect his own familiarity with the scene. Cowper, moreover, did not attempt to profit by publication of *The Task*: he could feel that his own independence was not compromised as, he suggests, was the landowner's who sought a sinecure or sold his vote in order to pay for the landscaping of his estate (his own independence, however, also depended on financial assistance from others).

In attacking Brown's landscape gardening Cowper helped to establish a fashion. The theorists of the picturesque, Uvedale Price, Richard Payne Knight, Humphry Repton and William Gilpin all went on, in the 1790s and 1800s, to attack Brown and the aesthetics for which he stood. They preferred as had Cowper a landscape which displayed a certain wildness and, ultimately, the squire's paternal duty to his tenants. Wordsworth also responded to this debate, on which I shall focus in chapter three. But Cowper's own attack is more than a discussion of gardening: from his anxiety at the loss of a landscape of great private importance to him comes a discourse which treats the landscape of gentlemanly taste as a testing ground for the political mores of the nation. He had renounced poetic comment on political events in 1781; here, however, he analyses from the rural scene the political culture which, he claimed, was plunging Britain further into a corruption which it was his duty (as well as temptation) to identify and fight. Whilst his analysis is questionable (like Johnson and like the radical Cobbett it implicitly idealizes a lost idyll of local rural paternalism), it forges a new relationship between high politics, the politics of taste, and the poet's meditation upon himself.

Within *The Task*'s meditation upon the self the narratorial 'I' remains unstable, shaped by the different forms of address it manipulates as well as by the conflicting issues it locates in the national field. Cowper retires to rural domesticity, yet shows that pastoral retreat is too demanding for him. The peasant's cottage seems a 'nest', a secure refuge defended by trees, yet life there is too frugal for Cowper to wish to retire to it: 'If solitude make scant the means of life, / Society for me!' (bk 1, lines 248–9). Only by continuing on a restless journey can the poet find a position both of security and authority, solitude and social power. This journey (Cowper's task) is carefully staged in the verse as a progress through a picturesque scene towards a position of eminence (real but also rhetorical) from which command of a field more usually experienced as divided can be briefly taken. After rejecting the refuge of the peasant's cottage Cowper descends the hill by which it is situated. He steps out upon a mock-heroic odyssey, a journey like Milton's Satan's towards the hill of Eden. First 'we pass a gulph' but hence

> We mount again, and feel at ev'ry step
> Our foot half sunk in hillocks green and soft,
> Rais'd by the mole, the miner of the soil.
> He not unlike the great ones of mankind,
> Disfigures earth, and plotting in the dark
> Toils much to earn a monumental pile,
> That may record the mischiefs he has done.
>
> (p. 15; bk 1, lines 271–7)

Here there is an echo of Hamlet's 'Well said, old mole. Cans't work i' th'earth so fast?' – a challenge made to the elusive spirit of his father, a spirit which at that point in the play Hamlet imagines may have been a delusion sent by the devil. Cowper is half-humorously half-seriously viewing the landscape through which he climbs to gain an authoritative position as similarly undermined by the ghosts of past patriarchs and obstructed by the vain monuments of their contrivance and ambition. The allusion suggests that Cowper's words are haunted by Milton and Shakespeare himself, as well as by the political monarchs of the earth, whilst its humorous inappropriateness makes mountains out of molehills, but wins the reader's sympathy for Cowper by self-deprecatingly showing him to be aware that his heroic journey (and verse) is on a comically minor scale.

Cowper produces a delicate blend of comedy and seriousness so that, self-undermined in advance, he reaches a commanding position to imply that it offers only a hollow temptation, an illusion of grandeur absurdly vulnerable to the pretensions of other men to write their names upon the world:

> The summit gain'd, behold the proud alcove
> That crowns it! yet not all its pride secures
> The grand retreat from injuries impress'd
> By rural carvers, who with knives deface
> The pannels, leaving an obscure rude name
> In characters uncouth, and spelt amiss.
> So strong the zeal t'immortalize himself
> Beats in the breast of man, that ev'n a few,
> Few transient years won from th'abyss abhorr'd
> Of blank oblivion, seem a glorious prize,
> And even to a clown. Now roves the eye,
> And posted on this speculative height,
> Exults in its command.
>
> (pp. 15–16; bk i, lines 278–90)

The exultant narrator is all too close to the vulgar 'clown', his writing too near to the 'characters uncouth' to remain above the rustic tragicomedy of his fellow men's desire to immortalize themselves in script. The retreat is despoiled before it can successfully become a vantage point of power, by a comically bucolic violation narrated in a Miltonic style more appropriate for Satan's destruction of Eden. By the end of the extract the narrator implies that he himself resembles Milton's Satan, the Satan who from the 'abhorred Deep' and 'dark oblivion' of Hell had journey'd like a scout up to 'the brow of some high-climbing Hill' from which 'far and wide his eye commands' the world, but who is ultimately the self-deluding fool of a God who comically reduces him to a clown 'to dash [his] pride' (*Paradise Lost*, bk ii, line 87; bk vi, line 380; bk iii, line 546; bk iii, line 614; bk x, line 577).

Cowper, having written himself up to the commanding height of the hilltop, discovers himself still to be vulnerable and unstable. The scene on which he looks down becomes, in the light of this discovery, an index of a personal need for a harmonious world in which men and natural objects have their timeless places and properties and make them available to the discerning viewer without conflict. In Thomson similar views are demonstrations of the poet's power to describe the property on whose apparently natural order his politician-patrons' disinterested views are founded. Here, however, the scene reassures the poet that, foolish in his pride though he may be, he can locate for a moment an order in nature that reassures him of the benevolence of God. He views a prelapsarian Eden in which the river Ouse plays Eve's part:

> the lime at dewy eve
> Diffusing odors: nor unnoted pass
> The sycamore, capricious in attire,
> Now green, now tawny, and, 'ere autumn yet
> Have changed the woods, in scarlet honours bright.
> O'er these, but far beyond, (a spacious map

Of hill and valley interpos'd between)
The Ouse, dividing the well-water'd land,
Now glitters in the sun, and now retires,
As bashful, yet impatient to be seen.

(pp. 17–18; bk ɪ, lines 316–25)

It is a brief and fragile vision, threatened as it is by Cowper's sense of the
absurdity of man's claims to authority. But it is an important one, for it
transforms the prospect-poetry of Thomson, making the viewer's verbal
authority more delicate, more uncertain but more deeply human than was
the case in earlier eighteenth-century landscape-description. Proceeding from
a quiet dramatization of authorial instability to a prospect of harmony
Cowper was able to take an (admittedly idealized) view from which social and
political divisions and retributive patriarchal authority are briefly absent. In
so doing he provided an example which, I shall suggest in chapter five,
helped Coleridge to shape his poetic contemplation of the political and rural
landscapes of England.

'Good order': poetic style and public affairs

Cowper understood that the scene of discourse shaped the subjectivity of
those involved. That is to say, the circumstances in which words were used
and the traditions influencing those circumstances constrained but also
energized the speaker or writer. He noted in particular the tendency of the
political and legal arenas to produce power-seeking rhetoric. Commenting in
1788 on Burke's prosecution of the case against Warren Hastings for
corruption and tyranny when he was governor of the East India Company,
Cowper wrote:

The stile of a criminal charge of this kind has been an affair settled among Orators
from the days of Tully to the present, and like all other practises that have obtained
for ages, this in particular seems to have been founded originally in reason and in the
necessity of the case. He who accuses another to the state, must not appear himself
unmoved by the view of the crimes with which he charges him, lest he should be
suspected of fiction or of precipitancy, or of a consciousness that after all he shall not
be able to prove his allegations. On the contrary, in order to impress the minds of his
hearers with a persuasion that he himself at least is convinced of the criminality of the
prisoner, he must be vehement, energetic, rapid; must call him tyrant, and traytor
and everything else that is odious, and all this to his face, because all this, bad as it is,
is no more than he undertakes to prove in the sequel, and if he cannot prove it, he
must himself appear in a light very little more desireable, and at the best to have
trifled with the tribunal to which he has summon'd him. Thus Tully in the very first
sentence of his first Oration against Cataline, calls him a Monster; a manner of
address in which he persisted, 'till said Monster unable to support the fury of his
accuser's eloquence any longer, rose from his seat, elbow'd for himself a passage

through the crowd, and at last burst from the Senate house in an agony, as if the
Furies themselves had follow'd him.   (*CoL*, vol. III, p. 113)

Later in the letter he concluded that such 'inflammatory' speaking was not
altogether proper. Yet in analysing the reasons for its appearance he had
shown an implicit understanding of the way in which his own public voice
appeared in his poetry. Eight years earlier he had written of his reaction to
the Gordon Riots, anti-Catholic disturbances in London during which much
property was destroyed: 'were I to express what I feel upon such Occasions in
Prose, it would be Verbose, inflated, and disgusting, I therefore have recourse
to verse, as a suitable Vehicle for the most vehement Expressions my
Thoughts suggest to me' (*CoL*, vol. I, p. 353). Reacting in this case to the
rumour that the riots had been fomented by France, with whom Britain was
at war in America, Cowper had composed Latin verses after the example of
Horace. He later translated them thus:

> False, cruel, disappointed, Stung to th'Heart,
> France quits the Warrior's for th'Assassin's Part.
> To dirty Hands a dirty Bribe conveys,
> Bids the low Street & lofty Palace Blaze.
> Her Sons too Weak to Vanquish us alone,
> She Hires the worst & basest of our own. –
> Kneel France – a Suppliant conquers us with Ease,
> We always Spare a Coward on his Knees.
>
>   (*CoL*, vol. I, p. 364)

Here the power given to words by rhythm and rhyme and by the traditions
which give precedents and examples for vehement public criticism, allows
Cowper to find an authority not simply his own and not available in prose.
Like the tradition of the state prosecutions in court, beginning for Cowper
with Tully, poetic tradition allows him a vehement public voice he would not
otherwise dare attempt. The verse itself in this instance has, however, the
sound of a timid man posturing – it attacks an uncontroversial target by
attributing disorder at home to a foreign enemy and claims a moral
superiority by a gesture that, having no corresponding political reality, is
purely rhetorical ('We always Spare a Coward on his Knees').

Cowper's poetic comment on public affairs is all too frequently marked by
the attempt to compensate for his own distance from the stages of power by a
rhetoric borrowed from writers who had, like Milton (and like Burke in the
Hastings trial), been situated at the heart of public and political confronta-
tions.[39] The certainty of interpretation assumed by his evangelical friend
John Newton offered another rhetoric by which this distance could be
bridged. In November 1781 Cowper discussed with Newton the surrender of

[39] On Cowper and politics, see W.B. Hutchings, 'William Cowper and 1789', *Yearbook of English
Studies*, 19 (1989), 71–93.

British troops to the Americans at Yorktown as a 'catastrophe ... ordained beforehand'. God was punishing the British for their sins and Cowper and Newton, conscious of sinfulness whilst their countrymen ignored it, believed themselves as well qualified by this to prophesy doom as were politicians by their experience to predict success: 'you and we by our respective firesides, though neither connected with men in power, nor professing to wield the affairs of kingdoms, can make as probable conjectures, and look forward into futurity with as clear a sight, as the greatest man in the Cabinet' (*CoL*, vol. I, pp. 546–7). Cowper made more conjectures a month later, viewing Britain's failure in America as divine punishment and constructing an interpretation in which either pursuing or abandoning the war would leave the country 'squeezed to death' (*CoL*, vol. I, p. 555). In politics as well as in personal religion Cowper was enjoying the certainty of damnation whichever alternative was chosen – authority coming to exist in the certainty of its future loss.

Cowper joked in his letters about his claims to political wisdom but nevertheless, as in *The Task*, made from self-deprecation a strength-in-weakness. He not only exhibited through humour his awareness of his lack of political authority but showed himself able to bear the necessity of weakness – proof of his self-knowledge and strength contrasted with what he viewed as the blind and effete leadership of the men of political power. Within the rhetoric of the poetry and letters, at least, the struggles of the suffering writer make him an antidote to the prevailing weakness that he diagnosed in the nation's public and political culture. So, in *The Task*, Cowper views the world as God's creation, 'a capacious reservoir of means / Form'd for his use, and ready at his will' (bk II, lines 201–2). Gaining strength from his conviction that he sees God's will in the world he launches into a moralizing tirade against England's effeminate leaders, contrasting them with great soldiers and leaders of the past and with his own inner struggle, bravely borne:

> To shake thy senate, and from heights sublime
> Of patriot eloquence to flash down fire
> Upon thy foes, was never meant my task;
> But I can feel thy fortunes, and partake
> Thy joys and sorrows with as true a heart
> As any thund'rer there. And I can feel
> Thy follies too, and with a just disdain
> Frown at effeminates, whose very looks
> Reflect dishonor on the land I love.
> How, in the names of soldiership and sense,
> Should England prosper, when such things, as smooth
> And tender as a girl, all essenced o'er
> With odors, and as profligate as sweet,
> Who sell their laurel for a myrtle wreath,

And love when they should fight; when such as these
Presume to lay their hand upon the ark
Of her magnificent and awful cause?
Time was when it was praise and boast enough
In ev'ry clime, and travel where we might,
That we were born her children.

(pp. 56–7; bk II, lines 216–35)

Cowper renounces combative public rhetoric only to launch an attack on contemporary political government with as much rhetorical colouring as he can muster, using stereotypical versions of patriotism and manliness. Reference to his own 'true ... heart' makes him implicitly as sensitive and caring towards his country as 'any thund'rer'. From this assumed position Cowper was able to claim that he could trace the nation's failure in the American war and its selfish cruelty in India to a moral corruption. This corruption stemmed, as it did in Britain, from the undermining of a disinterested paternal authority over the people by a culture of commercial exploitation intended to enrich the governors at the cost of the governed.[40] Lack of discipline, he continued, was the cause, and he idealized discipline as another of the stern patriarchs to whom submission was a virtue: 'his gentle eye / Grew stern, and darted severe rebuke; / His frown was full of terror, and his voice / Shook the delinquent with such fits of awe / As left him not' (bk II, lines 719–23). And, as in his discussions of religion and the rural scene, Cowper associated his own rhetoric strongly enough with the sublimely stern Father that he was briefly able to assume his tones. In the next book of the poem he speaks, via a gardening metaphor, as an authoritarian landowning lord: 'All hate the rank society of weeds / Noisome, and ever greedy to exhaust / Th'impov'rish'd earth; an overbearing race / That like the multitude made faction-mad / Disturb good order, and degrade true worth' (bk III, lines 670–4).

Good order, for Cowper, shifts from a social and religious authoritarianism and a Miltonic sublime style at the one extreme to a sympathy for distress based on his exploration of his own vulnerability at the other. In the process he redefines the discourse in which public authority had been produced for the writer by his presentation of a commanding view of the social, natural and literary landscapes. Vexed by his conflicting desires to identify with, submit to and propitiate paternal figures, Cowper made of his inability to resolve contradictions a new definition of authority as an endless inner struggle. In this definition irresolution is not simply a reflection of a readership's indecision over social and political issues but a token of an inner warfare waged by Cowper on its behalf. It confers dignity upon and acts as a purgation of the doubt that a polite and gentlemanly audience were likely to

---

[40] On Cowper's patriotism and his criticism of the slave-trade see Peter Faulkner, 'William Cowper and the Poetry of Empire', *Durham University Journal*, NS 52 (1991), 165–73.

exhibit with regard to public affairs as a result of their own increasingly conflicting loyalties. At the same time, Cowper was careful to isolate himself from some of the conflicts that had compromised Thomson's and threatened Johnson's authority. He had, in *Table Talk* (1781) attacked poetry

> Distorted from its use and just design,
> To make the pitiful possessor shine,
> To purchase, at the fool-frequented fair
> Of vanity, a wreath for self to wear.
>
> (lines 754–7)[41]

And he remained reluctant to be tempted either by the prospect of patronage or by financial success. In 1763 he had retreated from the prospect, arranged through the influence of his uncle Ashley, of taking the post of Clerk of the Journals in the House of Lords. In 1779 he criticized Johnson's acceptance of a pension from the King, claiming that it clouded the independence of his judgement of Milton by obliging him to disapprove of Milton's republicanism. Although Cowper himself received a pension from George III from 1794, it was sought for him by William Hayley as a way of curing the depression into which he had fallen. It failed to effect a cure, and he plunged into deeper despair, writing little and continuing to depend on the domestic and financial support of friends and family members. He had sought and received no remuneration for his writings before 1792, when Joseph Johnson, the publisher, paid £1,000 for his translation of Homer. He had even used friends to act as intermediaries in his dealings with Johnson (as he did in all his financial affairs). Gentlemanly disinterest and moral independence demanded a financial as well as physical distance from patrons and market-power and profit. This independence was, however, only achieved by the acceptance of gifts from friends and relations.

Cowper made his anxious distance a sign of a moral sensitivity that he could contrast, on his readers' behalf, with the apparent insensitivity of the rulers who had led the nation into the affairs in which love of England's land seemed incompatible with morality – exploitation of India, slave-trading, divisive war in America, commercial farming at the peasants' expense. This was a limited achievement: it both conceded, as Feingold has noted, that 'virtue cannot be an element of the political order'[42] and claimed to relocate that virtue in the poet's doubt and moral sensitivity. Doubt and sensitivity stopped, however, if submission to social and religious authority was threatened by rebellion from below – either from the sinner's foolish search for power or from 'the multitude made faction-mad'. Cowper, in the end, was unable to generate a vision of personal or social authority not based at least partly upon the subordination whose effects he so frequently regretted in

---

[41] In *The Poetical Works of William Cowper*, p. 17.
[42] Feingold, *Nature and Society*, p. 143.

rural and colonial politics. It was, nevertheless, Cowper's relocation of authority in inner struggle and doubt that drew the attention of Wordsworth and Coleridge. More prepared than was Cowper to endorse imaginative rebellion against existing authorities, more prepared to articulate social protest from the rural 'multitude', they formed from *The Task* a discourse in which intervention in the divided fields of the public realm was made more not less authoritative by the poet's exploration of the conflicts and weaknesses in his own position as a writer.

Cowper and Johnson

Cowper understood that the authority granted his writing by the public depended upon its critical reception. And this understanding led him both to desire the approval of Dr Johnson, the most eminent critic of the age, and to resent Johnson's power. Cowper's conception of post-Miltonic blank verse and his understanding of the proper style for political poetry were both shaped by his need to resist Johnson's views on these matters. It was over the work of Prior that Cowper disagreed with Johnson's verdicts on political verse.

Every man conversant with verse-writings, knows, and knows by painful experience, that the familiar stile, is of all stiles the most difficult to succeed in. To make verse speak the language of prose, without being prosaic, to marshall the words of it in such an order, as they might naturally take in falling from the lips of an extemporary speaker, yet without meanness; harmoniously, elegantly, and without seeming to displace a syllable for the sake of the rhyme, is one of the most arduous tasks a poet can undertake. He that could accomplish this task was Prior; many have imitated his excellence in this particular, but the best copies have fallen far short of the original. And now to tell us after we and our fathers have admired him for it so long, that he is an easy writer indeed, but that his ease has an air of stiffness in it, in short that his ease is not ease, but only something like it, what is it but a self-contradiction, an observation that grants what it is just going to deny, and denies what it has just granted, in the same sentence, and in the same breath?   (*CoL*, vol. II, p. 10)

These comments, from a letter of January 1782 in which Cowper recommends the poetry of Milton and Thomson as models for a young scholar, show him formulating a defence of his own verse in reaction to Johnson's *Life* of Prior. In defending 'familiar stile' Cowper was implicitly defending his own and Prior's conception of political poetry. A month earlier he had declared: 'I learn'd when I was a Boy, being the Son of a staunch Whig and a man that loved his country, to glow with that patriotic Enthusiasm which is apt to break forth into poetry, or at least prompt a person if he has any inclination that way, to poetical endeavors. Prior's pieces of that sort were recommended to my particular notice' (*CoL*, vol. I, p. 551).

Prior's patriotic pieces combined a familiar, even humorous, style with anti-French sentiments. They were occasional pieces, taking as their points of departure particular incidents in the war and praising the monarchy in Britain. One such is 'An English Ballad On the Taking of Namur by the King of Great Britain, MDCXCV'.

> If *Namur* be compar'd to *Troy*,
>   Then BRITAIN's boys excelled the GREEKS:
> Their Siege did ten long Years employ:
>   We've done our Bus'ness in ten Weeks.
> What Godhead does so fast advance,
>   With dreadful Pow'r those Hills to gain?
> 'Tis little WILL, the scourge of *France*;
>   No Godhead, but the first of Men.
> His mortal Arm exerts the Pow'r
>   To keep ev'n *Mons's* Victor under:
> And that same Jupiter no more
>   Shall fright the World with impious Thunder.
>
> (lines 41–52, Prior, vol. I, p.143)

Johnson noted of it 'the burlesque of Boileau's "Ode on Namur" has, in some parts, such airiness and levity as will always procure it readers' but declared that 'his Occasional Poems necessarily lost part of their value, as their occasions, being less remembered, raised less emotion' (*Lives*, vol. II, p. 203).

Cowper had himself, he told Newton, 'produced several halfpenny ballads' under Prior's influence (*CoL*, vol. I, p. 551), and although he decided that occasional political verse was too likely to be overtaken by events his 'A Present for the Queen of France' responds, in the manner of Prior, to events in the American War:

> The Bruiser e'er he Strikes a Blow,
> (Such is his Friendship for his Foe)
> Cordially shakes him by the Fist,
> Then Dubbs him his Antagonist,
> And Bangs him Soundly if he can,
> To prove himself the better Man.
> So Queen of France in Loving Mood,
> Feeling a Thirst for British Blood,
> E'er she began her Tilting Match,
> Sent Queen of England first a Watch.
> As who should say, Look sharp, take care,
> Ma très Aimable et ma Chère,
> For you and I must go to War.
> The Inference is short and sweet,
> Tho' Navies Join, and Armies meet,
> And Thousands in the Conflict fall,
> There was no Malice in't at all.
>
> (lines 1–17, Cowper, vol. I, pp. 219–20)

Prior, a gentleman of the bedchamber and secretary to King William, changed, under the influence of Bolingbroke, from a Whig supporter of war to an anti-Walpole satirist. Johnson, who privately told Boswell that William was 'one of the most worthless rascals that ever existed' and who remained a staunch Tory, had little reason to admire Prior's earlier political writing (Boswell, vol. II, p. 342).

Johnson attacked Prior's diction: his love poetry was 'cold and lifeless', without 'gallantry or tenderness', 'dull and tedious' (*Lives*, vol. II, pp. 202–3) and he damned the encomium on King William, 'Carmen Seculare', with the faint praise 'he exhausts all his powers of celebration . . . he probably thought all he wrote, and retained as much veracity as can be properly exacted from a poet professedly encomiastic' (*Lives*, vol. II, p. 185). Cowper, defending Prior against such attacks, was attempting to clear a space for a public voice which could combine familiarity, response to current events and morality without compromising the veracity and independence of the poet. He declared that Prior's introduction of Venus and Cupid into his poetry did not, as Johnson judged, show his passion to be insincere – they were legitimate poetic devices. And of 'Henry and Emma' he wrote 'But when the Critic calls it a dull dialogue, who but a Critic will believe him? There are few Readers of Poetry of either Sex in this Country, who cannot remember how that enchanting piece had bewitched them' (*CoL*, vol. II, p. 5).

Cowper's response consisted of an attempted defence of Prior's style on the basis that it enchanted rather than subordinated its readers, a defence which sought to make a space for familiar style in public as well as domestic verse. 'Henry and Emma', a tale of two lovers, ends with a speech by the goddess Venus. It is a speech which gives the romantic tale a patriotic political conclusion, combining the fanciful allegory that Cowper defended in Prior with an anti-French rhetoric that he imitated:

> Now, MARS, she said, let Fame exalt her Voice;
> Nor let thy Conquests only be her Choice:
> But, when She sings great EDWARD from the Field
> Return'd, the hostile Spear and Captive Shield
> In CONCORD's Temple hung, and GALLIA taught to yield.
> And when, as prudent SATURN shall compleat
> The Years design'd to perfect BRITAIN's State,
> The swift-wing'd Power shall take her Trump again,
> To sing Her Fav'rite ANNA's wond'rous Reign;
> To recollect unweary'd MARLBRO's Toils,
> Old RUFUS' Hall unequal to his Spoils;
> The BRITISH Soldier from his high Command
> Glorious, and GAUL thrice Vanquish'd by his Hand:
> Let Her at least perform what I desire;
> With second Breath the Vocal Brass inspire;

And tell the Nations, in no Vulgar Strain,
What Wars I manage, and what Wreaths I gain.
And when Thy Tumults and Thy Fights are past,
And when Thy Lawrels at my Feet are cast;
Faithful may'st Thou like *British* H E N R Y prove:
And, E M M A-like let me return Thy Love.

(lines 737–57, Prior, vol. i, pp. 299–300)

Cowper was unable either to ignore Johnson's criticism or to subordinate it to his own poetic practice. He remained uneasy as he tried to write in a manner of which Johnson had disapproved when it appeared in the writers to whom Cowper looked as sponsors. In September 1781 he was worrying that 'my doctrines may offend this King of Critics' and draw forth 'one of his pointed Sarcasms' which would 'spoil the Sale' (*CoL*, vol. i, pp. 520–1). Johnson was a critical patriarch unlikely to be easily propitiated, with power over public opinion and over Cowper's own estimation of himself. In 1788 Cowper was pleased to find 'that though on all other occasions he wrote like nobody, in his Letters he expresses himself somewhat in the stile of other folks' (*CoL*, vol. iii, p. 191). Johnson had been human after all, and Cowper was glad to think that his poems had been read by the Doctor, and favourably reviewed by a friend at the Doctor's behest.

Johnson, however, had too much power for Cowper to be able fully to regard him as a fellow man, and he remained an object of admiration and resentment. Cowper said of Boswell's *Journal of a Tour to the Hebrides, with Samuel Johnson* that 'now and then the Doctor speaks like an Oracle, and that makes amends for all' but also found that Johnson was made a coxcomb by his friends' flattery (*CoL*, vol. iii, pp. 289–90). Only in religious matters did he feel superior to Johnson; of the Doctor's posthumously published *Prayers and Meditations* he wrote 'I am sorry that He who was so manly an advocate for the cause of virtue in all other places, was so childishly employed and so superstitiously too, in his closet' (*CoL*, vol. ii, p. 371). Feeling more deeply experienced in the necessity for and delusion of hope than Johnson, he could patronize him and sympathize with him rather than remain in resentful thrall to his critical and moral word.

Cowper's struggle with Johnson's authoritative discourse was most intensely fought on the battleground of Milton. Whereas Prior was a poet Cowper held in affection, his style a malleable material from which his own was shaped, Milton was the writer towards whom he felt awe. As a translator of Homer, and later of Milton's Latin poems, as an imitator of Miltonic blank verse in *The Task*, Cowper had invested his own poetic authority in Milton's. Johnson's faint praise of Milton threatened Cowper's own work too, whilst it also gave him an opportunity to defend, like a dutiful son, the poet whose authority he respected and whose name he wished to be worthy of. In a letter of October 1779 Cowper doubts Johnson's good faith in his *Life* of Milton, attributing his prejudice to political bias and a placeman's need to flatter his master: 'A Pensioner is not likely to Spare a Republican, and the Doctor, in order I suppose, to convince his Royal Patron of the Sincerity of his Monarchical Principles, has belabor'd the great Poet's Character with the most Industrious Cruelty' (*CoL*, vol. I, p. 307). Cowper portrays the *Life* as a battle of giants: Johnson had trampled Milton's muse 'under his Great Foot'. It is a battle into which he is prepared to enter rhetorically on behalf of the blank verse of *Paradise Lost*:

I am convinced by the way that he has no Ear for Poetical Numbers, or that it was stopp'd by Prejudice against the Harmony of Milton's. Was there ever any thing so delightfull as the Music of the Paradise Lost? It is like that of a fine Organ; has the fullest & the deepest Tones of Majesty, with all the Softness & Elegance of the Dorian Flute. Variety without End! & never equal'd unless perhaps by Virgil. Yet the Doctor has little or nothing to say upon this copious Theme, but talks something about the unfitness of the English Language for Blank Verse, & how apt it is, in the Mouth of some Readers, to degenerate into Declamation. Oh! I could thresh his old Jacket 'till I made his Pension Jingle in his Pocket. (*CoL*, vol. I, p. 307)

Here critical disagreement becomes personal combat in Cowper's imagery. The prize is at once critical and political independence (as opposed to Johnson's jingling pension) and the re-emergence of Milton's sublime style as viable for Cowper in his own times. It was a battle Cowper continued to fight till the end of his writing life, a battle for his own authority as well as for that of the master in whose image his was shaped. In 1791 he told a correspondent, 'I am happy, and feel myself honourably employed whatever I do for Milton' and then attacked Johnson's criticism of Milton's Latin pastorals: 'he who never saw any beauty in a rural scene was not likely to have much taste for a Pastoral' (*CoL*, vol. III, p. 597). Failure to appreciate the poetry of rural scenes stemmed from an aesthetic – and perhaps moral – failing on Johnson's part, a limitation upon Johnson's claim to survey with supreme authority the whole landscapes of poetry and nature.

Cowper could not pretend to Johnsonian authority. His own style was not dominant but locked in struggle with and deference towards literary masters – Johnson and Milton especially – and with itself. Cowper did, however, find a poetic landscape over which Johnson's critical sway could be contested – the rural scene, from which London, for Johnson the centre of power and civilization, could be ignored or criticized as he desired. For Cowper the politics of landscape were, at least partly, critical politics. And in one sense he, from the retreat of rural Olney, won the battle to speak powerfully from and for a landscape over which Johnson's authority did not extend. He, surviving the Doctor, wrote his epitaph:

Here Johnson lies – a Sage by all allowed
Whom to have bred may well make England proud.

Whose prose was eloquence by Wisdom taught,
The gracefull vehicle of virtuous thought.
Whose Verse may claim, grave, masculine, and strong,
Superior praise to the mere Poet's song.
Who many a noble gift from heav'n possess'd,
And Faith at last – Alone worth all the rest.
Oh man immortal by a double prize,
By Fame on earth, by Glory in the skies!

(*CoL*, vol. ii, pp. 317–18)

Here Cowper speaks for the particular ground in which Johnson is interred and for all England. Johnson, bred from and returning to England's earth, is a source of patriotic pride, a national natural resource rather than a combative and divisive critic and moralist. Cowper's ability to absorb him into English nature and to speak for it is untroubled by Johnson's former personal rhetorical dominance of the public. Indeed, he quietly beats Johnson at his own game of writing magisterially impersonal epitaphs in which judgement and criticism are implicitly present within the formal tone. He makes Johnson a 'Sage' by virtue of others' allowance, rather than by his subordination of his readers. He acknowledges Johnson's verse to be 'grave, masculine, and strong' but permits it only to claim, rather than receive, 'superior praise'. And he leaves a doubt as to whether it does, after all, amount to poetry, albeit that it might in certain respects be stronger than 'the mere Poet's song'.

Cowper seldom achieved rhetorical control of this kind over Johnson. He perceived Johnson as too authoritative to be able consistently to subject him to his own discourse as an object in a fictional landscape. In this perception he shared the common public view, although for Johnson himself his authority had seemed more precarious and divided than it came to appear to others by the 1780s and 1790s. But Cowper also displayed towards Johnson what he displayed towards Milton and towards his God, a tense mixture of deference, rebelliousness and emulation. The result of this mixture was a new formulation of authority, played out in landscape poetry in which power to preach to the political and religious realms was asserted but undercut and reformulated as inadequacy and deference. By admitting weakness Cowper made his contradictions evidence of a minor heroism, an inner struggle, in which the poet's contemplative self, for the first time, became powerful in its instability. Taking vulnerability and anxiety – political, religious, poetic – upon himself, Cowper elevated it into a sign of his human profundity, of his ability to suffer in order that his readership, purging their own moral and political anxieties and weaknesses through him, should not. It was a strange achievement, by which the blank verse of Milton and the landscape poetry of Thomson were bequeathed, changed, to Wordsworth and Coleridge. And it was an achievement that brought about a change in the way in which an author addressed the public. Cowper's landscapes stage for a reading public the confession of weakness, the anxiety at sinfulness, the temptation of and regret at using the gift of language to subordinate others, all issues of which Johnson wrote in his private prayers and meditations. Cowper's landscapes enhanced his authority by allowing him to claim the reader's sympathy for his repeated struggles with his particular version of human inadequacy. For Johnson landscape was a place in which he could fight, and win, struggles for mastery, enabling him to dominate, through the exertion of rhetorical control, the threatening forces of others' (and his own) weakness and disorder. As such it was a place against which not only Cowper but later poets and critics had to define themselves, so that the scenes of their own very different writings came to be marked by it.

2

Johnson: the usurpations of virility

Tory rather than Whig, Johnson held in common with Thomson and Cowper belief in a society based on the legitimate inheritance of property, on the traditional and established law, and on what he called subordination. Like Thomson and Cowper again, he was a self-made writer whose authority derived from his own efforts rather than from inherited wealth or title. As a consequence his writing, like *The Seasons* and *The Task*, although in a way more directly assertive than either, forms a drama of different and sometimes conflicting sources of power. Johnson's need to formulate an independent and masterful voice often made him argue with belief in established authorities. He defined himself against them as he did against the powerful aristocrats who would be his patrons, aristocrats whose possession of political power he supported in theory and in a number of combative political essays. Less accommodating than Thomson, Johnson confronted conflicts of loyalty in similar areas without necessarily resolving them. He too supported landowners' power, but often attacked their exercise of it in the landscapes he visited. He wrote in discourses traditionally patronized and read by the nobility (and taken by them to reflect and perpetuate their educated values). And to an unprecedented degree he confronted the difficulty of so doing when his own sense of proper authority arose from his awareness of the independence of his own rhetorical, and other men's actual, deeds.

In this chapter I shall be investigating the drama of conflicting authorities in Johnson, considering the effects it had upon his conception of himself as a writer. I shall contend that the need to consider discourse as a contest affected his discussions of other writers, particularly Shakespeare, and helped to shape his ideas about authority too. He used the vocabulary of landscape-description to enhance that authority over other writers by portraying their work as a natural scene to be admired but also controlled by the order the critic 'discovers' in it. Beating Thomson and other landscape poets at their own game by this means, he nevertheless found his power threatened when Shakespeare and Milton proved too various and contradictory to be laid out as ordered scenes – or even landscapes in which a certain ultimately controllable wildness is admired as a token of natural power. In his criticism of the two greatest poets Johnson exposed the inadequacy of a critical authority based on laying out a poem, as poets and gardeners did a landscape, as a collection of beautiful or sublime tableaux. Johnson was himself divided between supporting powers that sought to control nature, and idealizing an older Highland culture that seemed to reflect the wildness of the landscape and to challenge the political order of Hanoverian England. In all these discourses the nature of Johnson's own authority as man and writer was formed, questioned and reformed, a drama of which Johnson was both the hero and victim – one repeated by subsequent writers who faced similar difficulties of authorship and who sought to negotiate them by reference to him. Johnson's social and political writings, with which I begin, mix independent authority with deference to establishments, reshaping our understanding of the mediation of power through discourse in later eighteenth-century England.

Fredric Bogel has argued that Johnson's authority is increased, rather than undermined, by the existence of irreconcilable tensions in his writing and in his position as an author.[1] I wish to summarize Bogel's argument here, and to extend its scope in my own consideration of Johnsonian tensions, particularly those surrounding the location of authority and the assumption of mastery. Bogel presents a Johnson who is aware that the basis of his authority is rhetorical. It is his control over a masterly prose style and his powerful wit that have brought him respect and even cultural power. Yet these rhetorical assets are dangerously individual and self-created. In a brilliant analysis of the *Life* of Savage, the illegitimate writer and self-publicist who spent his life trying to reclaim the parents who disowned him, Bogel suggests that Johnson reveals a man whose predicament exemplifies something of his own, as a man and as the writer of the *Life*. Savage is shown both to need external, parental forms of legitimate authority from which he can derive himself, and to declare himself independent of such authorities – unique, self-created. So too, Bogel argues, Johnson asserts his independence, his self-created authority, but still needs external and legitimate powers from which to derive it. Johnson's gratified acceptance of his Oxford degree and later of a pension from the Crown could be seen as an expression of this need. So too for Bogel, his self-punishing act of standing hatless in the Lichfield rain in penitence for past neglect of his father is a sign of guilt at neglect of proper authority in favour of self-assertion. Indeed, Bogel writes that 'for Johnson the assumption of authority was both necessary and necessarily guilt-ridden, and that he sought ways to assume and disclaim that authority in a single gesture'. For Bogel these ways amount to a redefinition of authority, a Johnsonian achievement of 'a stabler authority [which] will disclose, paradoxically, its internal division

---

[1]   Fredric Bogel, 'Johnson and the Role of Authority', in Felicity Nussbaum and Laura Brown (eds.), *The New Eighteenth Century* (New York and London, 1987), pp. 189–209. An expanded (and more diffuse) form of the article appears as English Literary Studies Monograph 47: *The Dream of My Brother: An Essay on Johnson's Authority* (University of Victoria, Canada, 1990).

and imperfection'.[2] The *Life* of Savage, he claims, ends *more* not less power-fully because it both exculpates and judges, sympathizes and criticizes. It has, in this view, two endings, dramatizing the author's difficulty in forming a single, absolute position. Similarly, when Johnson's remark 'the woman had a bottom of good sense' produced unintended laughter and he followed it by saying gravely 'the *woman* was *fundamentally* sensible', reducing the company to funereal composure, Johnson was not just asserting his authority by daring them to laugh, but reflexively demonstrating that his authority stemmed from his mastery of language: to assume control of his audience he follows an unintended pun with one still worse, but clearly intended (Boswell, vol. IV, p. 99). Bogel comments: it 'is a certain drama of power that allows Johnson to play the role of authority, to acknowledge that he is playing a role, and still to keep anyone from saying so'.[3]

So far Bogel. My own development of his argument concerns not so much Johnson's guilt and his rôle-playing, as the different forms of rhetoric by which he tried to negotiate tensions in his conception and experience of authority. I shall be concerned with the political, literary, and economic discourses in which those tensions presented themselves. I shall look at the power-relations involved in Johnson's public writing and in his conception of the sublime. And I shall examine the patterns of deference, assertion and mastery which appear in his treatment of his subjects.

Dictionaries and patrons

Johnson's great work, his *Dictionary, with a Grammar and History of the English Language* (1755), brought him fame not only for the accuracy of its definitions, but for the fact that he, with a few clerical assistants, had completed it within a decade.[4] The French had required a whole academy and a period of thirty years to produce a dictionary for their own language. There was a mixture of national pride and complacency at the achievement epitomized by Garrick's epigram which ends with the lines 'And Johnson, well arm'd like a hero of yore, / Has beat forty French, and will beat forty more!' (Boswell, vol. I,

---

[2]   Bogel, 'Johnson and the Role of Authority', p. 205. Robert Folkenflik also observes tensions in the *Life* of Savage; for him they are 'the expression of separate traits of character in the same man, and by holding them in perilous balance through his rhetoric, Johnson shows us what becomes of his life after all extenuation'. In *Samuel Johnson, Biographer* (Ithaca and London, 1978), p. 211.

[3]   Bogel, 'Johnson and the Role of Authority', p. 204. For a contemporary view of Johnson's need to assert his verbal power see Sir John Hawkins, *The Life of Samuel Johnson, LLD*, ed. Bertram H. Davis (London, 1962), pp. 71, 185.

[4]   For a useful collection of contemporary reviews of and reactions to the Dictionary, see James L. Clifford, *Dictionary Johnson: Samuel Johnson's Middle Years* (London, 1979), pp. 138–48. Robert DeMaria, Jr, relates the definitions to Johnson's wider reading and writing in *Johnson's Dictionary and the Language of Learning* (Oxford, 1986). The most comprehensive assessment of the Dictionary, including its relation to lexicographical tradition, is James H. Sledd and Gwin J. Kolb, *Dr. Johnson's Dictionary: Essays in the Biography of a Book* (Chicago, 1955).

p. 301).[5] Boswell endorsed these feelings by making it clear that Johnson's work had been completed without noble patronage. Instead, Johnson had worked for, and been supported by, the free market, emerging in Boswell's account as an embodiment of the commercial and enterprising spirit which British liberty fostered:

He had spent, during the progress of the work, the money for which he had contracted to write his Dictionary. We have seen that the reward of his labour was only fifteen hundred and seventy-five pounds; and when the expence of amanuenses and paper, and other articles, are deducted, his clear profit was very inconsiderable. I once said to him, 'I am sorry, Sir, you did not get more for your Dictionary.' His answer was, 'I am sorry too. But it was very well. The booksellers are generous liberal-minded men.' He, upon all occasions, did ample justice to their character in this respect. He considered them as the patrons of literature; and, indeed, although they have eventually been considerable gainers by his Dictionary, it is to them that we owe its having been undertaken and carried through at the risk of great expence, for they were not absolutely sure of being indemnified.

(Boswell, vol. i, pp. 304–5)

For Boswell and Johnson the traditional noble patron has been replaced by the venture capitalist. Success depends on sales rather than on pleasing the patron, and even the risk of poverty is preferable to the necessity of flattery. The booksellers, as venture capitalists, are not blamed for the small profits of the Dictionary, even though Johnson's finances were so little helped by it that he was arrested for debt in the year after publication. Boswell even sees Johnson's lack of a noble patron and the consequent dependence on the market as a salutory stimulant to self-help and the work ethic. To his neglect by patrons, 'operating to rouse the natural indolence of his constitution, we owe many valuable productions, which otherwise, perhaps, might never have appeared' (Boswell, vol. i, p. 304).

If Boswell's remarks and Johnson's actions represent the increasingly capitalist values of the late eighteenth century, they also show that the expansion of the reading public and the book trade had made new relations between writer, publisher and reader possible.[6] By 1769 Johnson could take as an example of the amazing ignorance on certain points of eminent men the fact that Sir Fletcher Norton 'did not seem to know that there were such

---

[5] On Johnson's Dictionary and the rise of nationalism see John Cannon, *Samuel Johnson and the Politics of Hanoverian England* (Oxford, 1994), p. 237.

[6] For a discussion of the eighteenth-century literary market and reading public, see Terry Belanger, 'Publishers and Writers in Eighteenth-Century England', in Isabel Rivers (ed.), *Books and Their Readers in Eighteenth-Century England* (Leicester, 1982), pp. 5–25. Edward A. Bloom, in *Samuel Johnson in Grub Street* (Providence, RI, 1957) provides extensive information about Johnson and the battles over copyright consequent upon the expanding book market (pp. 207–32). See also Jan Fergus, 'Eighteenth-Century Readers in Provincial England: The Customers of Samuel Clay's Circulating Library and Bookshop in Warwick, 1770–72', *Papers of the Bibliographical Society of America*, 78 (1984), 155–213.

publications as the Reviews' (Boswell, vol. II, p. 91). Boswell notes elsewhere the dramatic increase in booksellers' advances and purchases of copyright. Faced with an expanding market, the author appears as a free agent whose wealth (and moral health) depend upon his industry – a matter in his self-government not in the hands of a patron who determines when and what he writes and who acts, at least partly, as both publisher and reader. There are obvious objections to this rather narrow view of authorship, both on economic and moral grounds. Rather than rehearse them here, I wish to examine the conflicts of authority which Johnson's work for the market caused, both in his attitude to authorship and in his writing.

Johnson's famous letter to Lord Chesterfield does not at first seem to exhibit conflicts within the writer. On the contrary, Johnson seems certain of his own rôle, master of his independence and of his rhetoric. He attacks the nobleman who had offered to be his patron, but failed to perform his duties, only to have the effrontery to claim credit when the Dictionary appeared:

Seven years, my Lord, have now past, since I waited in your outward rooms, or was repulsed from your door; during which time I have been pushing on my work through difficulties, of which it is useless to complain, and have brought it, at last, to the verge of publication, without one act of assistance, one word of encouragement, or one smile of favour. Such treatment I did not expect, for I never had a Patron before.

The shepherd in Virgil grew at last acquainted with Love, and found him a native of the rocks.

Is not a Patron, my Lord, one who looks with unconcern on a man struggling for life in the water, and, when he has reached ground, encumbers him with help? The notice which you have been pleased to take of my labours, had it been early, had been kind; but it has been delayed till I am indifferent, and cannot enjoy it; till I am solitary, and cannot impart it; till I am known, and do not want it. I hope it is no very cynical asperity not to confess obligations where no benefit has been received, or to be unwilling that the Publick should consider me as owing that to a Patron which Providence has enabled me to do for myself.

Having carried on my work thus far with so little obligation to any favourer of learning, I shall not be disappointed though I should conclude it, if less be possible, with less; for I have been long wakened from that dream of hope, in which I once boasted myself with so much exultation,

My Lord,
Your Lordship's most humble,
Most obedient servant,
SAM. JOHNSON.

(Boswell, vol. I, pp. 261–3)

Chesterfield had treated the subject of independence lightly in the anonymous papers he had written recommending the Dictionary. Declaring that his was not an 'interested puff of this work' he denied that Johnson had offered *him* 'the usual compliment of a pair of gloves or a bottle of wine', an ironic and, for Johnson, insulting reversal of the support author might expect from patron. And Chesterfield illustrated the need for a Dictionary with a tale of an assignation 'between a fine gentleman and a fine lady' that had failed because misspellings in their notes had sent them to the wrong houses.[7] The hints here of immoral sexual intrigue, for which Chesterfield himself was known before and still more after the publication of his letters to his illegitimate son (1774) trivialized the Dictionary, and confirmed Johnson in his resentment of his supposed patron. This resentment had grown in 1747 when Johnson, seeking an audience with the Earl, had seen others preferred to him.

In his famous letter Johnson's resentment is a matter of rhetoric, of the 'gathering of figures' which Longinus defines as sublime:[8] the repetitions emphasize his independent existence ('I am indifferent', 'I am solitary', 'I am known') whilst incorporating it in a structure that moves to a deliberate anti-climax which reinforces rejection. The syntactical structure based on verbal repetitions emphasizes Chesterfield's tardiness – ('till' . . . 'till' . . . 'till I am known'). When we finally arrive at the sentence-end the resolution of the verb, having been delayed through a series of repetitions, appears all the more powerfully negative: 'do not want it'. It is Johnson's independence that emerges strongly from the sentence, declared both by repeated positive statements and by the accrued weight of repeated negatives ('cannot', 'cannot', 'do not'). Independence, then, is not just a matter of self-declaration, but of an assertion of limits, the acceptance of which brings freedom from desire ('do not want') and therefore from dependence on others. It may be not unconnected with this rhetorical self-limitation that Johnson, often a heavy drinker, chose to deny himself alcohol for several periods in his life. To deny desires and needs is to achieve independence of them, the sort of independence that allows Johnson to sign his letter to Chesterfield with a sarcastic parody which declares his freedom from the conventional forms of polite deference and the real servitude implicit in them: 'Your Lordship's most humble / Most obedient servant'.[9]

There is an undercurrent of bitterness in Johnson's great declaration which arises from the acknowledgement that to achieve independence he has had to abandon 'that dream of hope' that he would be helped by his fellow men. The safety of a secure and independent ego is bought at the price of sacrificing desires and hopes of support from others. Something of this bargain, and the sad and grim acceptance of human selfishness it brought, can be observed in his comment on a man's friends. Despite their sympathy,

---

[7] *The World*, nos. 100, 101, quoted in Boswell, vol. I, p. 258.

[8] James A. Arieti and John M. Crossett use Johnson's Letter to illustrate Longinus's point in their edition: *Longinus on the Sublime* (New York and Toronto, 1985), p. 112.

[9] A comprehensive account of Johnson's relations with Chesterfield in the Dictionary affair is provided by Sledd and Kolb, *Dr Johnson's Dictionary*, pp. 85–104. An astute analysis of Johnson's letter can be found in H. H. Erskine-Hill, 'Johnson and the Petty Particular', *Transactions of the Johnson Society (Lichfield)* (1976), 40–6 (p. 42).

'if he should be hanged, none of them will eat a slice of plum-pudding the less'. And as for the cult of sensibility: 'You will find these very feeling people are not very ready to do you good. They *pay* you by *feeling*' (Boswell, vol. II, pp. 94–5). Views of this kind offer a glimpse of a conflict within Johnson's position in the letter, as well as between him and Chesterfield, for they implicitly question whether patronage is viable at all. Ostensibly the letter attacks Chesterfield for failing to fulfil his obligations as a patron. It is not, apparently, the authority of the nobleman over him that Johnson resents, but Chesterfield's refusal to fulfil that authority as it is traditionally fulfilled. It is this neglect that leads him into sarcastic redefinitions of the word 'patron', both in the letter and the Dictionary itself. Johnson is not rejecting patronage and deference, but deference expected when the patron is not properly paternalistic. Nevertheless, such is the rhetorical control exerted by him over Chesterfield, so strongly are limits placed around the writer's self, that it is difficult to imagine his accepting any patron, or any accepting him.

Here Johnson faces conflicts in his assumptions about authority, conflicts which have political implications. For Johnson was a consistent supporter of political subordination, of a society governed by willing deference to established power, that power being concentrated in the hands of the nobility:[10]

But, Sir, as subordination is very necessary for society, and contentions for superiority very dangerous, mankind, that is to say, all civilised nations, have settled it upon a plain invariable principle. A man is born to hereditary rank; or his being appointed to certain offices, gives him a certain rank. Subordination tends greatly to human happiness. Were we all upon an equality, we should have no other enjoyment than mere animal pleasure.

(Boswell, vol. I, p. 442)

Whilst this remained his political view, he was not easily able to follow it in his own dealings with men of rank and power. Not only does the letter to Chesterfield assume control over the Earl from Johnson's own, rhetorical, resources, but it satirizes the forms of humility and servitude. Similarly, Johnson's actual encounter with this patron suggests that he not only resented Chesterfield's neglect of his duties, but wanted to redefine their relationship from the start as a meeting of gentlemen on equal footing. He objected to being made to wait in Chesterfield's antechamber on the grounds that the lord had company with him – as if he were not of sufficient rank to be accepted in that company. Worse, 'at last, when the door opened, out walked Colley Cibber; and . . . Johnson was so violently provoked when he found for whom he had been so long excluded, that he went away in a passion, and

---

[10] For a collection of eighteenth-century texts concerning subordination and society see Stephen Copley (ed.), *Literature and the Social Order In Eighteenth-Century England* (London, 1984). Johnson's politics are investigated by Donald J. Greene in *The Politics of Samuel Johnson* (New Haven, Conn., 1960).

never would return' (Boswell, vol. I, p. 56). Cibber was Laureate, placeman and flatterer of Walpole and George II widely thought to be shallow, and Johnson took his exclusion in his favour as an insult to his own literary and personal merit. This demonstrates Johnson's powerful consciousness of his independent worth, but also his reluctance to endure the deference to noble authority that he upheld in principle.

Johnson's reaction may also demonstrate a particular disillusion with regard to Chesterfield's politics, and with opposition politics more generally. As a young man in the 1730s Johnson had written satires upon Walpole's ministry, as had Chesterfield. *London* (1738) and *Marmor Norfolciensis* (1739) attack Walpole's foreign policy of peace, and his use of corrupt means to preserve his hold on power. Like Pope (who praised *London*) Johnson saw them as dangers to 'liberty and independence' (Boswell, vol. I, p. 29). And like Thomson he viewed the nation's compliance with Walpole's government as evidence of a national decline from the days of heroical and patriot kings, prepared to fight for Britain's interests. H. H. Erskine-Hill has suggested that Johnson, in this attack, alluded to Pope's line 'Old Edward's Armour beams on Cibber's breast', a line wherein Pope figures national decline in the image of Colley Cibber wearing in the pantomimes and plays in which he acted the armour of Edward III the warrior-king. Johnson wrote

> Illustrious EDWARD! from the Realms of Day,
> The Land of Heroes and of Saints survey;
> Nor hope the *British* Lineaments to trace,
> The rustic Grandeur, or the surly Grace;
> But lost in thoughtless Ease, and empty Show,
> Behold the Warriour dwindled to a Beau.
> (lines 99–104)[11]

For the Patriot opposition to Walpole Cibber was an emblem of a Court and ministry that ignored worth and valued flattery from men whose allegiance could be bought. Both Boswell and Sir John Hawkins associated Johnson with this opposition in the 1730s. Hawkins thought the topics of *London* had been drawn 'from those weekly publications, which, to answer the view of a malevolent faction, first created, and for some years supported, a distinction between the interests of the government and the people, under the several denominations of the Court and the Country parties'.[12]

Johnson may have shared the view of those 'weekly publications' (*The Craftsman* and *Common Sense*, instituted by Bolingbroke and Chesterfield amongst others). But he retained doubts, as a Tory with Jacobite sympathies, as to the motives of these politicians. Hawkins indicated the nature and

---

[11] In *The Poems of Samuel Johnson*, ed. David Nichol Smith and Edward L. McAdam, 2nd edn (Oxford, 1974), p. 73. I am indebted to H. H. Erskine-Hill for drawing my attention to this reference and to other matters Johnsonian.

[12] Hawkins, *Life of Samuel Johnson, LLD*, p. 34.

extent of these doubts: 'He could but just endure the opposition to the minister because conducted on Whig principles; and I have heard him say, that during the whole course of it, the two parties were bidding for the people'.[13] Doubting the disinterested patriotism of the men whose causes he was espousing, Johnson came to see many of them as less than sincere in their Country arguments. Chesterfield seemed particularly difficult to trust: he had both accepted place and honour from Walpole in 1730 and, in 1740, negotiated with the Old Pretender's representative, the exiled Duke of Ormonde, as the Patriots sought James's instruction to his Tory sympathizers in parliament to vote with opposition Whigs against Walpole at all times. In view of these doubts about the sincerity of the opposition in general and of Chesterfield in particular, Cibber's presence that day in 1747 very likely confirmed Johnson in a suspicion that the Earl, like many of the opposition Whigs of the 1730s, was politically as well as personally insincere. Waiting whilst Chesterfield spoke privately with the flatterer of Walpole revealed the distance Chesterfield had moved from the principles and supporters of independence.

Johnson had 'reported' for the *Gentleman's Magazine* (in fact, largely recomposed) the speeches made in parliament between 1740 and 1743. In the debate of 1 February 1743 Johnson has Chesterfield speak with great rhetorical power against the very abuses he had himself attacked in *London*, the 'incroachments of lawless power' threatened by the raising of troops without the 'consent of the Senate' by 'the despotic will of the ministers'. The employment of mercenaries threatened the Act of Settlement, Chesterfield declared, in that it constituted 'a tax laid upon the people, not by the Senate but by the Court'. He portrayed the independence of the nobility as essential in the defence of the native liberty of the British people:

I cannot but think it necessary, my Lords, that every man who values liberty, should exert that spirit by which it was at first established; that every man should rouse from his security, and awaken all his vigilance and all his zeal, lest the bold attempt that has now been made should, if it be not vigorously repressed, be an encouragement to the more dangerous incroachments; and lest that fabrick of power should be destroyed, which has been erected at such expence and with such labour; at which one generation has toiled after another, and of which the wisdom of the most experienced and penetrating statesmen have been employed to perfect its symmetry, and the industry of the most virtuous patriots to repair its decays.[14]

Chesterfield's Patriot defence of liberty is a Johnsonian construct, which roots the constitution in the labours of successive generations. Its symmetry, like that of his sentence itself, appears only at the end of long and difficult toils. In this rhetoric constitutional balance is reinforced by a syntactical resolution

[13]   Hawkins, *Life of Samuel Johnson, LLD*, p. 45.
[14]   See *Debates in Parliament by Samuel Johnson, LL.D*, 2 vols. (London, 1787), vol. II, pp. 278, 276.

which is also the result of labour. Johnson later said of his 'reports' (thought even-handed in their presentation of Whig ministerial and opposition speeches) 'I took particular care that the Whig dogs should not have the best of it'.[15] By 1755 he very likely wished that he had not given Chesterfield the best of it as an opposition speaker in 1743 when he was now revealed as a self-interested seeker of power and a patron of Walpole's former placeman.[16] Sir John Hawkins was in no doubt that Johnson realized within a few weeks of Walpole's fall that the Patriot opposition in which Chesterfield had been so prominent was motivated by personal hatred and ambition for power. Johnson's later definition of Patriotism as 'the last refuge of a scoundrel' confirms his disillusion with the Country-party and its leaders (Boswell, vol. II, p. 348).

Johnson's rejection of Chesterfield as patron is a declaration of authorial and political independence of view. It is to be contrasted with Thomson's tribute to the Earl and compared with Cowper who portrayed Chesterfield as the epitome of the immorality corrupting the governing classes to the nation's detriment:

> Thou polish'd and highfinish'd Foe to Truth
> Graybeard Corrupter of our list'ning youth,
> To Simmer and Scum off the Filth of Vice,
> That so refin'd, it might the more entice,
> Then pour it on the Morals of thy Son
> To taint His Heart, was worthy of thine own.
> Now, while the Poison all high Life pervades,
> Write, if thou canst, one Letter from the Shades,
> One, and One only, charg'd with deep Regret
> That thy worst part, thy Principles, live yet,
> One sad Epistle thence, may Cure Mankind
> Of the Plague spread by Bundles left behind.
>
> (*CoL*, vol. I, p. 435)

These lines of 1781 were published in 'The Progress of Error'. They portray Chesterfield's notorious letters of advice to his illegitimate son as a symptom of the vice of the age. Cowper's independence of such vice was demonstrated by his retreat from patronage and commerce to the support of family and friends.

Johnson's conceptions of himself as a moral and political commentator were based on the notions of free independent agency encouraged by success on the literary market. Publishing through booksellers, he enjoyed the new freedoms of an expanding economy and found, despite his

---

[15]   Arthur Murphy in G.B. Hill (ed.) *Johnsonian Miscellanies*, 2 vols. (Oxford, 1897), vol. I, pp. 378–9.
[16]   For an analysis of the Chesterfield affair in the context of opposition to Walpole see J.C.D. Clark, *Samuel Johnson: Literature, Religion and English Cultural Politics from the Restoration to Romanticism* (Cambridge, 1994), p. 187.

advocacy of a hierarchical society, that he possessed notions of authority and worth conditioned by his economic activity. His letter to Chesterfield makes clear the change in relation to the patron, but also to the landed nobility in general, that England's expanding commercial activity had produced. In the publishing trade, and in other trades too, men were learning to value themselves in ways which led, only thirty years later, to widespread fears amongst nobility, gentry and clergy of a revolution in England similar to that in France. Johnson's experience of publishing without noble patronage was accompanied not just by a sense of his independent worth, but by an appropriation to himself of the very basis of aristocratic power. Adam Smith argued in 1776 that the leisured man developed more extensive views because, free from the need to labour in one occupation, he was able to contemplate a greater variety of objects. Here, for Johnson, it is not the man of property freed by virtue of an independent income who arrives at such views but the writer for the booksellers, free to choose when, for whom and for how long to labour. The risk of such independence, as Johnson knew well enough, was penury and, at worst, imprisonment for debt. But he preferred it to dependence on patrons – noble and landed or not – and expressed it by an analogy with a soldier in an army imposing civilization on the British landscape. Here, in practice, he subverted the hierarchy of authority which his political views supported, for he assumed that, if he did not own land or wealth, he owned the history and properly derived lineage of *words*. This is evident from the plan which Johnson had written to his prospective patron when he had first proposed to compile a dictionary. There Johnson portrayed his work as a preservation of hierarchy and legitimate descent of meaning in language, and therefore of manners and morals in society:

By tracing in this manner every word to its original, and not admitting, but with great caution, any of which no original can be found, we shall secure our language from being over-run with *cant*, from being crouded with low terms, the spawn of folly or affectation, which arise from no just principles of speech, and of which therefore no legitimate derivation can be shewn.

(*JPP*, p. 129)

Proper authority here descends not through landed estates and families but through words. These are fixed and preserved by the lexicographer as a proper regulated estate reaching into the legitimate past.

Johnson himself, rather than the nobility, comes to embody the preservation of traditions of propriety and legitimacy. Rather than supporting the landed interest, this embodiment tends to replace it with a single figure of authority, who has achieved by his own efforts the guardianship of language and society. Johnson's choice of image to describe himself is significant in this respect:

When I survey the Plan which I have laid before you, I cannot, my Lord, but confess, that I am frighted at its extent, and, like the soldiers of Caesar, look on Britain as a new world, which it is almost madness to invade. But I hope, that though I should not complete the conquest, I shall at least discover the coast, civilize part of the inhabitants, and make it easy for some other adventurer to proceed further, to reduce them wholly to subjection, and settle them under laws.

(*JPP*, p. 138)

Starting as a soldier of Caesar, Johnson seems gradually to have become Caesar himself, the conquering general replacing native customs with a civilization based on force, then subordination, then law. Despite the modesty of the admission that he might not complete the conquest, the image transfers power from those who possess it by inheritance, like Chesterfield, to those who possess it through their own masterful conquest of language. It still, however, conceives power to come from the possession of property. And whereas the nobility depended upon laws that transmitted their property intact to the eldest male relative, Johnson recognized that the writer depended on the law of copyright. If success on the market was the key to wealth, it was also the means to gain public respect for one's language. To be acknowledged as a master of language it was necessary, in the commercial climate of competition and piracy, to be master of one's copyright (or at least to be free to sell it to a publisher of one's choice, free from pirated copies). Johnson achieved both when his Dictionary became generally known as 'Johnson's Dictionary'. Later he held out, when a copyright law was in the process of legal debate, for the term of 'the exclusive right of authours' to be enlarged to a hundred years (Boswell, vol. I, p. 439).

It is possible to speculate that Johnson felt some guilt at his assumption of independent mastery and at his consequent displacement of the established aristocracy which, in national politics, he supported. One possible interpretation of his anger at Chesterfield, at least, is that he was embarrassed by the fact that Chesterfield's public letter recommending the Dictionary displayed too openly a Johnson whose authority was self-created and absolute, whilst subjecting that authority to Chesterfield's frivolous play upon the common etymological root of 'Dictionary' and 'dictator':[17]

Good order and authority are now necessary. But where shall we find them, and, at the same time, the obedience due to them? We must have recourse to the old Roman expedient in times of confusion, and chuse a dictator. Upon this principle, I give my vote for Mr. Johnson to fill that great and arduous post. And I hereby declare, that I make a total surrender of all my rights and privileges in the English language, as a free-born British subject, to the said Mr. Johnson, during the term of his dictatorship.

(Boswell, vol. I, p. 259)

[17] Robert Folkenflik notices the etymological joke in 'That Man's Scope', in Isobel Grundy (ed.), *Samuel Johnson: New Critical Essays* (London, 1984), pp. 31–50 (p. 46).

The etymological conceit makes light of Johnson's serious lexicographical project of exhibiting the history and roots of words. Fulsome in its praise in taking up Johnson's own image of a Roman dictator and in dramatizing the nobility's surrender of power to him, it is nevertheless more perceptive than Johnson himself about his sources of authority. Despite his definition in the text of his Dictionary of the lexicographer as a 'harmless drudge' Johnson was, in his discussions of his own work, elevating himself to a position of independent power very close to that described by Chesterfield. It was a position from which he could neither give deference to the nobility in practice, nor abandon such deference as a necessary political theory.

If Chesterfield bore the brunt of the conflict in Johnson's experience of authority, others felt it too. Boswell notes often enough how Johnson's desire for victory would lead him to argue what he did not fully believe, and how, when apparently defeated in logic or knowledge, he would crush an opponent by wit. Against this deep-seated need, the image of the dictionary-maker as a harmless drudge seems to be a humorous fantasy: a picture of literary work which produces no subordination of others to one's desire for mastery, no challenge to existing authorities, but a mere recording of them. It remains a fantasy, for if Johnson did not directly challenge existing authorities, he appropriated the basis of their power and thereby refashioned his relationship to them. This process even occurs to some extent in his relationship with King George III whom he did accept as a patron. They met in 1767 when the young King, who had expressed a desire to meet Johnson, surprised him by coming to him informally in the library of the Queen's House, which Johnson had been invited to use some time before. George III had made it clear that Tories as well as Whigs would be acceptable to him as members of administrations: the old proscription of them as potential Jacobites was at an end. The Tory Johnson, having written in opposition to George II and retaining some sympathy for the Stuart succession, was nevertheless honoured that a King who, as the Patriots hoped, looked beyond party division should wish to see him. They talked for some time of literary matters; Johnson was impressed but retained his clarity of judgement. In Boswell's account he redefined the awe due from subject to sovereign as the respect due to a polite and fatherly gentleman:

During the whole of this interview, Johnson talked to his Majesty with profound respect, but still in his firm manly manner, with a sonorous voice, and never in that subdued tone which is commonly used at the levee and in the drawing-room. After the King withdrew, Johnson shewed himself highly pleased with his Majesty's conversation and gracious behaviour. He said to Mr. Barnard, 'Sir, they may talk of the King as they will; but he is the finest gentleman I have ever seen.' And he afterwards observed to Mr. Langton, 'Sir, his manners are those of as fine a gentleman as we may suppose Lewis the Fourteenth or Charles the Second.'

(Boswell, vol. ii, pp. 40–1)

Accepting George on these terms, Johnson was able to combine his own manly self-assertion with respect for a sovereign who deserved it as a regal gentleman. He was able to overcome the conflict between external and internal authority by reshaping power relations as a kind of polite equality. The King came to represent to Johnson a benevolent and personally known example of paternalism, a father who could respect and support him and the nation. Even at his most conservative, as in the pamphlet *The False Alarm*, defending the ministry's attempt to exclude the newly elected reformist MP John Wilkes from the House, Johnson dissociated the King from political repression, however necessary: he was 'a King who knows not the name of party, and who wishes to be the common father of all his people' (Boswell, vol. II, p. 112). On to the King, then, Johnson, through his understanding of their personal meeting, displaced the conflicts between internal and external authority, free-trading writer and deferential author. The King, for Johnson, licensed his own activity as a writer without humiliating him – he acted, in fact, in the conveniently vague, unspecific but generally benevolent way that, in the letter to Chesterfield, providence had acted. The King, like providence an agent of God, had 'enabled me to do for myself' (Boswell, vol. I, p. 263).

Johnson as critic

In Johnson's criticism enabling power is again important. Indeed, for Johnson part of the purpose of criticism was to provide rules by which others could write. As in his views on patronage, however, Johnson was divided as to how authority is transmitted, whether by provision of rules or by the example of geniuses who transcend rules. Johnson's Shakespeare and Milton frustrated but also fascinated him for breaking the rules of legitimacy in language, and were condemned but also praised for so doing. The issue of breaking or conforming to rules is at the heart of Johnson's conception of the sublime. In his Dictionary he defined *sublime* in terms which suggest that it is compatible with natural and literary order. It is 'the grand or lofty stile', a definition illustrated by a quotation from Pope: 'Longinus strengthens all his laws, / And is himself the great *sublime* he draws' (*An Essay on Criticism*, lines 165–6). Other quotations come from *Paradise Lost* and illustrate a Longinian, rhetorical view of the sublime as 'high in excellence; exalted by nature' and 'high in stile or sentiment; lofty; grand'. However, Johnson also commended Burke's *A Philosophical Enquiry into our Ideas of the Sublime and the Beautiful*, and was prepared to entertain the view that the sublime arises in the experience of nature's power to exceed man's notions of order.[18] He accepted, but remained ambivalent about, the idea that writers should try to imitate that

[18] The relevance to Johnson of the accounts of poetry provided in the writings of Burke and Longinus on the sublime is assessed by William Edinger, *Samuel Johnson and Poetic Style* (Chicago and London, 1977), pp. 114–18.

excess by making their own work surpass accepted notions of order and justice. As a result he at times supported their departure from order, and at others condemned them for it. More subtly, I shall suggest, he formed an ordering strategy of his own that, whilst granting Shakespeare the power to exceed proper rules and exalting him for so doing, sought simultaneously to bring that excess within Johnson's control and nature's larger order. This strategy forms a mirror image of his letter to Chesterfield in that it seems to subordinate Johnson to another, only to reclaim mastery by translating Shakespeare into terms which Johnson controls. Johnson turns Shakespeare's writing into a landscape ordered by his critical tending, a landscape in which a degree of controlled wildness is allowable as a token of its naturalness, like the gardens and estates ownership of which, in Johnson's political theory, entitled the nobility to political power. He had contested that power by portraying the English language itself as a land the conquest of which would give him authority. Turning Shakespeare, the master of English, into a similar landscape allowed him to proceed in his conquest even as he admired the beauty and sublimity of the scenery. It allowed him critical authority as Shakespeare became his literary property, the scene which he commanded.

Johnson's strategy may be contrasted with his response to the landscape poetry of Thomson. Since it did not seem to him to exceed all order, Johnson could treat Thomson's language as a reflection in lofty style of the great and awe-inspiring in nature, confinable within the bounds of his own distinctive style of generalization and antithesis. 'His descriptions of extended scenes and general effects bring before us the whole magnificence of Nature, whether pleasing or dreadful'; his mind 'at once comprehends the vast, and attends to the minute' (*Lives*, vol. III, p. 299). The episodic and general nature of *The Seasons* ensured that Johnson did not have to count the co-presence of the vast and minute as a threat to moral and critical order. Nevertheless in his Dictionary Johnson implicitly criticized Thomson's use of words which had little or no historical authority. As Thomas B. Gilmore has shown, Johnson regarded Thomson as one of the most poetical of poets, as a man endowed by nature with a poet's eye, giving him 'the power of viewing everything in a poetical light' (Boswell, vol. III, p. 37).[19] And Johnson illustrated over six hundred definitions in the Dictionary with quotations from Thomson, many of them illustrating 'poetic' words such as 'corse' and 'philomel'. But whilst Johnson's recourse to *The Seasons* as a source of illustrations signifies his approval of the poem as a whole, many of the words so illustrated are shown to have no precedent other than Thomson himself. Johnson gives Thomson as the source of 'raptured' and calls it 'a bad word'. He defines a sense of 'to spring' derived from Thomson as 'barbarous'. And many Thomsonian words are said to lack any other authority. Excessive linguistic innovation is

[19] Thomas B. Gilmore, 'Implicit Criticism of Thomson's *Seasons* in Johnson's *Dictionary*', *Modern Philology*, 86 (1989), 265–73.

apparently a Thomsonian vice that attends his attempt to find a poetic style that will surprise and astonish readers by comprehending the vast and the minute. Such innovation, stemming from Thomson's power 'of viewing everything in a poetical light' may be a source of pleasure, but it threatens to disturb the order, slowly created by historical precedent, by which language is generally agreed to reflect an order present in empirical reality. Johnson, preserving and clarifying that order by his Dictionary-making, resists Thomson's too individualistic attempts to put into words a nature in which vast and minute are irreconcilably co-present.

In the Dictionary Johnson could master the linguistic threat posed by Thomson's verbalization of a man/nature relationship conceived as turbulent, inclusive of extremes. He could separate Thomson's discourse into a series of quotations, separate the authorized from the unauthorized, exhibit the difference between propriety and peculiarity in diction. Thomson's poetry becomes a resource, a scene from which verbal illustrations can be separately drawn – ultimately a collection of verbal objects collected by Johnson and displayed in his own text with its own lexiographical (but implicitly critical) order. Whereas in his *Life* of Thomson Johnson depicted *The Seasons* by comprehending its turbulent landscapes in his own prose generalizations, in his Dictionary he did so by displaying its separate parts as objects in a verbal scene of his own, in which minute examples illustrate but do not threaten (at least not without criticism) the vast authority of linguistic law. In his reading of *King Lear*, however, empirical reality, the representations of language, and moral law became so irreconcilable that Johnson's own rhetorical control and his mastery as writer disappeared. 'I know not,' he declared, 'whether I ever endured to read again the last scenes of the play till I undertook to revise them as editor' (*JW*, vol. VIII, p. 704). He regrouped on the ground of his editorial rôle, assembling a self that was genuinely and honestly reduced temporarily to a painful humility. The editor was able to make the small revisions and corrections that belong to the drudgery of his profession, this itself being a small act of bravery when, as a reader, the scenes were too painful to be endured. But the editor was not able to make the larger revision that would express a return of critical power. He was not able to replace the final scenes all together. Johnson accepted, then, that Shakespeare surpassed the ordering power of the would-be dictator of the English language. In breaking rules of poetic justice, in reshaping them in his own terms Shakespeare beat Johnson at his own rhetorical game, leaving the doctor unable to dismiss or accept him.

Johnson had similar difficulties with the famous description of Dover cliff in the fourth act of *King Lear*. The awe-inspiring natural scene, dependent literally upon great height, was diminished by a language not lofty enough: 'He that looks from a precipice finds himself assailed by one great and dreadful image of irresistible destruction. But this overwhelming idea is dissipated and enfeebled from the instant that the mind can restore itself to the observation of particulars, and diffuse its attention to distinct objects' (*JW*, vol. VIII, p. 695). The choughs and samphire-man destroy the equivalence of great word with great object. Characteristically though, Johnson was soon impatient with such proper correspondence. He said of Thomson's imagery that it 'sometimes may be charged with filling the ear more than the mind' (*Lives*, vol. III, p. 300). He remained prepared to contemplate if not to endorse explicitly a sublime style based on a mixing of high and low, order and disorder.

Landscaping the poets

Johnson did not only use eighteenth-century conceptions of sublimity in language as a standard by which to criticize Shakespearian disorder. He also used the vocabulary of landscape-description as a strategy, a means of persuading his readers by emotion as well as reason of the rightness of his views when he could not triumph by logic. In a complicated movement this strategy both aims to convince the reader that the author's views are powerful truths of nature and to establish the authors under Johnson's critical scrutiny as authoritative and awe-inspiring objects, only simultaneously to control their authority by placing them in a scene of which the critic is the master. It projects on to the authors whom Johnson is criticizing his own needs and those of his society for order, harmony and power.

Bogel points out that Johnson often wrote for others, offering them his words to use as their own, as if this assuaged the guilt or shared the burden of his personal and egotistical assumption of authority.[20] The practice could also be seen, I suggest, as a way for Johnson to give that personal assumption the appearance of still greater objective authority than did his famous literary style. As he told Boswell, in writing for others he did not consider himself as bound to utter his own sentiments. Neither simply his own, nor the ostensible author's, such writings were disembodied, oracular. Disembodied voices of confidence and power, they were attractive to a Johnson who was satisfied neither by locating authority solely in himself, nor in existing institutions. They represent the nearest he could get to the only voice of authority that would have satisfied him (though he would have regarded its assumption as blasphemous), the voice of God. It was perhaps through a mixture of desire to achieve such a voice vicariously and a need to chasten such feelings that he was most oracular and sublime in the personae of others – as in his conclusion to Goldsmith's *The Deserted Village*, where the certainty with which he speaks of nature puts a stop to Goldsmith's increasingly desperate pursuit of the poetic muse through a ruined landscape: 'trade's proud empire hastes to swift

---

[20] Bogel, 'Johnson and the Role of Authority', p. 203.

decay, / As ocean sweeps the labour'd mole away; / While self dependent power can time defy, / As rocks resist the billows and the sky' (lines 427–30; Goldsmith, vol. IV, p. 304).

Johnson's discussion of Shakespeare approximates not so much to the voice of God as to the voice of nature. He deploys sublime imagery which locates the powers of Shakespeare in landscape. The *Preface* and the notes on Shakespeare reveal him depicting the playwright as a rugged country, an elemental natural force:

... the uniform simplicity of primitive qualities neither admits increase nor suffers decay. The sand heaped by one flood is scattered by another, but the rock always continues in its place. The stream of time, which is continually washing the dissoluble fabricks of other poets, passes without injury by the adamant of Shakespeare.

(*JW*, vol. VII, p. 70)

By portraying Shakespeare as a 'primitive quality' and as 'adamant' Johnson shifts the perspective to the vast power of elemental nature. His portrait appears to be a tribute to Shakespeare's lasting greatness, but it has another rhetorical purpose. By treating Shakespeare as a great object of nature Johnson is able to affirm Shakespeare's power while he avoids answering all the questions Shakespeare might set his beliefs if he always treated him as a *writer*, as a man proposing arguments.

At the end of *The Deserted Village* Johnson's shift to a wider natural perspective quelled Goldsmith's anxiety, but also transcended the vexed social arguments into which Goldsmith had ventured. His attacks on trade, on luxury, on enclosures – all vital contemporary debates in politics and economics – were left behind in Johnson's lofty appropriation of natural power. In Johnson's lines the voice of poetry is identified with a view so long and omniscient that the 'swift decay' to which 'trade's proud empire' hastes takes as long as the ocean takes to erode the 'laboured mole'. In his comments on Shakespeare Johnson uses a similar strategy to dismiss (albeit temporarily) the critical conflicts caused by Shakespeare's 'heterogenous modes' of composition. By contrast he vindicates Shakespeare's comic language as 'settled and unaltered', as the adamant which will remain for all time. This strategy allows Johnson to endorse certain aspects of Shakespeare's language. Shakespeare, the adamantine rock, is apparently a force of nature in his use of a 'natural' language of propriety. By contrast, the 'heterogenous' discourse of his tragedy, which offends propriety by mixing noble and base vocabulary, sublime and ridiculous passions, is unnatural. It seems that Johnson was so determined to show that propriety is not a temporary cultural code but a moral force present in nature (especially in the nature of language) that he was prepared to reshape Shakespeare into a natural embodiment of that force, thus conferring on him the authority of imagery which he could expect would inspire awe.

Yet Johnson's characteristic attention to detail prevents him from defining Shakespeare in this way without reservation, and he admits that there may be considerable exceptions to his description. Again he presents his point by using analogies drawn from landscape-description:

Shakespeare's familiar dialogue is affirmed to be smooth and clear, yet not wholly without ruggedness or difficulty; as a country may be eminently fruitful, though it has spots unfit for cultivation: His characters are praised as natural, though their sentiments are sometimes forced, and their actions improbable; as the earth upon the whole is spherical, though its surface is varied with protuberances and cavities.

(*JW*, vol. vii, pp. 70–1)

By virtue of this imagery Johnson suggests that those parts of Shakespeare which do not conform to his aesthetic ideal of smoothness, clarity and cultivation are the necessary exceptions to general truth that are found in nature itself.[21] This is the statement of an empiricist who relies on the general and predominant rather than seeking the absolute, and believes that his reliance is justified by the scheme of nature. Indeed, the very practice of describing Shakespeare in extended similes drawn from nature epitomizes Johnson's belief that knowledge comes from observation of the object world. This belief was itself in potential conflict with his belief in divine moral justice as his comments on the end of *Lear* showed.

Johnson's stress on the word 'cultivation' derives a human and social virtue from the practice of agriculture, thus basing social practice on ideas of an organic and natural fertility and production. But this, in effect, is to apply cultural values to nature, to judge it as better and more 'fruitful' to the extent that it provides food for the stomach and illustrations for social arguments. Nature has become valued as most natural when a resource for human use, as less good (although still itself) when its protuberances resist the values which eighteenth-century culture wishes to derive from (or impose on) it. When applied to Shakespeare the procedure allows Johnson to transform playwright into nature itself, identifying the parts that resist his aesthetics as the inevitable exceptions within it. They are objects in the larger scheme, to be noted and to be accepted as part of nature's variety. By a rhetorical sleight of hand Johnson thus praises Shakespeare by comparing him with nature itself, whilst at the same time reducing him to a landscape, a collection of objects, his words now no longer able to question whether notions such as 'cultivation' are social or natural virtues at all.

It is noticeable that Johnson's imagery associates all Shakespeare's faults with the barren parts of nature – difficulty is linked with ruggedness, forced sentiments and improbable actions with the protuberances and cavities which

---

[21] For a debate on these comparisons of Shakespeare to nature see Murray Krieger, 'Fiction, Nature, and Literary Kinds in Johnson's Criticism of Shakespeare', *Eighteenth Century Studies*, 4 (1970–1), 184–98 (p. 190).

vary the spherical earth. This strategy is that used in theories of the sublime and, later, the picturesque – the wild and uncultivated is first of all isolated as the exception to natural productive order and the virtues that are derived from that order – smoothness, harmony. Then it is restrained from challenging these notions of order by the theory that makes the wild governable by proposing a worked-out and therefore safe scheme of response to it. Disorder can thereby be acknowledged and contained, without threatening the idealization of order and cultivation that one wishes to make in response to the cultivated landscape. The sublime, then, exists for Johnson as a resource whereby tensions within his theories about nature and about poetry, between order and disorder, cultivation and wilderness, can be held in suspension. Shakespeare's disordered language and action, which had left Johnson in such critical distress at the end of *King Lear*, is both exalted and mastered within the *Preface* by a Johnsonian critical strategy. It is translated into a landscape in which wildness becomes a source of safely controlled and theorized pleasure. Transformed into a great natural object, it is part of a discourse by which Johnson rhetorically enforces his own critical beliefs, reaffirming his own power as master of order and right in language. It was in reaction to such enforcement that Adam Smith described the *Preface* as 'the most *manly* piece of criticism that ever was published in any country'.[22]

Johnson on Milton

Sublimity and mastery were again connected by Johnson in his *Life* of Milton. Discussing *Paradise Lost*, Johnson wrote 'The characteristick quality of his poem is sublimity.' Such sublimity, moreover, was itself a gift of nature, which made Milton a personification of its sublime power:

He seems to have been well acquainted with his own genius, and to know what it was that Nature had bestowed upon him more bountifully than upon others: the power of displaying the vast, illuminating the splendid, enforcing the awful, darkening the gloomy, and aggravating the dreadful; he therefore chose a subject on which too much could not be said, on which he might tire his fancy without the censure of extravagance.

(*Lives*, vol. I, p. 177)

Sublimity may be nature's gift, but it is Milton's self-knowledge, his acquaintance with his own genius that allows him to deploy it in art. His poetry may be grounded on his own nature and nature at large, then, but it is self-grounded by a self-conscious act: not simply an effect of nature but a harnessing of nature by an art that speaks in its name. Johnson implies that sublimity arises in a rhetoric, a language willed by a self-conscious act to look

---

[22] Quoted in W. Jackson Bate, *Samuel Johnson*, (London, 1978), p. 399.

like an outpouring of the nature on which it is based. Power is at root natural, but has to be reconstructed to appear so.

As the *Life* progresses, Johnson does begin to censure the extravagance of Milton's lofty style. The very individuality of its genius reveals too openly its constructed, rhetorical basis: Milton 'never fails to fill the imagination. But his images and descriptions of the scenes or operations of Nature do not seem to be always copied from original form, nor to have the freshness, raciness, and energy of immediate observation' (p. 178). Milton saw nature 'through the spectacles of books'. He violated the nature on which he knew his genius to be based by revealing too clearly that the source of that knowledge was not nature but his own learning: 'Milton was able to select from nature, or from story, from ancient fable, or from modern science, whatever could illustrate or adorn his thoughts. An accumulation of knowledge impregnated his mind, fermented by study, and sublimed by imagination.' It seems, then, that nature and knowledge pull apart in Johnson's account: knowing one's power stems from nature threatens not only to denaturalize it but to expose nature itself as a rhetorical construct, a concept used by men of learning (including or even especially Johnson) to legitimize and make familiar their own language of power. Milton's grand style is, for Johnson, so unusual, so far from what is conventionally accepted as natural English, that its lofty power declares it to be an individual rhetoric: 'he was master of his language in its full extent' (p. 191). The danger of so openly revealing the self as the unique source of verbal mastery is that it simultaneously derives its power from and usurps nature, thus preventing it being a common source from which all can draw: 'we read Milton for instruction, retire harrassed and overburdened, and look elsewhere for recreation; we desert our master, and seek for companions' (pp. 183–4). The reader is subordinated to a tyrant, overpowered by a unique language which in deriving itself from the source shows that source to be a figure of language. The place from which men believe their language and genius comes, which they share with their companions, is captured by a master whom one either obeys or deserts.

Johnson declares himself mastered by Milton, and expresses both admiration for and discontent with his master. It seems to me, though, that in so doing Johnson is confronting an aspect of his own use of language and attempting to understand and even purge himself of its dangers. Johnson knew the pleasure of talking for victory but also regarded it as a dangerous temptation. His written style too is like his description of Milton's, a masterful and astonishing style that seemed to contemporary readers to be as unusual and unique as Milton's seemed to him.[23] Elizabeth Montagu, the blue-

---

[23] Here my argument is similar to that of Dustin Griffin, who takes a Bloomian view of Johnson's Milton by suggesting that Johnson felt intimidated, and resisted intimidation, 'not so much by Milton's literary works as by his achievement as a man – his self-discipline, devotion, and religious

stocking Shakespearian critic and friend of Johnson's, discussed the critical terms of the *Preface* to Shakespeare with their mutual friend Mrs Carter:

words must certainly be weighed with scrupulous exactness, but I do not think they should astonish by their novelty, nor glitter by quaintness, which to tell you the truth, I think Mr. Johnson's are apt to do. The worst fault of language is to be equivocal, the next fault perhaps, is such a sort of novelty from new coin'd words, that the sense is not yet ascertained. Books written in the mother tongue should if possible be intelligible to those who know no others.[24]

Astonishing the reader with a unique style may have given Johnson immense critical authority but it risked isolating him from the 'mother tongue' from which all (and women in particular since they were less likely to know others) could feel they derived. When the last volume of Johnson's *Lives* was published Montagu came to feel that it had also led Johnson to humiliate the subjects of his biography. Lord Lyttelton, she felt, had been the victim of 'malicious falsehoods' by Johnson and she noted that 'some friends to one of the poets he has ill treated have begun such a satyrical account of Johnson's person and manner, and so ridiculous a representation of his style ... as will make him run mad if published'.[25] Since his unique style was the source of his personal authority parody was the best weapon against him, for Johnson's response when challenged directly was to become even more subordinative. When Weller Pepys stood up for Lyttelton at a dinner party Johnson became angry enough to declare 'Come forth, man! If you have anything to say, let's hear it. Come forth, man, when I call you!'[26] After the quarrel Johnson was contrite enough to take quietly a rebuke from Mrs Thrale, the hostess, accepting that his demonstration of verbal aggression had been out of place. Lyttelton, like Chesterfield, had been one of the leaders of the Patriots with whose attacks upon Walpole Johnson had sympathized. Lyttelton's subsequent abandonment of Patriot opposition for a place in the ministry made him, for Johnson, an embodiment of the betrayal of liberty. Johnson's continuing bitterness stemmed too from memory of Lyttelton's dealings with opposition writers: Thomson's independence had been compromised by his patronage just as Johnson's own had been threatened by Chesterfield's.

Writerly independence of establishments is, in the *Lives*, a virtue. Yet it is also a sin if over-indulged. In the *Life* of Milton Johnson both admires and resents the epic poet's 'peculiar power to astonish' in a style that is out of place, being formed 'by a perverse and pedantick principle' of using English words with a foreign idiom (*Lives*, vol. I, pp. 177, 190). His praise is ambiguous, and suggests that the critic is disempowered: Milton's 'call is

conviction' (all virtues that Johnson prized and struggled to practise himself). See Dustin Griffin, *Regaining Paradise: Milton and the Eighteenth Century* (Cambridge, 1986), p. 204.

[24] Quoted in Reginald Blunt, *Mrs. Montagu 'Queen of the Blues'*, 2 vols. (London, 1923), vol. II, p. 143.
[25] *Ibid.*, pp. 157, 160.
[26] *Ibid.*, p. 159.

obeyed without resistance, the reader feels himself in captivity to a higher and nobler mind, and criticism sinks in admiration' (p. 190). Milton's perversity is displayed for Johnson in the passage in which he chose to personify Sin and Death: 'This unskillful allegory appears to me one of the greatest faults of the poem, and to this there was no temptation, but the author's opinion of its beauty' (p. 186). Yet earlier in the *Life* Johnson had admired 'the sublimity of his mind' as evidenced by the fact that he sent 'faculties out upon discovery, into worlds where only imagination can travel, and delighted to form new modes of existence, and furnish sentiment and action to superior beings, to trace the counsels of hell, or accompany the choirs of heaven' (p. 178). It seems, then, that Johnson both admired the personifications of the forces of evil as instances of Milton's sublimity, and regretted them as examples of his perverse and peculiar opinion of what is beautiful. As such the Miltonic aesthetic disabled conventional criticism and surpassed the interests of the common reader: '*Paradise Lost* is one of the books which the reader admires and lays down, and forgets to take up again' (p. 183). Here, allying himself with the common reader, Johnson gains critical revenge for the experience of being overmastered to which he knew he himself subjected others. For Johnson, Milton's Sin and Death are figures of the sin of the independent writer, examples of his need to make everything (even the forces of evil which were for Johnson powerfully operative in the world) arise anew in his own unique literary practice. In making Sin and Death speak, Milton not only gives evil power, but makes them allegorical of his own perverse usurpation of the powers of nature *from* which he should show himself to derive. In doing so Milton becomes more like Satan than an angel, becomes an author claiming to be author of himself, to be guiltily admired but also viewed with horror: 'for what other author ever soared so high, or sustained his flight so long?' (p. 187).

There were political reasons for Milton's Satanism: Johnson described the poet's republicanism as founded in 'pride disdainful of superiority', a phrase that echoes Milton's description of Satan's 'high disdain' (p. 157; *Paradise Lost*, bk. I, line 98). Indeed, as Bruce Redford has argued, Johnson had already characterized political rebels against established governments as Satanic in his pamphlets *The False Alarm* and *Thoughts on Falkland's Islands*. This rhetorical tactic was attended with its own dangers, for the characterization threatened to glamorize Wilkes and the opposition, to make their resistance heroic as was Satan's, rather than simply to crush them beneath Milton's Abdiel rebuke. In his political pamphlets Johnson avoided the danger by using Milton's own tactic of bathos, reducing the Satanic rebels to dismally hissing serpents. But in considering Milton directly this tactic was less easily available, since the poet was authoritarian and rebel both. Using Milton's sublime poetry against the republican politics Milton embraced, Johnson tried 'to align himself with Milton yet repudiate him at the same time, to perform an

act of literary pietas that recoils upon the venerable ancestor'.[27] For Johnson
the price to be paid for so openly defying the natural elements and the
monarchial order is, in the name of the common reader, death: Milton
astonishes but is not read through to the end.[28]

Johnson's Shakespeare had presented him with a language so different
from his own and so disordered that he could scarcely bear to read the end
of *King Lear*. He half-heartedly accepted the substitution of a happy ending
for the original one and then mastered Shakespeare by making him a figure
(albeit a figure of greatness) in the landscape structured by his own critical
discourse. Johnson's Milton is a mirror image of his Shakespeare. Milton's
language is so like Johnson's that the doctor is first mastered and then
worried by it. It too openly reveals the individual, rhetorical and potentially
rebellious basis of the authority that he wished to be derived from nature
and from established traditions (including that of the monarchy which
Milton had opposed). Caught between admiration, resentment and self-
recognition, Johnson again had recourse to the rhetorical fiction of 'the
reader', in whose name he dismisses Milton's hold on the imagination and
rebukes himself: too open a display of the sources of one's power will crush
and then alienate the reader. In the process of his *Life* of Milton, then,
Johnson both opens a space in which the conflicting elements of his own
authority appear, and modifies our understanding of masculinity, power and
rhetoricity. Sin and Death are best left obscure, even more obscure than
Milton leaves them, because to bring them into focus displays too clearly
that they are controlled by the writer. Good and evil and nature itself had
better be left as forces presumed to exist beyond our discourses about them,
lest they become nothing but rhetorical figures in the language of the poet
with the most powerful imagination. That poet would then be able to make
the world in his own terms and subordinate us to his own peculiar power.
At least, he would if not challenged in the name of the common reader by a
critic wielding a similar language. Johnson makes that challenge, and makes
morality a battle for critical masculinity in the process: he both has to
master Milton in his own rhetorical terms, and suggest that power, mastery
and authority exist somewhere beyond the self-assertive rhetoric of a

---

[27] See Bruce Redford, 'Defying Our Master: The Appropriation of Milton in Johnson's Political
Tracts', *Studies in Eighteenth-Century Culture*, 20 (1989), 81–91 (p. 88). See also Folkenflik, *Samuel
Johnson, Biographer*, p. 126, who shows that Milton was compared with his own Satan in the period
after the Restoration by Tory monarchists who, like Johnson, found his republicanism odious.

[28] My interpretation of Johnson on Sin and Death may be compared with Bogel's in *The Dream of My
Brother: An Essay on Johnson's Authority*, pp. 50–4. For Bogel, Johnson's objection to Sin and Death
stems from his feeling that they embody Milton's failure to sublimate his restless power into a
recognizable aesthetic form. To this I add that it is not just the rules of art, but the claims of art, of
civilization itself, to be founded on nature, that are violated by Sin's and Death's incest. In their
coupling the proper subordination of child to parent and the proper separation of the sexes upon
which Johnson's proper society depends are not destroyed but inextricably confused, leaving him
unable simply to blame the female, whether Eve or the 'fatal Cleopatra' for their collapse.

particular writer.[29] Otherwise the world is a battleground of competing rhetorics, each seeking mastery by parading its self-generated power. In the words of the *Preface* to Shakespeare, there can be no repose save on the stability of truth, and it is in the name of truth, propriety and the commonly accepted that Johnson seeks to master Milton's and his own tendency towards a display of rhetorical mastery.[30] Johnson's tendency to describe the poets by analogy with natural scenes was, then, necessary to counteract the 'perverse' independence of Milton's and his own peculiar rhetoric, although once 'nature' is seen to have been a rhetorical figure it is difficult to restore it to awe-inspiring objectivity and stability. Wordsworth, I shall argue, followed a similar course. Coleridge, on the other hand, tried both to master Wordsworth as Johnson had Milton, and to find terms in which authority would no longer arise in the battle for mastery, but would be gathered from and shared in a social community of discourse.

Propriety and desire: the fatal Cleopatra

Johnson's own defence of social community appears most strongly in his defence of propriety and in the imagery that defines it as a masculine language under threat from the seductive disorder of the female. In *Rasselas* Johnson shows that lack and desire are essential to endeavour and happiness: ' "That I want nothing," said the prince, "or that I know not what I want, is the cause of my complaint; if I had any known want, I should have a certain wish; that wish would excite endeavour, and I should not then repine ..." ' (*JW*, vol. xvi, pp. 16–17). We might call this a capitalist psychology since desire for objects is made the condition of happiness and activity. But it is also male, as Johnson describes it, and it is also at the root of the sublime because it can never be satisfied, seeking always another object. Johnson seems to have appreciated this as early as his *The Vision of Theodore*, where he describes an allegorical mountain of existence:

Encouraged by this Assurance, I looked and beheld a Mountain higher than Teneriffe, to the Summit of which the Human Eye could never reach; when I had tired myself with gazing upon its Height, I turned my Eyes towards its Foot, which I could easily discover, but was amazed to find it without Foundation, and placed inconceivably in Emptiness and Darkness. Thus I stood terrified and confused; above were Tracks inscrutable, and below was total Vacuity.

(*JPP*, pp. 148–9)

---

[29] For a similar view of Johnson attacking Milton for a selfish egotism he detected and wished to defeat in himself see Stephen Fix, 'Distant Genius: Johnson and the Art of Milton's Life', *Modern Philology*, 81 (1983–4), 244–64.

[30] Martin Wechselblatt notes that authority in Johnson is suspended 'across a rhetorical space pulling in two directions at once ... toward an absolute, unquestionable origin ... and toward its utter dissolution': 'Finding Mr Boswell: Rhetorical Authority and National Identity in Johnson's *A Journey to the Western Islands of Scotland*', *ELH*, 60 (1993), 117–48 (p.133).

Here Theodore looks in a way that epitomizes the sublime. He desires to know the limits of the scene and is unable to find them or exert mastery over it, and is left astonished. It is a movement that was later to characterize both Burke's and Kant's discussions of the sublime. Johnson is different, though, in making the mountain-vision not just a particular type of aesthetic experience, but an allegory for existence itself: it is an object that can never be fully defined, never wholly possessed. But it is at least, by virtue of Johnson's allegorical landscape, an object, and is therefore susceptible to further attempts at definition – leaving the writer to renew, like Johnson's dictionary-maker, his attempts at conquest.

In *The Vision of Theodore* the protector's voice intervenes to guide the hero. In *Rasselas*, published a decade later, there is no semi-divine patriarch to guide and check the wanderings of desire. Johnson provides instead a cautionary tale in which the acceptance of limitations and duties, rather than the pursuit of happiness, is endorsed. Pursuit of desire is shown to be an abdication of paternal responsibility. Imlac discourses on the folly of the pyramid builders and the insatiability of desire: 'Whoever thou art, that, not content with a moderate condition, imaginest happiness in royal magnificence, and dreamest that command or riches can feed the appetite of novelty with perpetual gratifications, survey the pyramids, and confess thy folly!' (*JW*, vol. XVI, p. 119). Yet he says this from inside the pyramid, and it becomes clear that he and the prince and princess (the prince's sister) have repeated the folly of the kings who built the pyramids, allowing their desire for novelty to rule them. For when they return to daylight, their defenceless companions and servants have been attacked, and the women carried away by Arabs. Abduction and rape seem to be the price of indulgence of limitless desire, and Johnson appears to take a stand firmly against it. He does so by confronting the desire for mastery of the new with another masculine ideal: exertion of proper authority and protectiveness over vulnerable women. Protectiveness is preferred to self-assertion, but the pill is sugared by the fact that protectiveness expresses masculine desire in another form: mastery of the new is replaced by the endeavour to master what is already possessed lest another man take it. It is a myth in which women no longer symbolize the alluring truth that is still to be known, but the existing order which has always to be protected. Chivalry, both a duty and an implicitly sexual pleasure, replaces the unstable discourse of desire and the potentially ungovernable objects and scenes it seeks to control.[31]

---

[31] Isobel Grundy, *Samuel Johnson and the Scale of Greatness* (Leicester, 1986), pp. 163–4, discusses 'paternal vigilance' in *Rasselas*, suggesting that, by the tale's end, it is not viewed without irony. Jean H. Hagstrum, in *Samuel Johnson's Literary Criticism* (Minneapolis, 1952), pp. 130–1, suggests that *Rasselas* adopts Burke's distinctions between the sublime and the beautiful. Robert G. Walker relates *Rasselas* to theological arguments for the existence of an afterlife in *Eighteenth-Century Arguments for Immortality and Johnson's Rasselas* (Victoria, Canada, 1977).

It is a lesson to be learnt by the prince, but principally by the princess, whose keen desire to see inside the pyramid led her to abandon her companion. But if she has to learn her place under male authority, so does the writer. For Johnson makes it clear that the allegory applies especially to those who indulge in fictions and allow their imaginations to rule them:

> To indulge the power of fiction, and send imagination out upon the wing, is often the sport of those who delight too much in silent speculation. When we are alone we are not always busy; the labour of excogitation is too violent to last long; the ardour of enquiry will sometimes give way to idleness or to satiety. He who has nothing external that can divert him, must find pleasure in his own thoughts, and must conceive himself what he is not; for who is pleased with what he is? He then expatiates in boundless futurity, and culls from all imaginable conditions that which for the present moment he should most desire, amuses his desires with impossible enjoyments, and confers upon his pride unattainable dominion. The mind dances from scene to scene, unites all pleasures in all combinations, and riots in delights which nature and fortune, with all their bounty cannot bestow.
>
> (*JW*, vol. xvi, pp. 151–2)

The restlessness of imagination, even Shakespeare's, must be checked before it destroys one's acceptance of proper limits and duties. And so Johnson creates allegorical natural scenes to understand the endless inventiveness of imagination and to illustrate restlessness of existence, but carefully incorporates them in a discourse that reinforces traditional social precepts and duties. Rasselas is checked by chivalric duty, Shakespeare by Johnson's rhetorical manipulation of nature-description itself.

Johnson seems to have been prescient here. It is as if his discourse foresees both the Romantic location of desire in a potentially limitless scene – the restless yearning for something evermore about to be – and the problems of hysteria, madness and isolation that come with it. In avoiding these problems, though, he creates others in his understanding of nature, truth and language. He wished to see these concepts as attractive feminine forms, to be mastered by his power as a writer. Words, he wrote, were 'the daughters of earth'. They were subordinate to ideas, and then to things, which were 'the sons of heaven' (*JPP*, p. 304). Here both ideas and things are masculine, derived from the patriarchal God. In their superiority over 'female' words, they reproduce the actual social and property relations of contemporary Britain: women and mother earth are owned, defined and protected by men. Johnson develops the implications of contemporary empiricism in deriving value and meaning first from things, and in assuming that ideas (reason) are masculine. As in his proposal for his Dictionary, he exerts his mastery of words in terms which borrow from a nobleman's ownership of his family estate (terms of ownership and patronage he found it hard to bear from noblemen in practice). He put it firmly in *The Rambler*:

It is, however, the task of criticism to establish principles, to improve opinion into knowledge; and to distinguish those means of pleasing which depend upon known causes and rational deduction, from the nameless and inexplicable elegancies which appeal wholly to the fancy, from which we feel delight, but know not how they produce it, and which may well be termed the enchantresses of the soul. Criticism reduces those regions of literature under the dominion of science, which have hitherto known only the anarchy of ignorance, the caprices of fancy, and the tyranny of prescription.

(*JW*, vol. IV, p. 122)

Mastery of the scene of literature seems easily achievable here, yet Johnson's acceptance of limits to the desire for possession means that some truth – and therefore some language – remains beyond what can be properly striven for. A consequence of this acceptance is that truth becomes double. When idealized as a woman, truth is dressed charmingly, attracting the man within proper bounds and aiming at a respectable match in which his possession is expressed within recognized social codes. Socially unacceptable truths, ones which might challenge respectable orthodoxy, are dressed indecorously, wantonly displaying their charms in a dress code which says that they are exciting but can only be bought for a price – both in money and in the risk of bringing infection into the world of proper responsibility. Like the verbal conceits to which, Johnson claimed, Shakespeare was addicted, they resemble the 'fatal Cleopatra' for whom he lost the world and was glad to lose it.

Johnson compared women and landscape again in a passage which contains an ironic glance at his own persuasion of an older woman to marry him. He saw spinsters as similarly out of the common order, an order that was both social and natural, since even their bodily fertility cried out for a husband. And it is worth noting of a passage about rhetoric that Johnson's own style abhors singularity: everywhere he either unites opposites or chooses between them. There is no room in Johnson's nature for single women because there is no room in the language with which he shapes and knows nature. Single women, like words, truths and the landscape (in metaphors drawn from which he portrays them) are to be united with the master who knows them and brings them within the discourse of proper order. And, he points out, they are allowed by society no terms in which they can signify independently for themselves – their 'truth' is constituted by society's expectation that women should define themselves in terms of proper regulation of their uncertain bodies (their 'natural infelicity' as Johnson puts it) by the protective and masterful institution of marriage. Single women, Johnson argues by comparing them with nature, 'seldom give those that frequent their conversation, any exalted notions of the blessing of liberty' for whether they are conscious that like barren countries they are free, only because they were never thought to deserve the trouble of a conquest, or imagine that their sincerity is not always unsuspected, when they declare their contempt of men; it is certain, that they generally appear to have some great and incessant cause of uneasiness, and that many of them have at last been persuaded, by powerful rhetoricians, to try the life which they had so long contemned, and put on the bridal ornaments at a time when they least became them.

(JW, vol. III, p. 212)

Society, Johnson recognizes, has no place for singleness within its scheme of order which is, therefore, defined as barrenness in nature. Women themselves are eager to signify in the proper terms, being allowed no place beyond them other than that of a barren, savage country, hence their 'uneasiness' at their own individual state. But to move into those terms, to marry too late is, like the nature-woman with ill-adjusted dress, to take on the appearance of propriety only to undermine it by failing to observe its underlying assumptions – in this case not that of self-restraint but those of beauty and fertility. The late-married woman is thus more of an embarrassment to the discourse of propriety than the single, for unlike her she cannot be dismissed as beyond the pale as a woman with no meaning. Rather, she stands within the institution by which she assumes her proper social meaning as a woman, but only just, her age and possible infertility refusing the predominantly male equation of bridehood and married femininity with beauty and fertility. Like a countryside about to be made into a landscape garden, the woman needs both to be owned and to be dressed as if the signs of that ownership (the 'bridal ornaments' or landscape improvements) were her natural qualities.[32]

James Thomson, a bachelor happiest in men's company, made clear the sexual implications of the comparison. If the poet dressed nature as did the gardener, both could do so to stimulate male desire for a female plaything rather than to portray propriety. Thomson remarked to William Shenstone when visiting his landscape garden in 1746:

You have nothing to do (says he) but to dress Nature. Her robe is ready made; you have only to caress her, love her; kiss her; and then – descend into the valley. Coming out into the court before the house, he mentioned Clent and Waw-ton Hill as the two bubbies of Nature: then Mr. L. observed the nipple, and then Thomson the fringe of Uphmore wood; till the double entendre was worked up to a point, and produced a laugh ... We now passed into Virgil's Grove. What a delightful place, says he, is this for a person of a poetical genius. I don't wonder you're a devotee to the Muses. – This place, says Mr. L. will improve a poetical genius. – Aye, replied Mr. T. and a

---

[32] It should be noted, however, that Johnson was prepared to allow women within marriage the right to share 'that concordia discors, that suitable disagreement which is always necessary to intellectual harmony' (JW, vol. v, pp. 123–4: quoted in Jean H. Hagstrum, Eros and Vision: The Restoration and Romanticism (Evanston, IL, 1989), p. 124). Hagstrum's chapter (pp. 121–37) provides a useful analysis of Johnson's views on marriage.

poetical genius will improve this place ... He denominated my Virgil's Grove there Le Vallon occlus.[33]

Shenstone encouraged a more decorously sensual response by placing a copy of the Medici Venus in his garden, describing it in an inscription as an emblem of the garden as a whole:

> Fresh from the foamy tide,
>   She every bosom warms;
> While half withdrawn she seems to hide,
>   And half reveals, her charms.
>
> Learn hence, ye boastful sons of taste,
>   Who plan the rural shade;
> Learn hence to shun the vicious waste
>   Of pomp, at large display'd.
>
> Let sweet concealment's magic art
>   Your mazy bounds invest;
> And while the sight unveils a part,
>   Let fancy paint the rest.[34]

Like Thomsonian landscape-description, the metaphor of a clothed nature goddess implicitly establishes a safe and titillating area in which controlled emotional responses can be glimpsed and indulged. In the *Essay on Criticism* Pope also connects the dressing of nature by gardening with that done by writing. 'True Wit is Nature to Advantage drest' and 'Expression is the *Dress* of Thought, and still / Appears more decent as more suitable' (Pope, vol. I, pp. 272, 274; lines 297, 318–19).[35] Propriety in writing contains, however, not only decency but a controlled male sexual excitement: it is decent in order to ornament nature more pleasingly and seductively. The author of *Cursory Remarks on Tragedy* wrote in 1774: 'Let it not be advanced as a merit, let it not be urged even as an excuse, that Shakespear followed nature in the busy walks of men; that he presented her, as he found her, naked and unadorned: for there are parts of nature that require concealment; there are others too that by the thin transparent veil, by the light, the careless drapery, are greatly heightened and improved.'[36]

Pope and Johnson, by stressing the metaphor of truth and nature as a dressed woman, introduce to the ancient idea of truth's veiled appearance a peculiarly eighteenth-century sexual and cultural politics, a displacement into

---

[33] Quoted in James Sambrook, *James Thomson 1700–1748: A Life* (Oxford, 1991), p. 254.

[34] Quoted in Simon Pugh, *Garden, Nature, Language* (Manchester, 1988), p. 111.

[35] The dress/style analogy in Pope and other writers of the period is viewed as a mercantile commodification of both poetry and women by Laura Brown in *Ends of Empire: Women and Ideology in Early Eighteenth-Century English Literature* (Ithaca, NY, 1993), pp. 108–27.

[36] Quoted in R. D. Stock, *Samuel Johnson and Neoclassical Dramatic Theory* (Lincoln, NB), p. 68.

the language/nature relation of their desired model of a society based on the subordination of pleasure to restraint, desire to decorum. In this disguised form of mastery Christian moralists construct ideals of women, nature and language which subsume the tension between pleasure and instruction in an air of decorum which, they hope, appears to be natural. It is an irony that Johnson the empiricist should have created so idealized a view, but it is one inherent in the impossibility of deriving from the empirical world a validation of all the cultural practices and beliefs that Johnson the moralist wished to uphold.

The legitimacy of writing: the journey to the Western Isles

Boswell was always keen to establish Johnson's mastery as observer of and moralist upon nature and culture. When he persuaded Johnson to accompany him on a tour of the Highlands and Hebrides in 1773 he was triumphant. He had confirmed the intimacy of their relationship, and would be able to record the sayings of the great sage as he encountered new scenes of wildness. Johnson himself found that his reputation extended to educated men in the wilds of Scotland, although, like the authority imposed by the London government after the Jacobite rebellion of 1745, it was not unquestioned by the lairds and ministers whom they visited. And if Johnson met resistance from the inhabitants, he also encountered it from the land they inhabited: its wildness forbade one to say, factually or metaphorically, that man was master of his inheritance, his estate or his fate.

Their tour was late in the year, and Johnson was exposed to gruelling journeys on horseback and on foot across moors and through bogs. The landscape resisted him physically, and, more threateningly, it resisted his capacity to write of it as a natural order which might act as the foundation for a social or moral order. The comparatively gentle scenery of the Lowlands disconcerted him because it lacked trees, so that, as he noted in his account, 'the whole country is extended in uniform nakedness' (*JW*, vol. IX, pp. 9–10). This nakedness amounted not only to a lack of decorous ornamentation, but to a threat to proper distinctions. The traveller had 'nothing to contemplate but grounds that have no visible boundaries' (p. 9). Lacking trees, the land lacked those marks of gentlemanly ownership which revealed that it was *property* and, moreover, the property of separate families who bequeathed cultivation to their descendants. Instead, it was uniform and open in revealing agriculture, and therefore commerce, to be its organizational principle. Lacking the dress of foliage, it revealed a cultural impoverishment that Johnson found both socially and politically disconcerting. Families had not planted for their descendants' benefit, a sign of the possible destruction of the legitimate transmission of land and values that sustained order in society. Such an omission spoke of a loss either of hope or civilized values amongst the gentry: 'for that negligence some excuse might be drawn from an unsettled state of life, and the instability of property; but in Scotland possession has long been secure, and inheritance regular, yet it may be doubted whether before the Union any man between Edinburgh and England had ever set a tree' (p. 10).

Johnson attributes the cause of this failure to a custom begun 'in times of tumult', when possession and inheritance of land was insecure. What he does not admit here, though, is a matter which concerned him deeply as the tour continued. For Johnson the insecurity and dispossession evidenced by the lack of trees seemed to be an evil consequence of a society that was nevertheless in many respects better than the legitimate Georgian authority which replaced it. The Act of Union and the establishment of English and Hanoverian power in Scotland were, in replacing traditional Scottish authorities, creating insecurities and dispossessions of their own. As Johnson saw in the Highlands and Islands, for each of those given the security and the civilization to plant a tree for his descendants, there was a chief dispossessed of land and power in punishment for his support of Prince Charles in the rebellion. And this presented Johnson with a political dilemma which went to the heart of his beliefs about the legitimacy of authority, including his own.

One side of this dilemma can be discerned in Johnson's response to the wildness of the Scottish landscape and people. He found the countryside to be a threat to his belief in a productive and cultivatable nature, from which values of order, cultivation and improvement could be derived for the human world: 'an eye accustomed to flowery pastures and waving harvests is astonished and repelled by this wide extent of hopeless sterility. The appearance is that of matter incapable of form or usefulness, dismissed by nature from her care and disinherited of her favours' (p. 39). The highland natives were also uncivilized, since their remote and mountainous situation left little opportunity for intercourse with others: 'the manners of mountaineers are commonly savage, but they are rather produced by their situation than derived from their ancestors' (p. 44). In a world remote from London and the prosperous south, it was difficult to found an ordered society on a productive nature. But to accept that nature is barren as well as productive would be to question the very derivation of cultivation, improvement and order from it, and from the God who created it. Johnson reacts instead by making the landscape illegitimate, 'disinherited' from nature. He preserves the legitimacy of his view of nature and culture by making Scotland an exception to the rule, an aberrance whose savagery is reflected in that of its native inhabitants. Having done so, he is able to learn from it by treating it as an instructive source of realities with which to confirm one's pre-existent ideas. It conveys images upon which to found our abstract ideas of barrenness and desert:

It will very readily occur, that this uniformity of barrenness can afford very little amusement to the traveller; that it is easy to sit at home and conceive rocks and heath, and waterfalls; and that these journeys are useless labours, which neither impregnate the imagination, nor enlarge the understanding. It is true that of far the greater part of things, we must content ourselves with such knowledge as description may exhibit, or analogy supply; but it is true likewise, that these ideas are always incomplete, and that at least, till we have compared them with realities, we do not know them to be just. As we see more, we become possessed of more certainties, and consequently gain more principles of reasoning, and found a wider basis of analogy.

(p. 40)

By this means a language systematic and legitimate (because apparently derived from empirical reality) is reaffirmed; Johnson has restored Lockeian empiricism and the values of order and judgement implicit in it in the face of the Highlands' challenge to them.

That challenge had a direct bearing on Johnson's conception of himself as a writer. He describes in pastoral terms the company's journey through Glenshiel, a mountain valley which leads them to a bleak resting-place: 'I sat down on a bank, such as a writer of Romance might have delighted to feign.' But, as he continues, the pastoral changes into the sublime, the scene into a place of desolation and terror, in which the wildness of nature reveals human insignificance:

We were in this place at ease and by choice, and had no evils to suffer or to fear; yet the imaginations excited by the view of an unknown and un-travelled wilderness are not such as arise in the artificial solitude of parks and gardens, a flattering notion of self-sufficiency, a placid indulgence of voluntary delusions, a secure expansion of the fancy, or a cool concentration of the mental powers. The phantoms which haunt a desert are want, and misery, and danger; the evils of dereliction rush upon the thoughts; man is made unwillingly acquainted with his own weakness, and meditation shews him only how little he can sustain, and how little he can perform. There were no traces of inhabitants, except perhaps a rude pile of clods called a summer hut, in which a herdsman had rested in the favourable seasons. Whoever had been in the place where I then sat, unprovided with provisions and ignorant of the country, might, at least before the roads were made, have wandered among the rocks, till he had perished with hardship, before he could have found either food or shelter. Yet what are these hillocks to the ridges of Taurus, or these spots of wildness to the desarts of America?

(pp. 40–1)

'Here,' Johnson adds, 'I first conceived the thought of this narration.' His writing is prompted, then, by a desire both to record the sublime wildness of Scotland, and to control it. At the very moment when his own importance and centrality is most powerfully questioned, Johnson decides to write a journal, a document which sorts personal experience into an order of times and places, and which can be read by others. The act of intended communication that constitutes authorship here serves to reassert Johnson's own language, and all human language and society, against the threatening silence of the hills.

Absent from Johnson's published description of the scene is any acknowledgement that it was the site of a battle during the Jacobite rebellion of 1719. In Boswell's account the place is of historical significance, its wildness associated with the native courage and independence of the Highlanders who had fought in 1719 and 1745 for a cause for which he had some political sympathy.

M'Queen walked some miles to give us a convoy. He had, in 1745, joined the Highland army at Fort Augustus, and continued in it till after the battle of Culloden. As he narrated the particulars of that ill-advised but brave attempt, I could not refrain from tears. There is a certain association of ideas in my mind upon that subject, by which I am strongly affected. The very Highland names, or the sound of a bagpipe, will stir my blood, and fill me with a mixture of melancholy and respect for courage; with pity for an unfortunate and superstitious regard for antiquity, and thoughtless inclination for war; in short, with a crowd of sensations with which sober rationality has nothing to do.

We passed through Glenshiel, with prodigious mountains on each side. We saw where the battle was fought in the year 1719; Dr Johnson owned he was now in a scene of as wild nature as he could see.[37]

Johnson himself, in a private letter to Mrs Thrale, had written that McQueen 'told us some stories of their march into England' whilst accompanying them towards Glenshiel and the battlefield (*J Letters*, vol. II, p. 73). A few days later he wrote again, giving Mrs Thrale details of an event omitted from his published narrative: 'I slept in the bed, on which the Prince reposed in his distress. The sheets which he used were never put to any meaner offices, but were wrapped up by the Lady of the house, and at last, according to her desire, were laid round her in her grave. These are not Whigs' (pp. 90–1). Clearly Johnson, like Boswell a Tory, retained a certain sympathy for the Stuart succession and the Jacobite cause, a sympathy he was prepared to display in a private letter but not in a published narrative. But the deliberate omission leaves a question hanging over the published description of Glenshiel. Was his decision to respond to the desolate valley by writing 'this narration' an attempt, by subjecting the wild landscape to the order of a travel journal, to control the divided and disordered political loyalties that the place prompted in him? Imposing upon the Scottish wild a textual order intended for publication, Johnson was, perhaps, controlling his remaining Jacobite sympathies by displacing them into a scenic realm, a naturally disordered landscape over which writing could hope to gain power. If so then his narrative, an Englishman's

---

[37] See *Boswell's Journal of a Tour to the Hebrides with Samuel Johnson LL.D. 1773*, ed. Frederick A. Pottle and Charles H. Bennett (London, 1966), pp. 106–7.

version of Scotland, written up and published in London, was mastering both the Highlanders' political culture and the writer's sympathy for it, colonizing the Jacobite North and Johnson's Tory self at once. It was rewriting a landscape marked, as Johnson noted in private, by political rebellion as a place of purely natural wildness to be described, and so controlled, by the uncontroversial discourse of the scenic tour. The natural sublimity of Glenshiel, threatening though it seemed, appeared containable so long as the tour narrative kept the more dangerous threat of publicly mourning for Jacobitism there out of the picture.

Threatened by the social and political cultures of the Highlands, which refused to present themselves in terms (and words) familiar to an English visitor, Johnson responded to the native practice of the Highland clans with support of a system which, like Lockeian empiricism and his own writing, he perceived as ordered and civilized. Like them it emanated from Lowland Scotland and from England, and like them it had the authority of legitimate and established writing. Written and universal law was, for Johnson, a proper system replacing the clan loyalties and word of mouth by which Scottish chieftans had formerly governed their localities:[38]

> In the Highlands, some great lords had an hereditary jurisdiction over counties; and some chieftans over their own lands; till the final conquest of the Highlands afforded an opportunity of crushing all the local courts, and of extending the general benefits of equal law to the low and the high, in the deepest recesses of obscurest corners.
>
> (*JW*, vol. IX, p. 46)

By strict administration of the laws, he noted, cattle thievery was 'very much represt' (p. 45). Political authority, in the form of a written English-imposed system, went hand in hand with personal authority, which also controlled wildness by writing. Johnson was mastering the sublimity of the landscape and the oral culture of its inhabitants by imposing a fixed, established and improved language upon it. This language was created by writing, with the permanence it brings, but was fascinated, despite itself, with the disappearing culture which it ostensibly sought to regulate and replace. For it was a culture in the oral power and political affiliations of which Johnson privately recognized his own rebellious self. His battle to write Scotland in English Hanoverian discourse was shaped by his continuing need to gain written authority over himself – to fix his tumultuous imagination (and speech) into the stability of texts. Yet this stability, like the landscape-description by which he often sought to achieve it, was itself destabilized as soon as Johnson, finding his attempt to subordinate world and self to written law presumptuous, rebelled against it.

---

[38] For an assessment of Johnson and the law see E. L. McAdam, *Dr. Johnson and the English Law* (Syracuse, NY, 1951).

Johnson and the Ossianic culture

Shaped by his need for written authority, Johnson's battle to write Scotland
in loyal English reshaped his understanding of verbal power. His suspicion of
oral culture is evidenced in his attitude to the Highland language, Erse. He
doubted whether 'an Earse manuscript a hundred years old' even existed,
and added that 'there can be no polished language without books'. The
danger in an unwritten language was that since no author could fix or reform
meanings, no widely disseminated exemplary standard could exist. The
language was left as prey to the depredations of time and space: as it moved
from its origins it changed and declined. Erse 'merely floated in the breath of
the people, and could therefore receive little improvement' (p. 115). Just as
the uncodified clan law allowed thieving and favouritism to flourish, so the
unwritten clan language endangered the legitimate descent of knowledge: 'in
an unwritten speech, nothing that is not very short is transmitted from one
generation to another' (p. 116). Because of this, proper history and tradition
was vulnerable to time, to social disruption and to imposition. Johnson
focused his attention on the last, in the form of the controversy over
Macpherson's English 'translations'/forgeries of the Gaelic poetry of Ossian,
although the spread of English power and language after 1745 could be seen
as an imposition. It was, perhaps, to avoid taking this view that Johnson
concentrated on Ossian, whom he attacked for imposing a fake English
sublimity on the Gaelic, for misconstructing ancient Scotland and undermining the English literature which he imitated.[39] But Johnson was also
personally challenged by the newly 'recovered' bardic texts since, as the
acknowledged arbiter of legitimacy in English after his Dictionary, he wished
to be able to decide the authenticity of this Scottish manuscript too.

The poems of Ossian had been published in English translations in 1762–3
by James Macpherson. Macpherson claimed that he had discovered ancient
Scottish texts, and had put them into modern English.[40] Ossian, the ancient
bard, sang a Highland epic concerning the hero Fingal, capturing the mood
of the literary public who were eager for specimens of native folk epic and
who were prepared to make the bard a cult figure.[41] Written in a prose that
owed much to the style of the King James Bible, Macpherson's texts were

---

[39] On Ossian, Jacobitism and the romanticization of the Scottish past see Howard D. Weinbrot,
Britannia's Issue: The Rise of British Literature from Dryden to Ossian (Cambridge, 1993), pp. 523–56.

[40] Derrick S. Thomson in *The Gaelic Sources of Macpherson's 'Ossian'* (Edinburgh and London, 1951)
shows that *Fingal* was based on Gaelic poems, although not on an ancient epic as Macpherson
claimed.

[41] For a discussion of the bardic revival and the developing taste for touring the sublime scenery of
Wales and Scotland, see Malcolm Andrews, *The Search For The Picturesque: Landscape Aesthetics and
Tourism in Britain 1760–1800* (Aldershot, 1989), pp. 126–250. Macpherson's Ossian is placed in the
context of the Celtic bards in Edward D. Snyder, *The Celtic Revival in English Literature 1760–1800*
(Gloucester, MA, 1965).

regarded as the height of the sublime, narrating heroic deeds in high and lofty language against the backdrop of the wild mountains and moors of the Highlands:

As rushes a stream of foam from the dark shady steep of Cromla; when the thunder is rolling above, and dark-brown night on half the hill. So fierce, so vast, and so terrible rushed on the sons of Erin. The chief like a whale of ocean, whom all his billows follow, poured valour forth as a stream, rolling his night along the shore.[42]

Macpherson thoughtfully provided footnotes which compared such epic similes to those of the great poets: here to Pope, Virgil and Milton. And he also included a *Critical Dissertation on the Poems of Ossian, the Son of Fingal*, written by Hugh Blair, who became a friend of Johnson's shortly after publication (although Johnson was quick to reveal his disagreement with it). Blair defended the antiquity of the poems, stating that Macpherson's translation was a version of 'genuine venerable monuments of very remote antiquity' whose 'two great characteristics' were 'tenderness and sublimity'. He argued that Ossian was a bard who 'sung from the love of poetry and song', of scenery 'wild and romantic': a bard of 'the poetic inspiration'.[43]

Johnson's friend Thomas Percy took a similar view in his *Reliques of Ancient English Poetry* (1765). In an *Essay* in this collection of ancient ballads, Percy declared that the medieval minstrels were 'the genuine successors of the ancient bards' whose 'skill was considered as something divine; their persons were deemed sacred; their attendance was solicited by kings'.[44] The 'romantic wildness' (vol. I, p. lvii) of the northern ballads stemmed from the mountains and barren wastes of the scenery, as James Beattie, who wrote his popular poem *The Minstrel* after reading Percy, had noted in 1762. But it stemmed from a native British tradition too, from the Teutonic and Scandinavian rather than the Latin of classical civilization.

Rural, oral and native, the newly fashionable ancient poetry was little calculated to appeal to the London-based Latinate side of Johnson. Although he had written the dedication and the glossary for the *Reliques*, he was inclined to joke about Percy's ballads and decided that Ossian was a modern forgery, perhaps because it conformed so markedly to current theories of the sublime.

---

[42] *Fingal, An Ancient Epic Poem ... Composed by Ossian the Son of Fingal* (London, 1762), p. 10. Johnson, Blair and the Ossianic sublime are briefly discussed by Samuel H. Monk, *The Sublime: A Study of Critical Theories in Eighteenth-Century England* (Ann Arbor, Mich., 1960), pp. 127–9. Fiona J. Stafford, in *The Sublime Savage* (Edinburgh, 1988), relates Macpherson's sublime to eighteenth-century criticism, to Gaelic poetry and to Hebrew prosody as portrayed in the 1753 lectures of Bishop Robert Lowth (pp. 86–93). Eighteenth-century critical enthusiasm for Ossian and ancient bardic culture is assessed by Margaret Mary Rubel in *Savage And Barbarian: Historical Attitudes in the Criticism of Homer and Ossian in Britain, 1760–1800* (Amsterdam, 1978), pp. 39–101.

[43] The quotations are taken from the first edition (London, 1763), pp. 20–1.

[44] Thomas Percy, *Reliques of Ancient English Poetry*, 3 vols. (Edinburgh, 1858), vol. I, p. xxxii–xxxiii. The eighteenth-century fashion for Druids and bards is explored by A. L. Owen in *The Famous Druids* (Oxford, 1962).

He called on Macpherson to produce the original Gaelic manuscripts. Eventually Macpherson did so, having first fabricated them. But when Johnson made his trip with Boswell to the areas where Erse was still spoken, the issue was still being hotly debated. Johnson made many inquiries amongst the educated men with whom he and Boswell stayed, and became annoyed when, despite the lack of manuscript evidence for Ossian or for any ancient Gaelic poetry, ministers continued to believe in its authenticity:

> I asked a very learned minister in Sky, who had used all arts to make me believe the genuineness of the book, whether at last he believed it himself? but he would not answer. He wished me to be deceived, for the honour of his country; but would not directly and formally deceive me. Yet has this man's testimony been publickly produced as of one that held *Fingal* to be the work of Ossian.
>
> (*JW*, vol. IX, p. 118)

Johnson was haunted by a lost Gaelic culture and frustrated by its elusiveness since, being oral not written, it escaped his search for proper evidence. Ossian was still more annoying as a patriotic resurgence of that ancient oral culture which not only resisted his search for evidence, but focused Scottish pride against English authority (and the authority of English). The Ossianic poetry, because it was an epic idealization of a wild and barren Scottish landscape, was a cultural and linguistic threat. It was a poetry which, unlike that of Shakespeare, could not be pinned to a text and mastered by the strategy of portraying it as a natural scene in which barren areas proved the general rule of cultivation.

Still more frustrating, Ossian, as an English translation of oral Gaelic, seemed a poor mimicry of the Miltonic and biblical sublime. It seemed a parody of the great writing in English by criticizing which Johnson had established his own authority. Not only did Ossian miscontruct the Highland culture that Johnson idealized in a way he could not confute, but it also misconstructed the English writing in which his personal and England's national authority was contained. Revealing the colonial encounter as one of mutual misreading, Macpherson profited, at the expense of Johnson's deepest (and self-contradictory) desires – to see an older Jacobite oral culture and preserve it from English and Lowland Scottish Whig commercialism on one hand, and on the other to bring all of Britain under the empire of an English language which, guaranteed by the verbal judgement practised by poets and critics, would spread justice and truth rather than the sentiments and ideology of a colonizer. Johnson, unable to speak Gaelic and unable to see manuscripts, had his own authority as (in Chesterfield's words) the dictator of the English language threatened. His intention, announced in the plan of his Dictionary, to reduce the language to legitimacy was challenged not simply by this single case of possible forgery, but by its demonstration that there is a native oral culture which can be rendered into English in a mock sublime.

Johnson suspected it of being a poor copy of poetry he had himself endorsed (Milton, Shakespeare) but was unable, such was its oral basis, to subject it conclusively to his English criticism. Personal, political and linguistic authority were questioned simultaneously, hence the importance Johnson gave to the issue. Boswell describes the encounter with the learned minister in terms which reveal Johnson's view:

> Dr. Johnson proceeded, 'I look upon McPherson's *Fingal* to be as gross an imposition as ever the world was troubled with. Had it been really an ancient work, a true specimen how men thought at that time, it would have been a curiosity of the first rate. As a modern production, it is nothing.'[45]

Johnson's interest is an historian's or an anthropologist's, a matter of specimens of antiquity and of curiosities. Whilst, therefore, he maintains an interest in Gaelic poetry as evidence of the way men thought before language was improved, he is not willing to accord it power or legitimacy in his own age. Even had he accepted Ossian, it would have been on the basis of the accuracy with which Macpherson had translated the ancient manuscripts. To have accepted the power of oral culture and bardic recitation would have been to undermine the legitimacy of the written, and the established powers that rested upon it. Chief amongst these powers was the London government which was subordinating Scotland, with the assistance of Lowland Scots Whigs, by laws determining its judicial system and extending a network of military roads and forts across it.

And yet, despite Johnson's insistence on the written, his support of King George and his longstanding prejudice against the Scots, he retained a sympathy for the clan system and the Stuart succession – a sympathy that implied a criticism of the Whig commercialism introduced to the Highlands after 1745 by the Lowland agents of government. These included the Commission for the Forfeited Annexed Estates, which reformed tenancy rights on lands confiscated from Jacobites.[46] And, of course, he was well aware of the power as well as the elusiveness of speech since he was himself renowned as the most authoritative talker and wit of his day. Johnson was

---

[45] *Boswell's Journal of a Tour to the Hebrides*, p. 204.

[46] As part of a general attack upon assumptions that Johnson was solely Tory, Donald J. Greene has claimed that Boswell's account of his Jacobite tendencies is exaggerated. See *The Politics of Samuel Johnson*, pp. 231, 41–4. Weighing the evidence of independent accounts and of Johnson's own words, however, H. H. Erskine-Hill has largely vindicated Boswell's version. Erskine-Hill restores Jacobite sympathy to the centre of Johnson's concerns, showing in the process how the literary authority of his political poetry springs not from generality but from a comprehensive assimilation of present discontents to famous examples from the past. See 'The Political Character of Samuel Johnson', in Isobel Grundy (ed.), *Samuel Johnson. New Critical Essays*, pp. 107–36 and 'The Political Character of Samuel Johnson: *The Lives of the Poets* and a Further Report on *The Vanity of Human Wishes*', in Eveline Cruickshanks and Jeremy Black (eds.), *The Jacobite Challenge* (Edinburgh, 1988), pp. 161–76. See also Clark, *Samuel Johnson*, pp. 141–89. On Johnson's interpretation of Highland culture as a critique of Lowland Scots see Karen O'Brien, 'Johnson's View of the Scottish Enlightenment in *A Journey to the Western Islands of Scotland*', *The Age of Johnson*, 4 (1991), 59–82.

divided over Scotland and its ancient culture in a way which reveals divisions in his own authority. One part of him remained drawn to the Highland oral culture and the forms of social expression and power it produced:

Sir, let me tell you, that to be a Scotch landlord, where you have a number of families dependent upon you, and attached to you, is, perhaps, as high a situation as humanity can arrive at. A merchant upon the 'Change of London, with a hundred thousand pounds, is nothing: an English Duke, with an immense fortune, is nothing: he has no tenants who consider themselves as under his patriarchal care, and who will follow him to the field upon any emergency.

(Boswell, vol. i, p. 409)

Johnson's idealization of the feudal relation, and his accompanying sympathy for clan loyalty to Bonnie Prince Charlie, exemplify his essential interests in patriarchal society based upon legitimate descent and on the authority born of personal acquaintance. Familial and familiar fuse past and present, join institutionalized with personal power in a Tory ideal of a pre-commercial, pre-fiscal society. As a society based on personal contact it would require neither the formulation of written law nor the profession of author. Johnson yearned for it even as he recognized that its time had passed and that its very nature left it dangerously subject to loss.

If that recognition ensured that Johnson finally supported the political, social and personal authority that is based on codified law it also admitted the loss of a Tory Eden of clan (rather than class) relations, in which the chief is known and respected by birth and character as a benevolent patriarch, whose spoken word is law. Johnson was pleased to fancy himself in the position of clan chief, dominating his clan as he dominated his friends in conversation, but with the advantage that such dominance would stem not only from personal assertiveness (a trait which he sometimes regretted) but from birth too. Fancifully, Johnson saw the chief as an epitome of himself in an ideal rôle, possessing a mastery that is at once oral, social and political and in which personal and inherited authority fuse. The possessor of such authority would be exempt from the need to have such legitimacy conferred upon him by written degrees from established institutions – whether Dublin or Oxford Universities.

Johnson left the ideal as an enjoyable fancy because he knew that his own civilization and his place in it were based on writing, and on the division of labour that authorship symbolizes. It was as Johnson the published lexicographer and biographer, not Johnson the talker (however powerful that talk) that he had power to direct the moral and political beliefs of his fellow men and women. If this left him, in comparison with the clan chief, limited in power and rôle and indirect in effect, it at least sustained his words against the depredations of time and social disruption. His political support of King George, despite his Jacobite sympathies, was based on the understanding that in eighteenth-century England (and Scotland too after 1745) personal and political authority had to be disseminated beyond the range of speech. In the empirical rather than ideal world a 'merchant upon the 'Change' and a 'Duke, with an immense fortune' were the men of power, and their power depended on their separation from their goods and tenants. The merchant had become a stockbroker, a financial speculator, the duke an improving landlord who efficiently extracted (often by the intermediary of a steward) rents from tenants of whom he knew little. Division of classes and of labour was seen to allow the acquisition of a particular and limited form of power (in this case money) concentrated in the hands of a specialist. In each case 'patriarchal care' was lost, but a more complex and refined civilization found. Johnson, as an author, both participated in and benefited from this growing division of power from its source: by succeeding as a professional writer his word was heard beyond the limited scope of his voice. Hence the booksellers were to him valuable intermediaries, as the merchant or broker was to the farmer, even though, like all producers, he sometimes resented their particular actions and often regretted the division of producer and consumer which they epitomized.

Accepting the division of author from readership, lord from tenant, king from subjects Johnson was forced to embrace a subordination which, although it originated in feudal relationships, no longer emerged from an extant system of paternalism and respect. With characteristic honesty he accepted, to a degree which worried Boswell, that the maintenance of social subordination beyond the decline of paternalism would require the sacrifice of political and even personal liberty. He accepted too, that there was a possible contradiction between subordination and the independence he so powerfully asserted:

Why, Sir, I reconcile my principles very well, because mankind are happier in a state of inequality and subordination. Were they to be in this pretty state of equality, they would soon degenerate into brutes; – they would become Monboddo's nation; – their tails would grow. Sir, all would be losers, were all to work for all: – they would have no intellectual improvement. All intellectual improvement arises from leisure; all leisure arises from one working for another.

(Boswell, vol. ii, p. 219)[47]

Here independence and liberty are quietly replaced by intellectual improvement and leisure. Modifying Adam Smith's economic principles by claiming that leisure arises from labour for another, Johnson's answer nevertheless sidesteps rather than reconciles the contradiction. Elsewhere he not only resented working for another, but found in leisure not an opportunity for

---

[47]   James Burnet, Lord Monboddo had written that man and the higher apes belonged to the same species. Like Rousseau, he believed in the superiority of a simple life close to nature. See *Of the Origin and Progress of Language*, 6 vols. (Edinburgh, 1773–92 (facsimile rpt. Menston, 1967)).

intellectual improvement or disinterested and varied contemplation, but a temptation to indolence. Faced with the tensions inherent in his own unusual position of self-made literary independence, Johnson needed to define himself against a society in which such tensions were properly regulated. If he could not accept subordination for himself, he was left in a state of independent authority that was apparently outside normal social orders. It was, consequently, unique, but also lonely and vulnerable. By insisting on subordination for society at large Johnson increased his own unusual authority as an exception to the rule. And he simultaneously defended it against others who, in a society of free movement, might claim similar positions to his own. He was even able to turn his admission of inconsistency to his own advantage, claiming the merit of being able to hold disinterested views, above his own circumstances: 'I have great merit in being zealous for subordination and the honours of birth; for I can hardly tell who was my grandfather' (Boswell, vol. II, p. 261). This, of course, only claims greater power for Johnson himself: it humorously accepts that in freely deciding to promote subordination and heredity he shows his independence.

Johnson's wit allows him independent mastery in the guise of deference to authority. In fact, though, the joke also redefines subordination, for whilst ostensibly accepting the authority of birth, it wittily triumphs over those who accuse him of inconsistency. The doubters become subordinate to Johnson's verbal mastery, and to his personal authority, just as Lord Chesterfield did in the affair of the Dictionary. Beneath the humour, however, there were persistent anxieties. One of these was evident in his need for a society whose stable hierarchy allowed him to dominate it by his verbal mastery. He suspected the Methodists, for instance, because their reliance on the inner light allowed no criticism of their authorities for action and doctrine: 'When a person professes to be governed by a written ascertained law, I can then know where to find him' (Boswell, vol. II, p. 126). As was the case with his demand for the manuscripts of Ossian, it seems that Johnson insisted upon a society governed by written law because it was in such a society that his critical adjudication could fix his own and others' positions: Johnson as self-appointed and independent law lord. The challenge presented by the Methodists was not just a threat to the Bible then, but one to Johnson's own authority, based as it was on his exclusive mastery of the written word. And since this authority was freely offered in the service of the state, in the form of Church and King, it was also a challenge, in Johnson's eyes at least, to the mastery of religious and constitutional meaning on which the state depended. If the inner light eluded textual authority in this way, it represented a dangerous flux – despite the fact that Wesley strove with much success to ensure that the structure of his sect and the activities of its followers did not disturb social subordination.

It is in the process of mastery of and by writing that Johnson's redefinition of authority lies. Whenever an event (his own speech, his wife's death, the politics of a battlefield, the power of Shakespeare) threatens to exceed and disturb the self's limits with ungovernable power and wildness Johnson steps in to reassert the proper governing limits of authority, even at the risk of considerable strain to his prose, necessitating rhetorical sleights of hand. Such stepping-in is not simply a reassertion of traditional and legitimate authority (including the authority of writing), it is also (and often subversively) an assertion of Johnson's independent power to govern himself and others through writing. It is an assumption of syntactical control which is also a declaration of social power even to the point of challenging the legitimacy in whose name it is carried out. It is an elevation of the self as author which makes that self in its declaration of law as powerful as the event, in its original lawlessness, had been. In this process Johnson presages Wordsworth, whose encounters with wild nature, so different in appearance, show similar transfers of power. He also anticipates Coleridge, who envied and imitated (though with different results) Johnson's assumption of critical power through a discourse which is also a reassertion of the self.

But it is to the picturesque theorists and tourists I now turn in order to investigate their negotiation of the discrepancy between the aesthetic rules they wished to define and the social order they hoped to uphold. To many contemporaries picturesque landscapes, by including variety, wildness and disorder rather than removing them from the gentleman's prospect-view, threatened established aesthetic and political authority. Like Johnson, the picturesque writers wished to uphold the power of the landed gentleman – indeed, like Cowper they wished to recall him to his traditional paternalist rôle. But as their own aesthetic came to be linked with natural liberty and their rhetoric with the voices of the rural poor they seemed to challenge all subordination. For Gilpin, as for Johnson, it was in his confrontation with an older rural culture, on tour in the Lake District and Scotland, that his own rhetorical self-assertion became associated with local speech. And that speech resisted codification by the traditional rules of taste and eluded subordination to the social and political judgements of the gentlemanly classes.

3

Unreliable authorities? Squires, tourists and the picturesque

Thomson, in poetry, and Johnson, in criticism, had in related ways used landscape-description to recognize and also to control threatening disorder. When aesthetic, moral or political beliefs based on the legitimacy of property were challenged, these writers temporarily restored order by figuring the challenging force – women, another writer, an oral rural culture, an exploited social class – as objects in a scene constructed and organized, in the names of providential order, by their writing. This strategy both reaffirmed the power of written over oral authority and aligned it with the power of property holders. The writer owned his scene just as the landowner (for whom he was, in practice, often writing) owned his estate. And since Thomson's poetic scenes not only contained an apparently natural disorder but sought to reflect in verse the landscaped estates of the nobility, they seemed to confirm the legitimacy of the landowners' taste. The possession of taste for a cultivated order designed into and then read out of the owned landscape came to be a sign of one's legitimacy as a gentleman landowner. This taste was threatened in practice by its politicization in response to threats to its independence and assumed legitimacy from above and below, from ministry and peasantry.

Johnson had both supported legitimacy in the aesthetic and political realms and attacked it. He had sought to outdo his patrons by relying upon himself and aligning his voice with those of the poor, the dispossessed and the unregarded. The picturesque, the subject of analysis in this chapter, contained similar conflicts of authority. These arose as the picturesque writers took a theory of landscape on a tour of the rural Britain of the late eighteenth century. And, I shall suggest, they were conflicts which disturbed those writers' belief that they, as arbiters of taste and observers of nature, possessed a gentlemanly authority properly empowered to set, in the guise of aesthetic 'laws', social and political rules.[1] The picturesque was put forward and subsequently discussed in detail in the writings of William Gilpin, Uvedale Price, Richard Payne Knight and Humphry Repton. It was defined in Gilpin's *Essays on Picturesque Beauty* as a category of rural landscape characterized by variety, charm and wildness. Gilpin implied that such

---

[1] For a general discussion of these beliefs and their results see Tom Williamson and Liz Bellamy, *Property and Landscape: A Social History of Land Ownership and the English Countryside* (London, 1987).

landscape was aesthetically valuable in so far as it presented visual scenes which resembled, in their harmony of rustic elements, the pictures of Claude, Nicolas Poussin and, especially, Salvator Rosa. Gilpin included sketches in the tour narratives he published of his journeys to the wilder rural fringes of Britain. He gave readers advice as to where the best view could be taken, presenting the British landscape as a series of scenes to be consumed as staged prospects, essentially static and distant, pre-judged by the words of the guidebook and by the pictorial tradition which they were valued for resembling. Taste, in Gilpin's tour narratives and those of the many tour guides published in the 1780s and 1790s, came to be acquired through a voyeuristic consumption of landscape as a series of unrelated views. These views were made newly accessible to the middle classes since they could be obtained at relatively little expense: the reader/tourist neither had to own the landscape in which he saw aesthetic values reside nor did he have to tour Europe to absorb the scenery and artistic culture of classical and Renaissance Italy. When access to Europe became difficult and dangerous after Britain went to war with revolutionary France in 1793, the tour of Wales, Scotland or the Lake District became highly fashionable and the term 'picturesque' of general, although ill-defined, currency.[2] The picturesque became a popular mode of consumption, a leisure activity in which the middle classes were able, by enjoying their native land as a series of rustic scenes at little financial or social cost, to show that they too could afford and enjoy the disinterested view which had been a criterion for the exercise of cultural and political power by the landed interest. In this respect the picturesque was (as it remains) an aesthetic for the increasingly affluent town and city dwellers. By the end of the Napoleonic wars, both Humphry Repton and Wordsworth were complaining about the influx of newly moneyed townspeople into the rural areas, the traditional social and physical pattern of which they remembered and idealized.

That the tour narrative should have helped to produce a commercialization of rural society by an urban middle class is ironic, since the picturesque had first been designed as a response from the rural gentry to what they saw as the increasingly prevalent tendency of landowners to abandon their paternalist duties in favour of a newly commercial ethos in the organization of their estates. Uvedale Price and Richard Payne Knight were both gentleman landowners in Herefordshire. Price had inherited an estate of at least 3,844 acres at Foxley; Knight, from a family of ironmasters who had bought land earlier in the century, inherited a large estate at nearby Downton. Both men were assiduous landscape gardeners and estate managers; their version of the picturesque, whilst it acknowledged Gilpin's, was an aesthetic based on the continued possession of land and on the power

[2] On the picturesque as a vernacular tradition see David Watkin, *The English Vision: The Picturesque in Architecture, Landscape and Garden Design* (London, 1982).

that the landed gentry exercised in local society and the nation at large. For Price and Knight the landscape gardens produced for wealthy landowners by Lancelot 'Capability' Brown were the signs of an abdication of responsibility by the landed interest on whom political stability had, since 1688, depended. Smoothing and levelling grounds, removing roads, tilled fields and labourers' cottages from the view of the country house, Brown produced a manicured green desert, leaving the gentleman isolated from the historical patterns of agriculture and settlement in the locality of which he was squire. The resultant scenic uniformity was aesthetically barren and socially dangerous: the gentleman achieved privacy but was no longer a visible authority in rural society. He was secluded in his landscape or often absent in London or Bath. At the same time, the improved garden was often financed by the more efficient management of the farmed estate. Smallholders and labourers would often be deprived of land by enclosure or consolidation. This process brought increased profit for the landowner at the cost of destroying his paternal power over the local inhabitants, who were no longer physically or emotionally 'attached' to his land. And so for Price and Knight, Brown's landscapes were emblematic of the threat of rebellion by the newly landless. And they were also symbolic of the abdication by the gentry from the paternalist rôle which had helped give Britain political stability by ensuring that landowners could claim in parliament to represent the interests of the people, balancing those of the Court and City. As Foxite Whigs, Price and Knight viewed the liberty of the people as dependent upon their representation by men of property. As theorists of the picturesque, they sought to correct the taste of such men to ensure that they would again find aesthetic value in a rural estate visibly produced by the efforts, made over many generations, of the people they represented. These people were working under the constraints of the local natural conditions and under the supervision of the landowner and his ancestors.

Price's and Knight's picturesque was not without tensions. They nostalgically depicted the landed gentry in the manner of the Country Whigs with whom Thomson and Cowper had been associated but were nevertheless forced, in the tense political period of the 1790s, to defend themselves against the charge of revolutionary Jacobinism. So too was their friend, the leader of opposition to Pitt's ministry, Charles James Fox. Faced too with increasingly articulate self-representation by the rural labourers and farmers whom they claimed to represent, they could not easily offer the picturesque as a gentlemanly taste the possession of which naturally indicated landowners' fitness to speak for rural society in parliament. As the popularity of Paine's *Rights of Man* and of Cobbett's rural radicalism showed, the power of the landed interest was contested from below as well as divided from within. And the picturesque was further complicated by the attempt to make an increasingly moralistic and political idealization of traditional rustic landscape conform to patterns discerned in pictures. This attempt, criticized as impractical and restricting by Repton, led to further tension as Price tried to present the artist/patron relationship as a prerequisite for the production of tasteful landscape. Yet this relationship was itself prone to conflict and was threatened by the picturesque tour which appealed not only to patrons but also to a book-buying public of potential tourists.

I shall present the picturesque in this chapter as a discourse divided between tour narratives and the arguments of gentleman landowners, as one divided too over the changing politics of rural society and the nation at large. I shall argue that it reveals the gradually dying voice of eighteenth-century Country arguments about the constitution, as the landed gentry found other groups – middle-class town dwellers, professional men – claiming a greater reliability of disinterested judgement than that which a distant view of one's estate conferred on the squire. Placed on the defensive, the gentlemen theorists found themselves locked in dispute with each other and with a wider readership over the political implications of the picturesque. I begin with Uvedale Price, moving on to investigate the landscape of liberty idealized by Richard Payne Knight, before examining the career of Humphry Repton and his arguments with both theorists. I shall conclude the chapter with an extended discussion of William Gilpin's tours of the Lake District and Scotland. I shall present these as narratives containing social and moral anxieties about their reader-ship and about rural labourers. These anxieties make them indeterminate and self-conflicting texts, texts symptomatic of the dilemmas Wordsworth was to try to resolve as he sought to discover in the English landscape a national order that would not exclude the experience of the rural poor.

Price and the economics of the landscape

Stability of power had depended in Johnson's writings on its transmission through heritable property. The theory of Uvedale Price was beset by instabilities which occurred as he tried, and failed, to compensate through aesthetic theory for the loss of order that he feared gentlemen landowners and the rural society they dominated would suffer. Commerce, Price argued, threatened order as it rendered the landscape more obviously economically organized and more variously economically divided.

Edmund Burke, author of *A Philosophical Enquiry into the Origin of our Ideas of the Sublime and Beautiful* and supporter of landed property, had himself bought a country estate at Beaconsfield. As described by his friend Shackleton in 1780, it was a place in which the sublime and beautiful could be put into practice:

It is a most beautiful place, on a very large scale, the house, furniture, ornaments, conveniences, all in grand style – six hundred acres of land, woods, pleasure grounds,

gardens, Green-house &c. – for my part I stand astonished at the man and at his
place of abode – a striking parallel may be drawn between them – they are sublime
and beautiful indeed.[3]   (*B Corr*, vol. iv, p. 240n6)

When, a decade later, Uvedale Price wished to reform the theory and
practice of landscape gardening, it was to the aesthetics of Burke that he
looked. Acknowledging debts to Burke's *Enquiry*, he published works setting
out principles on which the new taste for the ruined, the unfinished and the
carelessly natural could be based. In Price's *Essays on the Picturesque* (1794–8),
nature was judged by the laws of pictorial composition as revealed in the
landscape paintings of Claude, Nicolas Poussin and Salvator Rosa.[4] The
formality of classical architecture and the decorousness of landscape gardens,
with their gravelled walks and carefully arranged vistas, were to be replaced
by an ideal of negligent yet harmonious wildness:

> there is one improvement which I am afraid almost all who had not been used to look
> at objects with a painter's eye would adopt, and which alone would entirely destroy
> its character; that is smoothing and levelling the ground. The moment this
> mechanical common-place operation, by which Mr. Brown and his followers have
> gained so much credit, is begun, adieu to all that the painter admires – to all
> intricacies, to all the beautiful varieties of form, tint, and light and shade; every deep
> recess – every bold projection – the fantastic roots of trees – the winding paths of
> sheep – all must go; in a few hours, the rash hand of false taste completely demolishes,
> what time only, and a thousand lucky accidents can mature, so as to make it become
> the admiration and study of a Ruysdal or a Gainsborough; and reduces it to such a
> thing as an Oilman in Thames-street may at any time contract for by the yard at
> Islington or Mile-End.   (Price, vol. i, pp. 31–2)

Price's attack on Capability Brown ventured to criticize the most popular
landscape-gardener for the very 'smoothing and levelling' that had made him
sought after by the gentry and nobility. They had paid Brown to re-order
their property by the dictates of propriety, to turn their fields from farmland
and 'wildness' into a park which demonstrated its owner's order, restraint
and harmony (an order supposed to be implicit in the nature he owned,
rather than imposed on it). It was an attack with which Burke may have
agreed, for when Price sent him a complimentary copy of the *Essays* he not

---

[3] On eighteenth-century applications of the sublime and the beautiful to landscape gardens see
   James A. W. Heffernan, *The Re-Creation of Landscape* (Hanover and London, 1984), pp. 1–53. On
   Burke at Beaconsfield, founding and maintaining a school for boys to compensate for the death of
   his own son, to whom the estate would have been left in a personal enactment of the patrilineal
   inheritance Burke supported in politics, see Conor Cruise O'Brien, *The Great Melody* (London,
   1992), pp. 576–7.

[4] The *Essay* first appeared in 1794. An edition incorporating additions, from which my quotations
   are taken, was published in 1810. On the picturesque in the period see Christopher Hussey, *The
   Picturesque. Studies in a Point of View* (London and New York, 1927); Malcolm Andrews, *The Search for
   the Picturesque: Landscape Aesthetics and Tourism in Britain 1760–1800* (Aldershot, 1989) and Sidney K.
   Robinson, *Inquiry into the Picturesque* (Chicago and London, 1991). On poetry and landscape
   gardening see John Dixon Hunt, *The Figure in the Landscape* (Baltimore, 1976).

only sympathized in his letter of acknowledgement, but assured Price that 'we do not in the main differ very essentially' over the sublime and beautiful (*B Corr*, vol. VII, pp. 547–8).

Price and Burke differed, but not very essentially, over the politics of landscape improvement. In his *Reflections on the Revolution in France* (1790) Burke had attacked Dr Richard Price for welcoming the French Revolution and for hoping that a reform would bring about in Britain the extension of liberty that was promised in France. Burke's response portrayed Price as a self-deluding theorist, one whose view of events was too distant for a proper understanding of the local and historical structures through which reform had to be effected if it was to be achieved without 'plots, massacres, assassinations'. Using the metaphor of the prospect-view, Burke attacked Price's 'bird-eye landscape of a promised land', his distant view from which the revolutionary chaos seemed 'moral, happy, flourishing' (*BWS*, vol. VIII, p. 115). Burke supported continued war with France in the mid-1790s, whereas Uvedale Price, a friend of Charles James Fox, felt that it was likely to drive the French to further Jacobinical excesses. Nevertheless, he formed a similar view of the distant prospect afforded by the landscape improvements of Capability Brown. For Uvedale Price, distant prospects from a commanding vantage point too easily became views of despotic authority, in which the landowner surveyed a park stripped bare of variety, history or social activity. Serving 'the vacancy of solitary grandeur and power' (Price, vol. II, p. 344)[5] such landscapes were militaristic: Brown's trademark planting of trees in clumps made them seem 'drilled for the purposes of formal parade' (Price, vol. I, p. 246). Against such vacant landscapes, Price emphasized, as had Burke, the importance of local traditions and familiar institutions as means by which the power inherited by landowners could be made visible as a paternal authority. Cottages should be 'protected, sometimes supported' by the landowner's trees rather than exposed or demolished by 'improvements' of Brown's kind which were likely to create resentment and rebelliousness amongst the cottagers (Price, vol. II, p. 351).

For Price distant prospects unbalanced by close views represented a despotism which might be exercised by revolutionary theorists or by the landed interest if either forgot the need to balance, within a traditional power structure guaranteed by the 1688 constitution, the needs of Court and Country, monarchy, nobility, gentry and people. Brown's levelling of estates was 'a principle that, when made general and brought into action by any determined improver either of grounds or governments, occasions such mischiefs as time slowly, if ever, repairs' (Price, vol. I, p. 374). Price advocated instead a landscape that connected high and low, distance and foreground, one that symbolized what it was produced by – the landowner's disinterested

---

[5]   Cf. *Thoughts on the Defence of Property* (Hereford, 1797), p.19.

regard for all the elements of the countryside under his ownership and authority. This was a reactionary idealization of a local rural paternalism that some large landowners in practice left to their stewards whilst they resided in London or Bath. It was also avoided – at least when it came to the increasingly onerous task of being a magistrate – by many of the smaller squires (although not by Price himself).[6] Price's idealization was unlikely to stem the fashions in landscape-gardening or the social and political changes to which they were related.

An extension rather than a refutation of Burke, Price's criticism of fashionable improvements did not challenge all the cultural illusions and social exclusions created by contemporary taste. In fact he sought to subjugate landscape to rules which idealized, if they did not exclude, the facts of production and the labourers who produced crops and husbanded livestock. He presented them as part of a hierarchy apparently natural so long as it was governed by a paternalist squire who accepted his traditional rôle.[7] This hierarchy and the landscape which it shaped had to seem so old and traditional as to be unplanned by a single hand – 'what time only, and a thousand lucky accidents can mature'. Price's ideal landscape was that of Burke's idealized British constitution – a distribution of power produced so slowly and incorporating such a variety of historical forms and local conditions that it seemed an expression of nature, rooted like an English oak tree in the land in which it still grew. Only then would it be worthy of the attention of a great painter, a Gainsborough or Ruysdael, an artist painting scenes the variety of which was a tribute to the squire's perpetuation of a traditional rural order inherited with his estate. Brown, by contrast, was figured as a commercial tradesman who imposed his own and his patron's desire to see only the power of their new wealth to command the rural world they governed. In the passage quoted above (p. 120) Price uses the metaphor of landscape painting to show that Capability Brown's gardening reduces the estate 'to such a thing as an Oilman in Thames-street may at any time contract for by the yard at Islington or Mile-End'. There is snobbery in this remark, directed at Brown's humble origins as a servant. There is also a gentleman-squire's distaste for the bridging of social barriers allowed by the interdependence of economic relations. It is not just that Brown is from the lower classes and like one of the artisans who supplied materials by contract from the less than refined areas of Islington or Mile-End. Nor is it solely that

---

[6]   Details are given in John Rule, *Albion's People: English Society 1714–1815* (London and New York, 1992), pp. 40–1.

[7]   For discussion of the removal of the facts of labour from the landscape, see Raymond Williams, *The Country and the City* (London, 1973), John Barrell, *The Dark Side of the Landscape* (Cambridge, 1980) and Roger Sales, *English Literature in History 1780–1830: Pastoral and Politics* (London, 1983). And see also Anne Janowitz (*England's Ruins: Poetic Purpose and the National Landscape* (Oxford, 1990), p. 57) for whom 'the picturesque, rather than framing the natural in the image of a painting, masks the historical, producing it *as* natural'.

employing Brown brings the manners of the city and the East End to the country. It is also that employing him turns the squire into a man of commerce, a man whose estate is produced by piece-work mass productions 'by the yard'. Brown and professional landscapers were of insufficiently wide or disinterested views: lacking the taste, local knowledge and education of gentlemen and motivated by profit, they produced landscapes which were no longer expressions of the independence conferred by centuries of inheritance. The landowner could, then, no longer expect his landed power to be rewarded by the attention of a master of painting: 'the admiration and study of a Ruysdal or Gainsborough'. Brown, by contrast, not only mass-produced landscapes, working on several at once, but contracted out the actual work rather than using his own labourers and plant nurseries. Employing him, the landowner was no longer a patron of an artist, but merely the first employer in a chain in which labour was divided, the artefact mass-produced and Brown almost a middleman. Instead, Price advocated that landscaping should be effected by 'men of liberal education, who passed much of their time at their own country seats' (Price, vol. III, p. 120). This was a forlorn hope, save in his own and Knight's case, and the contrast between employing a professional landscaper and patronizing an artist was itself fraught with difficulty.

Gainsborough was a friend of Price's family; he visited Foxley, painted its trees and particularly enjoyed depicting the cottages left amongst the woods. Yet this relationship should not obscure the more general truth that Ruysdael and Gainsborough were themselves in an economic relation to the landowners they painted for. They accepted commissions not as independent equals or masters conferring the privilege of their 'admiration and study', but as paid workmen. In Gainsborough's case his resentment of this position led him to destroy several paintings before patrons' eyes when he felt insulted by condescending treatment. It is also true that when painting portraits rather than rustic scenes Gainsborough sometimes employed a drapery painter to work on a picture as the most fashionable contemporary portraitist, Reynolds, often did. Late eighteenth-century practice, then, does not bear out Price's discussion, in which the intimacy of patronizing a single painter, and the individuality of the painting produced, is to be contrasted with the 'coarser' and less dominant relationship of employing a large number of workmen, paid according to quantity not unique quality, who will produce a landscape looking very like Brown's other landscapes. Humphry Repton, himself a professional gardener, complained that it was often his patrons who insisted on his producing a fashionable landscape that mimicked the features of the typical Brownian park and disregarded local features. And he noted, too, that gentlemen patrons were quite capable of withholding payment for work done: the artist/patron relationship seen from the artist's side was not necessarily free from the tyranny of commercial values which characterized that of employer and tradesman.

Price's picturesque was, in fact, an attempt to renew through aesthetics an ideology that was rapidly giving way in the changing social and economic relations of late eighteenth-century England. He tried to persuade landowners to shape their estates (and their image of themselves) on lines which appeared new but were in fact a re-expression of landed independence and personal patronage. Thus, for example, he perpetuated Pope's and Johnson's treatment of natural beauty as an attractive female clothed in a dress which half-concealed, half-revealed her charms to the male landowner:

> Many persons, who take little concern in the intricacy of oaks, beeches, and thorns, may feel the effects of partial concealment in more interesting objects, and may have experienced how differently the passions are moved by an open licentious display of beauties, and by the unguarded disorder which sometimes escapes the care of modesty, and which coquetry so successfully imitates.   (Price, vol. I, p. 22)

The picturesque was 'the coquetry of nature; it makes beauty more amusing, more varied, more playful' (Price, vol. I, p. 89). In making his estate into a picturesque landscape garden, the landowner was supplementing Burke's aesthetic, mollifying the sublime by 'loosening those iron bonds, with which astonishment chains up the faculties', and varying the beautiful by a partial concealment that always left something to be desired. As Vivien Jones has argued, the picturesque incorporates an implicit sexual politics in which the landowner 'must disrupt domesticity: for desire and pleasure, "the otherness of the land" ... must be perpetuated, if only in fantasy'.[8] For Price the variety and 'intricacy' of the scene produces a playfully exciting blend of the known scene with an alluring otherness, partially concealed in the familiar dress of modesty. Whilst, as the sexual metaphors suggest, the onlooker is still in a position of male cultural power as the owner of the scene, he is constantly tempted by its partial escape from 'the care of modesty', by its part-concealment, part-uncovering of its charms to the gaze. Here mastery is re-figured as a voyeuristic fantasy in which, whilst ultimately aware of his control of the scene he owns, the landlord fantasizes its tendency to escape the bounds of propriety as a sexual temptation. The scene is, to pursue his metaphor, a wife. Its natural intricacy is, like her 'unguarded disorder', a spontaneous tendency to escape the restrictions of propriety which yet never overturns them by an 'open licentious display'. Desire remains unconsummated and the viewer fascinated, yet since he, like Rousseau in *La Nouvelle Heloise*, owns the scene (the wife) he is not in thrall to its/her seductive charms. Moreover, he knows how to reproduce the exciting natural disorder

---

[8] Jones, '"The Coquetry of Nature": Politics and the Picturesque in Women's Fiction', in Stephen Copley and Peter Garside (eds.), *The Politics of the Picturesque* (Cambridge, 1994), pp. 120–44 (p.122). Jones develops a point first made by Martin Price in stressing the importance in the picturesque of playfulness. See Price's 'The Picturesque Moment' in F. W. Hilles and H. Bloom (eds.), *From Sensibility to Romanticism* (New York and Oxford, 1965), pp. 259–92 (pp. 270–1) and *To the Palace of Wisdom* (Carbondale, Ill., 1964), p. 364.

of his possession: if 'coquetry so successfully imitates' the blend of modesty and allure then his landscape gardening is 'the coquetry of nature'. Gardening becomes the artful imitation by feminine wiles of nature's female tendency to excite the male by offering glimpses of herself that cannot be immediately commanded (as could a prospect of Capability Brown's) by his gaze. And so, for Price, the gardener encourages nature to play the coquette, to imitate artfully the sexually appealing disorder she tends spontaneously to produce. And the cottagers who lived in his garden themselves became part of this appealingly natural but unthreatening disorder, their cottages artfully encouraged by Price's careful planting of trees to half-appear, half-disappear to the gaze, to emerge and retreat as traditional parts of nature's variety whilst ultimately remaining under his ownership, as they did under his ancestors'.

Price's picturesque was an attempt, in the guise of an extension of the rules of polite taste, to root into the patterns of land ownership and gentlemanly manners an aesthetic that both confirmed the squire in his power and ensured him perpetual pleasure in the objects subordinated to him, a pleasure without the danger of thraldom involved in the sublime. This attempt could only work by disguising economic change, even when it had benefited the landowners, as part of a beautiful, historic and natural scene to be preserved. Improving landowners had increased their wealth and power by enclosing common land. They charged higher rents to tenants to encourage greater production, at the cost of reducing those unable to pay to unbonded wage-labourers, often no longer with commons on which to graze their own livestock. Such actions were welcomed by the improving farmer John Billingsley of Ashwick Grove, for whom the traditional rights of grazing on common land allowed wage-labourers a dangerous independence:

The possession of a cow or two, with a hog, and a few geese, naturally exalts the peasant, in his own conception, above his brethren in the same rank of society. It inspires some degree of confidence in a property inadequate to his support. In sauntering after his cattle, he acquires a habit of indolence. Quarter, half, and occasionally whole days, are imperceptibly lost. Day labour becomes disgusting; the aversion increases by indulgence; and at length the sale of a half-fed calf, or hog, furnishes the means of adding intemperance to idleness.[9]

Price urged paternalist squires to check the rapacious self-interest of such improving farmers and opposed this open advocacy of economic domination. He showed the landscape produced by an earlier period of improvement – sheep-farming fields, the creation of which had enriched landowners in the sixteenth century – as part of an unchanging aesthetic scene *threatened* not produced by economic change: 'the fantastic roots of trees – the winding

---

[9]   John Billingsley, 'Uselessness of Commons to the Poor', in *Annals of Agriculture*, 31 (1798), p. 31. Quoted in Pamela Horn, *The Rural World 1780–1850* (London, 1980), pp. 52–3.

paths of sheep – all must go; in a few hours, the rash hand of false taste completely demolishes what time only, and a thousand lucky accidents can mature'. The irony of this is that Brown's 'false taste' was itself employed by landowners to remove the appearance of economic production from their land. Often they were able to afford the non-arable park that Brown created because their income came not only from the cattle and sheep that grazed in it but from other remoter sources – colonies in India and plantations in the West Indies, banking, coal mines and iron works, the profits of war and politics.[10] Price objected to Brown and to the shift of landowners from a locally based agriculture: like Cowper he idealized the farming squire and worried that the nobility were becoming absentees, speculators and nabobs. And yet despite his attack on Brown his taste was in one respect similar to that he regarded as 'false'. He too idealized a less obviously economically organized (because older and more familiar) landscape. In this ideal landscape labourers are not to be excluded but are to appear as subordinate elements in a scene whose 'natural' variety bespeaks the length of years that it has been worked and shaped by the tenants of the landowner and his forefathers. In Price's ideal estate the labourers are to appear as decorative images of bucolic roughness and dependence on the squire's paternal care. The improved landscape would, Price argued, ensure that 'the separation of the different ranks and their gradations', although 'like those of visible objects ... known and ascertained', 'is happily disguised'.[11] The 'connection' of large and small, high and low, near and far in the viewed scene was analogous to and even helped to perpetuate the connection between squire and tenant, preventing the known difference in rank and property turning into a mutually distrustful separation. Price, in the manner of Bishop Butler's conservative Christian apologetics, saw the connectedness of nature as evidence of God's creative power and as support for the principle of attachment in human society. It was, for Butler, 'a natural principle of attraction in man towards man ... having trod the same tract of land' that reflected 'this most astonishing connection' of 'the course of nature'. For Butler this natural connectedness was too complex and interdependent to be seen whole by any one individual. The constitution, itself a complex production of generations past, was likewise too interconnected to be understood – or replaced – by any one political improver.[12] Improvement would come by gradual and small changes rather than universal schemes.

Butler influenced Burke's conservative view of change; it is not surprising therefore to see Price, his picturesque avowedly a supplement to Burke's

---

[10] On income from grazing in the landscape park see Tom Williamson, 'The Landscape Park: Economics, Art and Ideology', *Journal of Garden History*, 13 (1993), 49–55.

[11] Price, *A Letter to H. Repton, Esq.* (London, 1795), p. 160.

[12] Joseph Butler, quoted in Nigel Everett, *The Tory View of Landscape* (New Haven and London, 1994), pp. 15–17.

aesthetics, developing Butler's arguments. Price termed the 1688 settlement 'the steady, considered and connected arrangement of enlightened minds'.[13] He adhered to the principle of connection in his woodland management. In doing so he nevertheless suggested that what was for Butler a natural analogy between human society and the course of nature had, by the 1790s, to be artificially reproduced. In the improved estate Price re-ordered the scene to disguise what it might, if not carefully gardened, reveal – the increasing consciousness of separation rather than connection between men of property, their tenants and the landless. In face of this increasing consciousness, felt by landowners, farmers such as Billingsley and labourers too, Price's picturesque would reassert the rural traditionalism of the Whig landed gentry by rendering their rural traditionalism an aesthetic category arising from apparently natural scenes in which taste could take pleasure. He attempted thereby to provide reassurance that taste could operate over the whole social field and that aesthetic judgement had priority over economic analysis or political opinion as a source of generally shared public values. But that taste had to be defended against groups whose increasingly organized self-representations – as well as their social inferiority – made them too threatening to be aestheticized. Not in his theory of the picturesque, which remained ostensibly unpolitical, but in a pamphlet of 1797 written during alarm over a possible French invasion, Price called upon all local property holders, large and small, to make common cause against any of the unpropertied poor who should rebel: 'It is well known, that nothing so intimidates a mob, or so readily disperses them, as cavalry advancing upon them in a compact body.' He also idealized the inhabitants of the cottages whose dilapidation made them so agreeably picturesque: 'even the cottager, with a few acres which he has tilled and manured – who sees part of their produce in his small barn, and part flourishing on the ground – has at least as much attachment to his little spot, as the greatest lord to his immense domain'.[14] Here the social field which aesthetics can claim to cover has narrowed. The cottager is within it, because he is thought to be interested in the perpetuation of property, both economically and emotionally (as 'attachment' suggests). But the landless are not to be judged by the standards of taste – Price recommends a ferocious attack upon them. Johnson, similarly, supported war against the American revolutionaries who had threatened his conception of authority (whilst resembling in their political action his own rhetorical defiance of that conception) by claiming that the ownership of property did not demand loyalty and self-subordination to an established property hierarchy of which the King was head.

[13] On Price and 'connection' see Stephen Daniels, 'The Political Iconography of Woodland in Later Georgian England', in Denis Cosgrove and Stephen Daniels (eds.), *The Iconography of Landscape* (Cambridge, 1980), pp. 43–82 (pp. 61, 79). Price's remark on the Glorious Revolution, quoted by Daniels, can be found in the *Essays on the Picturesque*, 2 vols. (London, 1796–98), vol. II, pp. 175–6.

[14] *Thoughts on the Defence of Property*, pp. 9, 19–20.

Less penetrating about the conflicts in his own authority than Johnson, Price tried, in his aesthetic theory and in the practical landscape gardening he carried out on its principles, to perpetuate the ability of an apparently disinterested gentlemanly taste to see disorder as a source of pleasure. Natural wildness was to be indulged by but contained within the discourses by which landowners ordered their property. In a valuable study of Price's management of his land at Foxley, Stephen Daniels and Charles Watkins have investigated in detail the methods by which he sought to include and contain natural disorder in an estate in which he also sought to maintain the principle of social connection without sacrificing an improved profit from farming. One example of the activities to which these not necessarily reconcilable aims led him was his improvement of the local lanes. Here-fordshire's roads, notoriously bad and clogged with mud in the winter, proved a major obstacle to the growth of the cider industry. Price had the sunken lanes of his Foxley estate widened to improve transport, but himself remedied the work of a labourer who had made too neat and vertical a cut into the bank. By judicious use of the spade Price was able to retrieve its bucolic and aged appearance, to make it look 'as ancient as any year old bank did', as he told Sir George Beaumont, the friend and patron of Wordsworth.[15] He was also prepared to sacrifice some profit from agriculture in order to preserve a certain wildness. An agreement of 1813 between Price and his neighbour Thomas Andrew Knight establishes that Knight had permitted, 'at the request and for the accommodation' of Price, his lands overlooking Foxley to remain uncultivated and that for the purposes of exchange they would nevertheless be valued at the rate of cultivated land. Price paid to preserve the wild woodland around his estate. And he devoted years to arranging this woodland as 'fine pictures' and 'compositions', thinning and planting and intending by his personal supervision to reconcile profit and the picturesque: 'as I must have an eye to profit I leave a number of trees which do no other harm than that of hiding what is at last to be displayed'.[16]

Price sought a similar reconciliation in the organization of the farms and smallholdings on his estate. Although an opponent of the hiring of professional landscapers such as Brown and Repton, Price employed the land agent Nathaniel Kent in 1774 to survey and improve his property. Kent, later an advocate in print of the social and economic benefits of small farms, nevertheless produced at Foxley a reorganization which tended to consolidate holdings, increasing the number of larger farms, enlarging fields by the removal of hedgerows and reducing the number of small farms. The rented

---

[15] A letter of 24 July 1812, quoted in Stephen Daniels and Charles Watkins, 'Picturesque Landscaping and Estate Management: Uvedale Price and Nathaniel Kent at Foxley', in Copley and Garside, *The Politics of the Picturesque*, pp. 13–41 (p. 23).

[16] *Ibid.*, p. 33.

return on this improved land increased as a result from £2,031 to £2,461 per annum. This drive for increased agricultural efficiency also increased the amount of land under Price's direct control, diminishing that let to tenants. It was, however, combined with a respect for local circumstances. Kent noted of a smallholding at Stoke Lacy that it was large enough 'for an industrious man being just enough to enable him to keep one cow',[17] and whilst some cottagers had their holdings reduced, and most had their rents increased, it does not appear that they were deprived of land on which they could support themselves. Price's improvements kept his tenants under his control, but he attempted neither to remove them from his view nor from attachment to his land. The hills surrounding the estate, fringed by the woodland Price strove so hard to increase, created a physical and psychological enclosure within which his paternal economy could be sheltered, its blending of profit and the picturesque secured against threats from the outside world. Price, riding along one of his carefully planned hilltop paths, could view that world through the trees as a distant prospect contrasting with the varied scene within his own valley.

Sheltering the picturesque within the defences of a secluded and secure gentleman-squire's estate could not, in the face of the increasing commercialization and mass production of the wider rural world, provide a sustainable model of how profit and paternalism, aesthetics and economics could be reconciled in the nation as a whole. As the employment of Kent and, elsewhere, Brown indicated, these forces could not easily be harmonized within the estates of the gentry. At the same time the growing tendency of many of the landed interest to give up their paternal duties in the countryside for an absentee life threatened their ability to claim that their tastes were formed by a general view of rural society. And this in effect diminished their legitimacy as parliamentary representatives of that society. Price was worried by the tendency of landowners to allow tenant farmers to deprive cottagers of their smallholdings, all in the name of improvement. His picturesque excludes the landless but remains haunted by the spectres of the rebellious poor whom it has had to banish from its purview lest their poverty lead to a political disorder that threatens all property. Such a disorder would also threaten the ability of property holders to believe that the aesthetic order they design into their land is a reflection of natural order and thus that their shared tastes and judgements are legitimately rooted in reality. For Price, then, landscaping disorder into nature – in theory and practice – makes a gentleman-writer into only an uneasy master of the scene, a patron worried by mass production and a landowner threatened by revolution. As a result, although Price does not admit it within his picturesque writings, the realm of taste is drawn more narrowly: no longer can it pretend to speak for the whole cultural field but

[17] Quoted in *ibid.*, p. 26.

only for those with some property in land. Gentlemanly taste can no longer speak paternalistically for or extend its patronage over all men. The landless poor, relief of whom was once a duty men of property and taste agreed was naturally theirs, were now a threat.

Knight: the Jacobinism of taste?

Richard Payne Knight owned an estate at Downton in Herefordshire less than twenty miles from Price's. Bought earlier in the century by a family engaged in iron smelting, its resources were more closely linked to the development of industry. Knight himself, although he retained interests in ironmaking, had enough inherited wealth to become a gentleman of leisure, devoting himself to the study of antiquity and the definition of aesthetic law. Wordsworth and Coleridge read his *Analytical Inquiry into the Principles of Taste* (1805) and annotated it critically. By that time Knight had already acquired a reputation as a controversialist (he argued with both Price and Repton over the picturesque) and as a libertine and freethinker. A member of the notorious Dilettanti Society, Knight had published in 1786 *A Discourse on the Worship of Priapus*, a work which had scandalized reviewers by its illustrations of phallic symbols, by its treatment of the Christian Church as a cult influenced by such worship and by its application to ancient cults of theological terms normally reserved for the Trinity: 'the characteristic properties of animals and plants were not only regarded as representations, but as actual emanations of the Divine Power, consubstantial with his own essence'.[18]

Knight's writings on landscape might be expected, in view of his reputation and mode of life, to present the rural scene as a pleasure ground in which the man of taste finds a sexual symbolism in the wildness of nature. In his poem *The Landscape* (1794) Knight did just that, declaring in the manner of Price (with whom he frequently discussed the picturesque) that nature should be made to resemble a coquette:

> For as the cunning nymph, with giddy care
> And wanton wiles, conceals her study'd air;
> And each acquired grace of fashion tries
> To hide in nature's negligent disguise;
> While with unseen design and cover'd art
> She charms the sense, and plays around the heart
> So every pleasing object more will please,
> As less the observer its intention sees.[19]

Knight's couplets aim at the polished and urbane style of Pope, a style in

---

[18] *A Discourse On the Worship of Priapus* (London, 1786), p. 50.
[19] *The Landscape*, 2nd edn (London, 1795); p. 55, bk I, lines 314–21.

which serious things might be said playfully, showing the author to be sufficiently disinterested to present his views with a nicely judged degree of humour. Here, as in Pope's injunction to 'treat the Goddess like a modest fair / Nor over-dress, nor leave her wholly bare' (Pope, vol. III, pt ii, pp. 141–2; 'Epistle to Burlington', lines 51–2) the sexual simile presents the landscape wittily by comparison with the familiar, yet still seductive, artifices of women. The lines appeal to gentlemen's experience and indulgence of feminine charms, charms which they allow and even encourage the scene/woman to reproduce.

Knight's attempt to portray the landscape in the playful verse-style established by Pope indicates the distance of his picturesque from Price and from Wordsworth, for both of whom the representation of the rural scene – in writing or gardening – was a more morally earnest affair. And it was, perhaps, this playfulness, combined with an emphasis on liberty rather than hierarchy, that caused contemporary readers to see Knight's picturesque as an endorsement of levelling and Jacobinical principles. For conservative reviewers, fearing a revolution of the lower orders to follow that of France, the constitutional order established in England since 1688 needed to be defended. The social hierarchy had to be reaffirmed rather than playfully disguised or suspended in landscapes that valued natural energy and liberty. *The Landscape* attacked the Brown style of park, in which the great house was isolated amongst lawns from rougher woodland and from surrounding cottages, and preferred a mixed scenery in which the wild forest represented 'native liberty' (bk II, line 40). It included a justification of revolution by analogy with nature. When a 'stagnant pool' is released it will first 'tear up the soil' but then fertilize the meadows: 'So when rebellion breaks the despot's chain, / First wasteful ruin marks the rabble's reign / ... Then temperate order from confusion springs' (bk II, lines 395–7). Published after the Jacobin Terror and the rule of Robespierre, this view, held by many aristocratic Whigs and middle-class reformers in 1789, seemed, in a climate of war with France, to betray an almost seditious enthusiasm for revolution in general and the enemy over the Channel in particular. As Knight's friend the Whig leader Fox found at this time, the traditional Whig defence of Liberty and the People and opposition to Pitt's war policy suddenly became radical. Fox seceded from parliament in 1797 in despair of effecting reform or preventing the war. He, like Knight, tended his country estate and cultivated his taste by reading classical authors. He also found that his Whig claim to represent the people against Court and ministry, a claim that was founded on those of opposition Whigs from 1688 and the 'Patriot boys' of the 1730s, a claim made by powerful aristocrats and country gentlemen, now made him popular with radicals appealing to the lower classes and campaigning outside parliament. In 1798 Fox toasted 'Our sovereign, the People' at a public dinner in the company of John Horne Tooke, the veteran radical. Fox explained that he meant by the toast 'that sovereignty under which alone, King William and the Brunswick kings have held their throne'. But his association with a man tried for treason in 1794 as a republican led conservatives to see Fox as a fellow traveller with those who would undermine king, nobility and the unreformed parliament.[20] Pitt suggested he should be sent to the Tower. It was in the polarized and alarmist political situation of 1794 that Knight's *Landscape* of liberty was read. Anna Seward found in it 'the jacobinism of taste'; Horace Walpole saw Knight as a popular tyrant – a 'dictator to all taste, who Jacobinically would level the purity of gardens, who would as malignantly as Tom Paine or Priestley guillotine Mr. Brown'.[21] Taste was now explicitly politicized and the landscape of liberty, in which gentlemen had formerly viewed their disinterestedness and their right to represent the nation as a whole, now seemed revolutionary and treasonable. Shared aesthetic values could no longer, whilst apparently remaining above politics, act uncontroversially as criteria for access to political power.

Alarmist readings of Knight's aesthetic, like those of Foxite Whiggism, soon seemed in retrospect to be exaggerated. Humphry Repton, having found Knight's picturesque a danger to the English constitution, came by 1806 to feel that they did not differ substantially concerning the organization of landscape. Similarly, political radicals of the lower classes such as Thomas Spence and Francis Place came to feel that Fox was serving his own search for power, was 'always willing to sacrifice [the people] to get a place'.[22] In 1795 Knight published a revised edition of his poem, in which he tried to set the landscape of liberty in the tradition of Britain's constitutional limited monarchy. Echoing Burke and Bishop Butler, he argued 'No decoration should we introduce, / That has not first been naturalized by use' (bk I, lines 310–11). Slow and gradual reform was necessary, rather than sudden change of the kind Brown had introduced to landscape gardens and despots (popular or monarchical) introduced to human society. Knight, like Fox, continued to hope for some good from the French Revolution if it was no longer forced to extremes by Britain's war against it. But he condemned Jacobinism as popular despotism. He portrayed the oak tree as a symbol of a constitutional British monarch paternally sheltering lesser trees grouped around it. The cedar by contrast was shown to resemble an Eastern despot, destroying everything in its shade. In *The Progress of Civil Society*, published in 1796, he regretted 'the fate which moderate and impartial men always have suffered in times of turbulence and prejudice, that of being condemned by all parties'. He also defended 'respect to private rights' and property as the basis of liberty, idealized tradition as the extender of order and celebrated the fall of

---

[20] Quoted in L. G. Mitchell, *Charles James Fox* (Oxford, 1992), pp. 150, 152.

[21] Quoted in Daniels, 'The Political Iconography of Woodland', p. 66. See also Frank J. Messmann, *Richard Payne Knight: The Twilight of Virtuosity* (The Hague, 1974), pp. 83–9.

[22] Quoted in Mitchell, *Charles James Fox*, p. 153.

the Jacobins. The poem is, in fact, a restatement of country Whiggism as a matter of impartiality and taste, rather than political ideology. Claiming moderation and supporting a polity of 'balanced interests',[23] its understanding of society flows from Harrington's Commonwealthsman arguments, from Locke's connection of rights and property and from Burke's defence of chivalry and tradition. Anti-clerical, as many Whigs in this tradition had been throughout the century, it represents the survival of Country party opposition to Court that J. G. A. Pocock has detected in the 1770s.[24] As Moyle, Bolingbroke and Chesterfield had done, it attacks commercialism, corruption in Parliament, and expensive alliances with German states, whilst supporting gentlemen of rank and wealth as men of sufficient independence and breadth of view to hold the monarch in check and prevent the degradation of labourers into a mob of 'swinish drunkenness' (bk vi, lines 396).

Knight's politics are essentially backward-looking, as is his vision of landscape. Faced with the political divisions that made his aesthetic a subject of dispute, he increasingly places liberty in a landscape of the past, a lost scenic idyll in which a disinterested observer (a gentleman with nothing to gain from improving it, unlike Brown and Repton) can view a society whose order reflects nature's own hierarchical liberty. His picturesque hopes to recreate such landscapes, but can do so only if in retreat from the vexed arguments about its contemporary political implications and if kept as a gentleman's preserve. Knight attacked Brown's followers as a 'tasteless herd' and likened Repton to a 'prudent mechanic'.[25] Without a gentleman's education, serving their own desire for profit, professional improvers lacked the taste to design a proper garden. They were incapable of respecting the local characteristics and traditional elements essential to the necessary combination of historical order and natural liberty. Knight declared in the 'advertisement' to the second edition of *The Landscape* that his purpose was to overcome the degradation of taste that Brown and Repton helped to cause. He declared: 'to ascertain and extend ... good taste in the art on which he has written, is the sole wish of the author upon the subject' (p. vii). He attacked Repton for introducing politics into their dispute, returning to the safer ground of a poetic version of his estate. Thus he could reassert the cultural power of gentlemanly taste without pursuing arguments as to what particular vision of contemporary Britain as a whole the gentleman should take.

Knight and Price, like Fox and the Burkeian conservatives who opposed them, were Whigs for whom liberty was founded on the possession of property and inherited, like land, through traditional institutions. Knight's advocacy of wildness and liberty in the landscape garden should be seen not as a revolutionary sympathy, but as an attempt to design into the English

[23] *The Progress of Civil Society* (London, 1796), p. xxii; bk i, lines 437–9; bk iv, line 150.
[24] J. G. A. Pocock, *Virtue, Commerce, and History* (Cambridge, 1985), pp. 78–9.
[25] *The Landscape* (1795), pp. 101, 103.

landscape the freedom which the rights to own, bequeath and exchange it had established for the nation. For such men, freedom and security of property depended on each other and had been confirmed by the Glorious Revolution of 1688 which limited royal power in Britain to an extent never achieved in France. Price and Knight, then, had as much sympathy with Burke as with Fox; or rather, all of them, as Whigs of various kinds, viewed property as the basis of political liberty and expected the gentry and aristocracy to preserve both against monarchical absolutism on the one hand and revolutionary democracy on the other. Price not only sent his work to Burke but, as Alan Liu points out, exercised his paternalist duties as a local squire, becoming, as did other picturesque theorists, a sheriff and justice of the peace. He defined his position as a Whig carefully in response to criticism of the picturesque: 'He who expresses warmly his love of freedom, and hatred of despotism – however carefully he may distinguish freedom from licentiousness, and despotism from limited monarchy – must never hope for candor. He will be treated by zealots, as a friend of anarchy and confusion, as an enemy to all order and regularity.'[26]

It was not for revolutionary France that the picturesque stood, but for the traditional political legitimacy of gentlemanly taste nurtured by an emotional attachment and (although picturesque theorists were less keen to admit it) by an economic subordination, to the power of property. It stood against an increasingly commercial England, one to which the Whigs were not opposed in principle but which threatened the values of the local squire, whether Tory or Whig. The picturesque idealized the natural, the ancient, the ruined in opposition to the mass production of landscapes by the hired man Brown and by the enclosure for agriculture which the squires were themselves practising. Masters and beneficiaries of a newly commercial and efficient farmland, the squires planned the picturesque garden as a place where older, more traditional and paternalist values could still have root in the pleasures of exercising one's taste.[27]

Repton: the picturesque as profession

Humphry Repton viewed landscapes from a different perspective to that enjoyed by Price and Knight. As they pointed out in their public argument with him, they were connoisseurs, he was a professional. They were disinterested, deriving their picturesque from the paintings they collected – from acknowledged models of taste. He was obedient to his own need for profit, restricted by his more limited education, limited by the desires of his patrons. That this position precluded him from gardening with taste and

---

[26] Liu, *Wordsworth: The Sense of History* (Stanford, 1989), p. 96. Price's comments are quoted in Robinson, *Inquiry into the Picturesque*, p. 80.

[27] A conclusion supported by Robinson, *ibid.*, pp. 68–9, 76–89.

propriety Repton never accepted. Indeed, he used the variety of experience his profession gave him as an argument against the picturesque: to judge landscape solely in relation to pictures was, he suggested, restrictive and limiting – the experience of an estate could not be framed as a series of views. Motion on the part of the observer and the observed, lapse of time, changes in light, human use of the land were all excluded by the framed picture. Yet, despite the advantages of working in many landscapes, using different skills, Repton did increasingly find his professional position divisive and often precarious and, as a result, became more conservative, moralistic and nostalgic in his view of landscape.

Repton began his career in 1788, after finding his income insufficient to sustain the life of a country gentleman. The basis of his interest in landscape, and of his method as a gardener, was what he called 'the rapid facility of sketching landscapes',[28] whereas his great predecessor Brown had based his work upon the maps he carefully made. Repton's approach brought him to the attention of Price and Knight and led to discussions and eventually to public disagreement about the importance of pictures in designing landscape. Repton's *Sketches and Hints of Landscape Gardening* (1795) made clear his dislike of landscaping based solely on pictorial tradition. He argued that Price's aesthetic was that of a dilettante unaware of its social and political implications: it ignored 'the happy medium between the wilderness of nature and the stiffness of art', a happy medium present in 'the English constitution'.[29] Knight's response to this was to parody Repton's own sketching, implying that it was vitiated by his lack of taste, by his debts to Brown's vulgar style and by his use of it to persuade clients to part with money. Repton's designs, and thus the landscapes produced from them, were commerce rather than art. Here Knight identified one of the major tensions in Repton's position, a tension which Repton himself found harder to bear as he grew older. To understand why, and to see how Repton's difficulties were similar to those experienced at the time by Wordsworth and Coleridge, we need to examine his working methods.

Repton prepared for his clients 'Red Books', personally designed volumes which incorporated prose and verse descriptions of the proposed alterations to their estates. The descriptions were accompanied by watercolour sketches incorporating slides which, when lifted, showed the scene before and after improvement. The volumes were, like a commissioned picture, unique to the patron and Repton charged separately for them – one of the dearer for Antony, near Plymouth, cost £31. As such, they seemed to be expressions of

[28]   George Carter, Patrick Goode, Kedrun Laurie (eds.), *Humphry Repton Landscape Gardener 1752–1818* (Norwich, 1982), p. 16. On Repton see Dorothy Stroud, *Humphry Repton* (London, 1962) and E. Hyams, *Capability Brown and Humphry Repton* (London, 1971).

[29]   Quoted in Stephen Daniels, 'The Political Landscape', in Carter, Goode and Laurie, *Humphry Repton Landscape Gardener*, pp. 110–21 (p. 114).

the artist/patron relationship that Price had idealized when contrasting Gainsborough with Brown. Repton sent one to Edmund Burke to illustrate his ideas and hoped to send that for Antony to the King. Yet they were also self-promoting in that they were intended both to persuade the client to commission Repton's design and to advertise his skills graphically to other landowners in the client's social circle. They were not simply disinterested views and William Mason, the author of *The English Garden*, writing to William Gilpin, suspected their accuracy and the motives behind them: 'he alters places on Paper and makes them so picturesque that fine folks think that all the oaks etc he draws on Paper will grow exactly in the shape and fashion in which he delineated them, so they employ him at a great Price ...'.[30] Repton, in fact, had always been prepared to use his artistic talent to promote his self-interest. In 1789 he designed a 'Map of influence operating on the elections' in Norfolk for the Whig magnate and agricultural improver Thomas Coke.[31] He acted as William Windham's political agent in 1790, designing a banner. In both cases he charged for his political work but was prepared to regard the influence gained as the major form of compensation for his labour. Windham's influence led to commissions from the Duke of Portland and conservative Whig MPs in his circle, and may have provided access to William Pitt, whom Repton met in 1793 and through whose patronage he received further commissions.

Price and Knight certainly suspected Repton of pandering his artistic talents to the false taste of his clients. In the mid-1790s they regarded him as having reneged upon an earlier enthusiasm for the picturesque in favour of a more profitable use of the popular style of Brown. For Repton himself improvement was, at best, a harmonious interchange between the desires of the client, the art of the gardener and the limitations and advantages of the landscape itself – a relationship which could not be simply codified pictorially. Yet this often proved to be an illusion: in 1806 a dispute with Windham, long Repton's friend and patron, arose over money. Repton, remembering he had sometimes waived his right to payment from Windham in the 1790s, was angered that Windham insisted on payments being made to him from the solicitor's business Repton's son had taken on. Windham had broken the illusion that they remained in a gentlemanly friendship in which money matters were subordinated to mutual respect. Denying that he had ever thought Windham a 'Man of Parts', Repton was unable to sustain the comparison he had made of them both two years earlier as disinterested and self-sacrificial patriots serving their country by their arts:

When you determined to forego the ease of leisure to promote the welfare of the kingdom at large; I chose the more humble task of contributing to the comfort and

---

[30]   Mason quoted in *ibid.*, p. 21.
[31]   In Daniels, 'The Political Landscape', *ibid.*, p. 110.

pleasure of individuals: and while you studied to raise the glory and secure the best interests of the country; I was content to guide its taste and improve its scenery.

After Windham's death Repton declared 'I never got a shilling by W. W.'[32]

Repton's desire to be treated as a disinterested artist and gentleman by his clients led to further disillusionment. For he was caught between the claims of art and taste and the crueller relationship of the market. It was a market in which he could less often promote his own interests successfully but which he could not stand outside (as could Price and Knight), save by the publication of works explaining the theories which he had fewer and fewer opportunities to put into practice. The Napoleonic wars reduced his income: in 1802 he earned half the amount he did in 1799; later still he feared eviction from his cottage as it became difficult to meet the terms his new landlord was demanding. Country squires, his potential clients, were paying heavy war taxes and turning their land over to the highly profitable growing of corn. Few were commissioning large-scale improvements, so that Repton was left feeling that 'my profession was becoming extinct'.[33] The 'country gentleman' of the last century was succumbing to corruption and selling his land: 'the habit of living in Lodgings or Watering-places, have of late changed his character and pursuits; and at the same time perhaps, tended to alienate half the ancient Landed Property of the Country'.[34] Those who bought land from the gentleman were, Repton complained, vulgar merchants and war profiteeers, who asked of him 'what will it cost . . . not how will it look?'. They worshipped money so that 'the taste of the country had bowed to the shrine which all worship'.[35] Such men tended to employ Repton for small consultations: 'a villa is to be built and Mr Repton must come to fix the spot (I can look back on many such concerns and one day is much like another)'.[36]

In reaction to what he called the sacrifice of 'beauty for gain', Repton sought, in a number of publications on the art of landscape improvement, to redefine taste as a conservative vision of social and moral order.[37] Renouncing the picturesque and the style of Brown, he now espoused views similar to Price's in that they saw the country gentleman's property as a field in which traditional paternal authority should be made visible. In his *Observations on the Theory and Practice of Landscape Gardening* (1803), he had drawn analogies between woodland management and such authority:

the man of taste will pause, and not always break their venerable ranks, for his hand is not guided by the levelling principles or sudden innovations of modern fashion; he

[32] In *ibid.*, pp. 24–5.

[33] Repton's *Memoir*, quoted in Stephen Daniels, *Fields of Vision* (Cambridge, 1993), p. 83.

[34] *Fragments on the Theory and Practice of Landscape Gardening* (London, 1816), p. viii.

[35] *Ibid.*, p. 191.

[36] *Memoir*, p. 169, quoted in Daniels, 'The Political Landscape', in Carter, Goode and Laurie, *Humphry Repton Landscape Gardener*, p. 115.

[37] *Fragments*, p. 192.

will reverence the glory of former ages, while he cherishes and admires the ornament of the present; nor will he neglect to foster and protect the tender sapling which promises with improving beauty to spread for future 'tenants of the soil'.   (p. 76)

'Good taste' also demanded a distinction in 'the character' as well as size of the gentleman's estate, so that his place at the top of rural society was visible. And whilst the 'features of farm and park' should be kept separate, 'greatness of character', he added in 1806, demanded not the improvement of land on the principles of paintings, but the inclusion in the squire's park of the cottages under his authority and protection.[38]

By 1812 Repton was devising means by which the connection between landlord and tenant could be made visible in activities as well as views. Not only did he oppose the removal of cottages and villages from the view, but advised his client to allow the cottagers to gather firewood from his plantations (a tradition to which Price was opposed). He also suggested that resentment of the Game Laws which penalized poaching so heavily would be tempered if the squire organized coursing matches: 'This promotes a mutual intercourse betwixt the Landlord, the Tenant and the Labourer ... This is the happy medium between Licentious Equality and Oppressive Tyranny.'[39] This 'mutual intercourse' was a staged ceremony through which the landlord rendered his authority familiar and benevolent: it suspended in a formal game his actual power just as the park, carefully landscaped to include cottages as 'a subordinate part of the general scenery', suspended it in a remodelling of the land itself.[40] Stephen Daniels comments on the Red Book for Sheringham (the estate for which the coursing matches were proposed) that it 'is a brief not so much for the exercise as for the display of paternalism'.[41]

Himself a cottager, Repton had few opportunities to exercise his views on paternalism. The Sheringham commission contrasted with many in which landowners were indifferent to his views. Shortly afterwards, however, he was able to propose plans for improving the workhouse in the Kent parish of which his son was curate. In these plans Repton's conservatism is apparent, as is his hope that a taste for gardening will lead to a patriotic attachment to the country. He wrote that the building's design should pay 'proper attention to the Comforts of the Poor'. The children kept in the workhouse should, as a 'reward of good conduct' 'be taught and exercised in the supervision of the Garden and perhaps drilled to become the future defenders of their

---

[38] *Observations*, pp. 55, 93; *An Enquiry into the Changes of Taste in Landscape Gardening* (London, 1806), pp. 7–8.

[39] *Fragments*, pp. 195–213, quoted in Daniels, 'The Political Landscape' in Carter, Goode and Laurie, *Humphry Repton Landscape Gardener*, p. 117.

[40] *Observations*, p. 138, quoted in Stephen Daniels, 'Humphry Repton and the Morality of Landscape' in John R. Gold and Jacquelin Burgess (eds.), *Valued Environments* (London, 1982), pp. 124–44, (p. 129). My discussion is indebted to Daniels's essay.

[41] *Ibid.*, p. 137.

Country'. At the same time Repton, like a rural Bentham, insisted on their supervision: the poor remained a threat if they did not acknowledge the benefits of the places given them. They were to be punished 'for misbehaviour and refractory conduct' by being confined in a backyard between the workhouse and a steep bank, unable to see the view towards Canterbury and the coast that their well-behaved fellow inmates enjoyed.[42] Here, then, landscape aesthetics are harnessed to a scheme for the control and reform of the poor, by a penal confinement and a utilitarian system of punishments and rewards. For Repton, in 1812–13, paternalism was systematized and institutionalized, a designed public scheme rather than the personal authority of the vanishing country gentleman. The prospect-view was, however, an ironic reward for the paupers, since it put them in the position of command that the gentleman formerly occupied, but only as a supervised reward for their acquiescence with their confinement in an institution whose very presence symbolized the breakdown of the gentleman's paternal care. Workhouses, which housed husbands and wives in separate dormitories, increasingly replaced the old system of poor relief in which paupers were maintained in their own cottages, often with additional charitable gifts from the squire.

In one respect, however, the reward of visual access to the landscape that Repton proposed for the paupers of Crayford hinted at his own sense of impoverishment and confinement. He was not simply an authoritarian conservative disguising the subordination of the poor as benevolence. His own status as hired landscaper left him closer to the poor tradesmen of his village in Essex than to the nobility for whom he worked with decreasing frequency. Lord Essex had called him 'a common tradesman';[43] in 1814 Repton's new landlord, a contractor enriched by supplying the army, threatened him with eviction in common with the village wheelwright, whom Repton called 'an industrious honest fellow'. Repton retaliated by criticizing his landlord *in the wheelwright's voice*. He articulated, in the village tradesman's colloquial speech, his own disgust at the landlord's refusal to act as a gentleman to his tenants:

Why you see sir, poor Widow Wards sow got into Mr B's park and what does he do? but takes and claps it into the pound! and there he keeps it till he starves it to dead! and then he drives it to Romford market and sells it for nothing at all – and he puts all the money into his own pocket, and never gives no account of nothing to nobody! – But he's a *cruel* man, he is Sir! and never was a gentleman! – I asked him what he meant by a gentleman, one as delights in seeing people happy – and will give up caring for himself to make them so.[44]

[42] *Fragments*, pp. 227–9.
[43] *Memoir*, p. 159, quoted in Daniels, 'The Political Landscape', in Carter, Goode and Laurie, *Humphry Repton Landscape Gardener*, p. 120.
[44] *Memoir*, pp. 74–5, in *ibid.*, p. 28.

Repton did not develop this into a Wordsworthian critique of gentlemanly values in the language of the rural poor. His own voice and his theory of landscape improvements remain generally conservative and paternalist, but also remain troubled by the divided allegiances his own precarious position produced. By 1816 he was even critical of the basis of the country gentleman's power, the power of 'appropriation' or 'command over the Landscape, visible from the windows, which denotes it to be private property belonging to the place'. Noting that such appropriation involved 'refusing that others should share our pleasure', he could only regretfully attribute it to 'human nature'. He developed no political analysis of the desire for appropriation as Coleridge, Cobbett and Spence, in different ways, did at this time, and the nearest he came to overcoming his regrets was in a wishful hope that the appropriated property of the powerful should be freely available to the eyes of all, for the continued unity of the nation: 'For the honour of the Country, let the Parks and Pleasure-grounds of England be ever open, to cheer the heart and delight the eyes of all, who have taste to enjoy the beauties of Nature.' Visual consumption of another's land is thus a substitute for (and a prophylactic against) the actual redistribution of property for which Spence and Coleridge, at different times, had called: 'if not our own property', Repton concluded, 'at least it may be endeared to us by calling it *our own Home*.[45]

Gilpin's proper audience

Price's picturesque was the theory of a landowner who wished landowners again to be able to play the parts of patrons and paternalists. A landscape gardener himself and a theorist about landscape as a source of aesthetic pleasure, he revealed property to be the foundation of taste. But in so doing he made taste into a defensive and embattled ideology rather than a general and disinterested discourse – in Price the landless are to be feared and hated whilst shared aesthetic values assure property owners of their common interest but no longer of their disinterest. On the basis of their shared attachments they are to make common cause against those beyond the fence within which property and taste is secure. And yet Knight, disputing the nature and political significance of taste with first Repton and then Price, had demonstrated that it could not easily unite men of property into a common view of their interest, authority and rôle. Repton, lamenting the destruction of the country gentlemen of the eighteenth century and of their beliefs, yet himself part of a world of trade and commerce, showed the almost unbearable strains under which the ideology of landscape was placed. As he accepted, the picturesque could not bear these strains and satisfactorily

[45] *Fragments*, pp. 233–4, 225.

reassert gentlemanly taste as an acquired view (of art and landscape) leading naturally to a paternal authority in society. But nor could the more explicitly moralizing and conservative 'connected' landscape that he and Price proposed in its place hold back the tide of changing patterns of ownership, belief and authority.

The work of Price, Knight and Repton, taken as a whole, reveals despite itself the destruction in the 1790s of taste as an apparently natural aesthetic of paternalism. William Gilpin, writing during the same period, but as a tourist rather than landscape gardener, attempted to renew that 'natural' aesthetic but from a more precarious position.[46] A minor clergyman rather than a country squire, Gilpin was in a similar authorial position to Johnson and to Repton. Like them he was between patrons and the market, although less dependent on the income from his works. Refining aesthetic theory and landscape-description so that it could contain a degree of disorder, Gilpin intended to renew the taste of the nobility, who would be his patrons, to suit more disordered scenes and times. But like Johnson, he discovered a source of authority within his own rhetorical efforts. He made this discovery as he articulated an exploited rural and oral culture (as when Repton spoke through the village wheelwright) rather than by the language of taste and propriety which he wished to write for his noble readers and patrons. He made it too by the alignment of his work with a readership of tourists.

Gilpin took the picturesque on tour, looking for pleasurably wild places in the wider countryside, both in the parks of the aristocracy and in the less intensively farmed Celtic fringes. In the wilds of Wales, the highlands of Scotland, the fells of the Lake District he sought the picturesque but also found the sublime. Gilpin's *Observations* on his tours were circulated in manuscript and then published.[47] The published narratives exhibit signs of his own fears that the picturesque might be socially dangerous. He apologizes to the noble landowners whose estates he presents as a series of views – afraid that he disrupts his professed discovery of an aesthetic and social order in those estates by selecting from them a few visual scenes for consumption by readers and tourists who, coming from elsewhere and merely passing through, are not bound by the rural order whose visual representation they merely observe. The independence of the reader and tourist allows him to consume the scene and move on. Neither the rural labourer governed by the squire of whose local power the estate is a sign, nor the squire designing his

---

[46] On the ideological splits opened in the picturesque by the difference between the tour narrative and the landowner's reworking of his own property, see John Whale, 'Romantics, Explorers and Picturesque Travellers', in Copley and Garside, *The Politics of the Picturesque*, pp. 175–95 (p. 191).

[47] Gilpin's publications include *Observations relative chiefly to Picturesque Beauty made in 1776, on several parts of Great Britain, particularly the High-Lands of Scotland*, 2 vols. (London, 1789 (facsimile rpt. Richmond, 1973)) and on the *Western Parts of England* (London, 1798) as well as *Three Essays on Picturesque Beauty* ..., 2nd edn (London, 1794). For an overall view of Gilpin's writings and drawings see Carl Paul Barbier, *William Gilpin: His Drawings, Teaching, and Theory of the Picturesque* (Oxford, 1963).

estate as a landscape to illustrate that local power, Gilpin's tourist judges in accordance with an aesthetic law derived from elsewhere – from pictures. Whilst Gilpin is worried by the implications of this – dedicating his work to noble patrons – he is also energized by his own alignment, as a touring writer and artist, with the tourists who will buy his works. Like Johnson deriving his writerly authority from his own efforts for the market rather than from patronage, Gilpin, though more timorously, produces a narrative whose restless movement threatens to undermine the established patterns of power that he supports politically. Not only are the estates of the great reproduced as easily consumable separate scenes, but those scenes are often criticized for their lack of conformity to picturesque aesthetics. They are treated as parts of a procession of scenes which the picturesque tourist, by virtue of having seen so many, will be better placed to judge disinterestedly than the lord of the manor himself. The tourist as consumer becomes a more reliable source of aesthetic judgement than the landed gentleman. And so, as landscape becomes a commodity, wealth (expressed as the collection of as many scenes or views as possible) rather than landed property (a single landscape owned, governed and heritable) becomes the source of power.

Gilpin's commodification of landscape could be seen as a reflection of (and a minor contribution to) the rise of commercial and mercantile values at the end of the eighteenth century. This rise challenged the hegemony of the traditional landed interest and the values of Country Whiggism (although the landed interest was often quick to embrace the benefits of commercial enterprises in practice). It could be seen as an inadvertent application of the account of value made by political economy to the rural landscape. Adam Smith, as I suggested in my introduction, regarded the man of leisure – the philosopher – as able, because he is exempt from a 'particular occupation', to contemplate 'an almost infinite variety of objects' and so to attain a 'comprehensive' understanding not available to the man who labours. Here the tourist, and Gilpin himself as his representative, more closely resemble the leisured man than does the local squire, whose contemplation is limited to the view of his own estate. But they do so only if the landscape is seen not as a complex of social, political and aesthetic parts but (in what Smith saw as a mercantile definition of value) as a collection of vendible commodities, to be viewed, compared and exchanged with others. In Gilpin landscape is viewed in this way: it is uprooted from its local origin and judged according to a central standard. By its representation in his text, it is to be hoarded as a collection of scenes, until sufficient are possessed for the tourist to become a connoisseur, acknowledged, like a collector of the pictures to which landscape views are compared, to be a man of taste and authority. Thus Gilpin's tours offered a bourgeois democratization of land and taste: by reading and touring every middle-class townsperson of a little leisure and mobility could become a purchaser of an almost infinite variety of scenes. He or she could claim the comprehensive understanding (and perhaps the social and political power that were allowed to men of such understanding) formerly accessible only to those who owned and gardened country estates.

The liberalization of taste from land ownership conferred new authority on the judgements of middle-class readers. But if this challenged the cultural and political power of the landed gentry, it did not confer it upon the labourers and small farmers whom they governed in the shires. And so the picturesque tour was criticized by country gentry who wished to preserve a landscape which expressed their paternal authority over, and care for, their tenantry – as by Jane Austen in *Northanger Abbey* and *Persuasion*. But it was also criticized by radicals who wished the middle-class reading public to acknowledge the voices and authority of the rural poor rather than view them as objects in picturesque scenes – Wordsworth and Coleridge in *Lyrical Ballads*. Gilpin himself remained uneasy, not just about his text's alignment with tourists but about the commodification of landscape that he seemed to be aiding and abetting. His later moral discourses largely eschew the picturesque and avoid the mobility of the tour, advocating a rural paternalism intended to reinforce the squire's authority over his local domain. And in the tours themselves persistent anxieties are discernible about the moral effects of making the landscape picturesque. Gilpin notes the social costs for the tenantry of a landlord who treats them, as he does his land, as commodities to be efficiently exploited to create a picturesque view. And he remains fascinated by the narratives that local villagers themselves make of the landscape in which they live – narratives that remain unreliable, oral and evanescent rather than static and harmonious pictures. The villagers' overheard stories of events in the landscape are reported by Gilpin in a way which exhibits his continued preoccupation with a lived rural experience that cannot be categorized by the pictorial values, the tasteful tableaux, of the picturesque.

Gilpin's picturesque tours remain torn between sources of authority, making them symptomatic of conflicts Wordsworth (who owned a copy of the tour to the Lake District) first sought to dramatize and then overcome. I shall examine them in detail, since they exhibit tensions between his endorsement of a proper social hierarchy, whose aesthetic theory the picturesque is intended to be, and his interest in a violence in nature which is conveyed and controlled by the peasants whom he meets. It is a violence which breaches the supposed disinterestedness of the picturesque. It threatens its ability to present a rural landscape based on economic subordination as a realm of naturally shared aesthetic values. In its levelling implications and in its dependence on the spoken words of local peasants rather than established written authority, it is a founding text for Wordsworth and an example of why the picturesque, conservative in intention, could also be seen as Jacobinical. Like Johnson, although with less self-awareness than Johnson, Gilpin formed a critical and political authority in tension between the written and pictorial on one hand and the oral on the other. He was torn between the noble patron and the local source, between established propriety and disruptive voices in the landscape. And, as was the case in Johnson, his descriptions of nature constitute battles to master the self and the scene by overcoming these tensions.

Gilpin's picturesque legitimized, in the terms 'nature' and 'beauty', social exclusions designed to remove the fact of labour from the landscape: 'the laborious mechanic, with his impliments of labour, would be repulsed'. Yet there is ambiguity in Gilpin's view, for he accepts that despite his exclusion from the picturesque, 'in a moral view, the industrious mechanic is a more pleasing object, than the loitering peasant' (who is included within it) (*Observations*, vol. ii, p. 44).[48] This raises questions as to the possible amorality of Gilpin's picturesque and therefore of the nature from which it was supposed to stem, doubts which reflect Gilpin's unease about his position as a writer between the landowners whose estates he comments upon, and the labourers who work upon them.[49] He endorses propriety and convention as the standards of the landowners for whom he writes: 'A house is an *artificial* object; and the scenery around it, *must*, in some degree, partake of *art*. Propriety requires it: convenience demands it' (vol. i, p. xiv). But he also finds this propriety limiting: 'it should also partake of *nature*'. A tension arises between art and propriety on one hand, and 'the freedom of the natural scene' on the other, a tension which is played out for Gilpin not only in the country estates he observes, but in his own writing too. For he is most concerned that his discourse should not become too free in its comments and in its style. He has, he tells us in a long defensive preface, 'studiously checked all severity of criticism, where the improver *still enjoyed his scene*' (vol. i, p. xvii). He is anxious not to offend the nobility and so he reserves criticism for estates whose improver has died. He tells us that a sense of his works' imperfections had prevented 'any design of publishing them', but that the support of the Duchess of Portland, who had seen them in manuscript, had led him to let them appear, though still with 'apprehension'. The dedication is to the Queen, who, he tells us, 'condescended to look into the following papers, when they were in manuscript' (vol. i, p. i). Clearly, by marshalling readers as distinguished as this, Gilpin humbly places his work under their protection, underpinning his risky enterprise of publishing criticism of the legitimacy of the nobility's presumption that their taste, shown in the way they order their lands (microcosms of the ordering of the 'garden of England'), accurately

---

[48] On this ambiguity and the far from hostile attitude to industry in the early picturesque tour, see Stephen Copley, 'William Gilpin and the Black-Lead Mine', in Copley and Garside, *The Politics of the Picturesque*, pp. 42–61 (p. 49).

[49] Discussed in Horn, *The Rural World*, p. 28 and Everett, *The Tory View of Landscape*, pp. 53–8. For further investigation of the eighteenth-century poor, see John Rule, *The Labouring Classes in Early Industrial England 1750–1830* (London and New York, 1986), pp. 352–78.

reflects an implicit natural order. His intention is to reform and extend that taste (effectively perpetuating its claim to be natural and thus its belief in its legitimate power to decide and order). He wishes it to incorporate a greater degree of the wildness of nature than had previously been the case, without the terror and violence of the sublime. And so he recommends greater natural wildness in the landscape garden, and advocates tours to wild rural areas, masking any challenge this might pose to the existing authority of taste by sheltering under the protection of the Queen – the mother of the nation and the guardian of social hierarchy and national propriety.

Gilpin proceeds by defending his literary style: he is worried that 'the author has wrought up many of his descriptions, in the following work, higher than the simplicity of prosaic language may allow' (vol. I, pp. xvii–ix). This possible offence to propriety is excused as poetic licence, a kind of 'high-colouring' by which 'images of nature' are 'forcibly' rendered. Similarly, he apologizes for his errant and excessive digressiveness, claiming that 'this too is poetic licence', necessary to provide variety (vol. I, p. xx). In both cases literary freedom from conventional order is shown to approximate to nature, to be an escape from the bounds of propriety. The apology-in-advance works hard to claim that this is allowable, and not a real challenge to order, rank and decorum, even hoping that 'no one will be so severe, as to think a work of this kind (tho a work only of amusement) inconsistent with the profession of a clergyman' (vol. I, p. xxi).

Full of tortuous strategies to defend him against imaginary charges, Gilpin's preface works hard to incorporate literary and natural liberties within a conventional aesthetic realm. So too in the work itself, nature is indulged, only to be judged by the pre-existent criteria of art, by the colouring, form and harmony found in landscape painting of the kind owned by the nobility to whom Gilpin is addressing himself. But there are passages in the book that provide some explanation for the lengths to which Gilpin goes to apologize for himself. And these passages suggest that the conflict between propriety and freedom had social and economic implications which Gilpin could not openly admit. These implications disturb both his views and the style in which they are expressed by dramatizing too clearly the rôle of his aesthetic theory in renewing the cultural and political hegemony of noble and gentlemanly taste. Reforming taste so that it could reflect 'natural' wildness and violence without terror (the picturesque), Gilpin shows, in these passages, wildness itself to be a figuration of a possible social and political violence. And it is not clear that taste can successfully incorporate this figuration in its aesthetic order. Nor is it clear whether Gilpin is not, despite himself, more excited by this figuration's threat to that order, by its threat, that is, to his own theory and to its renewal of the political order based on the legitimacy of noble and gentlemanly values. Indeed as Gilpin sympathizes with untutored rural labourers who seem to embody natural destructive power, he comes close to revealing gentlemanliness (including his own politely deferential style) to be an inadequate formulation of the social self.

Gilpin describes the place that Wordsworth later made his home, the Lake District. He records the effect of a water-spout that hit Brackenthwaite on the night of 9 September 1760:

At first it swept the whole side of the mountain, and charging itself with all the rubbish it found there, made it's way into the vale, following chiefly the direction of the Lissa. At the foot of the mountain it was received by a piece of arable ground; on which it's violence first broke. Here it tore away trees, soil and gravel; and laid all bare, many feet in depth, to the naked rock. Over the next ten acres it seems to have made an immense roll; covering them with so vast a bed of stones; that no human art can ever again restore the soil. (vol. ii, p. 5)

Here nature is beyond the bounds of propriety imposed on it by the landscape gardener, but also beyond those of the picturesque. Variety, careless beauty and informality are criteria absent from Gilpin's account, which instead focuses on the inundation as an uncontrollable force, capable of undermining houses and sweeping away causeways: nature turning on itself in the fury of destruction. The passage might seem to be an exercise in the sublime, after the manner of the poet Gilpin was so fond of quoting, James Thomson. But it is noticeable that Gilpin fails to draw any aesthetic or moral conclusion from it. He neither labels it sublime nor reflects on the vulnerability of humanity in the face of nature as Thomson was wont to do. It is, at this point, an eruption into Gilpin's text of an event which obviously interests him, but cannot be assimilated into an aesthetic or moral category. As such it is, perhaps, one of the digressions for whose challenge to propriety Gilpin had apologized in his preface.

As the tour continues Gilpin records two more incidents of the same kind. One in St John's Vale moves him to the 'poetic licence' of 'high colouring' and again he apologizes in advance: 'I shall relate the circumstances of it, as they were given to me on the spot: but as we had them not perhaps on the best authority, they may, in some particulars, be overcharged.' This is an interesting comment, for the metaphor 'overcharged' describes Gilpin's own discourse in a word which is literally true of the events it depicts. The mountains, overcharged with water from a summer storm, unleashed a cataract whose appearance 'must have equalled the fall of Niagara' and whose effects resembled those of the inundation at Brackenthwaite:

One of those effects was astonishing. The fragments of rock, and deluges of stone, and sand, which were swept from the mountain by the torrent, choked one of the streams, which received it at the bottom. The water, thus pent up, and receiving continually vast accession of strength, after rolling sullenly about that part of the vale in frightful whirlpools, at length forced a new channel through a solid rock, which we were informed, it disjointed in some fractured crevice, and made a chasm at least ten feet wide. Many of the fragments were carried to a great distance; and some of them were so large, that a dozen horses could scarce move them. We were sorry afterwards, that we had not seen this remarkable chasm: but we had not time to go in quest of it.

(vol. ii, pp. 37–8)

Despite the fact that Gilpin has only heard about this flood at second hand, his writing is animated enough by his excitement to make it a visualized power. As in the Brackenthwaite description, there is no explicit aesthetic or moral reflection. The passage has the hallmarks of the sublime, but refuses to name itself as such: as if the very source of the excitement that enters Gilpin's writing is the fact that the event cannot be categorized – indeed that it cannot even be named as an event seen or experienced. In both passages Gilpin is representing a representation, retelling a tale of an event not seen, and he is freed thereby of the pretence that his aesthetic (the picturesque) is derived from his observation of nature. This freedom is dangerous (as his apologies for impropriety indicate) since it suggests that the rule of proper noble taste which the picturesque seeks to extend is also founded not on nature but only on a tradition of ideological representations, including other aesthetic theories and the works of art made under their aegis.

Although he does not admit it, Gilpin's writing discovers in these passages what he accepts is true of his discussions of the picturesque; just as they are derived from paintings, these stem from representations and may not be dependent upon observation of nature at all. Furthermore, in retelling tales of cataracts and floods, Gilpin is not only free of conformity to the visual scene, but also free of obedience to pictorial tradition and the ordered aesthetic it bequeaths. Relying on a local guide for an anecdote gives Gilpin the heady freedom of replacing deference to an authorized masterful tradition with reference to an oral source that may already be hyperbolic. It licenses his own hyperboles, and the torrent becomes a Niagara as representation feels free to invoke other travellers' tales. Of course, there is a social implication here too: the unreliable speech of a local guide proves a more energizing source than the works of the painters in which Gilpin and his landowning audience find nature properly represented. Through its oral narration nature becomes dangerously active, its power unfixed in time and space. Oral narration undermines the conventional and pictorial representations of time and space since the tourist cannot know where, when and with whom the tale originates and since the events described within it seem to become again present in their turbulent and disruptive violence. And since this narration comes from a local story, not a neo-classical pictorial tradition, its elusiveness and the disturbing powers revealed by it challenge the very basis of Gilpin's alignment of his aesthetic towards a certain audience and its understanding of what is the proper discourse for a gentleman. It is for this reason, I suggest, that he can neither admit them openly, contain them in the categories 'picturesque' or 'sublime', or reject them all together.

They recur in a third narrative about a devastating flood, although this time the scene is not the Lake District, but the border country north of Carlisle, near to Gilpin's birthplace. Gilpin relates 'on the best authority' the story of a great mud-slide that had occurred on 16 November 1771, when Solway Moss had burst out and engulfed a village: 'One house after another, it spread round – filled – and crushed into ruin; just giving time to the terrified inhabitants to escape. Scarce anything was saved; except their lives: nothing of their furniture: few of their cattle. Some people were even surprized in their beds, and had the additional distress of flying naked from the ruin' (vol. II, p. 137). Again the inundation seems to represent an unaccountable excess in nature, an energy unbounded and unpredictable, a force bearing the hallmarks of the sublime checked elsewhere in the landscape by the patterns of propriety. And, borrowed from unspecified authorities, Gilpin's narrative again becomes excited and energized in a way that he cannot then reincorporate in an extended realm of proper taste.

In this narrative, unlike the two earlier ones, Gilpin describes the means taken to control the flood. He notes that the local landowner, Mr Graham, employs one of his tenants to drain the bog, so as to prevent it bursting out again. There is a lesson here for the writer too: a steady discharge allowed to flow unchecked may obviate sudden and violent floods: 'If this continue to run, as it probably will, it may be a fortunate circumstance; and save the country from any further mischief, by draining this bloated mass through a perpetual discharge' (vol. II, pp. 140–1). Gilpin sympathizes with Wilson, the tenant engaged upon draining the Moss, presenting him as a hero working with nature. He is uneducated, deriving his engineering ability from natural genius, and he orders the great forces of nature according to his own will, draining the flow of the bog through channels of his own design. Gilpin (who had, he informs us, himself been born and brought up locally) identifies with Wilson so that he appears to be an epitome of Gilpin's ideal *author*, one who harnesses and redirects the free energies of nature in his own channels, rather than restraining it until a sudden burst occurs.

But this tentative identification leaves Gilpin himself in a quagmire, for his book is written for and about the owners of the land, seeking to instruct them in picturesque landscape gardening. So the admiration of Wilson is a problem, exacerbated by Gilpin's dislike of his master's control and exploitation of him and the other tenants. Gilpin is caught between approving Mr Graham's efficient exploitation of his workers and resenting his replacement of paternalism with Adam Smith's reliance on economic need:

On this well cultivated plain twenty-eight families had their dwellings, and little farms; every one of which, except perhaps a few, who lived near the skirts of it, had the world totally to begin again. Mr. Graham, agreeably to the prudential maxims he has ever observed, affords them little assistance himself; and discourages the bounty of others. He seems to wish his dominions should thrive by industry alone; and would have his subjects depend on this great virtue for the supply of every want, and the reparation of every loss. If the maxim, in so full an extent, be good; it requires at least, a great hardiness of resolution to carry it into practice.   (vol. II, p. 142)

Graham has maintained the absolute power of a feudal lord without the paternalistic kindness that should accompany it: 'their time and labour he commands, by their mode of tenure, whenever he pleases', yet 'while he makes them labourers, he keeps them slaves. – Perhaps indeed the rough manners of the people in those parts, could not easily be moulded by the hand of tenderness' (vol. II, pp. 129–30). Gilpin palliates Graham's economic tyranny by drawing narrower limits to the discourse of propriety: lacking gentlemanly manners, the tenants perhaps do not deserve or need gentlemanly treatment. They are seen to be self-excluded from the world which gentlemen accept as the social realm in which they properly share feeling and taste. Like the landless in Price's pamphlet, their feelings and needs can be disregarded by those who govern them.

If this is not convincing, Gilpin proceeds to imply that he himself was not wholly convinced. He notes that Graham had boasted that Wilson had undertaken to remove an unsightly knoll 'which made a disagreeable appearance before his windows' (vol. II, p. 143). Graham had paid him less than £20 for the work, when a contractor from Newcastle had asked £1300 for the job. Gilpin records that 'we regretted, that he was paid so inadequately to his worth', and is clearly worried that the achievement of a picturesque view from the landlord's house should involve such brazen exploitation of a man 'with so much genius about him' (vol. II, p. 144). Again Gilpin satisfies himself with the notion that gentlemanly fairness need not apply: 'we were assured, as his appearance indeed testified, that he had no higher idea of happiness, than to get drunk after his day's labour: and that better wages would only destroy him sooner' (vol. II, p. 145). But yet, if Gilpin is explicitly prepared to settle for this explanation, his narrative implicitly suggests some far more disruptive sympathies. He describes how Wilson removed the knoll by channelling water at it: 'He then charged again, and levelled against another part with equal success. In short, by a few efforts of this kind, he carried away the whole hill; and told Mr. Graham, with an air of triumph, that, if he pleased, he would carry away his house next' (vol. II, p. 144). Wilson's rebellious joke points out that by harnessing nature the tenant, in one respect, possesses power over the landlord, power to destroy his view and his property. Here the power of nature could be harnessed for social rebellion, literally for the erasure of property, the seat of power, and metaphorically for the erasure of the power of money to degrade human relations. It remains a threat, neither performed by Wilson, nor developed by Gilpin. The discussion of Wilson's drunkenness serves to divert the revolutionary implications of the narrative, ensuring that neither Wilson nor

Gilpin himself appear by their works to be masters of their masters through their representation and redirection of natural power.

Gilpin's uneasy ambivalence throws the very alignment of his text into question. Faced with a landlord who openly bases his power on money relations and market forces he finds it difficult to endorse the picturesque as a discourse of disinterested taste renewing natural or traditional order by aestheticizing disorder. His narratives, energized as they are by events that they cannot categorize, suggest, against his own explicit conclusions, that he was alarmed by the social consequences of landlords' economic power. And they also suggest that he was discovering in the voices of the poor men who were disadvantaged by that power an authoritative self-representation. And he seems to admire that self-representation precisely because of its unassimilable difference, its proud resistance to discourses which in the name of gentlemanly propriety would absorb and neutralize its local particularity and social protest. The unreliable oral authority of rural guides and exploited labourers persists in Gilpin's picturesque in voices which, harnessing the disordered natural forces of their native places, refuse to be patronized. Unlike Gilpin himself, who submits his own work to the patronage of the nobility as a way of demonstrating its propriety, Gilpin's Wilson explicitly reserves for himself an authority whose potential rebelliousness refuses to be contained with the purview of the taming picturesque – a kind of Johnsonian self-referring and self-empowering rhetoric.

Within the *Observations* as a whole Graham and Wilson function as a monitory example, a limiting case warning a gentlemanly readership that the realization in landscape of picturesque aesthetics must not be openly based on economic exploitation, lest it invalidate the ideological function of these aesthetics by creating social resentments too powerful to be regarded as pleasing forms of rustic disorder. At the same time, however, they leave Gilpin's own authority divided. Endorsing propriety on the one hand, destructive forces on the other, he threatens the ability of his own aesthetic theory to maintain the rule of gentlemanly taste as he sympathizes with a rural and oral authority which is untutored by that taste and seems to embody and redirect the power of nature.

Gilpin tried to repair his own authority as a rural vicar and that of gentlemanly taste in a number of moral discourses published during the wars with France. In these works Gilpin addressed his parishioners and thence the reading public. Eschewing the mode of the picturesque tour, he nevertheless used discussion of landscape improvement to entreat the gentry to exercise their traditional paternal authority and protection over their tenants and to tell the poor to remain content with the station in which God had placed them. In his *Moral Contrasts: Or, The Power of Religion Exemplified Under Different Characters* (1798) he wrote a parable of two young men who inherit country estates. One, Leigh, squanders his inheritance remodelling his park, abuses his servants, drinks and gambles and ends in failure – rejected when he stands for election to parliament. The message is clear: gentlemen who renounce their duties deserve to lose their power to represent the people. Leigh's tyranny is symbolized in a style of landscape improvement strongly reminiscent of Graham's at Solway: 'if a piece of rising ground stood in his way, instead of casting about, how to turn it into a beauty, he would immediately order it, tho' of considerable dimensions, to be removed'.[50] Willoughby, the dutiful squire, makes no hasty alterations, having resolved 'never to fight with nature'. He works with the social landscape he has inherited too, employing local labour only when it can be spared from the farms, personally paying allowances to the children of deserving tenants, ensuring that cottagers' rents remain fair and that their dwellings remain within 'the precincts of his park'.[51]

A year later Gilpin published sermons reminding the local squires to act like Willoughby, to treat their property as a 'talent' given by God, to be used 'to preserve peace and security'. The rich man, he declared, was 'only a *poor tenant*' to God, whilst the poor man was to 'receive with meek resignation God's holy will', even in times of scarcity.[52] Arguments of this kind were uncomplicated in their conservative endorsement of a traditional social order, although Gilpin took the analogy with landscape improvement further than most of the clergy. His position became more complex in his *Dialogues on Various Subjects* (1807). Here, like Repton, he was responding to a more acute sense of the breakdown of rural paternalism in the face of the massive increase in rural poverty and vagrancy. Like Cowper (whose 'Nature is but a name for an effect whose cause is God' he had quoted in 1792[53]), he fulminates against London as a place in which the gentry learn corruption and 'specious ideas of liberty'. He presents the country seat as a place of retirement, its prospect of the natural scene 'an endless fund of amusement'. And like Cowper he is anxious that prospects may not be enough to keep the gentry from the pleasures of the city: 'The works of nature, however, furnish many employments to the mind, more solid than looking at a prospect.'[54] They teach God's majesty and love, if their connected design is studied, as Butler and Paley suggested.

Gilpin faced a still more serious anxiety than that over the aristocracy's absences in the towns and cities. He faced the problem of the poor. The dialogues include a discussion of whether it is right to give charity to beggars. A 'Mr Hales' states the traditionalist case that it is the gentleman's Christian duty to relieve the distresses of his inferiors. A 'Dr Lucas', on the other hand,

[50] *Moral Contrasts* (Lymington, 1798), pp. 32–3.
[51] *Ibid.*, pp. 38, 42.
[52] *Sermons Preached to a Country Congregation*, 3 vols. (Lymington, 1799), vol. i, p. 47; vol. iii, p. 118.
[53] In *Essays on Picturesque Beauty* (London, 1792), p. 47.
[54] *Dialogues on Various Subjects* (London, 1807), pp. 163, 177, 181.

argues in the manner of Malthus that relief only increases their numbers, that many are dissolute and undeserving, that no relief should be given despite the risk of causing suffering to those in genuine distress. He speaks the language of agricultural improvement and political economy. Also using analogies with nature, he sounds like the conservative utilitarian William Paley in his use of the argument from design:

Particular cases must always give way to general advantages. You inclose a common. It is hard on many poor cottagers, who are deprived of the little pasturage it afforded for a cow, or a pig. But an extended cultivation is so general a good, that it preponderates over all partial inconveniences. You lay taxes, which often fall heavily in particular cases: but if the tax be good on the whole, the partial inconvenience must be overlooked. Besides, my dear Sir, you, whose maxim it is to imitate in all things, as far as you can, our Heavenly Father, cannot certainly with propriety, reject this doctrine. Thunder and lightening, storms, earthquakes, and inundations, fall often very severely on particular persons. But the Almighty Ruler permits these notwithstanding as the means, no doubt, of general good.[55]

Here analogy with the general good of nature is used, as it was in Johnson's criticism of Shakespeare and Thomson's depiction of the dying shepherd, to present a particular ideology as inevitable. In this case, as in Thomson's poem, it is the gentry who benefit, since it is the poor who are to suffer if the force of the analogy is accepted as proving the argument. And, although Hales retains some doubts, he is persuaded: Gilpin, not without anxiety, redefines traditional and personal paternalism as a duty not to interfere with the laws of 'nature'. Gentlemanly property is saved from the burden of charitable relief as the needs of the poor (afflicted by war, by poor harvests, by the price of corn, by population increase) are portrayed as part of the disorder of nature, explicable only as part of God's mysterious law.

And yet disorder was not so easily displaced into 'natural law' and mastered. It persists in Gilpin's moralizing later works in a sympathy for the poor that disturbs his endorsement of gentlemanly property. In the earlier tour narratives it reappears as a disturbing force of natural and textual power that Gilpin is reluctant to recognize formally by categorizing it. Disorder continued to threaten and to tempt as he struggled to negotiate a verbal path between the written authorities of proper tradition and the unreliable oral reports of destructive local forces.

Gilpin in Scotland

On tour in Scotland in 1776, Gilpin had noticed that one unreliable local and oral source had already been incorporated into a process whereby the wildness of the countryside was domesticated. Ossian had already been re-

---

[55] *Ibid.*, p. 525.

presented to the gentlemanly view as part of a carefully controlled myth of national character. Reporting his journey in 1780, Gilpin objected to the Duke of Atholl's 'improvements' of the landscape around the River Braan. The Duke had turned the wild scene into a fashionable park, creating a path along one bank, 'decorated with knots of shrubs and flowers'.[56] Along the path the Duke had seats, vantage points and buildings placed, presenting the river as a series of formal views. One of the vantage points, supposedly a hermit's cell, showed a waterfall through panes of coloured glass. Gilpin likened it to a summer-house and complained of the 'forced openings, formal stands, white seats, or other artificial introductions preparatory to the several scenes' along the path, 'which has neither nature in it, nor art' (vol. I, p. 126). Within this pleasure ground of fashionable and, Gilpin implies, vulgar noble taste was 'a gloomy cell, on the banks of the river' containing the following inscription:

> Wake, Ossian, last of Fingal's line;
> And mix thy sighs, and tears with mine.
> The shell is ceased in Oscar's hall,
> Since gloomy Cairbar saw thee fall.
> The roe o'er Morven playful bounds,
> Nor fears the cry of Oscar's hounds.
> Thy four grey stones the hunter spies
> Peace to the hero's ghost he cries.   (vol. I, pp. 126–7)

This lament for Ossian, like Ossian's own lament for Fingal, celebrates a heroic bardic past. It presents the landscape as a ground of nostalgia for deeds formerly done, for an oral poetry formerly springing from it. But it is a safely controlled fantasy, contained by its appearance in a tamed park in which the wild landscape has been reorganized by the latest taste. To Gilpin's regret the inscription is juxtaposed with another on a rock in the river bed, commemorating a drinking exploit 'by a set of gentlemen, whose names are inscribed at length' (vol. I, p. 127). The Ossian inscription, in the light of its bathetic companion, seems an affectation rather than a serious lament for a native Scottish heroism still present in ghostly form in the wildness of the landscape.

Gilpin, as a result of such discoveries, displays considerable ambivalence with regard to the Highland landscape and to the great landowners whose estates he visits. He begins, as he had in his *Observations* of the Lakes, by a dedication to a nobleman – the Earl Harcourt. Here he apologizes for his criticism of the landscaped parks of the nobility, and declares that he has endeavoured to use a plainer style than in that work which 'your Lordship' had criticized for transgressing 'its proper bounds'. But he also declares that

---

[56] William Gilpin, *Observations on the High-Lands of Scotland*, vol. I, p. 120. Tourists' reactions to the gardens are discussed in Christopher Dingwall, 'Gardens in the Wild', *Garden History, The Journal of the Garden History Society*, 22 (1994), 133–56.

his less-than-plain prose had stemmed from an attempt 'to adapt my language to my subject', that of 'picturesque description' (vol. i, p. v). His style, then, chafes at the restrictions of noble taste to which he submits it, just as his taste for the picturesque leads him to criticize the improvements made by individual noblemen. And in the tour itself, Gilpin finds himself excited by narratives of a native warrior-like wildness that the contemporary Scottish landowners domesticate. He explicitly aligns himself with those landowners and with the Hanoverian order they represent and urges them to make their landscaping more subtle in its remodelling of the scenery. But he nevertheless remains fascinated by sites whose natural wildness bespeaks a native liberty that once manifested itself in rebellion. Thus the Duke of Atholl's seat at Dunkeld contained 'cascades, and slopes, and other puerilities [which] deform a scene which is in itself calculated to receive all the grandeur of landscape' (vol. i, p. 114). Similarly Lord Breadalbin's house at Taymouth was not located, as it should have been, in one of the 'noble situations' fit for 'the Scotch nobility', being placed so that it had none of the 'noble distance' of view 'which a great house should wish to command' (vol. i, pp. 158–9).

As Gilpin progresses around the Highlands he uncovers, by a criticism of their estates, a lack of confidence in the Scottish nobility. The Duke of Atholl, he notes, had unaccountably committed suicide: 'when we see a man of virtue, and piety under these terrors of mind ... human nature stands abashed in the midst of all its precarious enjoyments' (vol. i, p. 129). Lord Breadalbin, despite his power under Hanoverian rule, had not expressed his authority in the location of his house. Breadalbin's tenants, Gilpin noted, were emigrating to America, despite his paternal benevolence, owing to 'a discontented spirit got abroad' (vol. i, p. 169). Only the Duke of Argyll seemed able to express his authority in a fitting manner. He was continuing the improvements of his ancestor (an ally of Sir Robert Walpole who in the 1730s was, as a result, the most powerful peer in Scotland). These improvements consisted of an enlargement of the castle and park at Inverary which involved removing 'the whole town of Inverary ... a dirty, ill-built hamlet' and rebuilding it at a proper distance (vol. i, pp. 186–7). Johnson had admired 'the total defiance of expense' of the improvements in 1773.[57]

Far less politically astute than Johnson, Gilpin does not attribute the power of the Argylls to their alliance with Walpole Whiggery and the Hanoverian succession. Nor does he relate emigration to the poverty and depression afflicting many Highlanders after the failure of the Jacobite rebellion of 1745 and the subsequent redistribution of land and extension of English and Lowland military power. He praises the Highlander's 'independent spirit' that makes him reluctant to 'live on the labour of others' unlike English peasants who will 'often forge pretences' to gain poor relief (vol. i, p. 214).

---

[57] Johnson quoted by Boswell in Pat Rogers (ed.), *Johnson and Boswell in Scotland* (New Haven and London, 1993), p. 286.

The lack of poor rates in Scotland is thus seen as a benefit, rather than a cause of emigration. At the same time the 'serious, and religious deportment among the common people' is credited to George II's gift of £1,000 a year, from the income of estates forfeited to the Crown by the rebels of 1745, for the promotion of Christianity in Gaelic. Yet despite his uncritical endorsement of Hanoverian and Whig power in Scotland, Gilpin is repeatedly excited by scenes and stories which symbolize a political rebelliousness by their own wildness. The Grampian hills lead him to relate the story of the battle fought there by the ancient Britons against the Romans. He notes that, having lost the battle, the Britons 'had themselves, with barbarian fury, set fire to their own houses, and villages; and many of them had even put to death their wives and children. So innate a love of liberty burned within them, that when that was lost, they thought all was lost' (vol. I, p. 103). Highlanders became embodiments of an ancient British liberty which survived only in the rural fringes unaffected by the corruption that emanated from the London government. A description of the 'rough and picturesque scenery' of the pass of 'Killicranky' shows it as the seat of Jacobite valour, terrifying enough in its own wildness to intimidate the foreign troops employed by the government: 'in the last rebellion a body of Hessians having been detached into these parts of Scotland, made a full pause at this strait, refusing to march farther. It appeared to them as the *ne plus ultra* of habitable country' (vol. I, p. 136). Viscount Dundee had died gloriously there in William's reign, leading a Jacobite rebellion that found little support, but destroying the English army in the process. For Gilpin the scene is a memorial to Dundee's native Scottish heroism: 'An old highlander shewed us a few trees, under the shade of which he was led out of the battle; and where he breathed his last' (vol. I, p. 137). This was a more natural memorial than the inscription to Ossian in Athol's pleasure grounds, and Gilpin sanctifies it further with a quotation from Burns.

Elsewhere Gilpin describes the massacre at Glencoe in 1691, revealing it to have been an act of brutality designed by King William and his court as punishment for those clan chiefs who had delayed swearing their allegiance to the Crown. And whilst he welcomed the ending of clan warfare and cattle raiding by established law, he saw the clan system to have fostered bravery and loyalty, approving of the risks taken by poor Highlanders to shelter Bonnie Prince Charlie after his defeat at Culloden. Gilpin, then, has a continuing sympathy with the ungoverned independence of the Highlanders and with the wildness of the landscape, rough and picturesque, which fosters it. This sympathy does not translate into an endorsement of Jacobitism, but it does stand against his criticism of the taste of the Hanoverian Scots nobility. Their landscape parks, domesticating the wildness of the scene and avoiding commanding views, seem to show the nobility's abandonment of the duty of the clan chiefs to embody and direct the independent and brave spirit of their clansmen and country. These are themes worked out more acutely in Johnson's tour, but in both writers there is an alignment of the Highlands' native independence and unboundedness with the power of their own writing. Despite the apologies of his dedication to Earl Harcourt, Gilpin does come close to breaching the bounds of propriety when describing wild scenes and rebellious outbreaks. His picturesque description is energized by the disorder of the scenery and its people, even whilst he defends the political status quo and the aesthetic rule of gentlemanly propriety. And in this respect he opened a path for Wordsworth to use his own return to the Lake District and tour of Scotland to challenge explicitly what Gilpin threatened implicitly – gentlemanly taste and the hidden political and social exclusivity of its distant views.

4

Wordsworth: the politics of landscape

Wordsworth's tour of Scotland was made in 1803, and he visited many of the places seen by Gilpin in 1776. And throughout his career he retained an interest in Gilpin (he bought the *Observations* on the Lakes in 1796), as he did in Price (with whom he corresponded and whose picturesque estate he visited in 1810) and in Thomson and Johnson (whose critical ideas he modified in his own discussion of the poetry of inscriptions). The responses he made to these writers changed, however, for reasons to do both with his own changing conception of his social rôle as a poet and with his altered perspective on the politics of landscape (the landscape of Britain and of Europe). In this chapter I want to examine those changing conceptions as they manifest themselves in his poetry, in his thinking about poetry and in his politics. And I shall examine Wordsworth's politics in the light of Johnson's conflict between support of property, paternalism and patronage on the one hand, and his self-empowering rhetoric on the other. I shall focus too on the conflict between written tradition and unreliable oral culture that was already evident in Johnson and Gilpin.

I shall not, however, simply be attempting to show Wordsworth as a writer under the influence (amongst others) of Johnson, Thomson and Gilpin. Rather, I shall be exploring Wordsworth's search for authority, a search structured by the difficult and self-conflicting examples of those earlier writers as well as by his interpretation of the rural society in which he grew up and by his need for a national readership. In the process I hope to open some new perspectives on some of the most recurrent, and most important, questions about Wordsworth. These are questions about the nature of the power he confers upon himself as a poet and about the rôle that poetry (and the aesthetics that theorize about it) should have in the political realm. These questions, first asked by Coleridge and by Hazlitt, have recently been asked again by critics under the banner of New Historicism. In the second half of this chapter I shall challenge some of the conclusions of these critics directly. I shall try, through extended analysis of *Home at Grasmere*, 'Yew-Trees' and the Scottish poems to think through the questions revived by New Historicism in terms more open to the complexity with which Wordsworth addressed what were already complex issues. To

157

understand Wordsworth's authority in relation to political and social issues
we need to appreciate that it was through an ambivalent engagement with
aesthetic criticism that he sought both to enhance *and question* the cultural
authority of poetry. He sought power through art and through theory but
also counted the cost, for the artist and his subjects, of so doing. And these
subjects included the cultural and political heroes in relation to whom
Wordsworth formulated ideas, as well as the relatively unknown men and
women on whose voices he founded his own. I shall conclude the chapter by
examining Wordsworth's attempt to master Johnson in his criticism – to
found his critical authority upon Johnson's voice and arguments whilst
ostensibly rejecting the doctor's views. The *Essays upon Epitaphs*, I shall
suggest, reveal that the difficulties of speaking in poetry for another were
also present when speaking in literary criticism. In both discourses the
author's authority remained unstable. It emerged from conflicts, familiar in
the eighteenth century, between written and oral culture, between the writer
and the propertied classes for whom landscape poetry was traditionally
written. Wordsworth, who saw himself not as a Romantic or Lake poet but
increasingly as a successor to Thomson, Cowper, Burke and Johnson,
continued, as he faced the new dilemmas thrown up by the French
Revolution and Napoleonic War, to seek for his writing a cultural authority
based on his authority over the landscape. And so authority had to be
achieved, as it was for the authors I have already examined, through
negotiation of the troubled fields of patronage, propriety and taste and
through a (more or less deliberate) restoration in his own rhetoric of the
voices excluded from those fields.

I begin, though, with an examination of Wordsworth's earlier work in the
Lyrical Ballads. In investigating these poems I shall suggest that they are
structured, at least in part, by Wordsworth's attempts to resolve the dilemmas
revealed in Gilpin's *Observations*, dilemmas that arose as Gilpin tried to sustain
an aesthetic theory in the face of social and economic exploitation that
challenged its legitimacy. Speaking to a gentlemanly readership in a proper
manner in order to renew the legitimacy of its judgements, Gilpin had found
himself haunted by an excess in his narrative. This excess stemmed from
unresolved sympathy with local voices whose potentially destructive articulation of natural power could not easily be rewritten as aesthetically pleasing
natural wildness. Wordsworth, in choosing to broadcast similar voices, from
the same locality, found the local people already spoken for by Gilpin and the
other picturesque tourists in a way which uncovered, but then struggled to
contain, their potentially rebellious difference. Rejecting the prospect-view
and the aesthetics of the picturesque, Wordsworth was nevertheless
challenged by the authority its theorists claimed over the Lakeland landscape
and society in which he wanted to root his own power. He returned to them
in his later more conservative years in publishing his own guidebook to the

Lake country, but in the 1790s and early 1800s worked against their grain. And he did so without being able entirely to escape the cultural power their discourse had achieved and the tensions it had exhibited. Approaching Wordsworth through an understanding of that power and those tensions, then, will allow us to focus with clarity on some of the conflicts that arose in his authority – as he sought to speak for the locals whose voices had been vestigially present in Gilpin without, as Gilpin had done, retreating from their disturbing difference into known aesthetic categories and gentlemanly propriety.

Seeking to speak for – and like – those locals was a difficult and even self-counteracting task because, like Gilpin, Wordsworth was representing their voices for a readership largely drawn from the gentlemanly classes. For these classes poetry was a language of propriety to be judged by taste not a discourse challenging both propriety and taste by rendering the voices of rustics socially significant and politically threatening. More difficult still was the fact that, since Wordsworth was also drawing his poetry from the work of past poets who were accepted as aesthetically and socially proper, he had different sources of authority which were not necessarily compatible. His absorption of past poetry into a discourse that spoke of and for rural labourers threatened – for arbiters of traditional taste such as Francis Jeffrey – to devalue both that poetry and the art's very ideological purpose of appealing to and thus renewing the cultural legitimacy of the disinterested aesthetic judgements of the gentlemanly class. At the same time, from a radical perspective, the absorption of past poetry aligned Wordsworth with the gentlemanly class and appealed to it, as Gilpin had done, even as he spoke for the rural poor. Unable to escape these difficulties, Wordsworth made them his subject. He pondered the conflicts and betrayals that occur as the poet empowers himself to speak for the people who had made his landscape socially and for those who had remade it through the discourses of picturesque tourism and past poetry.

The *Lyrical Ballads*, Wordsworth explained, 'were written with a view to show that men who do not wear fine cloaths can feel deeply' (*WL* (*EY*), p. 315). They present such men, I shall argue, in alignment with Gilpin's presentation of them as figures whose disruptive authority is registered only to be contained, occluded or dismissed. They present them too in response to those in the 1790s who tried to derive from Adam Smith's economics a law justifying a change in public policy towards the poor. Wordsworth presents figures who, like Gilpin's Wilson draining Solway Moss, act and think in ways which challenge the validity of the economic system which, in practice, leaves them poor and, in theory, assumes that it is itself natural and inevitable. Wordsworth explained to John Wilson that the class-based limitations of property and gentlemanliness caused his poems, and the language of the people they portrayed, to be disregarded:

some cannot bear to see delicate and refined feelings ascribed to men in low conditions of society, because their vanity and self-love tell them that these belong only to themselves and men like themselves in dress, station, and way of life: others are disgusted with the naked language of some of the most interesting passions of men, because it is indelicate, or gross, or vulgar, as many fine ladies could not bear certain expressions in The Mad Mother and the Thorn, and, as in the instance of Adam Smith, who, we are told, could not endure the Ballad of Clym of the Clough, because the author had not written like a gentleman.   (*WL (EY)*), pp. 354–5)

Smith's inability to endure the ungentlemanly voice of rural verse was, for Wordsworth, an indication of the failure of his (and others') economic theory. It codified as natural law the commercial relations which suited merchants and it equated the extensive views necessary for political wisdom with the possession of leisure. For Wordsworth it did so because it simply ignored the voices of the lower classes. They were improper, beyond the bounds of nature and society, an assumption which, Wordsworth believed, led to degrading and repressive legislation to control the poor. Objecting to the Poor Law of 1834, Wordsworth added a postscript to his poems which was still hostile to the tendency of economics to describe human relations and decide social policy: there was 'a right in the people (not to be gainsaid by utilitarians and economists) to public support when, from any cause, they may be unable to support themselves' (*W Prose*, vol. III, p. 242).

Adam Smith's picture of economic relations as a natural law governing human conduct had led in the 1790s to national discussions of poverty, which was rising so rapidly with increased population and agricultural change that poor relief increased from less than £2 million in 1783 to almost £8 million in 1817 (between 12s. and 13s. per head of the population). Smith himself had addressed the poverty question, but his admirers later developed his views in different directions. In the 1790s Burke applied Smith's scepticism about the usefulness of government direction of trade into an attack on the system of poor relief. In his essay *Thoughts and Details on Scarcity* (1795) he declared that those able to labour should not be called poor: they were 'only poor because they are numerous' (*BWS*, vol. IX, p. 121). Their labour was a 'commodity' to be priced, as were traded goods in Smith, by the laws of supply and demand. Government relief and pity interfered with 'the common doom of man that he must eat his bread by the sweat of his brow' and would teach labourers 'to seek resources where no resources are to be found, in something else than their own industry, and frugality, and sobriety' (*BWS*, vol. IX, p. 355). Charity to those incapable of work should replace institutionalized relief to those capable of it; all should perform the tasks imposed by the sublime Lord, the 'great Master Workman of the World'.

Religion, Burke declared, restrained the desires and discontents of the poor. In his *Letter to a Noble Lord* (1796) he stated that 'the preventive police of morality' ensured stability if endowed with both the 'awe and terrour' of

Cato and the youthful ornament of Scipio: the sublime and the beautiful (*BWS*, vol. IX, p. 163). The awe and fear that aesthetic theories, including Burke's *Enquiry* and Gilpin's *Observations*, had viewed as disinterested emotional responses to the sublime in art or nature were now, as in Price's picturesque, to be deployed as part of a corrective social policy. They were to help prevent the possible disordered rebellion of the unpropertied – a rebellion that would be too menacing to be regarded as a charming rustic wildness.

Wordsworth's *Lyrical Ballads* sought to resist this structuring of social policy by the discourses of economic and aesthetic theory by demonstrating that the social plight and affective experience of the poor was not cognate to them – a demonstration which thereby challenged the assumption that those theories were an accurate codification of human experience in general and therefore legitimate sources of judgement and policy. Instead those aesthetics appeared, for Wordsworth as for other radicals, to form a self-perpetuating ideology disguising itself as truth and allowing the propertied classes to believe themselves possessors of legitimacy. The men of *Lyrical Ballads* were to unmask the 'truths' of economists and policy-makers by feeling deeply but also differently.

The *Lyrical Ballads* attempted to effect a politicization of feeling in opposition both to commercialist economics and to gentlemanly paternalism. They were not, as some critics have suggested, an evasion of politics via an escape into nature nor were they a Burkeian idealization of organic tradition.[1] They were instead the culmination of Wordsworth's development of a particular kind of English radicalism, one which used a view of rural landscape and society to make arguments about the government of the nation. Wordsworth's Lake District poems can be compared with Thomson's Patriot location of a pre-Norman native English liberty in an untamed Northern landscape. But whilst Wordsworth shared the Patriots' interest in the Harringtonian derivation of liberty from property ownership, and whilst he too aimed his northern scenes at the values of the metropolitan government, his landscapes developed a more radical Commonwealthsman critique than had Thomson.[2] Wordsworth's idealization of the small free-holders of the Lakes not only derived liberty and independence from land ownership, as Country-party readings of Harrington did, but endorsed the rustic speech of the farmers themselves. Here Wordsworth resembles John Horne Tooke, the radical campaigner tried for treason in 1794, whose

---

[1] See Marjorie Levinson, *Wordsworth's Great Period Poems* (Cambridge, 1986) and James K. Chandler, *Wordsworth's Second Nature: A Study of the Poetry and Politics* (Chicago and London, 1984).

[2] On Wordsworth and the 'Norman-yoke' ideology of eighteenth-century opponents of ministerial and monarchical power, see David V. Erdman, 'Milton! Thou Shouldst Be Living', *TWC*, 19 (1988), 2–8 and Christopher Hill, *Puritanism and Revolution: Studies in Interpretation of the English Revolution of the Seventeenth Century* (London, 1958), pp. 50–122.

etymological work *The Diversions of Purley* (1786–1805) attempted, as part of an attack upon the political and literary establishments, to derive the English language from the native vigour of Anglo-Saxon rather than the polite formality of Latin. Tooke illustrated his derivations with sentences that attacked monarchy in general and Pitt's ministry in particular. He sought to restore the native independence he found in Anglo-Saxon words as part of an attempt to renew in England a constitution of native liberty that, he and other radicals argued, had been encroached upon after the Norman conquest by absolutist monarchs. For Tooke, as for Wordsworth, speech was itself politicized: a preference for the concrete nouns and dialect forms of uncultivated rustic speech was an attack upon the abstract language used by Courts and ministries to claim, define, and preserve legitimacy.[3]

Wordsworth's *Preface* to *Lyrical Ballads* derives the power of rustic speech from its closeness to the 'permanent forms of nature' that its words designate – a Lockeian view of words as names of things found, politicized, in Tooke (*W Prose*, vol. I, p. 124). In making that closeness depend upon land ownership for its effective continuation, he adds a Harringtonian dimension. Wordsworth's Harrington is not, however, the Patriots' Harrington of the 1730s, since he shows the small farmer, rather than the landed gentleman, and a 'mountain republic', rather than the existing constitution, as the model of a society of liberty (*W Prose*, II, pp. 206–7). As Zera Fink has argued, Wordsworth was exposed to Harrington in a revolutionary context in France in 1792.[4] Harrington and Algernon Sidney were popular with the Girondins; the model constitution put to the National Convention in September adopted the proposals of *Oceana*. Wordsworth's friend, Michel Beaupuy, to whose ideals he paid tribute in *The Prelude* (1805, bk IX, lines 329–38), was himself influenced by Harrington, Milton and Sidney. Wordsworth's 1793 *Letter to the Bishop of Llandaff* shows the importance of the French Harrington in arguing for 'a modified representation in order to adapt free government to the large state'.[5] The Girondins had been interested in Harrington because his vision of government by assemblies elected by property holders showed how classical republican models could be adapted to large states. Wordsworth also considered Harrington's agrarian law, whereby property was divided and preserved in the hands of the many. He rejected this law as unfitted to complex and commercial societies, whilst recognizing the ideal of widespread property ownership that it was designed to realize. In 1794 he planned essays on the Commonwealthsman republicans and as late as 1803 advanced their names as British heroes.

---

[3] On Tooke, see Olivia Smith, *The Politics of Language in England 1792–1819* (Oxford, 1984), pp. 110–53.

[4] On Wordsworth, Harrington and the Commonwealthsmen, see Zera Fink, 'Wordsworth and the English Republican Tradition', *Journal of English and Germanic Philology*, 47 (1948), 107–26.

[5] See *ibid.*, 112.

By 1803 and indeed by 1798, when *Lyrical Ballads* were published, the major intellectual influence on Wordsworth was Coleridge, who had himself developed a radical version of Commonwealthsman arguments on property. Coleridge, as I shall show in the next chapter, favoured in 1795 and 1796 the abolition, or at least equalization, of property ownership. His Pantisocracy scheme, as Nigel Leask and Peter J. Kitson have argued, was for an agricultural commune modelled on Harrington's and Moses Lowman's view of the ancient Hebrew commonwealth.[6] Leask understands Coleridge's nature poetry, and the *Lyrical Ballads* too, as a development of this radical form of dissenting ideal. He sees it as a poetry of an agrarian commonwealth (or 'visionary mountain republic' as Wordsworth put it), designed as a model of social equality and independence. Part of a native tradition of British republicanism and livable in rural England, it represents, Leask argues, a political alternative both to French Jacobinism and to the repressive monarchy of George III and Pitt. Harrington and Moses Lowman had argued that the Jewish priests, the Levites, did not form a separate social order or political interest in the early Mosaic commonwealth. Unitarian radicals such as William Frend and Coleridge's hero, Joseph Priestley, had used these arguments to attack the established church.[7] Coleridge did so too in his Bristol lectures on revealed religion, whilst Wordsworth's republican *Letter* was addressed against the conservative polemic of the Bishop of Llandaff.

To the Commonwealthsman and dissenting radicalism of Harrington and the Unitarian radicals Coleridge added the work of Bishop Robert Lowth. Whilst Lowth was not himself radical, his understanding of the power of Hebrew poetry, to one excited by the social ideal of the Mosaic commonwealth, was. Lowth suggested that the language of ritual and liturgy in the scriptures was obscure and unpoetic.[8] The best Hebrew poetry was that which employed images and prosodic structures derived from the simple agricultural life of the Hebrew tribes. Coleridge read Lowth in 1796 and attempted a translation of the Song of Deborah following his ideas. When Wordsworth quoted lines from the Song in his 1800 note to 'The Thorn' as examples of how repetition could be beauty 'of the highest kind' and evidence of 'the interest which the mind attaches to words' (*WPW*, vol. II, p. 513) he was indirectly acknowledging the extent to which his own poetic articulation

[6] See Nigel Leask, 'Pantisocracy and the Politics of the "Preface" to *Lyrical Ballads*', in Alison Yarrington and Kelvin Everest (eds.), *Reflections of Revolution: Images of Romanticism* (London and New York, 1993), pp. 39–58; Peter J. Kitson, ' "The electric fluid of truth": The Ideology of the Commonwealthsman in Coleridge's *The Plot Discovered*', *Prose Studies*, 13 (1990), 36–62.

[7] The significance in the 1790s of Harrington's *The Art of Lawgiving* (London, 1659) and Lowman's *Dissertation on the Civil Government of the Hebrews* (London, 1740) is considered in Nigel Leask, *The Politics of Imagination in Coleridge's Critical Thought* (London, 1988), pp. 19–41.

[8] On the importance of Lowth's *On the Sacred Poetry of the Hebrews*, see Leask, 'Pantisocracy and the Politics of the "Preface" '.

of the speech of rural societies was indebted to his friend's dissenting radicalism. Behind the politicized poetic of *Lyrical Ballads*, behind its claim that the language of rural freeholders is exemplary in its moral depth and independent feeling, is Coleridge's fusion of Harringtonian and Unitarian idealizations of the Mosaic commonwealth with Lowth's views on Hebrew poetry.[9] The result is a social and political argument about the location of morality and independence in the speech of certain disadvantaged classes, and an alignment of poetry with that speech. It is a distinctly and self-consciously English and rural radicalism – an alternative to the French revolutionary emphasis on natural rights which the arguments of Burke and the militarism of Napoleon suggested led to tyranny.

Wordsworth's mountain republics, like Coleridge's Somerset communities, were imagined places in which the radical hopes of the earlier 1790s, defeated by government repression and the inadequacy of revolutionary doctrine, could be preserved in more deeply rooted form for the benefit of the nation. But a difficulty remained: to develop an account of how such visionary agrarian commonwealths could be adopted by contemporary Britain. Neither Coleridge in his 1795 lectures nor Wordsworth in the *Preface* was able to show how the nation at large could be transformed into the kind of society they admired in the rural fringes. Not only was property unequally distributed, unlike the Mosaic and Harringtonian commonwealths, but it was not simply held in land. Paine and Priestley, leading radicals of different positions, had rejected the equalization of property. Burke, attacking the French Revolution's redistribution of property, had associated radical intellectuals with financial speculators. The unlimited circulation of speculative ideas, like the inflationary expansion of paper credit, uprooted settled patterns of thought and of land ownership, leading to anarchy and, ultimately, despotism.[10] Wordsworth could answer this charge by showing his radical arguments to be defending a traditional pattern of land ownership (albeit one of small freeholding farmers rather than that composed of the aristocracy which Burke supported). But he could not show how this pattern and the culture of independence and liberty it produced would be adopted in Britain, other than by dispossessing the gentry and nobility. He could, however, envisage a symbolic, if not an actual, redistribution, through the medium of poetry. Coleridge's Unitarian emphasis that the Levites were not a separate order in the Mosaic commonwealth allowed him to imagine the poet too as part of the equal community for and of which he spoke. Like a bard, a poet of this kind developed the speech of the community of which he was a member, as Lowth argued the Hebrew poets had done in the

---

[9] For further discussion of Lowth, see my *Coleridge's Figurative Language* (London 1991), pp. 83–6, and chapter five below.

[10] On Burke's arguments, see J.G.A. Pocock, *Virtue, Commerce and History* (Cambridge, 1985), pp. 193–214.

scriptures. And Wordsworth too claimed to speak the language of the Lakeland farmers, representing their speech for the reading public and hoping thereby to disseminate the liberty and morality which their mountain freeholds fostered in them. The poet, like the Levites in Harrington's and Lowman's idealizations of the Mosaic commonweath, like Lowth's biblical writers, formalizes the language of the agrarian republic and vouchsafes it to others – spreading its values without requiring the actual redistribution of land.

But Wordsworth's reading public was largely drawn from the gentlemanly classes accustomed to regard their property and the cultural authority it gave them as legitimate. Even if many of them disagreed with the particular arguments of economists about poor relief, they were reluctant to accept that their taste was invalid as a source of judgements about experience in general or poetry in particular. Nor were they disposed to accept that morality and freedom best inhered in the language of the rural lower classes whom they were used to governing at both local and national levels. In 1801 Wordsworth tried to overcome the resistance of the influential public to his poetic language, at Coleridge's instigation, by sending copies of *Lyrical Ballads* to important men. These were accompanied by letters drawing attention to the poems' social message. The letter to Charles James Fox, the leader of the Whig opposition, attacked the institutions which dealt with the poor and the language which portrayed those institutions as benefits:

By the spreading of manufactures through every part of the country, by the heavy taxes upon postage, by workhouses, Houses of Industry, and the invention of Soup-shops etc., superadded to the increasing disproportion between the price of labour and that of the necessaries of life, the bonds of domestic feeling among the poor, as far as the influence of these things has extended, have been weakened, and in innumerable instances entirely destroyed. The evil would be the less to be regretted, if these institutions were regarded only as palliatives to a disease; but the vanity and pride of their promoters are so subtly interwoven with them, that they are deemed great discoveries and blessings to humanity.   (*WL (EY)*, pp. 313–14)

This letter reveals both Wordsworth's sympathies and his difficulties. Fox was a wealthy aristocrat remote from the social life portrayed in the poems. He praised some but, schooled to believe in decorum and propriety in poetry, he thought blank verse unfit for simple subjects. And in 1801 his return to parliament and subsequent period in administration was short lived. Pitt, who had, since the early 1790s, dominated government, left a changed political scene. And Pitt's original policy of relieving the poor had been reshaped by the *laissez-faire* economics Wordsworth resented.

Wordsworth's verse was too closely bound to the concerns and dialect of those poor families to appeal to the aristocrats who held power, or to the middle class who had influence. And yet it would not be read by the rural poor themselves. He was, then, unlikely to succeed on the literary market: he later wrote that a lifetime's poetry had brought him less than seven score pounds. It was in response to this economic marginalization that Wordsworth adapted his style. In *Lyrical Ballads* he conferred authority on the rural poor; in much of his later poetry he conferred it on himself, giving himself the power of genius when the age did not. And the age did eventually recognize this authority: he found a patron in Lord Lowther, escaping from the economics of the market to the security of support by the Tory landowner for whose cousin Wordsworth's father had worked as steward. His letter of application made his reasons clear and signalled his shift to a conservative position of support for the paternalist squire who protects his tenants from economic pressures: 'I had erroneously calculated upon the degree in which my writings were likely to suit the taste of the times' (*WL* (*MY*), vol. II, p. 3).

'The Female Vagrant' and 'The Last of the Flock'

In 1798 Wordsworth, like Gilpin observing Graham and like Johnson in Lowland Scotland, had found it difficult to see contemporary paternalist landlords as supporters of rural independence. There were personal reasons for this, since he was engaged in a lawsuit trying to recover salary owed his dead father by the Earl of Lonsdale. He saw paternalism as a mask for love of personal and economic mastery, a mask that slipped to reveal tyrannical oppression if the master's will was resisted. In 'The Female Vagrant' he attacked the acquisitive landlords who tried to increase their wealth by buying land, turning small independent farmers into tenants:[11]

> Then rose a mansion proud our woods among,
> And cottage after cottage owned its sway,
> No joy to see a neighbouring house, or stray
> Through pastures not his own, the master took.
>
> (*LB*, p. 42, lines 39–42)

The narrator's father 'dared his greedy wish gainsay', determined to remain a statesman (a class of small farmers with heritable land that survived in the Lake District in Wordsworth's day). In return 'His little range of water was denied; / All but the bed where his old body lay, / All, all was seized' (lines 51–3). Wordsworth appends a note to the phrase 'his little range of water': 'Several of the Lakes in the north of England are let out to different Fishermen, in parcels marked out by imaginary lines drawn from rock to rock.' The landlord had denied the farmer's fishing rights, a vital part of his subsistence, supplanting traditional locally established agreements between

---

[11] On the increase in enclosure in the Lake District, as a result of landowners, including Lonsdale, seeking improved returns, see C. M. L. Bouch and C. P. Jones, *A Short Economic and Social History of the Lake Counties: 1500–1830* (Manchester, 1961), pp. 227–39.

farmer and paternalist squire by the letter of financial contract – a move to a commercial relationship of a kind that Price in Herefordshire and Johnson in Scotland had regretted.

The note suggests that in forming a poetry intended to be resistant to the aesthetic values of paternalist gentlemen Wordsworth was also resisting the claims of the picturesque to reset those values in relation to the Lake District. Gilpin, in the *Observations* Wordsworth had purchased in 1796, had noted the same practice occurring on Windermere in his tour of the Lakes. But for him, writing earlier and more concerned with amusing and picturesque views, the practice simply illustrated the fishermen's dependence on chance:

> But tho the space of each fishery is nearly equal, yet the produce is otherwise; the fish running in shoals sometimes in one part of the lake, and sometimes in another. – When the farmer rents land, he can judge of his bargain by the surface. When he rents water, he must take his chance.   (*Observations*, vol. i, p. 153)

Wordsworth's poem is an attempt to develop into an instance of economic and social injustice what remains in Gilpin a natural chance, noted by the tourist as an instance of pleasingly different rustic customs. It resists the picturesque by forcing the gentlemanly reader to encounter, in an art form he would expect to appeal to disinterested judgements of taste, political arguments. However, Wordsworth's demonstration that the chances of nature are complicated by a deliberate and cruel monopolizing of property and labour, can also be seen as a more systematic and universal development of Gilpin's quiet concern about the exploitation on Graham's estates at Solway Moss. It can be seen as a development of that disturbing sympathy in the picturesque which threatens its declared support for the legitimacy of the aesthetic values of gentlemen.

In 'The Last of the Flock' Wordsworth uses the pastoral and Christian associations of the shepherd to criticize the system of parish relief as part of the exploitation, not help of the poor. In 1795 the justices of Speenhamland in Berkshire had decided that 'every poor and industrious man' whose earnings fell below a given amount (calculated in proportion to the price of bread and the size of his family) was entitled to a subsidy to bring his earnings to that minimum subsistence level.[12] Wordsworth's poem depicts what happened if the level was fixed too low, or if a poor man's basic and long term assets were taken to be realizable for income:

> 'Ten children, Sir! had I to feed,
> Hard labour in a time of need!
> My pride was tamed, and in our grief
> I of the parish ask'd relief.

[12] The Speenhamland system is discussed in Gertrude Himmelfarb, *The Idea of Poverty in England in the Early Industrial Age* (London, 1984), p. 65, and in Horn, *The Rural World 1780–1850* (London, 1980), pp. 102–7.

> They said I was a wealthy man;
> My sheep upon the mountain fed,
> And it was fit that thence I took
> Whereof to buy us bread:'
> 'Do this; how can we give to you,'
> They cried, 'what to the poor is due?'

(LB, p. 78, lines 41–50)

The shepherd speaks from poverty but not with pastoral contentment. As occurs elsewhere in the *Lyrical Ballads* Wordsworth harnesses through his voice an articulation of deep feeling. Gilpin had registered similar articulations as energizing excesses of representation challenging but explicitly contained by his aesthetic. By representing the ungoverned local speech of shepherds and the dispossessed in a poetry which dramatized its origin in their ungentlemanly voices Wordsworth aimed to relocate their speech in his own writing, making it awe-inspiring for a gentlemanly readership who would otherwise have regarded it as uncouth and beneath notice. Wordsworth hoped thereby to challenge the legitimacy of the reading public's taste and to appeal to that public to recognize a common language and humanity shared with those whom widening class and political divisions led it to view as merely a social problem or political threat. Finding the public reluctant to accept the inadequacy of its existing values to judge the poor and his representation of them, Wordsworth added the theoretical *Preface* for the second edition of *Lyrical Ballads*. This *Preface* only exhibited the conflicts facing Wordsworth as it both claimed that the language of rural Lakeland was the best part of language and conceded that the poet had to select from that language, removing its impurities (and thus rendering it more proper and gentlemanly). Faced with real social division and the implication of poetry in that division as it sought a gentlemanly readership, Wordsworth was left hoping, with more passion than immediate reward, that the acts of writing and reading the *Lyrical Ballads* would make poetry the reviver of a language held in common. Poetry, he hoped, would thereby become a guarantor of a community of Englishness, overcoming the inequalities of property-ownership that prevented a Harringtonian commonwealth of liberty being realized. It would make him, if not Johnson's Caesar conquering the English language then at least a 'prophet of nature' speaking a 'lasting inspiration' to the people as he united their land in his poetry (*Prelude*, bk XIII, line 442).

Home at Grasmere

In the *Preface* and the *Essay Supplementary* to it Wordsworth dramatized the difficulties of speaking for local authorities, implying in the process that it is poetry's relation to its public that often causes it to misrepresent for profit their strange power. Wordsworth thought the gentlemanly discourses which appeal through established aesthetic categories to be determined by the economic appeal of the familiar rather than by taste. Dramatizing the organization of the realm of aesthetics by economic forces he undermined the appearance of disinterestedness necessary for it to seem a legitimate source of judgements. He portrayed popular approval and financial reward as temptations leading writers to emasculate their socially dangerous local authorities through a familiarly marketable style – collapsing local and oral virtues into properly tasteful writing.

The difficulties experienced by earlier writers remain pertinent to the landscape poetry Wordsworth composed as the eighteenth century ended. Like Johnson Wordsworth attempted to find a voice which would be free of deference to patrons whilst he also sought to found his power on established authority – on the authority of the past masters of poetry whose words he hoped to renew if not on that of the masters of the land. Until his later years, when he accepted Lowther's patronage, Wordsworth sought to master the masters of the land by articulating it in a way they could not. Like Johnson his verbal power was founded upon his ability to speak for past poets and for the unregarded poor. And he learnt from Thomson and Gilpin as he made his poetic subject-matter out of his struggle to define his authority in relation to the rural voices for whom he spoke and to the landowning classes. He criticized these classes but could not ignore their power over the social and aesthetic realms. At his best Wordsworth created a complex politics of landscape in which he was able to ponder his authority, showing it to be unstable and achieved only at the cost of multiple usurpations. In particular *Home at Grasmere* conceives poetry as a usurpation-through-language of the power of the landowner (of his claim upon the land and of his claim to possess a language which legitimately empowers him to decide). But the poem also makes a usurpation of the voices of the local authorities through whom Wordsworth resists the landowners' power (authorities like Gilpin's Wilson resisting his master Mr Graham). And it is divided again as it shows Wordsworth's authority to be produced by usurpation of the words of other poets – Milton, Thomson, Cowper, Coleridge.

The Wordsworth who emerges from this self-questioning is one who himself considers the implication of his own authority (and poetry's authority in general) in social and historical realms for which he cannot speak without the danger of betrayals. It is a Wordsworth more aware and more complicated in his understanding than some recent critics have allowed – not a poet who seeks to escape or transcend the social and historical realm via a self-empowering flight to his own inner self but one who, in examining his conflicting loyalties and struggles for power, counts the cost of the authority achieved by a man speaking in and for his culture. It is a cost that he shows to be, at least in part, paid – and worth paying – when art reveals that it is implicated in politics.

The politics of landscape dwelt upon in *Home at Grasmere* can be brought into focus through an examination of Wordsworth's difficult personal negotiation of the social dispossession he himself suffered as a member of the rural economy. This negotiation is reminiscent of Johnson's with his patron Chesterfield. Wordsworth's father was the land agent and steward in Cumberland and Westmorland of Lord Lowther, the Earl of Lonsdale. Lonsdale was the most powerful landowner in the Lake District. He controlled several members of parliament, and employed numerous lawyers to act in the court-cases he frequently brought. When Wordsworth senior died, in 1787, Lonsdale refused to pay a debt of nearly £5,000 owed to him. This refusal left the orphaned Wordsworth children without patrimony, and threw them on the charity of relatives. Letters written by Dorothy at the time reveal that the servants enjoyed the downfall of the children of Lonsdale's steward: 'my Brs can not even get a pair of shoes cleaned without James's telling them they require as much waiting upon as any *Gentlemen*' (*WL* (*EY*), p.4). The Wordsworths attempted to recover their inheritance by taking legal action against Lonsdale, but although he settled out of court in 1791, he had still not paid the debt upon his death in 1802. The Wordsworths blamed their disinheritance, and their fall from the gentlemanly class, on Lonsdale's feudal power: 'We in the same moment lost a father, a mother, a home, we have been equally deprived of our patrimony by the cruel Hand of lordly Tyranny' (*WL* (*EY*), p. 88). William's resentment helped to push him towards radical politics. He announced that he was a democrat, and included these lines on Lonsdale in a satire attacking the King: 'Must honour still to Lonsdale's tail be bound? / Then execration is an empty sound' (*WL* (*EY*), p. 158).

If Lonsdale's political patronage epitomized the political corruption to which the young Wordsworth objected, his control of land and money symbolized the economic tyranny which Wordsworth portrayed in 'The Female Vagrant'. The resentment expressed there, and in a number of the other lyrical ballads, is of a landlord who uses his property to disinherit and dispossess others. Here the disinheritance of the poor can be seen as a theme arising from Wordsworth's own disinheritance – a more general form of protest than direct attack on Lonsdale and an elevation of the dispossessed to heroic status. Wordsworth had been warned by his brother in 1794 to be cautious in writing his political opinions since Habeas Corpus had been suspended. Lord Lonsdale, he added, 'has so many Spies in every part of the country' (*WL* (*EY*), p. 121).

As late as 1805 the Wordsworths were still fighting against a sense of their dispossession at the hands of the Lowther family, a sense expressed by others in the area. Nicolson's and Burn's *History of Westmorland*, which Wordsworth probably acquired in 1796, noted that in 1682 Sir John Lowther had 'pulled down and demolished' cottages and tenements in Lowther village 'to inlarge his demesne, and open the prospect to his house'. And the village and manor of Whale 'was drawn within the vortex of the house of Lowther, from age to age purchasing, and never selling again'.[13] As a letter of 1805 shows, Wordsworth and Dorothy still regretted the fact that the house in which they had spent their earliest years had belonged not to their parents, but to Lonsdale. They had lost it upon their father's death, and it had been left vacant:

Talking of Lord Lowther reminds me of Mr. Satterthwaite whose Father now lives at Cockermouth in the house where my Brothers and I were born and where our Father died one and twenty years ago. It is at the outskirts of the Town, the garden bordering on the River Derwent or rather a *Terrace* which overlooks the River, a spot which I remember as vividly as if I had been there but the other day, though I have never seen it in its neatness, as my Father and Mother used to keep it, since I was just six years old, a few months before my Mother's death. I visited the place again at the age of twenty three and all was in ruin, the terrace-walk buried and choked up with the old privot hedge which had formerly been most beautiful, roses and privot intermingled – the same hedge where the sparrows were used to build their nests. Nobody lived in the house for many years after my Father's death – at length Lord Lonsdale (perhaps in a whim) had it repaired, and put a Tenant in it; and now Satterthwaite's Father is there. (*WL* (*EY*), p. 616)

If grief for their parents' deaths is here displaced into grief for a lost childhood-garden, its ruin is attributed to Lonsdale. Its subsequent repair only confirms his absolute and arbitrary power ('perhaps in a whim') over what is, for Dorothy, a sacred place from which she is exiled. Similarly William regretted that the new Lord Lowther's landscape improvements would obliterate a wild woodland path on which he, as the steward's son, had been able to pace 'many an hour when I was a Youth, with some of those I best love' (*WL* (*EY*), p. 626). *Home at Grasmere*, recreating these landscapes of youth as Wordsworth's own, not only re-possesses the past as Dorothy sought to do, but regains property alienated by the power of the Lowthers.

Home at Grasmere was written between 1800 and 1806, and was intended to form part of *The Recluse*. Unpublished in Wordsworth's lifetime, like *The Prelude*, it underwent considerable revision, a process which is observable in the differences between the first manuscript (MS B) and the latest (MS D).[14] In both manuscripts mastery of one's own land and proper inheritance is a prerequisite of freedom, peace and the self-worth on which a sense of one's own authoritative masculinity depends. Wordsworth included a hymn to the

---

[13] Joseph Nicolson and Richard Burn, *The History and Antiquities of the Counties of Westmorland and Cumberland*, 2 vols. (London, 1777), vol. I, pp. 440–1.

[14] Beth Darlington, in her Cornell Wordsworth edition, views lines 1–457 and 859–74 of MS B as from 1800, whilst Jonathan Wordsworth, in *William Wordsworth: The Borders of Vision* (Oxford, 1982), p. 427, views almost all the poem as having been originally composed in that year. The issue is sensibly summarized in what remains the best account of the poem, Kenneth R. Johnston's *Wordsworth and The Recluse* (New Haven and London, 1984), pp. 370–1.

'Freeman' of the Lake District, 'sound and unenslaved' because 'he who tills the field, / He, happy Man! is Master of the field / And treads the mountain which his Father trod' (Darlington, MS B, lines 443, 462–4).[15]

Wordsworth acknowledged that the local farmers and shepherds have identities of their own, and he accepted that they should not be viewed through the false tenderness of a 'romantic hope' to find only love and a 'majestic frame of mind' (lines 400, 403). Yet he, by virtue of his own insight, found in them a symbol of sublimity, of the profound and menacing power that resides in nature. It is a process which suggests that it was here, rather than in *The Prelude*, that Wordsworth most explicitly rewrote a social and historical speech as a voice of nature audible to him alone. Rewriting of this kind allowed him to challenge the assumption that properly polite language was sufficient to comprehend society accurately. It confronted gentlemanly readers with a revised version of rural speech, a version closer to the language which was conventionally accepted to be proper for poetry. And in this way it made it harder for readers to disregard the words and experience of rural labourers – at least when those words were subsumed in Wordsworth's own 'voice of nature'.

> An awful voice,
> 'Tis true, I in my walks have often heard,
> Sent from the mountains or the sheltered fields,
> Shout after shout – reiterated whoop
> In manner of a bird that takes delight
> In answering to itself, or like a hound
> Single at chase among the lonely woods –
> A human voice, how awful in the gloom
> Of coming night, when sky is dark, and earth
> Not dark, not yet enlightened, but by snow
> Made visible, amid the noise of winds
> And bleatings manifold of sheep that know
> That summons and are gathering round for food –
> That voice, the same, the very same, that breath
> Which was an utterance awful as the wind,
> Or any sound the mountains ever heard.
>
> (lines 407–22)

The voice is like the bird's (a creature whose sublimity Wordsworth has already revealed at this point) in that it is self-sufficient and independent of the presence of another ('answering to itself'). It is, like the hound, 'single' among 'lonely' woods. Paradoxically, then, it is like these inarticulate creatures in being different from them and all else, in being single, individual. Like the thorn in the poem of that name it is powerful in its inexplicable and irreducible individuality, the same as nothing else save itself: 'That voice, the

---

[15] All subsequent quotations are from the MS B text unless otherwise specified.

same, the very same'. As such it is not *like* nature, not *like* the wind, but seems to stand for them in its self-enclosed inarticulacy. For it is a voice, not speech, a sound before or beyond words yet to enter into the self-differentiation that words bring and therefore one of the inarticulate sounds of nature. But if it is inarticulate it is still a voice, still active, and it still communicates, even if not by language: The sheep 'know / That summons'. It excites Wordsworth with the sense that he is overhearing the communication of nature normally closed to man, a secret utterance which he, like the mountains themselves, can now hear. It is sublime ('awful' is used three times in the passage) because it cannot be delimited by language, being itself extra-linguistic. Through it the shepherd, or rather Wordsworth who hears in the shepherd's voice what the shepherd himself does not, is raised into participation with the mysterious communicative energies which animate nature and render all human distinctions tentative. Tentativeness is present in the passage in the disembodiment of the voice: the reassuring attribution of sound to a visible or nameable person cannot be made. It is also present in the qualifying adjectives, which almost contradict each other in an attempt to describe the extra-ordinary: 'when sky is dark, and earth / Not dark, not yet enlightened'.

Here Wordsworth sought to found the authority of his articulate language, his poetry, on his privileged hearing and understanding of an inarticulate communication, an original and single voice apparently as primal and ungoverned as the wind. In this movement the inevitable differentiation and loss of unity that enters with articulate language can seemingly be repaired by grounding that language on the original voice of nature, a speech beyond speech. Wordsworth had taken Gilpin's and Johnson's interest in untutored rural speech to an extreme, in a logical development of the theories that he elaborated in the same year in the *Preface* to the *Lyrical Ballads*. In that essay the speech of mountain dwellers is the best part of language because founded on the enduring objects of nature. Here, though, their voices not their words constitute an original and moral example, since voices are not subject to the self-differentiation that language introduces.

On crossing the Alps in *The Prelude* Wordsworth speaks for the peasant who had pointed out their way. He founds his words on the speech of a rustic who had been native to that vale. Here, in *Home at Grasmere*, he speaks for a rustic whose voice is still more original and native because pre-linguistic. In *Home at Grasmere* then, even rustic language becomes untrustworthy, ostensibly because it is often immoral but at root because it showed itself to be subject to historical and social difference, to be shaped by tradition, dialogue and argument rather than being an innocent and perfect representation of unchanging nature. The shepherd taints what Wordsworth has heard in his voice when he dares to speak: 'That Shepherd's voice, it may have reached mine ear / Debased and under prophanation, made / An organ for the sounds articulate / Of ribaldry and blasphemy and wrath' (lines 423–6).

Wordsworth's authority in this passage no longer depends on a vindication of the language of the rural poor over that of their masters but on a self-exalting discourse which claims to know better than the rustics themselves their significance, using them as disembodied and speechless voices of nature, symbols of a vocal purity to which his own writing aspires in its attempt to overcome its threatened exclusion by the language of propriety and its masters – owners of the Vale.[16] This exclusion is social, historical and linguistic at once: Wordsworth seeks a language immune to the betrayals of meaning experienced in the discourses on which he had placed his hopes. These discourses included the law which Lonsdale had callously manipulated to sever the Wordsworths from their home, the revolution whose ideals had proved so vulnerable to Robespierre's corruptions, and the gentlemanly taste, as defined by critics such as Smith and Jeffrey, which disdained ballad poetry. In the search, however, he broaches the danger of another betrayal, that of the local authorities through whose voices he was trying to make his challenge to these discourses. A pure and uncompromised voice could only be found beyond language, even a language as simple and enduring as he had thought the rustics' to be, and so Wordsworth's poem shadows and pursues a voice which it can never master.[17] The drama here is one of both powerlessness and power. Wordsworth accepts his powerlessness to delimit the voice of nature in words, hence its sublimity consists not only of limitlessness but 'awful' humbling strength. But he assumes the power, by virtue of having at least been able to delineate his hearing of the voice, to know better than other men (and other poets) what and where it is: 'this sublime retirement', as he calls it (line 723), depends upon the ability of his poetry to convince him (and us) that it knows what it cannot say.

Wordsworth, Cowper and the freeman

Knowing the voice of nature better than other men and poets was critical to Wordsworth's assumption of power. Yet for all its exclusivity his poetry shows itself to be dependent upon the voices of others, not only those of the shepherds, but those of other poets. The whole discussion of the freeman in *Home at Grasmere* is derived from a passage in William Cowper's *The Task*, about which Wordsworth declared in 1814 'with the exception of Burns and Cowper, there is very little of recent verse, however much it may interest me,

---

[16] See Johnston, *Wordsworth and The Recluse*, pp. 219–24, on Wordsworth's difficulty in turning a personal into a social vision in the poem. Also Jonathan Wordsworth, *Wordsworth: The Borders of Vision*, pp. 125–7.

[17] A process which brings Wordsworth closer than he would have cared to admit to the Coleridge of 'The Ancient Mariner' and 'Constancy to an Ideal Object'. See my 'Coleridge, Böhme and the Language of Nature', *MLQ*, 52 (1991), 37–52. Paul Magnuson, in *Coleridge and Wordsworth: A Lyrical Dialogue* (Princeton, NJ, 1988), p. 232, views the poem as an intended 'declaration of independence' from Coleridge, which nevertheless remains haunted by him.

that sticks to my memory' (*WL* (*EY*), vol. ii, p. 179). Wordsworth valued Cowper's passionate fondness for natural objects and the 'chaste' diction in which he described them. Analysing a Cowper poem in an appendix to the *Preface* to *Lyrical Ballads*, Wordsworth valued its 'natural language' and concluded that 'in works *of imagination and sentiment* ... in proportion as ideas and feelings are valuable, whether the composition be in prose or in verse, they require and exact one and the same language' (*W Prose*, vol. i, p. 164). A reviewer of *Lyrical Ballads* in 1801 found Wordsworth to have achieved the clarity and power he admired in *The Task*. Of a passage of the 'Old Cumberland Beggar' he declared 'there is all the moral pith and nervous force of Cowper ... without any semblance of imitation'.[18]

In *Home at Grasmere* Wordsworth hymns the independent Lakeland farmer whom, in the *Preface*, he had treated as the speaker of a language of 'nervous force'. Calling him 'A Freeman, therefore sound and unenslaved' (line 443), Wordsworth rewrites the 'fortunatus est' theme that originated with Virgil and Horace: 'he who tills the field, / He, happy Man! is Master of the field / And treads the mountain which his Father trod' (lines 462–4). The term 'freeman' had a political currency amongst radical opponents of Pitt's ministry, derived from its use by seventeenth-century republicans. Algernon Sidney, the republican nobleman executed in 1683 and a hero of the Girondins in the French Revolution, was invoked by Coleridge in 1795 and praised by Wordsworth in 1794 and in a sonnet of 1802. Wordsworth had probably encountered his *Discourses Concerning Government* at Cambridge, discussed them in France with Beaupuy, and borrowed their republican arguments in his 1793 *Letter to the Bishop of Llandaff*. In the *Discourses*, Sidney had argued that the people or 'multitude were freemen' (although he did not specify whether by 'freemen' he meant 'freeholders' or men free from slavery). Government, he argued, as Harrington also did in *Oceana* (also influencing Wordsworth), should be by an assembly representing the freeman: 'till the commonwealth be established', he reasoned, 'no multitude can be seditious, because they are not subject to any human law'. Like Lowth, Sidney idealized Hebrew society, declaring 'we cannot find a more perfect Picture of Freemen, living according to their own Will, than in Abraham and Lot'.[19]

Sidney had been revived by radical neo-Harringtonian Whigs at the end of the seventeenth century. Wordsworth knew the 1698 publication of his work. And in 1795 the *Discourses* were reissued by Joseph Johnson, Wordsworth's and Coleridge's publisher. Quoted by prominent radicals such as Thelwall (himself tried for sedition in 1794), associated with the French Revolution, Sidney's republicanism made public praise of his views a radical and dangerous step. Wordsworth, however, had left his *Letter to the Bishop of*

---

[18]   In *The Monthly Mirror*, 11 (1801), 389.
[19]   *Discourses Concerning Government* (London, 1698), pp. 75, 81, 76.

Llandaff unpublished and, by the time of his 1802 sonnet praising Sidney, was far from advocating a republic. He was, in fact, by then nearer to the neo-Harrington tradition evident in the earlier eighteenth century and used by the Country-party apologists. Thomson's Patriot poem 'Rule Britannia' had implied that Britons were and would remain freemen if an aggressive naval foreign policy was pursued (a hit at Walpole's reluctance to fight against Spanish attacks on colonial trade): 'Britons never never never shall be slaves.' And for Bolingbroke and Chesterfield a parliament and electorate of independent property-holders was vital for the nation's liberty. Freemen and freeholders were a bastion against ministerial and monarchical encroachment, as Harrington had argued.

Yet Wordsworth retained a radical edge not found in the arguments of the great noblemen of the Patriot opposition. He had, as they had, turned his back on the republicanism of seventeenth-century accounts of constitutional freedom, but his 'freeman' is not, as it is in their work, principally the landed gentleman, but the freeholding small farmer. And although he does not adopt Harrington's agrarian law to ensure that landholding remains in the hands of many small owners, in *Lyrical Ballads* and in *Michael* he shows the small farmers to possess a language the moral depth of which stems from their independence – they are freemen in that they are free from wage labour and from the landlord's coercion.

In *Home at Grasmere* Wordsworth's discussion of the freeman and the appropriation of the shepherd's voice (which immediately precedes it) further modify his Commonwealthsman republicanism of 1793. Not Sidney's freeman but Cowper's is to the fore, for Wordsworth's passages, in vocabulary and style, echo *The Task*. Cowper defines the freeman by an allusion to Jesus' words in John's gospel: 'And ye shall know the truth, and the truth shall make you free' (John 8: 32: Coleridge later used the phrase as a radical motto for his political journal *The Watchman*). Cowper also distinguishes the freeman's possessions from the property of the landowners:

> He is the freeman whom the truth makes free,
> And all are slaves beside. There's not a chain
> That hellish foes confed'rate for his harm
> Can wind around him, but he casts it off
> With as much ease as Samson his green wyths.
> He looks abroad into the varied field
> Of Nature, and though poor perhaps, compared
> With those whose mansions glitter in his sight,
> Calls the delightful scen'ry all his own.
> His are the mountains, and the vallies his,
> And the resplendent rivers. His t'enjoy
> With a propriety that none can feel,
> But who with filial confidence inspired,

> Can lift to heav'n an unpresumptuous eye,
> And smiling say – my father made them all.
> Are they not his by a peculiar right,
> And by an emphasis of int'rest his,
> Whose eye they fill with tears of holy joy,
> Whose heart with praise, and whose exalted mind
> With worthy thoughts of that unwearied love
> That plann'd, and built, and still upholds a world
> So clothed with beauty, for rebellious man?
>
> (*Task*, pp. 219–20; bk v, lines 733–54)

As Wordsworth was later to do, Cowper claims 'a peculiar right' over the land because his interest in it is aesthetic, moral and religious, not commercial. The glittering mansions of wealthy landowners may be evidence of their property rights, but propriety in ownership comes from a filial acceptance that all one's possessions originate in God the Father. Cowper enforces a moral distinction between 'property' and 'propriety' which allows him to subordinate the economic relations of master and servant, landlord and tenant to the moral discourse of filial duty and love: 'And smiling say – my father made them all!' In so doing, he opens a way for Wordsworth, for he makes the landscape the true possession of the poet whose 'exalted mind' enables him to apprehend its divine and paternal originator.

The power of the landlords is supplanted, whilst the liberty of the peasants is surpassed by that of a man who is closer to the meaning of the land than they. Cowper continues:

> Yes – ye may fill your garners, ye that reap
> The loaded soil, and ye may waste much good
> In senseless riot; but ye will not find,
> In feast or in the chace, in song or dance,
> A liberty like his, who, unimpeach'd
> Of usurpation, and to no man's wrong,
> Appropriates nature as his father's work,
> And has a richer use of yours, than you,
> He is indeed a freeman.
>
> (p. 220; bk v, lines 755–63)

Home at Grasmere is thematically and verbally similar to this. When Wordsworth discusses the shepherd's voice, profaned by ribaldry, as Cowper's farmers are by 'senseless riot', he too claims a superior understanding, and therefore truer possession, of the freedom of nature. Wordsworth also appropriates a spiritual origin in nature that he assures us is gained by no attack on others' property: 'The unappropriated bliss hath found / An owner, and that owner I am he' (lines 85–6). Cowper concludes that his spiritual freedom protects him against worldly oppression: 'to bind him is a vain attempt / Whom God delights in, and in whom he dwells' (p. 221; bk v, lines 777–8). Wordsworth also makes his possession by a paternal God the guarantee of his 'wealth / Inward and outward' (line 91). Thus by basing his discussion of the freeman on Cowper's evangelical definition of liberty as a spiritual possession of the retired and disinterested poet, ultimately evidence of God-in-nature, Wordsworth modifies his politics of the 1790s. Liberty, in *Home at Grasmere*, inheres in its representation by one whose place in the landscape affords him spiritual, rather than actual possession. The free-holding small farmer is an image of a freedom felt and understood more deeply by the poet who has no economic interests at all in the land. Like Cowper, Wordsworth here makes independence and disinterest depend not on the actual possession of land, not, as he had argued in 1793 after Harrington, on a commonwealth of freeholders, but on a *spiritual* possession of all the landscape that demands that one *actually* owns and profits from no part of it. Commercial self-interest, whether that of the large landowner or small freeholder, is here for Wordsworth, as for Cowper, a threat to disinterest. Owning nothing but representing all, the poet develops the extensive view of the large landowner without his domination of others for profit, whilst he has the detailed experience and self-reliance of the smallholder without the limitation of perspective that comes with attachment to a small part of the scene.

The change in Wordsworth's politics of landscape is also apparent in the prosody of *Home at Grasmere*, and here too Cowper was influential in offering Wordsworth a poetic style neither simply identifiable with the landowning classes nor with the local peasants. Cowper's prosody redeemed the gentlemanly voice for Wordsworth and, at the same time, familiarized Milton's epic style – making it a discourse adaptable to a first-person articulation of landscape. In adapting Miltonic and Thomsonian blank verse Cowper had retained some relatively formal and Latinate words but introduced the vocabulary of gentlemanly conversation. His verse, as a consequence, was more often polite than bombastic. But he had largely retained the syntactical structures that Milton had employed to give both drive and variety to his argument in the long verse paragraph. Since Cowper, however, spoke more familiarly and nakedly from the admittedly vulnerable position of a first-person narrator his syntax tended to dramatize an 'I' whose authority was displaced into subordinate and qualifying clauses, secondary subjects and complex syntactical relations.[20] Any conventional or pre-existent relationship between the subject 'I' and the objects of its verbal contemplation is removed, to be replaced by a disturbingly (but also, potentially, exhilarat-ingly) fluid and shifting pattern. At best this pattern, suspending the 'I' of the poem in varied and changing syntactical shapes, places it in new and

---

[20] On Cowper's syntax and Wordsworth's blank verse see Joseph F. Musser, Jr, 'William Cowper's Syntax as an Indication of his Relationship to the Augustans and Romantics', *Style*, 11 (1977), 284–307.

provisional representations of time and space. Nature and the self, in their conventional forms, are deconstructed and remade in new relations over and again. For Cowper the risk of this prosodic fluidity was that the suspended self would never again crystallize, never be deposited at the end of the complex verse sentence with its authority redefined. Here he differed from his master, Milton, who paid out a verbal and syntactical net of complication and entanglement to stage, for example, Satan's sophistical convoluted arguments, only to pull it taut with a resolving main verb in which the speaker's control over words (and the scene they represent) is decisively re-established.

Cowper opened a way for Wordsworth in that he deepened the instability and vulnerability of the 'I', leaving it suspended in the complex verbal scene but unable to dominate it since the verse-sentence comes to no grandly reassertive conclusion:

> Here unmolested, through whatever sign
> The sun proceeds, I wander. Neither mist,
> Nor freezing sky, nor sultry, checking me,
> Nor stranger intermeddling with my joy.
> Ev'n in the spring and play-time of the year,
> That calls the unwonted villager abroad
> With all her little ones, a sportive train,
> To gather king-cups in the yellow mead,
> And prink their hair with daisies, or to pick
> A cheap but wholesome sallad from the brook,
> These shades are all my own. The tim'rous hare,
> Grown so familiar with her frequent guest,
> Scarce shuns me; and the stock dove, unalarm'd,
> Sits cooing in the pine-tree, nor suspends
> His long love-ditty for my near approach.
> Drawn from his refuge in some lonely elm
> That age or injury has hollow'd deep,
> Where on his bed of wool and matted leaves,
> He has outslept the winter, ventures forth
> To frisk awhile, and bask in the warm sun,
> The squirrel, flippant, pert, and full of play.
> He sees me, and at once, swift as a bird,
> Ascends the neighb'ring beech; there whisks his brush,
> And perks his ears, and stamps and scolds aloud,
> With all the prettiness of feign'd alarm,
> And anger insignificantly fierce.
>
> (*Task*, pp. 246–7; bk vi, lines 295–320)

'I wander', Cowper declares, but within the scene that his verse envisages it is others who wander: the mist, the villagers, the hare, the stock-dove and the squirrel are united in their playfully active response to the 'play-time' of spring, itself conceived as calling to them. Spring is a time and place of playful unworried motion, as the suspension of narrative drive by a syntax full of descriptive phrases and qualifying asides slows the reader, whilst shifting his or her attention from activity to activity. And whilst, of course, it is the poet who is constructing this meandering narrative, he is not tempted to view it as an exemplification of his own artistic power. Indeed the 'I' is lost as an active force within the scene, defined instead as the passive object of others' activity, allowed access to the scene by the innocent unselfconscious energy of its native inhabitants, who are too playful to exclude him from it – they only feign alarm and anger. 'Those shades', it seems 'are all my own' only because the poet can vicariously enjoy (and represent) the activity of those who have generously shared their native place with him. Passages of generosity such as this remade the self, showing its passivity to contain a deep emotional investment in a varied and shifting scene. Rather than oppressing Words-worth with a powerfully conclusive discourse they enabled him to structure his landscapes so that the narrating 'I' is suspended in a scene apprehended as a pattern of shifting time/space relations. Bringing Miltonic prosodic tension home to a polite voice vulnerable in its retired passivity, Cowper left Wordsworth the unfinished task of re-establishing a gentlemanly voice in power over itself and over the scene when his verse had shown that it could no longer presume to authority over either in conventional terms. It was a task which, in *The Prelude*, he explicitly announced as his own as he sought to write an epic poem on the growth of his own mind. So too, in *Home at Grasmere*, *The Task* was for Wordsworth a pre-text, a language which would reach full articulation in his own later verse. In this respect it had a not dissimilar function to that of the inarticulate voice of the shepherd. The prosody and the politics of *Home at Grasmere* were founded on such texts, on others (including Thomson and Coleridge) for whom Wordsworth could confidently speak, as well as on a tussle with predecessors so great that their words could never easily be made one's own.

The fact that Wordsworth proved unable to finish *The Recluse* suggests that *The Prelude* and *Home at Grasmere* were successes of a kind he could not easily develop. In broaching the divisions that arose in his authority as he sought a poetic voice powerful enough to challenge contemporary taste, the poems throw a piercing light on the difficulties of authority in the culture which Wordsworth wished to change. They question the place and power of the poet in relation to his subjects and to his likely readership and they are illuminative of the personal and implicitly political conflicts arising from the attempt to speak for disregarded local authorities to the audience whose taste helped cause that disregard. In this respect the poems diagnose the destruction of the gentlemanly consensus in which disinterested agreement about aesthetic values had been used, by those capable of making the agreement, as a basis for their proper definition and rule of the social realm.

Diagnosis is not cure, however, and *Home at Grasmere* and *The Prelude*, without the explicitly public and historical vision which was to have been made in *The Recluse*, were too exploratory of the conflicts involved in speaking for the landscape to a divided society to be the kind of cure that Wordsworth increasingly wanted poetry to be. In the years 1800–5 he began to conceive an increasingly ideological rôle for his own voice. It would be a translation of local authorities into a self-consciously poetic shared language the figurative power of which was intended to move its readers towards a renewed sense of the national community that both radical and Westminster politics had failed to restore. This rôle was, as Jon Klancher has argued, limited by the fact that only the educated classes were likely to form Wordsworth's readership.[21] He could only hope that by the general diffusion of his poems the rural classes would also be awakened to the power of their language. And such awakening, even if, as he hoped, the rural poor did come across his verse in chapbooks and broadsheets, would in practice be likely to consist of the poor learning to value what the poet and the educated reader thought valuable in their experience.

Yet Wordsworth remained suspicious of the educated readers of his own times. The reading public, guided he thought by hostile reviewers, threatened his self-belief by remaining largely indifferent to his claims that the poet had, crucially, the ability to renew society. His suspicion was in part justified, at least until his later years when recognition and the Laureateship came, and in part a reflection of the fact that, because he had staked his poetic manliness on translating for himself and society otherwise unheard voices of authority, no reader could ever be relied upon to receive and return his words without misinterpretation and loss, whether the readership was the public or was his circle of admirers. In this respect Wordsworth's rural poetry was similar to Cowper's, written with a disdain for the market that became a token of the poet's independence of the culture of commercial self-interest he attacked in the nation at large. Despite his real desire for public success, Wordsworth preserved the appearance of a disinterested view by stressing his refusal to write in fashionable styles for popular applause. Allied with his independence of any gentlemanly or noble patron this position allowed him, until the reconciliation with the Lowther family, to criticize a nation defined by 'getting and spending'. He himself stood, meanwhile, with a clear uncorrupted view, in and for the independent and free community of the Lakeland freeholders. It was, nevertheless, a standpoint achieved only with the aid of Raisley Calvert's legacy, which gave Wordsworth a private income. He could write without subjecting himself to the demands of the market or the whims of a living patron with the aid of this 'Bequest' 'sufficient for my needs'. It enabled him 'to pause for choice'

---

[21] See Jon P. Klancher, *The Making of English Reading Audiences 1790–1832* (Madison, WI and London, 1987), p. 146.

(*Prelude*, 1805, bk XIII, lines 356–7) as Adam Smith had suggested the leisured man was able to do.[22]

Rejecting the existing reading public, Wordsworth needed an ideal audience which would be responsive to his words without criticism. Besides appealing to the spirit of the people in history as an ideal readership who would vindicate his poetry, Wordsworth returned to the aesthetic theories whose authority his poetry had done so much to challenge. As if to accommodate his poetry within the gentlemanly discourse by which the value of art was preserved as the prerogative of those capable of disinterested (because leisured) judgement Wordsworth corresponded with Uvedale Price. He declared that Price had been 'much pleased with what I said upon the Sublime' (*WL* (*EY*), vol. I, p. 35). In a manuscript discussion of the sublime and beautiful Wordsworth stressed his difference from picturesque theory, declaring that the sublime was dependent neither on novelty nor on taste for pictures. But in asserting the sublimity of gradual curves and stressing imaginative energy he also perpetuated some of the criteria laid down by Gilpin and Price in response to Burke.[23] Wordsworth mixed Burke, the picturesque and Kant in his theory as he made individual form, duration and a sense of power necessary parts of the sublime, which 'raises us to a sympathetic energy and calls upon the mind to grasp at something towards which it can make approaches but which it is incapable of attaining' (*W Prose*, vol. II, p. 354).[24]

The by now more gentlemanly and conservative Wordsworth was assimilating the dangerous incompleteness, the energetic grasping, of his poetry to a conventional aesthetic category. He tended to remove the social and political threat of showing that his poetry's dangerous energy emanated from the voices of rural authorities ungoverned by taste. Yet he did not completely become a traditionalist and, faced with the organization of an actual landscape by picturesque aesthetics, refused, even in the company of gentlemen and patrons, to endorse the legitimacy of their claim properly to reflect a rural locality. In 1810 he visited Price's landscaped estate at Foxley,

---

[22] The Smith/Wordsworth comparison is made at length by Stephen Copley, 'Real Jobs in the Real World: Wordsworth and Adam Smith', *TWC*, 25 (1994), 62–7.

[23] A.W. Heffernan (*The Re-Creation of Landscape* (Hanover and London, 1984), pp. 17–34) assesses Wordsworth's continuing involvement with picturesque aesthetics. See also Hugh Sykes Davies, *Wordsworth and the Worth of Words*, ed. John Kerrigan and Jonathan Wordsworth (Cambridge, 1986), pp. 198–221.

[24] Kant's analysis of the sublime in the *Critique of Judgement* (1790) shows the mind, defeated in its attempt to comprehend the almost-infinite object, rebounding upon itself and there finding true infinity in its own reason. For application of the Kantian sublime to Wordsworth, via a Freudian interpretation in which religion struggles to repress the imagination so that a divided but powerful self emerges, see Thomas Weiskel, *The Romantic Sublime* (Baltimore, 1976), pp. 38–44. Frances Ferguson makes an acute criticism of Weiskel's views as a recasting of Kant 'in empiricist terms, so that the infinite seems like the next stage up from the size or number that one can comfortably comprehend'. In *Solitude and the Sublime* (New York and London, 1992), pp. 86–7.

but was not impressed by its beauties. Price had, he thought, removed the variety of scenery that arises from 'the occupations and wants of life in a country left more to itself'. Enclosing farmland into a park 'which he keeps exclusively to himself, and which he devotes wholly or in part to ornament', Price had isolated himself from his tenants, 'impoverishing and *monotonizing* Landscapes' (*WL* (*EY*), vol. I, p. 506). Price was a Whig squire, knighted for political services, and Wordsworth was writing here to another country gentleman, his friend and patron Sir George Beaumont. But even in these circumstances Wordsworth was politely suggesting that the occupations of farmers and labourers, the work of a rural population, and not the gentlemanly taste for the picturesque, make the land aesthetically as well as economically productive.

A tour in Scotland, 1803

The Wordsworths had taken several opportunities of observing the gentlemanly taste for the picturesque during 1803 when, initially in the company of Coleridge, they toured the Highlands of Scotland. Their route took them to a number of the noblemen's estates visited by Johnson and by Gilpin and established as tourist sights by their inclusion in tour narratives. Dorothy's own narrative judges those estates in a manner similar to Gilpin's tour (which Wordsworth had owned since 1795 at least) preferring the appearance of wildness to landscapes either too formal or too fashionably ornamented. But Dorothy was not restrained, as Gilpin had been, by the dedication of the narrative to the nobility. Rather than repair their taste she was prepared for its inadequacy. Of the pleasure grounds by the Linn, she noted 'Along the whole of the path were openings at intervals for views of the river, but, as almost always happens in gentlemen's grounds, they were injudiciously managed; you were prepared for a dead stand by a parapet, a painted seat, or some other device.'[25]

Following in Gilpin's footsteps, the Wordsworths reached Inverary, to be impressed as he had been by the Duke of Argyll's improved castle and grounds, save where they exhibited the style of Capability Brown: 'we continued our walk a short way along the river, and were sorry to see it stripped of its natural ornaments, after the fashion of Mr. Brown, and left to tell its tale – for it would not be silent like the river at Blenheim to naked fields and the planted trees on the hills'.[26] Similarly, at Lord Breadalbin's grounds by the river Tay, Dorothy wrote of the gravelled walks: 'it seemed to us that a bad taste had been at work, the banks being regularly shaven and cut as if by rule and line'. Like Gilpin, she criticized the situation of the new

[25] Dorothy Wordsworth, *Recollections of a Tour Made in Scotland A.D. 1803*, ed. J.C. Shairp, 3rd edn. (Edinburgh, 1894), p. 38.
[26] *Ibid.*, p. 131.

house, 'in a hollow, without prospect either of the lake or river, or anything else – seeing nothing, and adorning nothing'.[27] And the Duke of Atholl's estate at Blair also met the same criticisms as those made by Gilpin: the house lacked prospect and the grounds contained 'wearisome' gravel walks, too wide and straight to afford any variety of prospect.[28]

Dorothy's criticisms are those of Gilpin, those of the picturesque tourist visiting known landscape gardens and judging them in relation to a standard of taste defined in previous tour narratives. Like Gilpin she objects to the smoothed parks of Capability Brown, to the dressing of the scene in an ornamenal style imported from fashionable London. She notes of Inverary that 'the author-tourists have quarrelled with the architecture of it', that the castle lacks the 'ideas of danger or security' which would befit the seat of 'an ancient Highland chieftan'. It is, however, suitable for a 'Duke of Argyle at the end of the eighteenth century' with his 'house in Grosvenor Square, his London liveries, and daughters flittering at St. James's'.[29] Her taste for wild landscape sometimes also owes much to the picturesque, with its tendency to view the landscape as a series of scenes of aesthetic value rather than moral import, provoking associations with a romanticized ancient past:

We hardly ever saw a thoroughly pleasing place in Scotland, which had not something of wildness in its aspect of one sort or another. It came from many causes here: the sea, or sea-loch, of which we only saw as it were a glimpse crossing the vale at the foot of it, the high mountains on the opposite shore, the unenclosed hills on each side of the vale, with black cattle feeding on them, the simplicity of the scattered huts, the half-sheltered, half-exposed situation of the village, the imperfect culture of the fields, the distance from any city or large town, and the very names of Morven and Appin, particularly at such a time, when Ossian's old friends, sunbeams and mists, as like ghosts as any in the mid-afternoon could be, were keeping company with them.[30]

If the above passage exhibits the tendency of Gilpin's picturesque to view agricultural inefficiency and rural poverty as a source of aesthetic delight for an uninvolved tourist, there are many others in Dorothy's narrative which exhibit her detailed interest in the experience and self-expression of the inhabitants of the Highland glens. And her narrative also presents William's response to the same scenes, in the form of comments made at the time and poems written later. For Dorothy 'the sound of a half-articulate Gaelic hooting' from a boy calling the cattle through the mist and oncoming darkness 'was in the highest degree moving to the imagination'. She notes that 'his dress, cry, and appearance [were] all different from anything we had been accustomed to'. For her brother these cultural differences not only

27   *Ibid.*, pp. 193–4.
28   *Ibid.*, p. 199.
29   *Ibid.*, p. 130.
30   *Ibid.*, pp. 158–9.

illustrated 'the whole history of the Highlander's life' but 'above all, that visionariness which results from a communion with the unworldliness of nature'.[31] Similarly, Dorothy's detailed observation of the lives and words of the girls at the ferry-house on Loch Lomond is followed by William's version of the encounter – the poem 'To a Highland Girl' – which transforms both Dorothy's nuanced social observation and the picturesque views of rural scenes:

> Sweet Highland Girl, a very shower
> Of beauty is thy earthly dower!
> Twice seven consenting years have shed
> Their utmost bounty on thy head:
> And these grey rocks; this household lawn;
> These trees, a veil just half withdrawn;
> This fall of water, that doth make
> A murmur near the silent Lake;
> This little Bay, a quiet road
> That holds in shelter thy abode;
> In truth together ye do seem
> Like something fashion'd in a dream ...[32]

The rhyme scheme creates a harmony from the objects of the scene whilst the syntax leads the reader through them to the 'true seeming' which the poet's simile is able to see in them. Prosody, structuring recollection, is able to transform the viewed objects which in their variety compose a picturesque scene into an image of the 'visionariness' which, William told Dorothy, 'results from a communion with the unwordliness of nature'. That visionariness is attributed to the girl, but realized fully only in Wordsworth's more self-conscious meditation. She is subsumed in the more self-aware vision that she has prompted in him by stimulating his poetic recollection. She thus loses her individuality and her social context, becoming instead an embodiment of the unworldliness of nature, a figure of its elusive spirit or an articulation of its voice, more ghost than person:

> Thou wear'st upon thy forehead clear
> The freedom of a mountaineer:
> A face with gladness overspread!
> Sweet smiles by human-kindness bred!
> And seemliness complete, that sways
> Thy courtesies, about thee plays;
> With no restraint but such as springs
> From quick and eager visitings

[31] Ibid., p. 116.

[32] Ibid., p. 113, cf. WPW, vol. III, pp. 73–4. On the contrast between Dorothy's journal observations and William's poetry on their Scottish tour, see Pamela Woof, 'Dorothy Wordsworth and the Pleasures of Recognition: An Approach to the Travel Journals', TWC, 22 (1991) 150–60.

Of thoughts that lie beyond the reach
Of thy few words of English speech:
A bondage sweetly brook'd, a strife
That gives thy gestures grace and life!
So have I, not unmoved in mind
Seen birds of tempest-loving kind,
Thus beating up against the wind

(lines 32–46)

The girl's limited English is shown here neither as social deprivation nor as evidence of the social and cultural difference of Scotland. Rather, like the shepherd's inarticulate calls in *Home at Grasmere*, it is portrayed as a sign of 'the freedom of a mountaineer', of, that is, a free natural energy which those native to a wild place are able to voice (if not speak). Such native liberty is not reconciled with the cultural order of language – the girl's struggles to articulate her thoughts in 'English speech' produce a powerful energy but no verbal issue. Wordsworth both values – as he does in *Home at Grasmere* – a voice whose inarticulacy makes it seem to emerge from a natural wildness rather than a cultural order and offers himself as one more capable of translating it into words. He can do what the girl cannot, deliver the thoughts prompted in her by the place into English. But he could not make the translation, any more than he could as he crossed the Alps in *The Prelude*, without a more original native utterance.

'To a Highland Girl' shifts the picturesque towards the sublime as it transforms the girl from an object in a scene valued for its aesthetic appeal into a voice of innermost natural freedom, more fully realized in Wordsworth himself. It does not, however, simply flee from history to nature, or 'landscape' the girl as a voice of the vale. Instead, it represents a cultural struggle brought about by the presence of the English tourists in Gaelic Scotland as being analogous to a natural one. The need to address the visitors in English is seen as a 'bondage' for the girl, but one which, 'sweetly brooked', brings an animating tension – just as the opposing energies of birds and wind allow them to rise in the air. By means of this analogy and the confidence in English of which it is an example, Wordsworth subsumes the Scottish/English encounter in a larger encounter of natural liberty/linguistic order. He exclaims 'What joy to hear thee and to see! / Thy elder brother I would be ...' (lines 58–9). He is sure that 'heaven' 'hath led me to this lonely place' in order that he may feel a joy that he will be able to recollect as he remembers the spot in the future. What the girl experiences as a tension between a native mountain freedom and an alien language is resolved only in the words of one who, remembering her and the scene from another mountain country, turns linguistic difference into a sign of a 'common neighbourhood' (line 57). That neighbourhood is a fraternal participation in the spirit of mountain nature which she embodies but only he can articulate, albeit only in a language foreign to her. It is, however, necessary that the girl is unable to command English – both so that she cannot, as did the shepherds in *Home at Grasmere*, prostitute her voicing of natural freedom in familiar and profane words and so that Wordsworth can claim a *spiritual* kinship with her. The lack of conversation that marks the encounter of native and tourist is here the ground for an affirmation of a deeper conversation, one overcoming cultural difference, distance and the lapse of time. It is one of a shared spiritual seeing, a second sight, which the poet's language can predict if not fully articulate:

> For I, methinks, till I grow old,
> As fair before me shall behold
> The Lake, the Bay, the Waterfall,
> And thee, the Spirit of them all.
>
> (lines 73–7)

Wordsworth's construction of the tourist's encounter with the Gaelic-speaking peasants can be contrasted with Johnson's. Gaelic's unintelligibility and the peasants' unfamiliarity with English were, for Johnson, frustrating in that they confounded his attempts to know and judge another culture. They were also fascinating in that they hinted at the survival of an ancient culture relatively untouched by the political and commercial order of England. For Wordsworth, however, Gaelic's obscurity to the tourist is a sign of the mountain dweller's sympathy with nature's elusive and withdrawing spirit, heard, voiced, but never fully decoded. Gaelic's unintelligibility makes it a voicing on which his own more articulate voicing of mountain energies can found itself. In 'Stepping Westward', the Highland woman's question 'What! You are stepping westward?', already noticed by Dorothy to be a characteristically Scottish way of judging direction, was 'a sound / Of something without place or bound; / And seem'd to give me spiritual right / To travel through that region bright'.[33] And in 'The Solitary Reaper' the 'Highland Lass' sings like a voice of nature, till 'the Vale profound / Is overflowing with the sound'.[34] Wordsworth cannot understand her Gaelic song, but its very foreignness makes it seem more truly a voice from nature's heart, both emerging from but also disrupting the scene:

> No sweeter voice was ever heard
> In spring-time from the cuckoo-bird
> Breaking the silence of the seas
> Among the farthest Hebrides.
>
> (lines 13–16)

The voice breaks but also gives definition to the place, directing Words-worth's own journey through it. As in 'Stepping Westward', his construction

---

of the encounter makes the woman his Muse: the paradox that her native voice also breaks the natural silence, focusing the nature of the place by speaking its secret, licenses his own voice, that of a tourist, to speak for it too:

> I listen'd till I had my fill,
> And as I mounted up the hill
> The music in my heart I bore
> Long after it was heard no more.

(lines 29–32)

The tensions that arise between traveller and foreign land, tourist and local, Gaelic and English speakers are here part of a larger tension between nature and culture, in which nature can only be known by the voice which, however local, translates it into human terms. But if even the local girl is a cuckoo in the nest as she turns the silent seas into song, her voicing, foreign as it is to the English-speaking Wordsworth, sponsors his own – foreign to her and to the place. In other words, the condition of foreignness is shown here to affect all languages, however native, as they speak for the inarticulate voices of nature, rather than to be an affliction of the tourist. At the same time, the fact that the girl's words cannot be understood makes them seem closer to the nature they voice, more inspiring, as 'music', for the travelling poet.

The political implications of Wordsworth's position are evident in the sonnet he wrote, in the year of the tour, about the Pass of Killicrankie. Dorothy, like Gilpin on his tour, reads the 'deep chasm' as a bleak refuge of Highland military courage. From the standpoint of 1803, however, with English fears of Jacobite rebellions long passed, Dundee's destruction of the English army at Killicrankie is viewed as evidence of a native valour now needed for Britain's defence against a likely Napoleonic invasion. Political and religious divisions between Scotland and England are overwritten by an account which rebukes Britain's generals:

> Six thousand veterans practised in War's game,
> Tried men, at Killicrankie were array'd
> Against an equal host that wore the Plaid,
> Shepherds and herdsmen. Like a whirlwind came
> The Highlanders; the slaughter spread like flame,
> And Garry, thundering down his mountain road,
> Was stopp'd, and could not breathe beneath the load
> Of the dead bodies. 'Twas a day of shame
> For them whom precept and the pedantry
> Of cold mechanic battle do enslave.
> Oh! for a single hour of that Dundee
> Who on the day the word of onset gave:
> Like conquest might the men of England see,
> And her foes find a like inglorious grave.[35]

[35] *Recollections*, pp. 207–8, cf. *WPW*, vol. III, p. 85.

Valour is a 'whirlwind', a mountain-storm, an attribute of 'shepherds and herdsmen' inspired by a harsh landscape rather than a matter of regimentation and imposed order. Scotland is here a source for Wordsworth's romantic nationalism, part of his campaign against the rule of society by 'mechanic' and rationalist disciplines. Local loyalty and mountain freedom are resources which Wordsworth, himself a mountain poet, can dedicate to the nation.

In other poems written after his Scottish tour, Wordsworth incorporated Ossian into a similar nationalistic voicing of landscape. And he did so in conscious reaction to the pleasure grounds which Gilpin, on his tour, had criticized. Dorothy and William visited the Duke of Atholl's grounds on the river Braan to see the waterfall. After following gravel paths and passing flower beds they were

conducted into a small apartment, where the gardener desired us to look at a painting of the figure of Ossian, which, while he was telling us the story of the young artist who performed the work, disappeared, parting in the middle, flying asunder as if by the touch of magic, and lo! we are at the entrance of a splendid room, which was almost dizzy and alive with waterfalls, that tumbled in all directions – the great cascade, which was opposite to the window that faced us, being reflected in innumerable mirrors upon the ceiling and against the walls. We both laughed heartily, which, no doubt, the gardener considered as high commendation; for he was very eloquent in pointing out the beauties of the place.[36]

Like Gilpin, the Wordsworths were surprised by the vulgarity of the taste exhibited in this commodification of the view. Ossian had become a stage effect, a mechanical contrivance installed to prepare for the still greater tourist attraction of the waterfall itself. In an 'Effusion' written about the experience, Wordsworth portrays it as a violation of Scottish poetry and history which ignores their remaining ghostly presence in the landscape:

> What He – who, mid the kindred throng
> Of Heroes that inspired his song,
> Doth yet frequent the hill of storms,
> The stars dim-twinkling through their forms!
> What! Ossian here – a painted Thrall,
> Mute fixture on a stuccoed wall . . .[37]

He appeals directly to a Nature 'ever averse to pantomime' whose rocks and streams, exalted by Ossian, should have 'wakened some redeeming thought / More worthy of this favoured spot' (lines 34, 42–3). He imagines an alternative design for the scene, in which an image of Ossian is carved out of the rock of the river bank, a realization of the 'ghost' native to the place, played upon by wind and water. Contrasting his own design with the 'affectations' of patrons, Wordsworth speaks against them for the wisdom of

[36] *Recollections*, p. 210.
[37] *Ibid.*, p. 294; cf. *WPW*, vol. III, pp. 102–5.

unornamented nature and for a land made to speak again, as Ossian made it
speak, of Scottish warriors, of a nobility uncorrupted (unlike the Duke of
Atholl) by the 'vain pleasures of luxurious life' (lines 108, 105):

> Thus (where the intrusive Pile, ill-graced
> With baubles of theatric taste,
> O'erlooks the torrent breathing showers
> On motley bands of alien flowers
> In stiff confusion set or sown,
> Till Nature cannot find her own,
> Or keep a remnant of the sod
> Which Caledonian Heroes trod)
> I mused; and, thirsting for redress,
> Recoiled into the wilderness.

(lines 119–28)

The unsatisfied bitterness of the final couplet goes deeper than a picturesque
tourist's distaste. Wordsworth leaves himself as a prophet in the wilderness,
doubly excluded since Scotland's nobility should cherish poets who sing of
its/their native wildness. It is national poetry – Wordsworth's and Ossian's –
as well as the picturesque view, that is prostituted and excluded by the taste
of which this landscape is a small example.

   In a companion poem written after hearing that Ossian was traditionally
believed to have been buried in the Narrow Glen, Wordsworth sets out his
view of an appropriate landscape to contain the nation's heroic past. It is
neither a violent place (although Ossian 'sung of battles') nor a picturesque
one:

> A convent, even a hermit's cell
> Would break the silence of this Dell;
> It is not quiet, is not ease,
> But something deeper far than these;
> The separation that is here
> Is of the grave; and of austere
> And happy feelings of the dead:
> And therefore was it rightly said
> That Ossian, last of all his race,
> Lies buried in this lonely place.[38]

The first couplet of this extract rejects the picturesque: Gilpin's fondness for
ruined buildings of the Gothic past is not indulged. Echoing 'The Solitary
Reaper', Wordsworth declares that such buildings would 'break the silence'
of the glen. It becomes instead a wilderness, a place of quiet desolation
imbued with 'perfect rest', with the utterly self-enclosed otherness of the dead
(line 22). It is, in fact, the unmarked, unhumanized quality of the landscape

---

[38] *Recollections*, p. 214, cf. *WPW*, vol. III, pp. 75–6.

that makes it a fitting place to contain Ossian, a poet whose now dead voice sung of the death of his race. Wordsworth speaks quietly and factually, rather than ecstatically, of the place, as if to break its silence would be to violate the otherness it contains, to disturb its ghostliness and its ghost. Yet he does speak, and in the final lines aligns himself with local tradition. By means of this alignment his own words seem to inherit and reproduce the local sources, rather than impose a tourist's view upon the scene. Thus Wordsworth positions himself as the quiet spokesman for a past poet vouchsafed to him by local tradition – for a poet who sang and is now part of death and the deathliness of place. And so Wordsworth's Scotland is made symbolic of what he, following the paths of dead warriors and the words of dead poets and local traditions, can represent, a past violence stilled and cherished in the form of a death at the heart of nature.

Local tradition is crucial, just as the reaper's song and the Highland girl's greeting were. Without them, his voicing of the Highland silence would seem too foreign, too much a tourist's imposition. Following their voices, Wordsworth displaces the burden of foreignness on to them: their words first break the silence, turn natural energies into human speech. This allows him at his best to speak of the Scottish landscape, in a way hostile both to the affected taste of the contemporary landowners and to the aesthetics of the picturesque tourist, as a visionary ground in which the death that surrounds life is manifest. In the process he uses the elusiveness of Gaelic voices and Ossianic poetry to his advantage: their unintelligibility and alien morality is made to sponsor his own writing – which resists the picturesque by offering itself as a *voicing* of the scene's ghostly energies rather than a view of its prospects. Appropriating Gaelic voices for his own speaking of the landscape, Wordsworth is to be contrasted to Johnson, for whom Gaelic poetry and culture was frustratingly resistant to explication and codification by his own and others' English. At worst Wordsworth's borrowing of Scottish voices is, however, an appropriation of the kind Johnson questioned, one which uses ancient Gaelic poetry, just as Macpherson had used it, to empower the contemporary English writer and his political agenda. In poems of 1824 and 1833 Wordsworth imagined Fingal's cave as a place where 'they could hear *his* ghostly song ... / While he struck his desolate harp' (*WPW*, vol. iv, p. 41). He acknowledged Ossian's presence animating the scene, only to appropriate its power for himself and other 'Bards of mightier grasp' (*WPW*, vol. iv, p. 39). It is in Wordsworth's rather than Ossian's poetic imagination that the local authorities of the past come to centre.

Wordsworth's Scottish poems reveal his tendency, seen in *Home at Grasmere* and *The Prelude*, to reject the prospect-view and instead to speak for local voices and traditions. They claim to articulate the native energies of place by criticism of the taste of the landowning classes and of its manifestation in their landscape parks. They succeed in transforming the genre of the tour narrative and, whilst sharing Gilpin's critical view of the noblemen's estates, surpass the criteria of the picturesque. But in offering so confidently an English voicing of a Gaelic culture and a Scottish landscape, they raise questions about the betrayals of translation and the appropriations of colonialism. It is not that Wordsworth denies historical and social issues for an escape into nature, but rather that he speaks for a native culture in a manner that offers his own voice as the realization of what was implicit in that culture. He claims, and often succeeds in claiming, to know, better than the unselfconscious peasants and their noble landlords, the true voice of Highland culture rooted in the wild landscape since Fingal's time.

The landlord as patron

Wordsworth continued to speak for and of the local inhabitants of mountain districts after the Scottish poems were written. But in the years after 1805, his ambivalent involvement with the landowning classes and his changing attitude to their aesthetic values helped to cause a change in his conception of his authority and place as a poet. I wish to examine this change in relation to the politics of his Lakeland landscape, arguing that these politics remain more complex and perceptive about conflicts of loyalty than many recent critics have suggested. To understand Wordsworth's complex politics we need to focus first upon his altered relations with the Lowther family.

By 1806 the Earl of Lonsdale had died, and Lord Lowther his cousin had inherited the estate and was proving fair-minded and honourable. The debt owed the Wordsworth family was settled and, when Wordsworth himself was disappointed in his efforts to buy a small estate in Patterdale, Lowther stepped in and presented it to him. Wordsworth was becoming a landlord; possessing heritable property from which he took rent but on which he did not live, he was claiming the rights and possessions his father had never had. Moreover, in accepting land from the new Lord Lowther he was accepting a benevolent paternalism from a successor who had paid the debt Lonsdale had refused to pay. The new Lord was accepted as a 'good father' who gave the land to Wordsworth that Lonsdale, if he had been a true paternalist not a tyrant, would have given to his father.

Accepting Lowther's patronage caused Wordsworth to change his social views. He no longer wrote of the landlord as a cruel disinheriting father. He became increasingly Tory, accepting the paternalism of the landed classes as a bastion against commercialism and the domination of human relationships by money. In 1818 he campaigned actively for Lowther's candidates in elections. He also accepted paternalism in his own writing, both economically and thematically. Asking Lowther to procure a sinecure for him through his influence with ministers, Wordsworth wrote that his poetry had never supported him financially. From the economics of the market he turned to noble patronage, appealing to a (somewhat fictional) history of inherited patronage: 'my Family has for several generations been honoured by the regard of that of your Lordship' (*WL* (*MT*), vol. II, p. 3). He was returning to the kind of relationship idealized by Price in his remarks on Brown and Gainsborough quoted at the beginning of chapter three (p. 120): the master of his art accepts the recognition, but also the social, economic and political authority of a landed patron. Wordsworth became a regular guest at Lowther Castle, and in 1814 dedicated *The Excursion* to its lord. He gave advice on the landscaping of the estate and this is reflected in the dedicatory poem, in which earlier fears that Lowther would destroy the forest path of Wordsworth's youth are turned to courtly praise of his domains:

> Oft, through thy fair domains, illustrious Peer!
> In youth I roamed, on youthful pleasures bent;
> And mused in rocky cell or sylvan tent,
> Beside swift-flowing Lowther's current clear.
> – Now, by thy care befriended, I appear
> Before thee, LONSDALE, and this work present ...
>
> (*WPW*, vol. v; p. 1 , lines 1–6)

Abandoning his earlier position Wordsworth here celebrates his patron's care in terms which, ironically, place himself on the same level as the garden. Both he and it are dedicated to and cared for by the lord who sees in them classical standards of pastoral wisdom. Both the 'sylvan tent' and the man who mused in it are decorative endorsements of the taste and classical order of the man who owns them: even the river bears his name. The poem illustrates a common feature of Wordsworth's later verse: its recourse to the very 'poetic diction' to which he objected in the *Preface* to *Lyrical Ballads* as a class of words simply inherited from other poets, rather than derived from a language really spoken, or from direct observation of nature. It is a deliberate choice, which reveals the extent to which for the later Wordsworth value inhered in standards passed down in proper tradition, and not in self-authenticating rebellions against it. It was an acceptance of paternal authority stemming from Wordsworth's own reconciliation with a paternalist landlord and the society which he dominated. It is not unconnected with this that the Wordsworthian God, as he appeared in *The Excursion*, was described by Hartley Coleridge as 'the popping in of the old man with a beard' (*CL*, vol. v, p. 95).

Yet, as I shall argue about 'Yew-Trees', the later Wordsworth at his best was questioning rather than reproducing the ideologies of the landowning and gentlemanly classes. Paternalist but questioning paternalism, patriotically Tory but questioning contemporary patriotism, Wordsworth formed not a stable – or staid – gentlemanly self but an authority which was closer to Johnson's in that it put into question the domination and violence on which it shows contemporary and historical versions of power to be founded.

At this point it is necessary to take more detailed stock of some of the recent arguments about Wordsworth's politics which I mentioned at the beginning of this chapter so that recurrent and major questions about his poetry can again be asked and at least provisionally answered – is the Wordsworthian poetic self liberating or enslaving, and does it challenge or perpetuate ideologies of conservatism? The question was answered in the criticism of the 1960s in terms of imagination. Wordsworth the visionary was shown to be a voyager into the imagination, the poet who could reveal to us, by his self-reflexive contemplation of his own mind, the sources within by which we shape the world in which we live and move. In the criticism of Geoffrey Hartman, in particular, Wordsworth is seen through the lens of the philosophy of Martin Heidegger as one whose voice apprehends a Being that exists nowhere save in its own articulation. Wordsworth becomes, in Hartman's brilliant account, not so much one of the 'Prophets of Nature' (*Prelude*, bk xiii, line 442) but the prophet of the ungrounded/self-grounding voice of imagination.[39]

The 1980s saw a reaction against what was perceived as the a-historical, a-political bias of such criticism. Jerome J. McGann, in *The Romantic Ideology*, proposed instead a criticism which interrogated Romantic poetry in terms of what he claimed was its attempt to transcend historical and political conflicts.[40] Contending that Wordsworth's lyrical poetry formed a disguised ideology, McGann sponsored a critical school who viewed not only Words-worth's later work as conservative but his early work too. Moreover, they argued that his hymning of nature and imagination was a denial of the historical realm which had the effect of, at best, ignoring and, at worst, legitimizing the prevailing distribution of social and political power that he had initially regarded as unjust. Rather than protest at injustice and its causes, the argument runs, Wordsworth (increasingly a Tory gentleman horrified by the violence that followed the French Revolution's attempts to amend the state) either portrayed social evils as natural ills, or compensated for them by seeking harmony instead in his own newly paternalist mind and home – a harmony readers could share as they too recoiled from social conflicts or enjoyed the benefits of their privileged class position.

Romantic New Historicism, as the criticism prompted by McGann has

---

[39] See Geoffrey Hartman, *The Unremarkable Wordsworth* (London, 1987), especially pp. 90–119 and 194–206. Heidegger's own meditations on the poetic singing of Being can be found in *Poetry, Language, Thought*, tr. Albert Hofstadter (New York, 1971). For a similar view of Wordsworth's imagination see Herbert Lindenberger, *On Wordsworth's Prelude* (Princeton, NJ, 1963), p. 269: 'In *The Prelude* this social dimension is largely missing, or, more precisely, it exists only as a shadowy and negative force against which the self struggles and which it ultimately transcends.'

[40] Jerome J. McGann, *The Romantic Ideology: A Critical Investigation* (Chicago and London, 1983).

come to be known, provided a powerful corrective to previous accounts, forming a counterweight like that provided in Wordsworth's own time by Hazlitt's attacks on the growing conservatism of his imagination.[41] But it has itself come under scrutiny. It has been argued that critics such as McGann and Marjorie Levinson have understood history and politics in too limited a sense and have wrongly assumed that Wordsworth's involvement in nature is a flight from political and social issues.[42] It has been suggested instead that, then and especially now, the relation of men and women to the 'green earth' is a vital, perhaps the most vital, political issue. Such suggestions attempt to answer the arguments of New Historicism by claiming that Wordsworth's vision of human community in nature amounts to a politics in which social well-being is seen to depend on respect for the environment in its local particularity.

This criticism is attractive, for it ably exposes some buried assumptions in the New Historicists' view of history and, more importantly, proposes a way in which Wordsworth's poetry (and Romanticism more widely) can be seen as something more than an attempted escape from social and political issues. In Jonathan Bate's account, for instance, Wordsworth again becomes a liberating force, as he was for Ruskin and J. S. Mill in the nineteenth century, through his emphasis on a 'revolutionary' community in nature, real (in the Vale of Grasmere) and symbolic.[43] And yet Bate's account of Wordsworth's local politics also has limitations; it largely downplays his Burkeian rural paternalism and his later Toryism, leaving the evidence of much of his work unexamined and leaving a question still to be answered: can we derive a political lesson about the importance of ecological consciousness from a Wordsworth whose rural Toryism is included in the account? It is a question I wish to consider through analysis of 'Yew-Trees'. This poem both confronts the local and national politics of landscape – politics of ownership and insurrection – and ponders Wordsworth's own place in those politics. It does so by a meditation on tradition made through an adaptation of images and motifs borrowed from poems he (amongst others) had quoted as instances of the sublime.

---

[41] As distinct from the Renaissance New Historicism of Stephen Greenblatt.

[42] See, for example, M. H. Abrams, *Doing Things With Texts: Essays in Criticism and Critical Theory* (New York, 1989), Thomas McFarland, *Wordsworth: Intensity and Achievement* (Oxford, 1992) and Nicholas Roe, *The Politics of Nature: Wordsworth and Some Contemporaries* (London and Basingstoke, 1992). The work of Levinson's which they criticize is *Wordsworth's Great Period Poems*.

[43] Jonathan Bate, *Romantic Ecology: Wordsworth and the Environmental Tradition* (London, 1991), pp. 12–35, 47, 57. For a similar claim for Wordsworth as an ecologist whose 'landscape vision' we can, however, no longer possess save through his language, see Karl Kroeber, *Romantic Landscape Vision: Constable and Wordsworth* (Madison, WI, 1975).

Arbours of the imagination: 'Yew-Trees'

'Yew-Trees' was probably begun in 1803 or 1804 and completed in 1814.[44]
It was published by Wordsworth as a poem of the imagination in his
collection of 1815. In the *Biographia Literaria* Coleridge singled it out as an
example of the 'imaginative power' in which Wordsworth 'stands nearest of
all modern writers to Shakespear and Milton' (*BL*, vol. ii, pp. 151–2). More
recently Theresa M. Kelley has linked it to 'The Thorn' as a later example of
'Wordsworth's most reiterated sublime landscape and figure' and Steven
Knapp has termed it 'a version of the sublime detached from the human
interests imbedded in traditional structures of confrontation and ambivalence'.[45] It is, however, as an example of Wordsworth's questioning of, rather
than detachment from, traditional structures of confrontation and ambivalence that I want to consider it.

> There is a Yew-tree, pride of Lorton Vale,
> Which to this day stands single, in the midst
> Of its own darkness, as it stood of yore:
> Not loth to furnish weapons for the bands
> Of Umfraville or Percy ere they marched
> To Scotland's heaths; or those that crossed the sea
> And drew their sounding bows at Azincour,
> Perhaps at earlier Crecy, or Poictiers.
> Of vast circumference and gloom profound
> This solitary Tree! a living thing
> Produced too slowly ever to decay;
> Of form and aspect too magnificent
> To be destroyed. But worthier still of note
> Are those fraternal Four of Borrowdale,
> Joined in one solemn and capacious grove;
> Huge trunks! and each particular trunk a growth
> Of intertwisted fibres serpentine
> Up-coiling, and inveterately convolved;
> Nor uninformed with Phantasy, and looks
> That threaten the profane; a pillared shade,
> Upon whose grassless floor of red-brown hue,
> By sheddings from the pining umbrage tinged
> Perennially – beneath whose sable roof
> Of boughs, as if for festal purpose decked
> With unrejoicing berries – ghostly Shapes
> May meet at noontide; Fear and trembling Hope,

---

[44] On the dating of the manuscripts of the poem see Mark L. Reed, *Wordsworth: The Chronology of the Middle Years* (Cambridge, MA, 1975), pp. 679–81. For transcripts of the manuscript versions see *The Cornell Wordsworth: Poems in Two Volumes and Other Poems 1800–1807*, pp. 665–71.

[45] Theresa M. Kelley, *Wordsworth's Revisionary Aesthetics* (Cambridge, 1988), p. 165; Steven Knapp, *Personification and the Sublime* (Cambridge, MA, 1985), p. 129.

Silence and Foresight; Death the Skeleton
And Time the Shadow; – there to celebrate,
As in a natural temple scattered o'er
With altars undisturbed of mossy stone,
United worship; or in mute repose
To lie, and listen to the mountain flood
Murmuring from Glaramara's inmost caves.

(*WPW*, vol. ii, pp. 209–10)

In a brilliant essay Geoffrey Hartman has said that 'Yew-Trees' 'is in many ways the most ghostly poetry ever written: one in which speech itself is near to fading out, like echo, or the voice of genius that dies with the tree it inhabits'.[46] Hartman makes the poem's disembodied voice that of an epitaph, which speaks for a tree so old that it is a funerary monument. In his account the tree becomes a symbol within nature of death: the likely death of nature under attack from war and industrialization. It is also an object in which Being reveals itself as self-enclosed, 'in the midst / Of its own darkness', as solitary and unassimilable. Wordsworth, placing himself towards it, becomes for Hartman 'the first poet to grant nature due process' as he risks reducing his voice to ghostliness in the attempt to articulate the always-receding never-grounded Nature of nature.[47] In this attempt is revealed the nature of human articulation in its heroic fragility; through it we grant life and meaning to ourselves as we attempt to speak for the darkness of a world that eludes and resists our discourse.

Hartman's criticism changed the course of Wordsworth studies. Yet his discussion of 'Yew-Trees', like that of *The Prelude*, left the political dimensions of the poem relatively neglected. I wish to examine these and to revise his discussion in the light of Wordsworth's engagement in the poem with the Miltonic narrative of authority and rebellion. I shall look first, however, at the relatively impersonal voice used in the poem, arguing that it allows Wordsworth to present his views with an appearance of objectivity. Wordsworth's abandonment of the narratorial 'I' in the poem aligns its voice with the spirit of the named place: it speaks as the genius of Lorton and Borrowdale, its persuasiveness founded upon its use of actual names of real places. Wordsworth speaks neither of his exclusive possession of nature's meanings nor of his own prophetic authority but through a style in which observation is presented as locally and traditionally vouchsafed truth. This quietly objective style bears some resemblance to that of the guide to the Lakes which he first published in 1810. In that work he appears to the reader as a well-informed local whose emotional responses are shared matters of fact. The 'mountain wanderer', he declares, will find the 'naked' mountain tarn a 'centre or conspicuous point to which objects, otherwise disconnected

---

[46] 'The Use and Abuse of Structural Analysis', in *The Unremarkable Wordsworth*, pp. 129–51 (p.150).
[47] *Ibid.*, p. 150.

or insubordinated, may be referred'. He will feel a 'not unpleasing sadness . . . induced by this perplexity, and these images of decay'.[48]

Like the guidebook, 'Yew-Trees' discovers, in a relatively impersonal voice, perplexity and sadness in the natural objects upon which it centres the landscape. It finds the trees, as the prose-guide does the tarns, to stand as 'permanent forms' at the heart of nature. Here the poem's voice (and the concern with sadness and age it seems to find in, rather than impose on, nature) also resembles that of the epitaph. In 1810 Wordsworth's abiding interest in funerary inscriptions led him to write his *Essays upon Epitaphs*. There he argued that epitaphs should speak faithfully of the dead person they commemorate in a voice which seems to emerge from the community who now mourn that person. Epitaphs must use only those species of composition which 'have been acknowledged by the human heart; and have become so familiar that they are converted into substantial realities' (*W Prose*, vol. ii, p. 76). 'Yew-Trees' seems a composition of this kind, a long-acknowledged discourse already accepted as the real truth about the landscape. The trees are described in a voice that is apparently neutral and disembodied but that is clearly informed by deep local knowledge. In a comment made to Eliza Fenwick years later Wordsworth reverted to the actual trees, 'still-standing', and one nearby, fallen and dead yet supporting from its 'decayed trunk' numerous young plants. Wordsworth recalled that this latter tree, an example of living death, was said by Hutton, the local guide at Keswick, to have existed before the flood (*WPW*, vol. ii, pp. 503–4).

In 'Yew-Trees' the narrator's description seems reliable because it suggests that it is founded on a local knowledge as detailed as that which Wordsworth later communicated to Fenwick. The narrator is a local authority to be trusted and his views seem as rooted in fact as is the tree in the landscape. Through this style, however, he is able to present a patriotic and nationalistic view as an apparently uncontroversial one. The political meanings he derives from the tree are offered as apparently objective and impersonal observations for the narrative makes the Lorton yew an object so steady, permanent and single yet so old and so rooted in a named English locality that it embodies English history. That history, as Wordsworth portrays it in the poem, is one of continuing valour, one worthy of patriotic pride. It is a conservative history for it suggests that a sturdy independence resulting from a rooted attachment to a local place is a defining characteristic of Englishmen. Rooted independence is shown, with an implicit nationalism, to bring martial success against foreigners: the Lorton yew is 'not loth to furnish weapons' for Umfraville and Percy, northern lords defending the independence of their locality against the Scots in the Border Wars of the late fourteenth and early fifteenth centuries. On King Henry IV's behalf Umfraville and Percy won

---

[48] *A Guide through the District of the Lakes in the North of England*, in *W Prose*, vol. ii, p. 186.

battles at Otterburn (1388) and Homildoun (1402), partly by the power of English archers. Although Henry Percy, Earl of Northumberland, and his son, Hotspur, later rebelled against King Henry IV and were killed, the Umfravilles fought on Henry V's part in Scotland and in his French campaign.[49] Furnished with longbows from the Lorton tree, their bowmen helped bring about the victory at Agincourt (an effort already used by Shakespeare to vindicate Englishness against the degeneracy and corruption represented by the French).

Wordsworth's restrained tone does not explicitly celebrate war – its allusion to Shakespeare is quiet for a period in which *Henry V* was being revived in London as a patriotic anti-French play. The tree, in one of Wordsworth's characteristic negative constructions, is 'not loth' rather than positively willing to be used as a source of arms. Nevertheless, in speaking for it in this quiet and apparently factual way, Wordsworth makes it, and the landscape in which it is rooted, sponsor an Englishness defined in heroic battle. As a result of this process the politics of war are licensed by the English landscape and by the historical rootedness in it that is Englishmen's legacy from the past. The quoted place names 'Lorton' and 'Borrowdale' are themselves evidence of this rootedness in the poem. Wordsworth defines them by reference to trees which have remained largely unchanged since Percy's time. They are examples of what he declared in the Preface to *Lyrical Ballads* to be 'a more permanent and a far more philosophical language' one 'incorporated with the beautiful and permanent forms of nature' (*W Prose*, vol. I, p. 124). Quintessentially English names, 'Lorton' and 'Borrowdale' exemplify in the poem Wordsworth's ideal English language – a language so historically rooted in a largely unchanging nature that it creates a stable and authoritative personal, local and national identity. The yew trees are resources for the authority of English and Englishness: from them grow reliably powerful words in which common cause can be made and expressed. The yews allow Wordsworth's English to dominate, just as they provide 'sounding bows' to defeat, the exotic and unstable French. 'Azincour', 'Crecy' and 'Poictiers' remain exotic names, unstable even in their orthography (Poitiers? Agincourt?). They are incapable of resisting the English empowered as it is/they are by nature. Wordsworth's act of speaking the being of the trees is a nationalistic one then, made in the context of Britain's war with Napoleonic France.

In several other poems of the period, Wordsworth offers the English names that his verse invokes as talismans of England's superiority to France.

---

[49] Some of this history is noted by Gene W. Ruoff, although he locates an earlier Umfraville, fighting at Halidon Hill in 1333. See 'Wordsworth's "Yew-Trees" and Romantic Perception', *MLQ*, 34 (1973), 146–60 (pp. 150–1). Kelley notes that the Lorton yew is in reality the same tree as the 'thorn' that, in *The Borderers*, is identified with rebellion against the King (*Wordsworth's Revisionary Aesthetics*, pp. 164–5).

Published in the *Morning Post* in 1803, his sonnet 'It is not to be thought of
that the Flood / Of British freedom' was a patriotic anti-French contribution
to a newspaper that supported war. It ends by founding freedom on our
inheritance of English, an inheritance imagined as descending through a
proper Burkeian family-line from the land itself:

> We must be free or die, who speak the tongue
> That Shakespeare spake; the faith and morals hold
> Which Milton held. – In every thing we are sprung
> Of Earth's first blood, have titles manifold.
>
> (*WPW*, vol. iii, p. 117)

Similarly the sonnet 'Great men have been among us' invokes Sidney,
Marvel, Harrington in the new context of anti-French sentiment: 'France, 'tis
strange, / Hath brought forth no such souls as we had then' (*WPW*, vol. iii,
p. 116).[50] Another sonnet ponders the politics of France by surveying its
landscape, concluding that the French not only act against their own best
interests, but perversely because they do not found themselves upon their
'chosen soil, where sun and breeze / Shed gentle favours' (*WPW*, vol. iii,
p. 118). In this context the act of speaking for named heroes and places in
'Yew-Trees' is a self-conscious appeal to national pride intended to foster a
sense of historical unity and superiority to the French, giving confidence for
continued war. As Wordsworth put it at the conclusion of his *Essays upon
Epitaphs*, the 'naked names' of Shakespeare and Milton 'and a grand
comprehensive sentiment of civic gratitude, patriotic love' inspired by them
are themselves a tribute to the past (*W Prose*, vol. ii, p. 61).

With their emphasis on nationality as a matter of family lineage,
Wordsworth's anti-French sonnets echo the Toryism of Johnson and the
1790s writing of Burke. Although 'Yew-Trees' is more complicated than they
are, nevertheless it has a nationalistic political dimension largely ignored in
Hartman's account of it (as in Jonathan Bate's notion of Wordsworth as a
revolutionary ecologist).[51] Wordsworth was, as Hartman points out, drawing
upon Cowper's poem 'Yardley Oak', which also uses a tree as a symbol of
time and history.[52] Yet Cowper uses the oak to rebuke politicians who pursue
their own power at the expense of the land they have inherited:

---

[50] The Romantics' assessment of these earlier radicals is analysed in Peter J. Kitson, ' "Sages and
patriots that being dead do yet speak to us": Readings of the English Revolution in the Late
Eighteenth Century', *Prose Studies*, 14 (1991), 205–30.

[51] Whilst Ruoff and Kelley see only the Lorton yew as being described in warlike terms, Knapp,
though he notes that the Borrowdale yews are described by allusions to Virgil and Milton, decides
that 'heroic narrative survives only in the poem's allusions to ancient battles … and even these
disappear after the eighth line', *Personification and the Sublime*, p. 127.

[52] *The Unremarkable Wordsworth*, p. 146. As Jonathan Wordsworth points out, it may have been the
receipt of 'Yardley Oak' in a volume of Cowper's poems sent to him, coupled with the sight of
Lorton yew in September 1804, that prompted Wordsworth to write 'Yew-Trees' (*Wordsworth: The
Borders of Vision*, pp. 279, 442). For Cowper's poem see *The Poetical Works of William Cowper*, ed. H.S.

But the axe spar'd thee; in those thriftier days
Oaks fell not, hewn by thousands, to supply
The bottomless demands of contest wag'd
For senatorial honours.

(lines 100–3)

There is perhaps a direct allusion here to the Earl of Northampton's raising of funds to buy votes for his candidates in parliamentary elections, to his bankruptcy and to the charge taken on his timber in Yardley Chase by Capability Brown. Wordsworth, by contrast, used the oak tree in the 1850 *Prelude* as an image of the rectitude of a parliamentarian whose disinterest had been doubted after he had accepted a pension. Wordsworth described Burke standing sublime 'to awe / The younger brethren of the grove' and insisting 'Upon the allegiance to which men are born' (bk VII, lines 521, 530). And his yew tree too is Burkeian, in that it epitomizes nature and Englishness as 'a living thing / Produced too slowly ever to decay'. It is an organic tree of Englishness opposed to (and subduing) the unrooted Liberty tree of France and its Napoleonic scion.[53] Here Wordsworth's oak resembles those of Uvedale Price and Richard Payne Knight, also anti-Jacobinical symbols of the English constitution.

Yet the yew tree is not simply patriotic and political. As the poem progresses, Wordsworth speaks of the 'fraternal Four of Borrowdale' in terms which deepen and trouble our apprehension of them. As Gene W. Ruoff notes, 'the poet looks *at* the Lorton yew but *into* the grove of Borrowdale'. And what he sees there is different too; for Ruoff different to the extent that the poem gives us 'two radically discontinuous structures of experience', passing from profane history to a time haunted by the sacred in the Borrowdale trees. And Ruoff's insight is deepened by Kelley, for whom the Borrowdale grove forms a Wordsworthian beautiful by which the dangers of the egotistical sublime of the Lorton yew can be recognized and contained: 'Unlike sublime figures and speakers, who absorb or deny their surroundings so that they may be isolated in their own darkness, beautiful figures are receptive, even sociable. The Borrowdale four are "worthier still of note" precisely because they entertain and contain such figures.'[54] Valuable though such interpretations are, they tend nevertheless to overemphasize the differences and discontinuities between the trees. It is worth remembering that they are, after all, yews rooted in a named and known Lakeland landscape, that all are said to be worthy of note, and that both Lorton and

---

Milford, 4th edn (London, 1934), pp. 410–14.

[53] On the oak tree as a symbol of English tradition and monarchical government, see William Ruddick, 'Liberty Trees and Loyal Oaks: Emblematic Presences in Some English Poems of the French Revolutionary Period', in Yarrington and Everest (eds.), *Reflections of Revolution*, pp. 59–67.

[54] Ruoff, 'Wordsworth's "Yew-Trees" and Romantic Perception', pp. 152, 157; Kelley, *Wordsworth's Revisionary Aesthetics*, p. 167.

Borrowdale trees are described by numerous allusions to *Paradise Lost*. These allusions are worth exploring in some detail since they complicate the poem's apparent affiliation to traditional aesthetic categories and nationalistic politics.

The Lorton yew, as Kelley notes, is hellish in its 'vast circumference and gloom profound'; as Knapp points out it has Satanic associations evoking Milton's description of the fallen hero when 'his form had yet not lost / All her Original brightness, nor appear'd / Less than Arch-Angel ruin'd' (*Paradise Lost*, bk I, lines 591–3).[55] Similarly, the Borrowdale yews have connections with Milton's sinful and rebellious warrior-angel: each trunk is 'a growth / of intertwisted fibres serpentine / Up-coiling, and inveterately convolved', a perverse snake-like motion that recalls Milton's description of Satan appearing to Eve (bk IX, lines 494–516) and his fight with Michael, where he 'writhed him to and fro convolved' (bk VI, line 328). They also resemble Milton's Sin who 'ended foul in many a scaly fold / Voluminous and vast, a serpent armed / With mortal sting' (bk II, lines 651–3).

The narrative concerning the Borrowdale yews takes place in the fallen world, for the trees 'threaten the profane' and their 'pillared shade' is one of postlapsarian sadness. Wordsworth alludes to Milton's sinfully dark and self-procreative Indian fig-tree in whose 'thickest' 'pillared shade' the fallen Adam and Eve find covering (bk IX, lines 1110, 1106). The phrase 'pining umbrage' further indicates regret and lament. And the grove is also a place of contradiction (it is decked for 'festal purpose' with '*unrejoicing* berries': poisonous fruit that bring death). The yew tree resembles the Miltonic tree of good and evil seen after the serpentine temptation to eat of its fruit has introduced 'Death the Skeleton' to Eden. The ghosts with which it is haunted are those introduced by desire and fantasy: 'Fear and trembling Hope, / Silence and Foresight; Death the Skeleton / And Time the Shadow'. These are Miltonic spirits, themselves derived from Virgil's description of hell-gate. Knapp quotes the *Aeneid* passage, with its population of 'Grief and avenging Cares', 'sad Age and Fear', Death and 'Death's own brother Sleep' and, at the centre, a shady elm tree in whose branches false dreams hang.

Virgil's description was frequently imitated by English poets who introduced Christian elements into the allegorical personifications waiting at hell-gate. Spenser writes of 'rancorous Despight ... trembling Feare ... Lamenting Sorrow'; Pope portrays 'pale *Terror*, gloomy *Care*'; Gray describes 'pallid Fear ... faded Care, / Grim visag'd comfortless Despair'. Wordsworth differs, however, from these poets in that he reduces the number of figures personified and removes the 'sublime confrontation' between the voyager and the guardians of hell-gate.[56] He shifts the scene to the familiar local

[55] *Ibid.*, p. 165; Knapp, *Personification and the Sublime*, p. 123.

[56] *Aeneid*, bk VI, lines 273–81; *Faerie Queene*, bk II, canto vii, lines 21–2; *Windsor-Forest*, lines 414–22; *Ode on a Distant Prospect of Eton College*, lines 57–9, 81; *Personification and the Sublime*, pp. 125–7.

ground of Borrowdale and offers a series of quiet allusions rather than a set-piece imitation which every classically educated gentleman-reader would recognize. His poem is left in an uncertain relation to classical poetry and the vision of hell found in that poetry: both are disturbingly half-present in its evocation of the Lakeland grove; neither is an authority safely located in the other-world of the dead and gone. In this respect Wordsworth is closer to Milton than to Virgil, for in Milton's poem the guardians of hell-gate, Sin and Death, are loosed upon the earth. Wordsworth's narrator does not voyage beyond the common earth to encounter them and Wordsworth's verse does not formally invoke the past poets whose words echo in his own. And so the local world depicted in the poem and the familiar language by which it is depicted are left haunted. Their sublimity is produced by the intimation of a mortality present at the heart of nature – present even in the apparently never-dying yews. And since that intimation is dependent upon the haunting half-presence of Milton's words in Wordsworth's, the poem implies that it is the capacity of the poet to be haunted by the words of dead poets which allows him this sublimity. It is, the allusions suggest, the poet's understanding that life – and language – is occupied by death that makes poetry an essential song of experience. And if the poet shows death to haunt the English landscape and the language that depicts it, then he shows those who dwell on that land and speak that language to be imbued with a sense which makes them strong in battle. To be properly English, 'Yew-Trees' suggests, is to be familiar enough with the trees of life and death from one's local knowledge to be prepared for the violence of patriotic war. Patriotism is shown to depend neither on desire for glory nor on a code of honour, but on a sense of death discovered in the local landscape and made explicit by the poet. War is the sinful yet necessary extension of a fallen nature already haunted by Sin and Death.

Nature in 'Yew-Trees' is complicated and ambivalent – a place where creative and political tension is explored in a way rarely to be found in Wordsworth's later, nationalistic, poems. It should not be seen as simply a means of legitimizing war and Tory politics. For it has betrayal as well as Sin and Death encoded within it, posing the reader a number of difficult questions. Why is the Satanic temptation and threat attributed to the tree itself? Why is Death a skeleton here, when Burke had, in a discussion of which Wordsworth approved, attacked artists who illustrated Milton's indeterminate Death by a skeleton? In Burke's opinion they violated the necessary obscurity of the sublime.[57] Why is the theme of temptation and

---

[57] Wordsworth's allusion in *The Prelude* to Burke's discussion is discussed by Gordon K. Thomas, 'Wordsworth and "The Mystery of Things"', *TWC*, 22 (1991), 118–24 (pp. 121–3). Lucy Newlyn, in *Coleridge, Wordsworth and the Language of Allusion* (Oxford, 1986), p. 30, points out that Wordsworth alluded to Milton's Death in the 'uncouth shape' of his 'Discharged Soldier' (line 38, cf. *Paradise Lost*, bk II, line 666–7 and 681 'execrable shape').

betrayal broached at all, and why by allusion to Milton? The answers, I think, are to do with Wordsworth's self-troubling investigation of his own poetic imagination, of the relation between his writing and those things – trees, nature, history, politics, other poets – through and for which it speaks. His Miltonic description of the Satanic and deathly trees articulates the danger that in speaking for others he betrays them and himself. The Lorton yew's self-enclosed darkness is violated by a poetry which describes it in order to empower the poet and his political ideas. The Borrowdale yews then act as symbols of an imagination haunted by its awareness of the betrayals and appropriations involved in such poetic (self-)empowerment. As growths haunted by ghosts and death they are emblems of an imagination which can realize itself only by clothing itself in the words and deeds of the dead.[58] And their growth also represents the threatening energy of Satanic fantasy: they are both tempter and temptation, serpent and bearer of fruit. They suggest that the temptation to betray the already existent world lies at the heart of nature. It is, of course, in Wordsworth that the temptation really lies as he seeks to found and ground himself by borrowing nature and history to establish his own voice. Together the Lorton and Borrowdale yews portray Wordsworth's tentative claiming of a historical Other (the trees, old battles and heroes) through and for which to speak with authority. The references to Milton's Satan and serpent suggest that claiming the past in this way also risks betraying one's poetic predecessors. Perhaps Wordsworth in re-using Milton's verse to enhance his own authority resembles Milton's Satan. Satan, after all, tried to usurp God's power. If so it would be Wordsworth's imaginative usurpation that caused the fall-story to be relocated in the tale of the Lorton yew. It would be the rebellious poet who introduced to the self-enclosed independent tree a haunting consciousness of Death, causing, as Satan had done, a fall which the world now suffers with him.

It is possible that there were political reasons for Wordsworth's troubled Miltonic language in the poem. Wordsworth had been an enthusiastic supporter of the early French Revolution and had formerly invoked republican radicals such as Sidney and Milton in arguments against the British monarchical state. Now he was using their names to define 'British freedom' 'faith and morals' against the 'perpetual emptiness' of France in his political sonnets (*WPW*, vol. III, pp. 117 and 116). Perhaps the Satanic energy of Wordsworth's patriotic yew tree stems from his awareness that he was enlisting these republican heroes in the kind of rhetoric he had himself

---

[58] Pertinent here is Wordsworth's use of the image of a tree to describe how epitaphs should commemorate the dead: 'The character of a deceased friend or beloved kinsman is not seen, no – nor ought to be seen, otherwise than as a tree through a tender haze or luminous mist, that spiritualises and beautifies it; that takes away, indeed, but only to the end that the parts which are not abstracted may appear more dignified and lovely; may impress and affect the more' (*Essay upon Epitaphs* in *W Prose*, vol. II, p. 58).

formerly opposed, a rhetoric of which they might not have appro\
Certainly Wordsworth's growing political conservatism[59] led him to fac_ _
difficulty that Burke's *Enquiry* had shown confronted those who would
represent and disseminate authority – natural or political. Burke had noted
that rulers and monarchs strove to increase their power by cloaking it in
mystery and obscurity: 'despotic governments ... keep their chief as much as
may be from the public eye' (*PE*, p. 59). Violating that mystery by defining
the image too precisely would threaten that power, revealing its mundane
limits: it would reduce Death to a skeleton (hence Burke's advice that state
executions should be few and carefully staged so as to preserve their terrifying
and coercive sublimity). Wordsworth, in 'Yew-Trees', confronts but also
explores the moral implications of a similar discourse of authority: betrayal is
the danger both if he too successfully and arbitrarily appropriates objects to
empower himself *and* if he too readily locates his power in those objects, so
losing the mystery that makes it awe-inspiring and enthralling. Neither sole
possession nor an objective discourse is satisfactory, and the yew trees
represent Wordsworth's difficulty in finding a ground for his poetry that will
neither undermine it nor itself be undermined. All 'objects (*as* objects)', wrote
Coleridge, 'are essentially fixed and dead' (*BL*, vol. i, p. 304) and yet, for
Wordsworth, it was only his deliberate hold on the objective world that
rescued him from an 'abyss of idealism' (*WPW*, vol. iv, p. 463). His
imagination operates between the death of objects and the abyss of ideas,
pondering the convolutions of its efforts to grant itself power by mystifying
things.

To sum up: the strangely real yet ghostly yew trees are figures of
Wordsworth's efforts to ground his imagination in a material, poetic and
political Englishness from which he can derive his writing and to which he
can return it. Yet to return to this ground, to root poetry completely in the
already existent landscape would be to lose independence, to escape from the
abyss of an ungrounded imagination only to submit to the authority of the
already established: to reduce the mysterious shadow to a substance,
imagination to a skeleton of materiality. The evanescence and indeterminacy
of overheard arboreal voices ('sounding bows') is replaced by 'looks / That
threaten', by an all-too-visualized tree. Overheard spirit becomes a seen
skeletal presence, independent of the need for a direct authorial presence to
overhear it. In a move from voice to script, the necessary obscurity of the
origins of heroic imagination (Percy's, Henry V's, Milton's, Wordsworth's
own) is betrayed, a course Wordsworth nevertheless takes such is his
attachment to materiality (although he tried to preserve voicing and hearing
above script at the end of the poem and, in general, by reading his verse
aloud). And in that materiality rhetorical and political authority would also

---

[59] See James K. Chandler, *Wordsworth's Second Nature*, pp. 15–92.

be lost: as Burke showed, the chief's power depended upon the obscurity and mystery thrown over him by the sublime. On the other hand, a successful appropriation of others by one's own voice threatened to betray them, to uproot them from the natural, historical and political rootedness for which one valued them: Shakespeare, Milton and Sidney becoming figures in a warlike Wordsworthian rhetoric, the Lorton yew becoming a figure of his own nationalism. What Wordsworth seeks in the yew trees is a figural real and a real figure, a Life-in-Death rather than Hartman's funerary monument, a grounded ungroundedness, an original yet material self, both Lorton-grown and Wordsworth-made. What he comes close to getting, however, is an attachment to materiality which shows itself to be a bowing to the authority of the real (and of Milton) lest imagination again betray it, lest it emulate too well Milton's own Satanic betrayal of established power (divine, monarchical and natural) by its own words. The ghosts of betraying imagination need confinement in the tree (as Prospero threatened Ariel), yet can at least be apprehended there.

At this point it is worth developing a point made briefly by Kelley, that Wordsworth's reference to Percy hints at the subject of rebellion against the King. Hotspur and his father both turned against Henry IV and died fighting him, as did their descendant Thomas Percy against Elizabeth I. This hint, taken with the allusions to Satan's rebellion in *Paradise Lost*, leaves the yew trees' symbolism divided from the start. Sources for national pride and power, they are also linked with a rooted local pride that led to treason against the monarch of that nation. Thus, as sites of imaginative power they are treacherous too: places which might figure to Wordsworth not only his patriotism, not only his fear that such patriotism betrayed his revolutionary Miltonism of the 1790s, but also that his localized imagination, his particular Englishness might, like the Percys' and like Milton's, have led him through his radical opposition to ministers into a treasonable attack upon the King.

What we are left with by such divided symbolism is a poetry that both discusses power, legitimacy and treachery and questions their relations in its reflection upon its own troubled and numerous sources. Although the voice of the narrator is less personal in 'Yew-Trees' than in *The Prelude* and *Home at Grasmere*, the poem is a microcosm of the strength-in-difficulty that Wordsworth attains in those long poems as he struggles to formulate an authoritative self. It has not the egotism detected by New Historicist critics, for whom Wordsworth transcends historical and material reality (by 'denial' or 'displacement') into the aesthetic safety of his separate imagination. Nor has it the post-Kantian post-Freudian pattern sketched out by those critics who, influenced by Harold Bloom, find Wordsworth to attain a transcendence for himself through repression of the desire to master the Father (the Father being Milton and/or the paternal landscape). Rather, although displacement and repression do operate here, there is no decisive move from history to imagination, from powerful others to a transcendent self. There is instead a voice which gains profundity and obscure power by troubling its own origins – finding only fall and betrayal and losing the sublime as conventionally defined (Death becomes skeleton). That troubling process discovers not one origin to be transcended or displaced, for history, geographical location, political and literary traditions all dispute for priority in the poem. And the voice transcends none of them, but reveals with a radically new power the nature of their intractable relationship, intertwined themselves, producing and produced by discourses of the self that are themselves intertwined with them. Wordsworth is more complicated, and probes more deeply into complications, than is allowed by the view that he simply displaces nature or history into imagination. Here – and this is why it is still powerful – the poem ends with a symbolic questioning in which obscurity is not thrown over complex and divided relationships of priority and origin in favour of a single account. The haunting presences of Fear, Hope, Silence, Foresight, Death, and Time (and of Percy and Milton, heroes and rebels) are not banished or subsumed, but share a voice that is *also* Wordsworth's. No longer the fixed personifications of Spenser and Pope, they emerge into a real and named place as 'ghostly Shapes' who are

> – there to celebrate
> As in a natural temple scattered o'er
> With altars undisturbed of mossy stone,
> United worship; or in mute repose
> To lie, and listen to the mountain flood
> Murmuring from Glaramara's inmost caves.

Although this gives up possession of the bower to the shapes imprisoned there it also almost offers to save the place (and all nameable Lakeland places) for an individualized imagination released from fears of multiple betrayals. For it is so tenuously syntactically linked to the rest of the poem that, as we read it, it seems more that it is the observing narrator (and the readers) and less the 'ghostly shapes' who are 'there to celebrate'. Read in this way, the last lines open an unlimited realm of possibility (governed only by 'or' and the infinitive 'to lie') within which, at last, the place willingly discloses its being, murmuring its inmost energies to us from its inner darkness. Glaramara's caves almost offer what Borrowdale's trees deny, a willing release of their being, but yet they communicate only after (and partly *to*) the ghosts that have been raised and confined by history, geography and imagination informing and informed by place.

Kelley has found the conclusion of the poem to 'belong to the Wordsworthian beautiful' rather than the sublime, since the trees 'speak for and of figures that aspire to contain meaning rather than those that work to displace it'.[60] While this finding is based on an important understanding that notions of displacement and transcendence are not the whole truth about Wordsworth, it is, it seems to me, a misattribution. Skeletons are not beautiful, still less if associated with Milton's Death. Nor is the return to listening at the poem's end beautiful, since it links the ghosts' (and narrator's) apprehension with *overhearing*. By this overhearing inner 'sounding' *is* displaced from Glaramara's caves to a voice – not, however, a single voice which achieves transcendence as a result, but one that is simultaneously that of the 'ghostly Shapes', of the poet, and of the local and Miltonic discourses through which the poem speaks. This voice is not solely Wordsworth's though it is Wordsworthian. It is powerful in the potential endlessness of its negotiation of the multiple and conflicting sources and voices which it raises and which the sublime conventionally obscures. A later flowering of 'The Thorn' in the sense that it finds a haunted sublimity in the slow-growing tree, 'Yew-Trees' also gives us a tree of Wordsworthian knowledge, knowledge of the dangers and betrayals as well as the benefits of the vital act of imaginative representation.

En-graving the author: Wordsworth, Johnson and the inscription

In 'Yew-Trees' Wordsworth had contained the tensions and divisions that he found to be present in his writerly authority by speaking in a disembodied and traditional voice: 'There is a tree ...' Speaking like an authoritative local guide, he temporarily displaced his personal struggle for mastery of the scene and himself into a voice his own yet not his own. Johnson, struggling likewise to found his voice on established authorities instead of his own rhetorical efforts, had spoken in the works of Goldsmith and others, as a disembodied anonymous voice, apparently an oracular declaration of nature. It is not surprising, in view of their common need to find a disembodied and apparently objective voice, that both Wordsworth and Johnson wrote, and wrote about, inscriptions for monuments and epitaphs for tombs. I shall examine these writings in this section, arguing that Wordsworth's praise of the apparently calm and objective authority of inscriptions conceals an attempt to master Johnson, to usurp his critical authority. This attempt involved similar strategies to those by which Johnson himself made Shakespeare and Milton into scenes his writing could dominate. At the same time, Wordsworth was absorbing Coleridge's voice into his own. A number of his examples of epitaphs on headstones had been observed by Coleridge and recorded in his notebooks. And one of the *Essays upon Epitaphs* appeared first in Coleridge's periodical *The Friend*.

For Wordsworth inscriptions and epitaphs gave the poet an opportunity to

---

[60] Kelley, *Wordsworth's Revisionary Aesthetics*, p. 166.

speak with finality from the landscape. Rather than mastering it in his own name, such writing, appearing on gravestones in village churchyards or on commemorative monuments, spoke from the land and the community who lived upon it generation after generation. To emerge powerfully from that community, it was necessary that the inscription spoke in common speech rather than self-consciously poetic terms. In his *Essays upon Epitaphs* (1810) Wordsworth uses Johnson's *Lives* as a point of departure for his discussions of what was proper for verse inscribed upon headstones and funerary monuments. Commenting on Johnson's treatment in his *Life* of Pope of that poet's epitaphs, Wordsworth takes the opportunity to declare his own poetic creed in opposition to what he construes as a Johnsonian attack on common language (although in fact Johnson was objecting to clichés, being himself an advocate of poetry based on the model of language as it is generally spoken).

it is not only no fault but a primary requisite in an Epitaph that it shall contain thoughts and feelings which are in their substance common-place, and even trite. It is grounded upon the universal intellectual property of man; – sensations which all men have felt and feel in some degree daily and hourly; – truths whose very interest and importance have caused them to be unattended to, as things which could take care of themselves. But it is required that these truths should be instinctively ejaculated, or should rise irresistibly from circumstances; in a word that they should be uttered in such connection as shall make it felt that they are not adopted – not spoken by rote, but perceived in their whole compass with the freshness and clearness of an original intuition. The Writer must introduce the truth with such accompaniment as shall imply that he has mounted to the sources of things – penetrated the dark cavern from which the River that murmurs in every one's ear has flowed from generation to generation.   (*W Prose*, vol. ii, pp. 78–9)

The passage echoes Wordsworth's statement of his own aims as a poet in *Lyrical Ballads* as being to put commonplace truths in an interesting point of view or, in Coleridge's phrase, 'to give the charm of novelty to things of every day; and to excite a feeling analogous to the supernatural' (*BL*, vol. ii, p. 7). And it contests the implications of Johnson's view, expressed in the *Life* of Milton as well as that of Pope, that dignity, grandeur and sublimity are produced by poetry that exceeds the common tongue. Indeed in the image of the 'dark cavern' and the river Wordsworth tries to practise what he preaches by transforming the ordinary truth of an inherited language, through imagery, into an awful and mysterious organic tradition.

Throughout the *Essays* Wordsworth can be found reacting in detail to Johnson, arguing over the epitaphs the doctor had chosen, attacking his view of the familiar in poetry. Epitaphs preclude all species of composition 'except those which the very strength of passion has created; which have been acknowledged by the human heart; and have become so familiar that they are converted into substantial realities' (*W Prose*, vol. ii, p. 76). In the process, however, he is responding to Johnson's suspicion that the poetic language of

Milton, precisely because it seems to exceed reality, crushes rather than awakens the reader, leaving him 'sunk' and 'harrassed'. Wordsworth's reaction to Johnson shows him searching for a language that intensifies common speech but does not violate the familiarity that makes it real to the community that speaks it. Such a language, in inscriptions but also in poetry in general, would place the poet amongst those of and for whom he writes, empowering rather than subjugating the reader. To envisage it he modifies Johnson's discourse on the metaphysical poets, whom Johnson had censured in his *Life* of Cowley for violating poetic dignity by introducing remote analogies, words which had only an arbitrary or casual connection with each other. Whereas for Johnson Milton had so far exceeded common ideas and language that he had produced an awesome but crushing and wearisome language, the metaphysicals had violated them with heterogeneous ideas pursued until their poetry was at worst ridiculous, at best witty. To Johnson's regret the language of propriety, based on what was generally spoken, was surpassed in both cases, although he added of the metaphysicals that 'they likewise sometimes struck out unexpected truth: if their conceits were far-fetched, they were often worth the carriage' (*Lives*, vol. I, pp. 20–1).

Even as he advocated a writing whose authority was of a communal, apparently objective kind, Wordsworth was subordinating Johnson, the most authoritative critic in the mind of the public. The headstones and monuments through which Wordsworth wished to speak from the rural community are also sites of an intensely personal battle for critical power – over epitaphs and poetry in general. Although built after Johnson's pattern Wordsworth's engraved monuments pay him no tribute, but seek power by obscuring his words. He remains silently en-graved beneath them. Wordsworth's criticism mirrors Johnson's own use of nature-imagery in his discussion of Shakespeare. Both men portrayed others as regions to be conquered and landscapes to be mastered to establish their own mastery: in Johnson's case over Shakespeare, in Wordsworth's over nature, the public and Johnson himself. Both men, mastering others by mastering the scenes they made of them, were also seeking to master themselves – to construct a stable authority by locating their authority in themselves when faced by divisions and tensions with regard to the patrons, landowners, public and peasants for and of whom they wrote. Asserting and displacing their power often in the same gesture, they also sought to locate authority outside their individual rhetorical discourses – in established powers in the landscape itself. Yet those powers were themselves divided and in conflict as landowners and the landless became increasingly alienated from each other. Thomson's prospect-views could no longer contain these divisions within a landscape poetry of propriety and taste – any more than could Cowper's moralizing from retirement or Gilpin's and Price's picturesques. Authority over the scene inevitably involved what Johnson termed 'the usurpations of virility' (*JW*, vol. II, p. 458) and

Wordsworth the 'strength / of usurpation' (*Prelude*, bk VI, lines 532–3) since the scenes themselves – the politicized landscapes and the writing that formulated the selves of writer and reading public in relation to those landscapes (real and imaginary) were increasingly understood to be divided by entrenched powers and ideologies.

Wordsworth's struggle for authority had its roots in eighteenth-century discourse and the conflicts that discourse negotiated. It did not deny or evade revolutionary violence and the problems it posed for his poetry, but incorporated it in other conflicts of longer English descent, which Wordsworth rewrote in his own image, often by borrowing the strategies which had been used by the powerful poets and critics who preceded him. I have outlined a number of perspectives on how that rewriting was achieved: the discourse on the poor, the Johnsonian critical landscape, Gilpin and the picturesque, the battle with paternalist landlords, the reworking of Milton, Thomson and Cowper, the struggles with patrons and public. All are connected in the issues of economic, social and poetic conflict, and it was out of those issues that Wordsworth made his exaltation of differing but essentially masculine versions of authority, embracing the disruptive verbal powers that Gilpin broached only to contain, but not without division or debts to the past.

Considered as an answer to the predominant ideologies of *laissez-faire* economics, gentlemanly taste and social authoritarianism, Wordsworth's discourse was, particularly in its post-1800 form, both personally intense and socially limited. It allowed Wordsworth to assert independence of landlords' power and elevated him and the readers who shared his vision or sought his protection to a position of authority that those ideologies cannot match. Yet it no longer gave such authority directly to the poor themselves. For not only was it easier for Wordsworth to speak for himself than the dispossessed, but his exaltation of his own imagination led him towards an assumption of paternal superiority that manifested itself increasingly in the patrician social attitudes he had formerly resented when they were evident in Lonsdale. In a poem of 1831, 'Highland Hut', for example, Wordsworth invites the passing traveller to enter and give charity: 'But love, as Nature loves, the lonely Poor; / Search, for their worth, some gentle heart wrong-proof, / Meek, patient, kind, and, were its trials fewer, / Belike less happy. Stand no more aloof!' (*WPW*, vol. III, p. 271, lines 11–14). Here poverty is not an economic condition, but a natural one. As in Thomson possible feelings of social injustice are assuaged by the georgic convention, which sees the inhabitants generically rather than individually, and reassures the visitor that their hardship makes them happy, virtuous and properly humble before their superiors. Thus the politics of Wordsworth's Scottish tour narratives are transformed by his growing willingness to speak for both nature and the local inhabitants in a generalized vocabulary familiar to the gentry. Rather than articulate the voices of Scottish peasants and poets as presences in a wild landscape that resists the aesthetic and political views of the Scottish landowners, as he had done in 1803 when invoking Ossian and Burns and narrating the voices of the Highland Girl and Solitary Reaper, Wordsworth frames Scotland through a doubly colonizing discourse. His poem provides a pseudo-spiritual justification of Scottish poverty for the English traveller who would at first be shocked by it and it finds a gentlemanly vocabulary and poetic convention adequate to narrate the experience of the peasant.

By 1831 Wordsworth's tour writing was less challenging than that of either Johnson or Gilpin although they, in Scotland before him, were ostensibly more nearly allied with the English and Lowland gentry and nobility. His Scottish poem endorses a gentlemanly paternalism closer to Thomson's and Uvedale Price's idealizations of the rôle and view of the independent country landowner, directing but also charitably relieving the poor amongst his tenantry. Like Gilpin's ideal landowners, Wordsworth's traveller is a bastion against the utilitarian and commercialist forces which would reduce poor relief and regiment the poor in workhouses. Wordsworth's Tory paternalism is thus the direct descendant of his Commonwealthsman republicanism of the 1790s. Like the Country-party Patriots who invoked Harrington's association of liberty with independent land ownership, Wordsworth saw the landed gentlemen, as he had once seen the Lakeland 'statesmen', as a defence against ministerial corruption and a national culture of commercial self-interest. The 'mountain republic' of freeholding farmers and shepherds that had formed his social, political and linguistic ideal proved too limited to work as a model for the complex, increasingly commercial and industrial nation at large. Wordsworth adopted a neo-Harringtonian position and located independence (as Bolingbroke, Chesterfield and Thomson had done) in a landed gentry and aristocracy freed by property-ownership from self-interest. He moved away from republicanism to a conservative endorsement of the 1688 balanced constitution, dominated as it was by the landowning classes. This endorsement was akin to that of Uvedale Price and opposed to the pro-reform radicalism of Brougham and Cobbett – both of whom also claimed to represent the voices of rural freeholders and tenants.

Wordsworthian poetic authority was by the end of his life a paternalist discourse that reinforced the values of Tory landowners. Yet it had not been ever thus, and it need not be viewed as solely thus now. Wordsworth settled in many late writings for an establishment of his discourse upon a traditional institution but was neither then nor earlier simply revising the traditional ideologies by which the propertied classes asserted the legitimacy of their judgement and rule. He was, perhaps, laying down a burden of usurping vision which had, at times despite himself, shown all institutions to be provisional and subject to revolutionary undermining. His writing is not a denial but an attempted redirection of history – as the power of fathers to legislate for and leave to sons – and claims to be the history (story) where this legislation is made. But it is at the same time the place where a lost legacy is repossessed, re-establishing destroyed continuities in place and time. Wordsworth creates by a Blakeian act of imaginative rebellion and appropriation from extremis a Johnsonian continuity of tradition, an organic national order modelled on a community of readers which itself reflects, but also finally replaces, a rural society in which community is always shown to be threatened with destruction. His writing is about the making of history through discourse too, about the making of political issues into story, as it challenges and invokes Thomson and Milton (two such makers) and ponders the gain and loss involved in their and his self-elevating acts of rhetorical transformation. Paradoxically for Wordsworth history is continuity and tradition, but these are only made through individual and arbitrary acts of will (and are therefore Satanic). In the end Wordsworth's writing is also about writing itself, as a force which affirms continuity only by disrupting it, by speaking for (but also instead of) shepherds and past masters. It achieves power for its writer only with guilt at his usurpation of the established power (in culture and nature) he tries to exalt – a guilt he became increasingly inclined to lay to rest by regranting power to established figures of paternal authority. He offered his verbal landscapes back to those who owned inherited estates rather than to the dispossessed who gained the awe-inspiring objectivity of the mountains from which their characters were derived.

Nevertheless, as 'Yew-Trees' and *Home at Grasmere* show, Wordsworth's poetry often discovers multiple sources of power, questioning each and striving for a renewed social discourse in which the self can be redefined alongside, rather than above, others. Wordsworth's writing remains ambiguous and (self-)challenging, that of a writer neither simply an ideologist nor a green revolutionary who, exposing the rhetorical and material figures of power, both opens them to revolutionary revision in his own voice and those of Lakeland dwellers and renews them in a willed perpetuation of tradition. This is the Wordsworth who both inspired and frustrated Blake and Hazlitt, empowering their political and literary imaginations with visions of the transformative power of words, searching for (and at the same time troubling and questioning) a recognizable common order in the fields of Britain.

5

Coleridge: fields of liberty

Coleridge's landscape-descriptions, made in dialogue with Wordsworth, searched for a common order conceived in terms that became increasingly different from those of the poet of *The Prelude*. In this chapter I wish to examine that search in order to focus upon the tensions that beset it. To do so I shall place Coleridge in a number of contexts that will illuminate the strategies he adopted in order to formulate discourses of poetic and critical authority. Many of these were developed from those used by poets and critics earlier in the eighteenth century. In particular, I shall argue, Coleridge learnt from Cowper, from the picturesque, and from a new understanding of biblical poetry as he sought to empower his voice to overcome his own divided loyalties and articulate a vision of national unity. Landscape poetry, fusing eighteenth-century traditions, became for Coleridge a way of retrieving a personal consistency endangered in his daily life and his political journalism. It became a radical nationalism as he preached, like Cowper before him but with a deeper intensity, of an England renewed as a moral and spiritual community of harmony and liberty, free from division and repression.

But Coleridge's own position as a writer was not free from conflict and repression and his landscapes of liberty often reinscribed, beneath their ostensible terrain of freedom, personal, religious and social subordination. Much of his landscape-description can, I shall suggest, be seen as an attempt to control the instabilities of his own authority. At his best, however, he was able to use his own experiences of instability and vulnerability to articulate the sense of dispossession felt by those for whom the loss of their native landscape was disastrous. On his Scottish tour Coleridge developed a new kind of landscape-description, indebted to Cowper and akin to Clare, which portrays the destruction of landscape as an uprooting of identity that destroys the love of the land, of the self, and of others. In what amounted to a new Romantic radicalism, social bonds and the local and national order are shown to be threatened from the root. Here landscape is not just a vehicle for political comment but a ground, real and symbolic, on which individual and social identity is shown to rest. When it is enclosed self and society face madness and chaos – a point Wordsworth had set out to make in *Lyrical Ballads*. But in Coleridge, as in Cowper, the poet's own vulnerability allows him to voice that madness as a demoralization – as a voice fading into silence, into depression and into emigration. It is a more fragile voicing than Wordsworth's speech, and one that remains a warning in today's age of ecological destruction.

Thomson, Cowper and the Bible

In a letter written to George Dyer in March 1795 Coleridge set out the basis of his moral and political creed:

It is melancholy to think, that the best of us are liable to be shaped & coloured by surrounding Objects – and a demonstrative proof, that Man was not made to live in Great Cities! Almost all the physical Evil in the World depends on the existence of moral Evil – and the long-continued contemplation of the latter does not tend to meliorate the human heart. – The pleasures, which we receive from rural beauties, are of little Consequence compared with the Moral Effect of these pleasures – beholding constantly the Best possible we at last become ourselves the best possible. In the country, all around us smile Good and Beauty – and the Images of this divine καλοκἀγαθόν are miniatured on the mind of the beholder, as a Landscape on a Convex Mirror. Thomson in that most lovely Poem, the Castle of Indolence, says –

> 'I care not, Fortune! what you me deny
> You cannot rob me of free Nature's Grace!
> You cannot shut the Windows of the Sky,
> Through which the Morning shews her dewy face –
> You cannot bar my constant feet to rove
> Through Wood and Vale by living Stream at Eve'

Alas! alas! she *can* deny us all this – and can force us fettered and handcuffed by our Dependencies and Wants to *wish* and *wish* away the bitter Little of Life in the felon-crowded Dungeon of a great City!

(CL, vol. ɪ, pp. 154–5)

The pernicious effects of city life and the restorative power of rural beauties upon the morals of society were themes that Coleridge explored in the nature poetry of 1796 and 1797, using phrases close to those of this letter. And he did so by a further modification of the aesthetics of the picturesque.[1] Here in the letter the practice of viewing the landscape in a convex mirror, made fashionable by the picturesque tourists, provides a metaphor for the mind's absorption of aesthetic and moral truths, divine in origin, from the unfettered freedom of the rural scene.[2] The picturesque view is not only a means of aesthetic and moral education but a microcosm of the relations that should

---

[1] On Coleridge's attitude to the theory of the picturesque, see J.R. Watson, *Picturesque Landscape and English Romantic Poetry* (London, 1970), pp. 108–14.

[2] Coleridge's combination of empirical observation with neo-Platonic aesthetics was influenced by Locke, David Hartley, Shaftesbury and, increasingly as the 1790s progressed, by Berkeley. See James C. McKusick, *Coleridge's Philosophy of Language* (New Haven and London, 1986).

exist between mind, world and God. The passage quoted from Thomson similarly speaks of the restorative power of nature and seeks to re-present it in microcosm by affecting the reader through the pleasurable variety and beauty of its own form.

Coleridge arrived at his understanding of the moral purpose of viewing and describing landscape through the aesthetics of the picturesque and the poetry associated with it. But, as the letter indicates, he felt that moral purpose to be under much greater threat than Thomson had thought it to be. His sense of the corrupting influence of city life, coupled with political tensions manifest in rural society, made him aware of an increasing vulnerability in landscape and in the discourses that sought to establish morality and social reform on the basis of the beauty and liberty they found in it. His awareness led him more to Cowper than to Thomson, and his understanding of the authority with which Cowper spoke from a position of vulnerable retirement was crucial to his modification of the picturesque view and to his nature poetry in general.[3]

Cowper, as I suggested in chapter one, revised the traditional topos of retirement so that it was an escape from the divided social field of the rural landscape itself. From his vulnerable Eden garden Cowper, having fled from the guilt that undermined his effort to speak for the landscape as a whole, was able to find a less compromised although still unstable voice. He preached to his polite readership of the nation's ills, tracing those ills to the moral failings of the ruling classes rather than to their domination of the political and social scenes. These included the rural scenes in which cottagers were left in a penury and hardship too real for him simply to aestheticize it through the georgic convention. Accepting his marginality with self-deprecating humour, Cowper made it a position of relative strength, albeit one that, he accepted, courted bathos. To Coleridge Cowper offered a position of rectitude, a retreat from the potential corruption of preaching for hire to the moral high ground. Cowper's recognition that the temptation of taking the moral high ground may itself lead to corruption appealed to Coleridge. It allowed him to develop his own exploration of vulnerability whilst he made his critique from retirement of the political realm. He told Hazlitt in 1798 that Cowper was the 'best modern poet' and admired *The Task* in the *Biographia Literaria*.[4] Ann Matheson has suggested that it was Charles Lamb who, in a series of letters in 1796, argued Coleridge into an appreciation of Cowper on the basis of the simplicity and clarity of his verse.[5] If so, then Coleridge's tribute to Lamb in

---

[3]   Coleridge was also led to the poetry of William Lisle Bowles. On Bowles and other minor poets who were, possibly, influences on his nature poetry, see Kelvin Everest, *Coleridge's Secret Ministry: The Context of the Conversation Poems* (Hassocks, Sussex and New York, 1979) and George Dekker, *Coleridge and the Literature of Sensibility* (London, 1978).

[4]   *The Complete Works of William Hazlitt*, ed. P. P. Howe, 21 vols. (London, 1930–4), XVII, p. 120; *BL*, vol. I, 25.

[5]   Ann Matheson, 'The Influence of Cowper's *The Task* on Coleridge's Conversation Poems', in

'This Lime Tree Bower My Prison', a poem which explores feelings of isolation and insecurity in a rural retreat after the manner of Cowper, was especially appropriate.

By the later 1790s Coleridge faced a social field whose divisions left his authority as deeply compromised as Cowper's. Active in Bristol as an anti-government radical journalist and orator, Coleridge was an admirer of much of what the French Revolution had achieved. But in rural Somerset, where he lived from 1796, he was seen as an atheistic Jacobin and dangerous revolutionary by landowning, churchgoing, polite society. Alarm at a visit by John Thelwall, the radical campaigner who had been acquitted in the treason trials of 1794, led to a spy being sent by the Home Secretary to watch Coleridge and Wordsworth. In such circumstances even nature poetry became a matter of suspicion – excursions made for the purpose of writing a poem, to be called 'The Brook', after the manner of Cowper, were viewed as attempts to ascertain the navigability of the local rivers for invading French ships. Britain was, after 1793, at war with France, and enthusiasm for the revolution and opposition to Pitt's ministry risked appearing treasonable. During 1797 and 1798, seeing Thelwall hounded from one rural area to another and finding that the Wordsworths' lease on the nearby Alfoxden House was not renewed owing to their reputation as radicals, Coleridge discovered that rural society was not a retreat from the political pressures that threatened his liberty. Habeas Corpus had been suspended; Treason and Sedition Acts passed; two radicals whom he knew and respected, Gilbert Wakefield and Joseph Johnson (the publisher of *Lyrical Ballads)* were imprisoned. Coleridge himself was then satirized in the *Anti-Jacobin*, a magazine supported by the ministry to attack its opponents.

Coleridge and Wordsworth escaped from the dangers of the English scene in 1798 by retiring to Germany where both sought to formulate an authority-in-writing free from political tensions by making descriptions of communities in harmony with the landscape. But before they left, both men had written landscape poems in which they sought to make rural retirement into a position of strength. Like Cowper Coleridge had, however, to retire not only into the country, but from the pressures experienced in the rural community to an unviolated refuge – that of a garden or picturesque scene whose natural wildness made it seem free from the traditional patterns of order legible in the cultivated landscape. Commonland, unmarked by the fences that enclosed landlords' fields, became a poetic refuge, retirement to which allowed Coleridge enough freedom from political pressure and social division to speak for a landscape. Developing Cowper, Bowles and other landscape poets he spoke for it as a place of harmony and liberty, as a natural moral economy, an ideal towards which Britain should be moving. His speech moralized but

Donald Sultana (ed.), *New Approaches to Coleridge: Biographical and Critical Essays* (London, 1981), pp. 137–50.

avoided specific political controversy. In this way it also avoided some of the pressures facing him in rural society and in his own mind, divided as he was between support of France and of his own countrymen at war with France.

Coleridge had, as Cowper had before him, the tradition of blank verse nature poetry available to him. He praised Cowper's 'divine Chit chat' (*CL*, vol. I, p. 279). The divinity – or rather the lofty spiritual and moral tone – of such colloquial verse came to Cowper from Milton and from the Bible. Coleridge, facing conflicting political loyalties in his Somerset retirement as he had in London and Bristol public activity, also tried to revise the style recognized to be sublime in scripture. He did so via Cowper but also via a new critical understanding of biblical poetry, trying thereby to find a language in which he could present the English landscape unmarked by social exclusion and political repression. By the representation of landscape he hoped to unite writer and readers into a community which would act as a model for what the nation should be. To this end he employed rhetorical strategies designed to gain the readers' sympathy rather than subjugate them to the writer's power.

Coleridge, property and the mosaic commonwealth

Coleridge's landscape poems of the later 1790s were a development of the commonwealth politics expressed in his Pantisocracy scheme and in his Bristol lectures of 1795. These politics themselves stemmed from a strain of dissenting radicalism shared by many of Coleridge's Unitarian allies and distinct from Paine's belief in natural rights and Godwin's emphasis on the reasoning individual. They borrowed the arguments of James Harrington, Algernon Sidney and Milton against absolute monarchies and established church. They derived liberty from the democratic representation of the propertied. Joseph Priestley, the Unitarian and radical philosopher and scientist whose emigration to America helped to inspire Coleridge's Pantisocracy scheme, echoed Harrington when distinguishing his own view of the Bible from Paine's. Claiming it as a liberating rather than, as Paine argued, a repressive book, Priestley idealized the Mosaic commonwealth as a republic of liberty: 'In the original institutions of Moses, there was no provision for a *king*, tho' all the neighbouring nations were governed by kings, and in the most arbitrary manner, and when the Hebrews wished to imitate their neighbours in this respect, as they did in every other, the prophet Samuel, speaking by authority from God, described to them the fatal consequence of adopting that form of government, in as earnest and emphatical a manner as you yourselves could now do it, viz. as leading to oppression and every species of abuse'.[6]

[6] Joseph Priestley, *An Answer to Mr Paine's Age of Reason* (London, 1795), p. 24.

Dissenting radicals formulated a political interpretation of early Hebrew and Christian communities that Coleridge echoed. Priestley himself declared Jesus' doctrines to be 'most favourable to the *liberty and equality of man*',[7] charged terms during a war with revolutionary France. Gilbert Wakefield contrasted Christianity, 'that system of *peace* and *love*', with the bloodthirsty British state and the preachers of the Church of England who supported it.[8] Regarding an institutionalized and paid priesthood as a corruption of the freedom and independence of Moses' and Jesus' teachings, William Frend, the fellow of Coleridge's Cambridge college tried and banished by the University for his Unitarian opinions, wrote that 'the established church of England can be considered as a political institution'. Frend derived his arguments on the Poor Laws from the Mosaic Law.[9] Coleridge, present in the gallery at Frend's trial, espoused such arguments eagerly in his Bristol lectures and in correspondence with the reformist agitator John Thelwall. Thelwall, himself atheistic, viewed Coleridge's religious radicalism as the rant of the conventicle but incorporated arguments of the same kind in his pamphlet *The Rights of Nature Against the Usurpations of Establishments* (London, 1796), noting 'the primitive Christians ... both upheld and practised, not only *equality of rights*, but *community of goods*: (a wild and absurd scheme, I confess, and not practicable upon any *large scale*)' (p. 67). In doubting its practicality he was, as was Priestley,[10] further from the seventeenth-century Commonwealthsmen than Coleridge himself.

Peter J. Kitson and Nigel Leask have shown that in favouring the abolition of private property, in advocating a society based on the communal sharing of land, Coleridge was a more levelling radical than either Thelwall or Priestley in 1795.[11] He encountered the work of Harrington in that year in James Burgh's *Political Disquisitions*.[12] And he read Moses Lowman's *A Dissertation on the Civil Government of the Hebrews* (1740), a work by a Unitarian which extended Harrington's arguments in a detailed assessment of the Hebrew commonweath. Lowman termed property 'the natural Foundation of Power' and argued that the Mosaic commonwealth was a model of freeholding liberty: 'if the Property be generally divided near equally among all Members of the Society, the true Power and Authority of such

---

7 *Ibid.*

8 Gilbert Wakefield, *The Spirit of Christianity Compared with the Spirit of the Times in Great Britain*, 2nd edn (London, 1794), pp. 11, 24–5.

9 William Frend, *Peace and Union Recommended to the Associated Bodies of Republicans and Anti-Republicans*, 2nd edn (Cambridge, 1793), pp. 37, 28–9.

10 Priestley accepted that 'every government ... is originally, and antecedent to its present form, an equal republic' but also accepted that inequalities of property and thence power were necessary. See *An Essay on the First Principles of Government and on the Nature of Political Civil and Religious Liberty* (London, 1768), pp. 41, 20–1.

11 Nigel Leask, *The Politics of Imagination in Coleridge's Critical Thought* (London, 1988), pp. 20–41; Peter J. Kitson '"The electric fluid of truth" ... ', *Prose Studies*, 13 (1990), 36–62.

12 On Coleridge and Burgh's *Disquisitions* (London, 1774–5), see *ibid.*, 37–46.

Government will naturally be in all the Members of that Society, whatever Form of Union they may have, for the better Direction of the Whole as a political Body' (pp. 33–4). Lowman also argued that the Levites were not originally a separate priestly class, their power having grown through a corruption of the Mosaic law – a point echoed by Coleridge in his Bristol lectures. It was important, Lowman declared, that priests were not allowed 'to invade the Property or oppress the Liberties of any Part of the Nation' (pp. 236–7). This argument may have helped to make Coleridge reluctant to preach for hire when offered the post of minister at the Unitarian church of Shrewsbury in 1798. In his ideal commonwealth, as he put it in 1795, every man was his own priest.

Commonwealthsman radicalism was most influential on Coleridge's politics of liberty in 1795 and 1796. He wrote to Thelwall in May 1796 that property 'is beyond doubt the Origin of all Evil' (*CL*, vol. I, p. 214) an extreme development of seventeenth-century arguments that its unequal distribution destroyed freedom. In his public statements of 1795 he imagined 'a pure Republic' as perhaps involving 'an abolition of all individual Property' (*LPR*, p. 116). The Mosaic commonwealth remained his model for its 'Admirable Division of Property' (*LPR*, p. 119). In his second *Lecture on Revealed Religion* he added, 'Every Hebrew was thus the Subject of God. Nor was an end proposed without means established. The Lands were restored. Property is Power and equal Property equal Power' (*LPR*, p. 126). Supporting redistribution of property, idealizing the Mosaic commonwealth, proposing the rotation of offices, Coleridge echoed Harrington. But he also modified Harrington in a way which should prevent our judging his and other similar 1790s radical dissent as merely an ineffectual echo of the Country-party Harringtonians of the 1730s. Coleridge exceeded Priestley, Price and Paine when he argued for the abolition of property. But he also accepted that such abolition could only be maintained, within the proposals of Mosaic law, in simple agricultural societies (like his own Pantisocracy): 'Commerce and Manufactures which might have made a more complex Code necessary were either expressly forbidden by the Law, or at least clearly contradictory to the Spirit of it' (*LPR*, p. 130).

Commerce was, of course, an increasingly powerful force in Coleridge's Britain, and his agrarian radicalism is adopted in conscious opposition to it. Agrarian radicalism allowed Coleridge an alternative model of human society, a model intended to preclude insincerity and self-interest. He asked the audience of his sixth lecture: 'If he be a Commercial Man, can he be always sincere? Can he always prevent a spirit of selfishness?' (*LPR*, p. 225). He attacked Britain's colonialist exploitation of India. But his vision of agrarian communism remains an ideal alternative, not a solution, to the evils of commerce as revealed by the selfishness, repression and self-interest of governors such as Lord Clive and Warren Hastings. As he admitted, commercial societies needed more complex codes than Moses' or Harrington's agrarian laws could provide. Nevertheless, the country, Coleridge told his listeners, could be a site of spiritual rule, centred on the viewer like a landscape in the mirror of a picturesque tourist:

> In the country, the Love and Power of the great Invisible are everywhere perspicuous, and by degrees we become partakers of that which we are accustomed to contemplate. The Beautiful and Good are miniatured on the Heart of the Contemplator as the surrounding Landscape on a Convex Mirror. But in Cities God is everywhere removed from our sight …
>
> (*LPR*, p. 224)

In this lecture context, more even than in the letter from which Coleridge borrowed the comparison, the apparatus of the picturesque is a means towards a spiritual politics that, Coleridge concludes, can only be fully realized at some future time when men conquer the avarice that leads them to want 'Emperor and King'. The republic of liberty and virtue is, by the lecture's end, an agrarian millennium for which radicals must wait, confident in the predictions of scripture, preparing to triumph over their own base desires (*LPR*, p. 228).

Without the conceptual or effective means to overcome the commercialist society he deplored, Coleridge, as Peter J. Kitson shows, continued a seventeenth-century commonwealth tradition, prophesying in radical jeremiads which derived from Milton.[13] The poem 'Religious Musings' and the pamphlet *The Plot Discovered* imagine the destruction of the agents of repression at the hands of God. But Coleridge also imagined communities that acted as models of agrarian republics, communities enjoying spiritual harmony and political liberty in a rural landscape. He planned in 1796 to write a hymn to the sun, a scheme probably based on reading about the Essenes, the Jewish religious communities who composed sacred hymns, the hymn to the sun being to a symbol of the deity (*CN*, vol. I, 174, 240–7). The Essenes, according to Josephus, the historian of the Jews, lived in rural communes, keeping all things in common, labouring until the late afternoon.[14] William Enfield, the Unitarian whose *History of Philosophy* was Coleridge's direct source, described them as having 'had a perfect community of goods'. They practised agriculture, and lived as brothers.[15]

---

[13] *Ibid.*, 54–6.

[14] *Of the Antiquities of the Jews*, in *The Famous and Memorable Works of Josephus*, tr. Thomas Lodge (London, 1670), pp. 614–15.

[15] William Enfield's *The History of Philosophy, from the Earliest Times to the Beginning of the Present Century*, 2 vols. (London, 1791), II, pp. 183–5. Coleridge had borrowed volume one of Enfield's work in 1795 and may have read the second volume in Bristol Library. See G. Whalley, 'The Bristol Library Borrowings of Southey and Coleridge, 1793–8', *The Library*, 4 (1949), 114–32 (p. 119). Coleridge would also have known of Enfield through his contributions to the *Monthly Magazine*. On these, see J.E. Cookson, *The Friends of Peace. Anti-War Liberalism in England, 1793–1815* (Cambridge, 1982), pp. 49, 90.

Coleridge's interest in their hymns evinced his need to find a connection between a radical political ideal and a spiritual poetry. The Essenes, like the Mosaic commonwealth, were a historical and religious model for a communal language and life of liberty and equality to be imagined in the fields of Britain as a mode of opposition to the prevailing social and political forces.

In imagining communities of language emerging from agricultural communes, Coleridge was a religious and political visionary at once. He had precedents other than those described by Enfield, Lowman and Harrington. His own father had published a discussion of the Book of Judges, in which he declared that 'the writings of the prophets and poets, in [the] divine books' were superior in their sublimity to other Eastern poetry: 'the words and expressions do not only there instruct, move the passions, and delight the reason of man, but often strike in the strongest glare of eloquence ... '[16] His son was to echo these comments in 1796 and subsequently. It was, however, not John Coleridge but Bishop Robert Lowth whose discussion of biblical poetry allowed Coleridge to formulate a poetry in which rural communities and their language are seen to be the source of greater sublimity and spirituality than others. Lowth's work, in other words, helped Coleridge to form a politics that envisioned rural life not simply as a retreat from urban and commercial vice but as the source of a language of liberty, equality and spiritual community. Coleridge's nature poetry strove, in the wake of his reading of Lowth and of Cowper (whose 'God made the country, but man the town' he inscribed in a notebook of 1800 (*CN*, vol. I, 815)) to speak the language of the spiritual and agricultural communes he had idealized in his political lectures. It could not do so, however, without anxiety and defensiveness, both at the demands of commerce and the shifting sands of politics. Suspicious of the compromises of newspaper writing, Coleridge wrote and published his own journal, attempting to win editorial independence and to unite an audience around his work. But he found, as he did in poetry, that changing political circumstances and his own changing views led to difficulties and inconsistencies which appeals to the sublimity of scripture could not resolve.

Coleridge arrived at his understanding of biblical poetry by reading, in 1796, Lowth's lectures (first given in 1741 and published in 1753).[17] Lowth's work isolated the elements of power in Hebrew verse – not regular metre or rhyme but loose repetitions and echoes of phrase – parallelisms as he called

[16] John Coleridge, *Miscellaneous Dissertations Arising From the* xviith *and* xviiith *Chapters of the Book of Judges* (London, 1768), p. 2.

[17] Coleridge read Lowth in Bristol in 1796. See George Whalley, 'The Bristol Library Borrowings of Southey and Coleridge, 1793–8', 123. On Coleridge and biblical criticism in Germany, see E.S. Shaffer, *'Kubla Khan' and The Fall of Jerusalem* (Cambridge, 1975), pp. 17–95.

them.[18] Coleridge even began a verse translation of the Song of Deborah in the manner of Lowth, who had termed it a 'perfectly sublime Ode' and whose translation of Isaiah he had read by 1795.[19] In a short preface Coleridge defined his understanding of the 'parallelisms of the Original': 'each Line or member of a sentence is counter-balanced by the following, either by difference, or similitude, or by the repetition of the same thought in different words or with a different Image'.[20] Lowth had written of parallelisms in his *Praelectiones de Sacra Poesi Hebraeorum* (1753). There he connected them with the Hebrew poet's imagination. Creating by verbal and rhythmic repetition similarities between apparently unrelated things, parallelisms exemplified imagination's operation: 'in those objects, which upon the whole have the least agreement, some striking similarity is traced out'.[21] Coleridge quoted from Lowth's translation of Isaiah in his 1795 *Lectures on Revealed Religion*. He not only adopted Lowth's connection of imagination with parallelisms, but found through him a way of treating the prophetic books as shaped human discourse. He regarded them not simply as a source of imagery sublime in itself or by association, but as a creation whose internal structure worked upon the mind and emotions of the reader, raising him to new heights of thought and feeling.

Lowth's arguments showed this poetry to have emanated from the simple agricultural life of the Hebrews, who enjoyed 'an equality of lineage and rank' and 'equal liberty' as a separate nation of 'husbandmen and shepherds'. The familiar objects of rural labour supplied them with their imagery of 'the grand and magnificent'.[22] The Old Testament, particularly the Psalms and Isaiah, became accessible as the embodiment in poetry of the agricultural republics Coleridge sought in politics; its structures could be adopted for works of Coleridge's own. Coleridge adopted them as did Blake, Macpherson and Smart, for whom the exploration of biblical style begun by Bishop Lowth was also a poetic starting point.[23] The result in each case was a poetry which understood the relation of religious insight and spiritual power to words to be a fragile one. Lowth argued that the rites and practices of the institutionalized

---

[18] Lowth, Professor of Poetry at Oxford, gave his ground-breaking lectures from 1741. They were published in Latin as *Praelectiones de Sacra Poesi Hebraeorum* (Oxford, 1753), summarized in Hugh Blair, *Lectures on Rhetoric and Belles Lettres* (London, 1783) and translated as *Lectures on the Sacred Poetry of the Hebrews*, 2 vols. (London, 1787), with notes by Michaelis, Professor at Göttingen. On Lowth's importance for the Romantics, see Stephen Prickett, *Words and The Word: Language, Poetics and Biblical Interpretation* (Cambridge, 1986), pp. 105–22, James C. McKusick, *Coleridge's Philosophy of Language*, pp. 57–61, and Tim Fulford, *Coleridge's Figurative Language* (London, 1991), pp. 83–6.

[19] Robert Lowth, *Isaiah. A New Translation* (London, 1778). For Coleridge's verse translation, see James C. McKusick, 'A New Poem By Samuel Taylor Coleridge', *Modern Philology*, 84 (1987), 407–15.

[20] *Ibid.*, 408.

[21] Lowth, *Lectures on the Sacred Poetry of the Hebrews*, vol. I, pp. 264–5.

[22] *Ibid.* pp. 144–7.

[23] See Morton D. Paley, *The Continuing City. William Blake's Jerusalem* (Oxford, 1983), pp. 44–9.

Hebrew priests made bad and obscure poetry. Sublimity came from images discovered outside the institution in the poet's own prosodic similarity to the language of a rural society. That society largely gone, it was left to the 1790s poets to imagine it renewed or to find sublimity in their own words. And to Burke and other defenders of traditional authority in church and state this seemed a dangerous and subversive independence hostile to all establishments.

In a letter of December 1796, Coleridge told Thelwall of the superior sublimity of Hebrew to Greek poetry and of 'Isaiah or St Paul's Epistle to the Hebrews' to Homer and Virgil. He quoted Paul's revision of Isaiah, 'ye are come unto Mount Sion, and unto the city of the living God, to an innumerable multitude of Angels, to God the Judge of all, and to the Spirits of just Men made perfect' (Hebrews 12: 22–3). He quoted Milton too against Thelwall's classicism and atheism: 'Sion Hill / Delights *me* more, and Siloa's Brook that flow'd / Fast by the oracle of God!' (*CL*, vol. I, p. 281; *Paradise Lost*, bk I, lines 10–12). This letter was written after reading Lowth's lectures, but in 'Reflections' (1795), when he knew only Lowth's *Isaiah*, Coleridge was treating Hebrew poetry, and Mount Zion in particular, as a source for a poetry intended to unite the English landscape, as reflected upon by its poet, into a place of divine harmony rather than political division:[24]

> But the time, when first
> From that low Dell, steep up the stony Mount
> I climb'd with perilous toil and reach'd the top,
> Oh! what a goodly scene! *Here* the bleak mount,
> The bare bleak mountain speckled thin with sheep;
> Grey clouds, that shadowing spot the sunny fields;
> And river, now with bushy rocks o'er-brow'd,
> Now winding bright and full, with naked banks;
> And seats, and lawns, the Abbey and the wood,
> And cots, and hamlets, and faint city-spire;
> The Channel *there*, the Islands and white sails,
> Dim coasts, and cloud-like hills, and shoreless Ocean –
> It seem'd like Omnipresence! God, methought,
> Had built him there a Temple: the whole World
> Seem'd *imag'd* in its vast circumference:
> No *wish* profan'd my overwhelmed heart.
> Blest hour! It was a luxury, to be!
> (*CPW*, vol. I, p. 107; lines 26–42)

A subtle progression of movement, rest and movement is achieved as words, rhythmic units and phrasal structures are stated, repeated and taken up again in modified form, so that each observation recalls and seems to include

[24] On the use made of biblical mountains in romantic poetry see Fred V. Randel, 'Frankenstein, Feminism, and the Intertextuality of Mountains', *SiR*, 24 (1984), 515–32.

something of the others, giving a kind of verbal omnipresence which sponsors the poet's recognition of a divine omnipresence. It would not have been possible had not Lowth's Isaiah revealed an imitable structure in scriptural poetry. Coleridge's authority depended on his secular development of holy writ into a malleable style capable of investing his poetry with spiritual power when faced by divisions in his political loyalties that left him uncertain whether to continue as a vocal opponent of Pitt's government. But the development was his to make: he surpassed Lowth and created a newly flexible blank verse poetry by adopting the intricate parallelisms of the Bishop's translations to the new and contemporary context of the subjective meditation on nature established by Cowper.

Coleridge's 'Reflections' seem to develop a passage at the beginning of *The Task* in which Cowper tries to reveal in detail nature's restorative power of harmony:

> Here Ouse, slow winding through a level plain
> Of spacious meads with cattle sprinkled o'er,
> Conducts the eye along his sinuous course
> Delighted. There, fast rooted in his bank
> Stand, never overlook'd, our fav'rite elms,
> That screen the herdsman's solitary hut;
> While far beyond, and overthwart the stream
> That as with molten glass inlays the vale,
> The sloping land recedes into the clouds;
> Displaying on its varied side, the grace
> Of hedge-row beauties numberless, square tow'r,
> Tall spire, from which the sound of chearful bells
> Just undulates upon the list'ning ear;
> Groves, heaths, and smoking villages remote.
> Scenes must be beautiful, which daily view'd
> Please daily, and whose novelty survives
> Long knowledge and the scrutiny of years.
>   (*Task*, pp. 9–10; bk I, lines 163–79)

Both poets use the picturesque mode; observing the scene from a hill, they use the course of the river to direct the eye into the view and present it as a series of separate but related objects.[25] The instructions 'Here' and 'There' ask the reader to see the place as a picture, the writer being a tourist guide. Coleridge's scene is also indebted to the views presented in William Crowe's *Lewesdon Hill* (1788). This poem, like *The Task*, combined picturesque prospects with Miltonic style, creating a Dorset landscape that is reminiscent of the harmonious Eden of *Paradise Lost* yet also vulnerable to the ravages of

---

[25] On the picturesque in this passage and in Cowper generally see Patricia Meyer Spacks, *The Poetry of Vision* (Cambridge, MA, 1967), pp. 180–2.

time.[26] Coleridge borrowed the poem from the Bristol Library in March 1795 and praised its 'genial influence' in *Biographia Literaria*. His 'Reflections' echo its opening view of 'hills, / And woods, and fruitful vales, and villages / Half-hid in tufted orchards, and the sea / Boundless …'.[27] Crowe, like Cowper, made the hilltop vantage point not only a place of retirement but a 'height' on which 'I feel the mind / Expand itself in wider liberty' (p. 4.). As in Thomson and the georgic mode generally, retirement allows a standpoint of authority, a view untrammelled by 'base compliance' with the desire for wealth and the demands of men of political power (p. 5). Crowe develops a patriotic vision of his local hill as a seat of native liberty, resistant to unnecessary war and to despotism – a vision which must have increased the attractiveness of his poem to Coleridge and to Wordsworth, opposed as they were both to what they saw as Britain's unnecessary war with France and to the tyranny of the Jacobins in the revolution there. For Crowe, Lewesdon Hill is a worthy resting place, a seat properly reminiscent of the 'glorious mount of Liberty' on which George Washington rests having delivered his country from British imperialism (p. 15). Such repose, he decides, is not allowed to 'such / As rise in causeless war' (p. 14). Speaking like Cowper in Miltonic tones, he condemns such men in what seemed, in the charged political atmosphere of the 1790s, a radical evangelical attack on the British monarchy and ministry:

> in fields of blood
> Hail'd victors, thence renown'd, and call'd on earth
> Kings, heroes, demi-gods, but in high Heaven
> Thieves, ruffians, murderers; these find no repose …
>
> (p. 14)

Crowe's own politics were not so extreme as they later seemed. His sympathy for the Americans in their war against Britain was shared by many Whigs, for whom the ministry's attempt to tax and to rule without allowing representation offended against the spirit of the 1688 revolution settlement. But his view of American liberty was shared by Coleridge, who had hoped to base his Pantisocracy in the countryside near the Susquehannah river. And Coleridge certainly used a Miltonic rhetoric to prophesy destruction for his political opponents in 'Religious Musings' and 'The Destiny of Nations'. Crowe's hilltop vision, like Cowper's moral high ground, offered Coleridge a symbolic treatment of the real English landscape, a country-mount from which to preach, as they had done, in Miltonic tones of the triumph of liberty and the destruction of tyranny.

In locating Miltonic and biblical prophecy in a visualization of a known

---

[26] A point made by Nicholas Roe in *The Politics of Nature: Wordsworth and Some Contemporaries* (London and Basingstoke, 1992), pp. 120–23. Coleridge's praise can be found in *BL*, vol. I, pp. 17–18.

[27] William Crowe, *Lewesdon Hill* (Oxford, 1788 (facsimile rpt., Oxford, 1989)), p. 1.

landscape, Crowe and Cowper helped Coleridge to overcome his tendency, later acknowledged and regretted, to a turgidity of diction remote from the real language and concerns of his contemporaries. In their poetry, Miltonic visions, spiritual and political, emerge from a narration of landscape the clarity and simplicity of which is a token of the poet's rooted love of his locality. And love of this kind is shown to be (as Coleridge agreed it to be when attacking Godwin) a prerequisite for a love of his country and countrymen. Cowper's Buckinghamshire fields, as here Crowe's Dorset, allowed Coleridge to derive his radical politics of liberty from a detailed and loving view of its land, in which natural order seems to protect vulnerable human independence:

> Then stand I in the hollow comb beneath
> And bless this friendly mount, that weather-fends
> My reed-roof'd cottage, while the wintry blast
> From the thick north comes howling: till the Spring
> Return, who leads my devious steps abroad,
> To climb, as now, to LEWESDON's airy top.
>
> Above the noise and stir of yonder fields
> Uplifted, on this height I feel the mind
> Expand itself in wider liberty ...
>
> (p. 4)

In the 'Reflections' Coleridge adds to Crowe's and Cowper's hilltop views a developing urgency, allowing a climax that transforms the picturesque scene into a sublime vision in which the view becomes a symbol of divine limitlessness. And by so doing he develops from retirement a language which allows him an authority which he is unable to attain in a world requiring political and social action. His phrase 'it was a luxury, – to be!' grants him full satisfaction of desire, contrasting him with Bristol's 'wealthy son of Commerce' with 'his thirst of idle gold'. The poet attempts to re-enter public life renewed by the authority gained in retirement, declaring 'I therefore go, and join head, heart, and hand, / Active and firm, to fight the bloodless fight / Of Science, Freedom, and the Truth in Christ' (*CPW*, vol. I, p. 108, lines 60–2). This affirmation is, however, pompous and stilted. Like Cowper, Coleridge finds that self-righteousness attends upon his desire to make political action depend upon a religious conviction that stems from a vision of spirituality in nature. Coleridge, as Kelvin Everest has shown,[28] made his affirmation as a way of gathering strength under the strain of carrying on his political journal *The Watchman*, in which he also addressed the issues of commerce, luxury and benevolence that divided his readers between Godwin

---

[28] Everest, *Coleridge's Secret Ministry*, pp. 222–42.

and London-based radicals on the one hand, wealthy Bristolian Unitarians on the other.[29]

The Watchman failed as its readership shrank in number and Coleridge grew tired of producing a journal almost single-handed. Coleridge's poetry proved similarly vulnerable to the indifference of a readership which, to judge by the reviewers, neither expected poetry to espouse radical and pacifist politics in the climate of war with France nor wished it to renounce neo-classical decorum for colloquial simplicity. And so Coleridge's newly formulated authority was fragile, as Cowper's had been. Because it depended upon his conviction that his language would repair social and political divisions by offering spiritual reconciliation in a landscape of harmony, it remained vulnerable to insecurity. In 'This Lime Tree Bower My Prison', written in 1797, Coleridge attempts to overcome insecurity by offering his poetic voice, self-consciously reflected upon, as the power which will rebind him to friends and audience by its envisioning of their relationship with each other and with nature as a shared community. The poem makes a movement from renewal of friendship to an invocation of nature which hopes to facilitate an apprehension of the divine:

> Yes! they wander on
> In gladness all; but thou, methinks, most glad,
> My gentle-hearted Charles! for thou has pined
> And hunger'd after Nature, many a year,
> In the great City pent, winning thy way
> With sad yet patient soul, through evil and pain
> And strange calamity! Ah! slowly sink
> Behind the western ridge, thou glorious Sun!
> Shine in the slant beams of the sinking orb,
> Ye purple heath-flowers! richlier burn, ye clouds!
> Live in the yellow light, ye distant groves!
> And kindle, thou blue Ocean! So my friend
> Struck with deep joy may stand, as I have stood,
> Silent with swimming sense; yea, gazing round
> On the wide landscape, gaze till all doth seem
> Less gross than bodily; and of such hues
> As veil the Almighty Spirit, when yet he makes
> Spirits perceive his presence.
>   (*CPW*, vol. I, p. 179–80; lines 26–43)

The poem follows the characteristic movements of Cowper's nature poetry as it launches a vision of spiritual renewal in the wide landscape from the refuge

---

[29] Coleridge's radicalization of Unitarian dissent, via his arguments over the equalization/abolition of property, was one of the reasons for his attraction of the sons of wealthy dissenters – the Wedgwoods, Charles Lloyd – wishing for a purer, more idealistic politics than that of their fathers.

of a garden-bower.[30] Like Cowper, Coleridge draws attention to the limitations of his position. His bower has 'Much that has sooth'd me' within it, but as a pastoral place of healing it is also 'my prison'. Nevertheless, freed there from social and political pressures the poet can, in isolated safety, envisage a nature which his friends can freely view and possess in harmony with the divine spirit present in it. As Wordsworth was to do in *Home at Grasmere*, Coleridge speaks from a refuge in the divided and owned larger landscape (in which he and the Wordsworths were viewed by local families with suspicion and spied upon by the ministry's man). And he envisages from that refuge a land shareable in common, free from the (spiritual) imprisonment of the metropolis, because it is common land – the unenclosed Quantock hilltops on which one may roam unrestricted by fences.

For Cowper nature offers a liberty and equality that he does not dare advocate politically precisely because it escapes the ability of pictorial tradition or proper taste to control it adequately. For Cowper a 'woodland scene' is attractive, though not beautiful, in its twilight variety:

> No tree in all the grove but has its charms,
> Though each its hue peculiar; paler some,
> And of a wannish grey; the willow such,
> And poplar, that with silver lines his leaf,
> And ash far-stretching his umbrageous arm.
> (*Task*, p. 17; bk I, lines, 307–11)

In 'This Lime Tree Bower' Coleridge also imagines a picturesque woodland scene in order to reveal a natural wildness that his friends can move through and rise out of into an unconfined natural freedom 'beneath the wide wide Heaven':[31]

> The roaring dell, o'erwooded, narrow, deep,
> And only speckled by the mid-day sun;
> Where its slim trunk the ash from rock to rock
> Flings arching like a bridge; – that branchless ash,
> Unsunn'd and damp ...
> (*CPW*, vol. I, p. 179; lines 10–14)

Coleridge, having learnt from the simplicity of diction and fluidity of movement manifest in *The Task* at its best, uses a less Latinate vocabulary and formal structure than Cowper to describe his wood. Like Cowper, he moves from such description to a vision of spiritual liberty rather than to a reinforcement of propriety, but only by virtue of having first seen through a

---

[30] On Coleridge and Cowper see Humphrey House, *Coleridge. The Clark Lectures 1951–52* (London, 1967), pp. 71–83.

[31] Here I modify the work of Anne K. Mellor, who has suggested that the poem moves through the established category of the picturesque to that of the sublime, in 'Coleridge's "This Lime-Tree Bower My Prison" and the Categories of English Landscape', *SiR*, 18 (1979), 253–70.

'guiltless eye' (*Task*, p. 18; bk I, line 333), an eye purged by the poet's tactical withdrawal from the divided social and political fields of rural England.

In 'This Lime Tree Bower' withdrawal allows a move uphill to a transcendent view of a land marked by churches, agriculture and commerce but briefly held in harmony. The view is also made possible by the use of structures derived from Coleridge's understanding of biblical poetry. Lines 32–7, ('Ah! slowly sink ... thou blue Ocean') adapt to Coleridge's own voice the diction and parallelisms of the Hebrew poetry that Bishop Lowth had taught him to value: 'each Line or member of a sentence is counter-balanced by the following', creating a pattern of syntactic and rhythmical echoes (based around the vocative phrases 'ye ...') which is interwoven with, but remains discernible in, that of the blank verse lines. Lowth had pointed out that Hebrew poetry did not depend on lines of equal metre; his own translations, like Coleridge's Song of Deborah, used lines of varying measure. In this instance Coleridge's lines imitate the form of address used in the Psalms as he assumes the power to invoke or even command the landscape, in order to dedicate it to Charles and thence to God: 'Give unto the LORD, O ye kindreds of the people, give unto the LORD glory and strength ... Let the heavens rejoice, and let the earth be glad; let the seas roar, and the fullness thereof. Let the field be joyful, and all that *is* therein: then shall all the trees of the wood rejoice' (96: 7–12).

Biblical visions could not, as the 1790s progressed, overcome the political tensions that resided in the landscape for which Coleridge wished to speak. These tensions, and the increasing difficulty of containing them in poetry derived from eighteenth-century landscape-description, are evident in the 'Recantation' poem he published in the *Morning Post* of 16 April 1798. 'France: an Ode' as it was later called, recanted Coleridge's sympathy for the French revolution and opposition to the war against France, in response to the French invasion of Switzerland. Published in a newspaper itself under government pressure for its support of radical causes, the poem opposes France but tries to justify Coleridge's earlier enthusiasm for the revolution; it tries to combine patriotism with a continued enthusiasm for liberty. It locates that enthusiasm in a progress through a landscape and in a style familiar from 'Reflections on Having Left a Place of Retirement' and 'This Lime Tree Bower'. The movement from the gloomy but inspiring wildness of a picturesque wood to a hilltop vision again adapts the language of Cowper and of the Bible:

> Through glooms, which never woodman trod,
>   How oft, pursuing fancies holy,
> My moonlight way o'er flowering weeds I wound,
>   Inspired, beyond the guess of folly,
> By each rude shape and wild unconquerable sound!
> O ye loud Waves! and O ye Forests high!

> And O ye Clouds that far above me soared!
>   Thou rising Sun! thou blue rejoicing Sky!
>   Yea, every thing that is and will be free!
>   Bear witness for me, wheresoe'er ye be,
>   With what deep worship I have still adored
>   The spirit of divinest Liberty.
>   (*CPW*, vol. I, p. 244, lines 10–21)

The tone is more defensive, the experience lonely, the invoked audience that of natural objects rather than the friends who might act as a model of a community reconciled.

The next stanza reveals that the progress from retirement through the picturesque to the biblical sublime vision is under political pressure. Coleridge claims it as a progress through which patriotic love of Britain is experienced, but has to defend such patriotism against his former opposition to Britain in its war with France, whilst now recanting that opposition:

> And when to whelm the disenchanted nation,
>   Like fiends embattled by a wizard's wand,
>   The Monarchs marched in evil day,
>   And Britain joined the dire array;
>   Though dear her shores and circling ocean,
> Though many friendships, many youthful loves
>   Had swoln the patriot emotion
> And flung a magic light o'er all her hills and groves;
> Yet still my voice, unaltered, sang defeat
>   To all that braved the tyrant-quelling lance . . .
>   (*CPW*, vol. I, p. 245; lines 28–37)

There is more anxiety here than Coleridge cares to admit. In attacking Britain and the European monarchies for trying to reimpose the spells of repression on 'disenchanted' France, he risked wishing for his own country's defeat. And the word 'magic', describing the light that 'patriot emotion' had spread for him over Britain's 'hills and groves' indicates that perhaps such emotion too was a spell cast 'by a wizard's wand', as if the love of country stemming from friendship and 'youthful loves' is suspect as another fiendish monarchical ideology. The enchantment of a patriotism arising from love of the English landscape would, following the implication of Coleridge's metaphors of magic, be less a vision of 'Liberty' than a spell closer to monarchical nationalism than he explicitly admits.

By the close of the poem liberty and patriotism cannot be reconciled and Coleridge can no longer claim to oppose Britain's policies in the name of a harmonious society envisaged as being naturally founded on a reconciled British landscape. The Quantock hill, as formulated by Coleridge's adaptation of Cowper and scripture, is no longer a place from which the poet commands a vision of a socially realizable freedom for his readers and countrymen. Coleridge climbs the hill again, but to experience in isolation a spirit of liberty latent in wind, waves, 'earth, sea, and air', a spirit now, however, equally remote from Britain and France, a spirit which, he declares, never 'Didst breathe thy soul in forms of human power' (line 92). It is for Coleridge a gloomy conclusion since it leaves him a lonely spiritual transcendence but no model by which his vision can be made present in social and political structures. It is the conclusion of a poet whose voicing of landscape no longer gives him a discourse by which he can speak with authority for a public audience – even by asking that audience to model itself on a community of intimate friends.

The fragmentation of Coleridge's sense of audience, the political pressure upon him, and his dependence upon Cowper's earlier attempts to negotiate similar difficulties, are apparent in a letter of circa 10 March 1798. Concerning himself with his political reputation in a country at war, Coleridge also reveals divisions within the anti-government radical movement. The letter is addressed to George, Coleridge's church and state-supporting brother, and does its best to find common ground with him:

I am inclined to consider the Aristocrats as the more respectable of our three factions, because they are more decorous. The Opposition & the Democrats are not only vicious – they wear the *filthy garments* of vice.

> He that takes
> Deep in his soft credulity the stamp
> Design'd by loud Declaimers on the part
> Of Liberty, themselves the slaves of Lust,
> Incurs derision for his easy faith
> And lack of Knowlege – & with cause enough.
> For when was public Virtue to be found
> Where private was not? Can he love the whole
> Who loves no part? He be a *nation's* friend
> Who is, in truth, the friend of no man there?
> Can he be strenuous in his country's cause
> Who slights the charities, for whose dear sake
> That country, if at all, must be belov'd?
>
> (Cowper)

I am prepared to suffer without discontent the consequences of my follies & mistakes–: and unable to conceive how that which I am, of Good could have been without that which I have been of Evil, it is withheld from me to regret any thing: I therefore consent to be deemed a Democrat & a Seditionist. A man's character follows him long after he has ceased to deserve it.

(*CL*, vol. i, p. 396–7)

The letter uses the quotation from *The Task* (bk v, lines 496–508) to assure George of Coleridge's discontent with the atheistic London-based democrats – with Paine, with Godwin. Like 'France: An Ode' and the poem Coleridge composed a month later, 'Fears in Solitude', it uses Cowper's Christian moralizing to imply that Coleridge is a lover of both his country and its religion. It uses it too to take a lofty view of aristocratic mores and a still loftier one of democratic mores. In *The Watchman* and his lectures of 1795 Coleridge had attacked Godwin's view that a free society must be based on reason, and that familial and domestic emotion was, since it prejudiced the judgement, a hindrance to the achievement of that society. Godwin attacked the institution of marriage, advocating free sexual partnerships that would not, as did marriage, prevent benevolent action by clouding the disinterested judgement of what was best for society as a whole. Here, as in his 'Reflections on Having Left a Place of Retirement', Coleridge develops from Cowper an argument that is aimed both at Godwin's utilitarian doctrine of benevolence and at aristocratic libertines who do not act upon the compassionate sensibility they claim to feel.

Yet Coleridge, defending himself on several fronts at once, could not sustain the moral view of the political sphere that he wished to take. Instead, faced with the possibility of imminent invasion by France and therefore by deepened divisions amongst those who had opposed war with France, Coleridge told his brother that nature poetry offers a retired and uncontroversial means of spreading love, liberty and benevolence.

The Ministers may have had in their possession facts which may alter the whole state of the argument, and make my syllogisms fall as flat as a baby's card-house – And feeling this, my Brother! I have for some time past withdrawn myself almost totally from the consideration of *immediate* causes, which are infinitely complex & uncertain, to muse on fundamental & general causes – the 'causae causarum'. – I devote myself to such works as encroach not on the antisocial passions – in poetry, to elevate the imagination & set the affections in right tune by the beauty of the inanimate impregnated, as with a living soul, by the presence of Life – in prose, to the seeking with patience & a slow, very slow mind . . . What our faculties are & what they are capable of becoming. – I love fields & woods & mounta[ins] with almost a visionary fondness – and because I have found benevolence & quietness growing within me as that fondness [has] increased, therefore I should wish to be the means of implanting it in others – & to destroy the bad passions not by combating them, but by keeping them in inaction.

(CL, vol. i, p. 397)

Following these remarks with a quotation from Wordsworth's 'Ruined Cottage', Coleridge envisages a vital public rôle for poetry. Retiring from political controversy to Cowper's fields and woods and Wordsworth's mountains, it will offer its readers a model of how benevolence grows by 'shadowy Sympathies with things that hold / An inarticulate Language', leading to a love capable of healing social division. This is a less pessimistic conclusion than the lonely pursuit of liberty at the end of 'France: an Ode' but similarly fragile in making social reform dependent upon a reform of

sympathy that could not be effected by political organizations and campaigns.
And it needed testing in public poetry.

In the month following his writing of the letter to his brother George,
Coleridge composed 'Fears in Solitude', putting it before the public in a
pamphlet published by Joseph Johnson (himself anxious to lose his dangerous
reputation for having pro-French sympathies). This poem can usefully be
seen as a modification of Cowper's landscape-description. It seeks to give
Coleridge a stable authority but, like 'France: an Ode' (published in the
month of its composition) and like the letter, reveals the increasing
inadequacy of eighteenth-century moralizing from nature in bringing a
divided and politicized landscape into harmony. The poet is left anxiously
aware of the inefficacy of his words as an intervention in the political realm,
choosing instead to find an uncontroversial familial harmony in nature which
might act as a microcosm of the social reconciliation he is unable to conceive
in political structures. Written 'during the alarm of an invasion' caused by
fear that French success in Switzerland would be followed by attack on
Britain, the poem has again to defend the poet's former opposition to war
with France. It does so by trying, on the basis of his love of a rural scene that
stands for Britain as a whole, to refute the charge that he is an enemy-within:

> Others meanwhile,
> Dote with a mad idolatry; and all
> Who will not fall before their images,
> And yield them worship, they are enemies
> Even of their country!
>
> Such have I been deemed. -
> But, O dear Britain! O my Mother Isle!
> Needs must thou prove a name most dear and holy
> To me, a son, a brother, and a friend,
> A husband, and a father! who revere
> All bonds of natural love, and find them all
> Within the limits of thy rocky shores.
> O native Britain! O my Mother Isle!
> How shouldst thou prove aught else but dear and holy
> To me, who from thy lakes and mountain-hills,
> Thy clouds, thy quiet dales, thy rocks and seas,
> Have drunk in all my intellectual life,
> All sweet sensations, all ennobling thoughts,
> All adoration of the God in nature . . .
>
> (lines 171–88)

Images from the same landscape are used in a rhetoric which seeks to prove
Coleridge's patriotism by advocating repulsion of the French invaders:

                              Stand we forth;
             Render them back upon the insulted ocean,
             And let them toss as idly on its waves
             As the vile sea-weed, which some mountain-blast
             Swept from our shores! And oh! may we return
             Not with a drunken triumph, but with fear,
             Repenting of the wrongs with which we stung
             So fierce a foe to frenzy!
                                                    (lines 146–53)

The images attempt to make defensive war into a natural process. Their
violence serves to suggest Coleridge's vehement patriotism whilst allowing
him to avoid reference to the 'bloody deeds' such a war would actually entail
– deeds he had formerly depicted in graphic terms in his anti-war writing.
Coleridge tries to seem a man of peace, still consistent with his earlier
opposition to war, and to prove his patriotism by portraying violence as a
natural product of the shores and hills of Britain for which he claims to speak.
At the same time those hills act in the poem as the moral high ground from
which Coleridge can berate the ministers and warmongers who, by provoking
France (stinging 'so fierce a foe to frenzy'), got Britain and those who wished
both to be loyal and lovers of liberty into the mess of war:

             Oh! 'tis a quiet spirit-healing nook!
             Which all, methinks, would love; but chiefly he,
             The humble man, who, in his youthful years,
             Knew just so much of folly, as had made
             His early manhood more securely wise!
             Here he might lie on fern or withered heath,
             While from the singing lark (that sings unseen
             The minstrelsy that solitude loves best),
             And from the sun, and from the breezy air,
             Sweet influences trembled o'er his frame;
             And he, with many feelings, many thoughts,
             Made up a meditative joy, and found
             Religious meanings in the forms of Nature!
             And so, his senses gradually wrapt
             In a half sleep, he dreams of better worlds,
             And dreaming hears thee still, O singing lark,
             That singest like an angel in the clouds!

                My God! it is a melancholy thing
             For such a man, who would full fain preserve
             His soul in calmness, yet perforce must feel
             For all his human brethren – O my God!
             It weighs upon the heart, that he must think
             What uproar and what strife may now be stirring

This way or that way o'er these silent hills –
Invasion, and the thunder and the shout,
And all the crash of onset; fear and rage,
And undetermined conflict – even now,
Even now, perchance, and in his native isle:
Carnage and groans beneath this blessed sun!
We have offended, Oh! my countrymen!
We have offended very grievously,
And been most tyrannous.

(lines 12–43)

Coleridge's spiritual high ground is recognizable from his earlier poems – the landscape of the Quantocks formulated through Cowper's version of the picturesque. From naturally wild (and therefore free) dells and nooks he moves upwards. But the 'better worlds' seen above are 'dreams' only, and the 'religious meanings' that he alone finds for the reader in Nature are haunted by the conflicting and guilty uses he makes of the landscape as he tries to claim moral and political consistency for himself. Landscape is too easily a resource both for visions of spiritual peace and for imagery which naturalizes violence.

At the close of the poem Coleridge reworks his characteristic progress through the landscape yet again. This time the move towards a transcendent climax is checked and instead, in a careful modification of Cowper, a picturesque view of domestic social harmony rather than a sublime vision of universal spiritual reconciliation is offered (lines 208–32). This view stills, though it does not overcome, the tensions and conflicts evident in the earlier use of the landscape to claim public and political authority. It develops from the passage quoted above from *The Task* (bk I, lines 163–79) both its poetic organization of the view and its retiring emphasis on domestic harmony as a quiet and uncontroversial model for society when more political visions are found to be flawed. It was, as I have already suggested, a precarious model, haunted like Coleridge's political visions both by his divided aims and by the pressures placed on it. The versions of retirement and the picturesque offered by Cowper (and of the sublime offered by scripture) intensified though they were by Coleridge, could not resolve to his own or his readers' satisfaction the conflict that divided the public realm. The landscape and the authority of those who wrote of it were left too divided to be places in which readers could imagine themselves and the nation at large to be in aesthetic or political agreement for longer than a few brief moments.

Coleridge on tour

'Fears in Solitude' exemplifies the deleterious effects on Coleridge's public poetry of the political tensions which left him and his dissenting readership divided and on the defensive. After 1800, Coleridge, his confidence shot by his anxiety over public reception and over Wordsworth's disapproval of his poems, turned away from landscape poetry. But he did not turn away from landscape-description. In the intimate medium of the tour journal, in writing not intended for publication, he continued to question self and society. He walked in the Lake District, climbing Scafell. He wrote as he went, stopping at the summit and making entries in his notebook. The result was prose full of spontaneity, unworried by the pressure of a public or of the landscape poetry that was popular with it. He recorded his involvement in prose which tried to convey the fast-changing experience:

I slipped down, & went on for a while with tolerable ease – but now I came (it was midway down) to a smooth, perpendicular Rock about 7 feet high – this was nothing – I put my hands on the Ledge, & dropped down / in a few yards came just such another / I *dropped* that too / and yet another, seemed not higher – I would not stand for a trifle / so I dropped that too / but the stretching of the muscle[s] of my hands & arms, & the jolt of the Fall on my Feet, put my whole Limbs in a *Tremble*, and I paused, & looking down, saw that I had little else to encounter but a succession of these little Precipices – it was in truth a Path that in a very hard Rain is, no doubt, the channel of a most splendid Waterfall. – So I began to suspect that I ought not to go on / but then unfortunately tho' I could with ease drop down a smooth Rock 7 feet high, I could not *climb* it / so go on I must / and on I went / the next 3 drops were not half a Foot, at least not a foot more than my own height / but every Drop increased the Palsy of my Limbs – I shook all over, Heaven knows without the least influence of Fear / and now I had only two more to drop down / to return was impossible – but of these two the first was tremendous / it was twice my own height, & the Ledge at the bottom was [so] exceedingly narrow, that if I dropt down upon it I must of necessity have fallen backwards & of course killed myself. My Limbs were all in a tremble – I lay upon my Back to rest myself & was beginning according to my Custom to laugh at myself for a Madman, when the sight of the Crag above me on each side, & the impetuous Clouds just over them, posting so luridly & so rapidly northward, overawed me / I lay in a state of almost prophetic Trance & Delight – & blessed God aloud, for the powers of Reason & the Will, which remaining no Danger can overpower us! O God, I exclaimed aloud – how calm, how blessed am I now / I know not how to proceed, how to return / but I am calm & fearless & confident / if this Reality were a Dream, if I were asleep, what agonies had I suffered! what screams! – When the Reason & the Will are away, what remains to us but Darkness & Dimness & a bewildering Shame, and Pain that is utterly Lord over us, or fantastic Pleasure, that draws the Soul along swimming through the air in many shapes, even as a Flight of Starlings in a Wind.

(*CL*, vol. ii, p. 842)

The prose deliberately forgoes the subordination involved in correct grammar and punctuation. It uses dashes and hyphens rather than create a highly structured paragraph, and by so doing avoids self-consciously persuasive rhetoric and the need for formal conclusion. The advantage of this informality is that Coleridge's reflections on reason and the will seem to emerge spontaneously from the experience, as one more event in the sequential narrative. The 'sight of the Crags' produces in him a response in accordance with those stipulated in theories of the sublime, but after his strenuous activity he is able to see that such responses depend upon a state of lassitude and rest. When he is still struggling down the rocks his reason and will are so involved in decision-making that he cannot enter the conventionally sublime state of being overpowered by fear and awe. Here, as for Thomson in *The Seasons* and Johnson criticizing Milton, the sublime depends upon a certain distance. But for Coleridge the distance is not a safe one and it leads him to consider the psychological conditions necessary for subordination to power, those, he suggests, pertaining in dreams, where the reason and will are suspended. Thus Coleridge's informal prose, intimately describing an actual experience of landscape, leads to a far more subtle understanding of power than the self-exculpatory rhetoric of the 'Recantation' ode. Coleridge, in fact, makes a penetrating criticism of the way in which fear and awe are evoked in the dream-world of his best poems. By banishing the ordinary conditions under which reason and will operate, by creating a world of fantasy, reverie and the supernatural, the poems produce the subordination that Coleridge identifies here as 'Shame' (echoing Christabel's 'mark of shame'), as mastery – 'utterly Lord over us' (cf. Christabel's 'Lord of thy utterance'), and as a masochistic mixture of pleasure and pain. Here Coleridge arrives at a new understanding of the sublime as an experience in which the potential instability of the self, and its need for stabilizing forces, is discovered by a writing which is both unstable and stabilizing: unstable in eschewing formal syntax, stabilizing in inscribing the self in an activity of description by which it discovers in the changing scene the nature of its own relationship with that scene and with itself. Coleridge's private and informal prose, unworried by his anxious desire to conform in public to contemporary aesthetic taste and religious prejudices, finds an authoritative self by showing self-knowledge to arise in the representation of the self's unstable and fluctuating relationship with a landscape in which it puts itself at risk. The danger of self-loss (from falling off the cliff or into panic), reproduced in words, brings self-redefinition.[32]

The following year Coleridge travelled with the Wordsworths to Scotland. The joint tour was not a success. Coleridge's illness, the wet weather, the bad inns, led to an increasing tension which manifested itself in entries in Coleridge's tour notebook. He lamented on hearing Dorothy quote her brother's poetry 'I have no dear Heart that loves my Verses – I never hear

---

[32] Compare Hartman in 'Reflections on the Evening Star', in Geoffrey Hartman (ed.), *New Perspectives on Coleridge and Wordsworth* (New York, 1972), pp. 113–22, especially p. 121: 'He felt ... a loss of substance, a passivity both shaming and sublime – and he recovers himself ... by the will of his voice; more precisely, by the willed intimation of a sublime voice.'

them in snatches from a beloved Voice ...' (*CN*, vol. i, 1463). On 29 August he parted from the Wordsworths, ostensibly to return to Edinburgh and the south. Revitalized by his departure from his friends, he went south only after a vigorous tour of the Highlands during which he recorded his impressions of the landscapes and the people he encountered. The results, in the informal prose of the notebooks, exhibit none of the anxieties that beset 'Recantation'. Nor does Coleridge simply present the landscape as a series of picturesque scenes, to be judged by the English gentleman-traveller. In recording the social and political circumstances of the highlanders he is most like Johnson; in his ability to articulate the activity of the landscape and his changing perception of it, he surpasses both Dorothy Wordsworth's and Gilpin's depictions of the mountains:

met with three good Highlanders, two understood & talked Gaelic, the third, an intelligent man, spoke low Scottish only – I went with him into a field to my right, & visited a noble waterfall – during rain it must be a most noble one / the Trees are old, & *army*, one on each side / it is one great *Apron* with an oval Pool at the Bottom, but above it you look up thro' a rocky Stream with trees & bushes, & the Fall itself is marked by two *great Cauldrons* delved out in the black rock, down which it falls – into which cauldrons it boils & rebounds / this is on the River of *Glenfalloch*, which word signifies the *Hidden Glen* – I talked much with the Scotchman – the oppressions of the Landlord – & he used these beautiful words – 'It kills one's affections for one's Country, the Hardships of Life, coming by change, & wi' injustice.' – The Hills on each side of me are low, for I myself am on very high Ground – they are almost cragless, an intermixture of beds of purple Heath, slumbring in its Beauty, & beds of green fern, always alive & fluttering – but to my right the Hill breaks, & lets in upon the view a triangular mountain of fine outline ... And in the break a little Stream with glimmering Waterbreaks & cowering Alders / wild Sheep-folds in the Hills but before me Ben More or the Huge Mountain / One of the highest in the highlands, shaped like a haystack, which dallies with the Clouds, that now touch, now hide, now leave it ...

(*CN*, vol. i, 1475)

In this note, unlike Wordsworth's 'Solitary Reaper' and 'Highland Girl', the Highlander's words are quoted. And the words redefine the rapidly yet subtly evoked character of the scene. They politicize the landscape, making its varied beauty and dynamic activity, so carefully narrated in the shifting tenses and viewpoints of Coleridge's prose, unavailable to the man native to the place. The Highlander shows the scene to Coleridge, who recreates it for the reader as an exhilarating experience rather than composed view, only then showing that the experience is not shared by the Highlander himself. The exclusion from the landscape of which the Highlander complains is thus dramatized for the reader by the passage's structure, creating an acute sense of his deprivation. Writer and reader share the scene courtesy of the Highlander's guidance and are thus able to feel what he has lost. Political oppression is rendered here as a stifling of the soul, of the ability to love and to share: sympathy with the Highlander's 'beautiful words' becomes a quiet act of political solidarity – feeling making common cause in place of argument. Coleridge quoted the Highlander's words again in his *Lay Sermon* of 1817 when arguing against the pauperization of the labouring classes by the forces of economic improvement. Feeling for the Scottish landscape, a birthright violated by economic forces and government policies, is for Coleridge a fundamental basis for loyalty to the political nation, an emotion to be evoked by him in conscious opposition to the forces and ideologies defining and governing contemporary Britain.

Coleridge's own vulnerability and marginality as a lone traveller isolated from his friends allows him to articulate the Highlander's isolation, to stage the mountain scenes as fleeting and precarious experiences, their beauty both vital to the inhabitant's sense of rooted identity and dangerously evanescent. He also stages the landscape as a dramatization of the distortion of meaning that endangers his and Wordsworth's mutual understanding and love: 'My words & actions imaged on his mind, distorted & snaky as the Boatman's Oar reflected in the Lake' (*CN*, vol. I, 1473). Both for Coleridge on a personal level and the Highlanders on a political one, it is the loss and perversion of social connection – of community – that destroys the love of the land. But this is a downward spiral: the loss of love for the land leaves the being isolated, unable to renew that connection. It is the scenario of the 'Dejection' letter and ode, written the previous year, enacted in Coleridge's own case and giving him an insight denied both to Gilpin and to Wordsworth into the politics of Scotland. Emigration is shown to be the demoralized and desperate recourse of a people crushed and alienated by the clearance of their communities for sheep-farming. In 1817 Coleridge quoted the words of a Highland woman: 'Within this space how short a time back! there lived a hundred and seventy-three persons: and now there is only a shepherd, and an underling or two … And do you think, Sir! that God allows of such proceedings?' (*LS*, pp. 209–10). At such moments Coleridge the tourist becomes a historian of the politics of feeling, reproaching the profiteering landowners for having turned Scotland's lonely beauty into an image, for its inhabitants, of their 'desolation dreamlike' (*CN*, vol. I, 1489).

Coleridge, like Wordsworth, represents the end of an eighteenth-century political tradition as well as the beginning of that movement which, originating in a challenge to that tradition, came to be called Romanticism. His *Lay Sermon* (1817) 'addressed to the higher and middle classes' reveals both aspects. In it Coleridge reconstructs some of the encounters with Highlanders he had made on his Scottish tour of 1803. And he does so, in Wordsworth's manner, to challenge the social and political assumptions of those 'higher and middle classes'. He makes the Highlanders speak directly of their dispossession at the hands of the landlords in words presented, as in *Lyrical Ballads*, as showing 'a propriety of phrase' and 'discrimination of tone' 'which strong feeling seldom fails to call forth in humble life' (*LS*, p. 209). Mrs Andrew McFarlan of Glengyle voices a local attachment to her native place, her political reproach emerging from an articulation of a feeling for nature not comprehensible by the language of economics to which Coleridge explicitly opposes it:

Well! but they are gone, and with them the bristled bear, and the pink haver, and the potatoe plot that looked as gay as any flower garden with its blossoms! I sometimes fancy, that the very birds are gone, all but the crows and the gleads! Well, and what then? Instead of us all, there is one shepherd man, and it may be a pair of small lads and a many, many sheep! And do you think, Sir! that God allows of such proceedings?

(p. 210)

The clearances had, as Coleridge shows by quoting another Highlander, succeeded by alienating the peasants from the laird in destroying the clan loyalty that fostered Jacobitism. And in doing so they had given good cause for a pro-French Jacobinism:

Why, that their fathers were all turned out of their farms before the year was over, and sent to wander like so many gipsies, unless they would consent to shed their gray hairs, at tenpence a day, over the new canals. Had there been a price set upon his head, and his enemies had been coming upon him, he needed but have whistled, and a hundred brave lads would have made a wall of flame round about him with the flash of their broad-swords! Now if the _____ should come among us, as (it is said) they will, let him whistle to his sheep and see if *they* will fight for him!

(pp. 210–11)

In 1803 Coleridge had termed the Highlander 'the Jacobite Traitor of a Boatman', later changing his pencilled note to read 'Jacobin' (*CN*, vol. I, 1469 and n.). In relating the incident in 1817 he is more sympathetic: he not only attacks the economic colonialism of the lairds loyal to the Hanoverian state, not only shows events in Scotland as symptomatic of the situation in Britain as a whole, but makes moral authority reside in the words of the peasants and not in the assumptions of the ruling classes.

Yet although such quotations revive the radical agenda of *Lyrical Ballads*, the *Lay Sermon* incorporates them in an appeal to, rather than an attack on or transformation of, the gentlemanly values of rural paternalism. Coleridge endorses the independent landed gentleman, as Uvedale Price, Gilpin and Wordsworth himself also did, as the repository of the values of duty and disinterested patriotism that protect the constitution by ensuring the loyalty of the tenantry. The landowner would be a gentleman if 'as the result of his own free conviction the *marketable* produce of his Estates were made a subordinate consideration to the living and moral growth that is to remain on the land' (*LS*, p. 218). It is neither to a democratic commonwealth of equal or shared property nor to a commercialist society that Coleridge turns in 1817, but, like the Country-party writers of the early eighteenth century, to an anti-commercialist idealization of the squirearchy as disinterested protectors of the land and the tenants who live on it. It is a rural ideal, an image of the nation which locates value in an almost feudal relationship, unwilling to accept commerce and industry as anything other than forces in need of counter-acting and enlightening powers. It is, therefore, a reactionary, though deeply human ideal, formulated in part by a revision of Coleridge's radical commonwealth arguments of the 1790s. In 1817 he again invokes the laws of 'the inspired Hebrew Legislator' as evidence that the state must counteract commerce with anti-commercial laws (*LS*, p. 223). And he quotes James Harrington, the great source of arguments for a state based on the laws of the Mosaic commonwealth (*LS*, p. 225). Yet it was now not a radical common-wealth, but the existing constitution in which landed gentlemen were seen as independent representatives in parliament, that Coleridge supported. He had moved to a neo-Harringtonian position, akin to that of Thomson and the Patriots in the 1730s, with a concern about the subversion of the values of landed gentlemen reminiscent of Cowper, Repton and Gilpin.

Quoting the Earl of Winchilsea, Coleridge argues that it is 'the generality of Farmers', wishing to maximize their profits, who refuse to let 'the Laborers rent any land' (*LS*, p. 226). The large landowner, Coleridge argues in the words of Winchilsea (himself an aristocratic agriculturalist), preserves social order in the nation because he is above the need to increase profit by enclosing and depriving the labourer of land. Winchilsea, who had written his arguments during the dearth year 1796, argued, as did Uvedale Price, that labourers should be allowed enough land to graze a cow or plant a garden, to make them 'more contented, and more attached to their situation'.[33] Coleridge, reviving his arguments in the depressed years after Waterloo, makes the large landowner's paternalist view essential to the maintenance of a peaceful and ordered society. It is a revival, of course, of an argument older than Winchilsea's *Letter*, one which is as conservative as Johnson in accepting subordination. By 1817 for Coleridge as for Words-worth liberty could only be preserved by a society in which land was unequally distributed and political power proportioned to that distribution. Peace and order had come, against the threats of commercialist ethics and rebellion by the impoverished, to seem dependent on the continued acceptance by the landed classes of the paternalist duty by which their independent wealth and their power over their tenants was made to foster a stable social order. The landlord's broad and protective view of his estate was still, as it had been for Thomson, a sanction for the authority of his views in the public sphere.

By 1817, however, that view was endangered by more than the

---

[33] *Letter from the Earl of Winchilsea to the President of the Board of Agriculture on the Advantage of Cottagers Renting Land* (London, 1796), p. 5.

blandishments of Walpole. Paternalism was threatened by the landowners' own embrace of commercialist ethics as they sought to maximize profit from their estates and industries to maintain their wealth and power in an increasingly commercialist nation. Cobbett accepted this in campaigning for a reform of parliament that would extend power beyond the landowners, realizing that his yearning for a return to paternalism by country gentlemen would not be fulfilled on the ground. Coleridge, like Wordsworth, both opposed the Reform and continued to exhort the gentry and nobility to return to their traditional (and idealized) rôle. In this respect his social and political arguments, like those of the eighteenth-century Country party they resembled, were more elegiac than effectual. It was his landscape-description rather than his prose sermons that effectually changed eighteenth-century traditions of representation (poetical and political). Seeking a community of readers beyond contemporary class and property distinctions, it transformed the legacy from Thomson as it showed moral, spiritual and political authority to arise from the common sharing, rather than exclusive possession, in deeds and words, of the landscape. And, showing that 'what no one with us shares, seems scarce our own', it found a voice for the self-uprooting, the personal and social dislocation that resulted when one was dispossessed of one's native land (*CPW*, vol. I, p. 396). And so, like the poetry of Clare, like the lyrical ballads of Wordsworth, it remains a warning of the terrible costs of the destruction of the ground on which men and women grow and stand. To lose the landscape, it reminds us, may be to lose oneself – one's mental and social as well as political fields of liberty.

Index

CAMBRIDGE STUDIES IN EIGHTEENTH-CENTURY
ENGLISH LITERATURE AND THOUGHT

General editors

Professor HOWARD ERSKINE-HILL LITT.D., FBA,
Pembroke College, Cambridge
Professor JOHN RICHETTI, *University of Pennsylvania*